HAMLET

AN AUTHORITATIVE TEXT
INTELLECTUAL BACKGROUNDS
EXTRACTS FROM THE SOURCES
ESSAYS IN CRITICISM

SECOND EDITION

A NORTON CRITICAL EDITION

William Shakespeare
HAMLET

AN AUTHORITATIVE TEXT
INTELLECTUAL BACKGROUNDS
EXTRACTS FROM THE SOURCES
ESSAYS IN CRITICISM

SECOND EDITION

Edited by

CYRUS HOY

UNIVERSITY OF ROCHESTER

W · W · NORTON & COMPANY · *New York* · *London*

Printed in the United States of America.

The text of this book is composed in Electra, with
the display set in Bernhard Modern. Composition and
manufacturing by The Maple-Vail Book Group.
Book design by Antonina Krass.

Second Edition.

Library of Congress Cataloging-in-Publication Data
Shakespeare, William, 1564–1616.
Hamlet : an authoritative text, intellectual backgrounds, extracts
from the sources, essays in criticism / William Shakespeare ; edited
by Cyrus Hoy. — 2nd ed.
    p.   cm. — (A Norton critical edition)
Includes bibliographical references.
ISBN 0-393-95663-6
1. Shakespeare, William, 1564–1616.   Hamlet.   I. Hoy, Cyrus
Henry.   II. Title.
PR2807.A2H68   1991
822.3′3—dc20   90-44697

ISBN 0-393-95663-6

W.W. Norton & Company, Inc., 500 Fifth Avenue, New York, N.Y. 10110
W. W. Norton & Company, Ltd., 37 Great Russell Street, London WC1B 3NU

1 2 3 4 5 6 7 8 9 0

Contents

Preface

Everything about *The Tragedy of Hamlet, Prince of Denmark* is problematic. Critical uncertainty concerning the character of the Prince, his attitudes, and the tragic quality of his highly dramatic situation is matched by a corresponding diversity of scholarly opinion regarding such matters as the date of the play, its precise relation to its sources, and its textual authority. An editor approaches his task with a proper awe that is the more profound from his steady realization that he is, after all, dealing with the most celebrated work in English literature.

The present edition includes a text of the play in modern spelling, with explanatory and textual notes; extracts from the only two pre-Shakespearean treatments of the Hamlet story that are extant; a selection of late sixteenth-century opinion on four subjects—melancholy, demonology, the nature of man, and death—which, in one way or another, bear directly, and crucially, on the play's meaning; and a selection of critical commentary on the play, ranging in time from the early eighteenth century to the present.

The text of the present edition of *Hamlet* is based on that of the second quarto, published in 1604–5. Since there is good reason to suppose that the second quarto was printed from Shakespeare's own manuscript, its authority is very high, and I have adhered to it closely, but not slavishly. The second quarto of *Hamlet* is, unfortunately, a very carelessly printed book. It exhibits a number of obvious misreadings, and it is riddled with omissions of all sorts, from single letters to whole lines. In such cases, an editor must turn to other textual authority, usually to the text of the play printed in the 1623 folio collection of Shakespeare's complete works. The folio must be consulted as well for some 80 lines, scattered throughout the play, which are omitted from the second quarto. My editorial practices will be evident from the textual notes, printed after the play, where a complete list of all substantive departures from the text of the second quarto is given. The editorial problem that the play poses is summarized, together with an account of the principles which have governed the preparation of the present edition, in the Textual Commentary section.

The relevant portions of the Hamlet story as it is recorded in the *Historia Danica* of Saxo Grammaticus and the *Histoires tragiques* of Belleforest are presented under the section dealing with Shakespeare's sources. In estimating the relevance of these to Shakespeare's tragedy, it is necessary to avoid either exaggerating or underestimating their importance. Since they provide us with the only pre-Shakespearean accounts of the story that are extant, their relevance to any serious study of the play is obvious. But they are sources of Shakespeare's tragedy only in an indirect sense. It is by no means certain that he knew either of them. Saxo's *Danish History*, written at the end of the twelfth century, was first printed in 1514, and had gone through a number of Continental editions by the end of the sixteenth century; but no edition is known to have been printed in England before or during Shakespeare's lifetime. Belleforest's *Tragical Histories* present a roughly similar case. His account of Hamlet's story is contained in volume 5 of the *Histoires tragiques*, and this was widely printed on the Continent after its first edition in 1576, but there is no known English edition prior to Shakespeare's play. *The Historie of Hamblet*, an English translation of Belleforest, was published in 1608, five years after the appearance of the first edition of Shakespeare's *Hamlet*. This, far from influencing Shakespeare's treatment of the story, has in fact been influenced by it, as the anonymous translator's departures from his French text (to which attention is drawn in the note on page 139) make clear. The immediate source of Shakespeare's tragedy was an earlier *Hamlet* play, presumably the work of the dramatist Thomas Kyd, which is now lost, but which we know from contemporary references to it—in Nashe's preface to Greene's *Menaphon* (1589), in Lodge's *Wit's Miserie* (1596), in Henslow's Diary (June 9, 1594)—was being acted on the London stage in the late 1580s and early 1590s. There has been much speculation concerning the nature of this lost play, and necessarily so. Between the Hamlet of Saxo and Belleforest, and the Hamlet of Shakespeare, a number of vast changes have been wrought, and the effort of critics to define the dramatist's intentions in this, the most ambiguous of all his tragedies, could proceed on very much surer ground if it were possible to know which of the changes were Shakespeare's own innovation, and which had already been introduced into the earlier dramatization of the Hamlet story. It is possible to conjecture something of the general features of the lost *Hamlet* play from the example of such other Elizabethan revenge plays as Kyd's *Spanish Tragedy* and Marston's *Antonio's Revenge*; from *Der Bestrafte Brudermord* (*Fratricide Punished*), a badly debased German version of what would appear to be Shakespeare's play but with traces of the *Ur-Hamlet*, carried to the Continent presumably by a touring company of English actors; and from certain elements in the remarkably garbled text of the first quarto (printed in 1603) of Shakespeare's *Hamlet*. But no amount of conjecture—clever and elaborate though much of it has been—can conceal the fact that the lost play is lost, and in the absence of it one must necessarily turn to Saxo and Belleforest in order to assess Shakespeare's source material.

Turning to them can be a salutary experience for the student of the play, if for no other reason than to witness just what an energetic fellow the Hamlet of the original saga is, by comparison with the highly introspective figure of the Prince which Shakespeare, or Shakespeare's critics, have made of him. It is only for the student to keep in mind the fact that, between the Hamlet story as it is narrated in Saxo and Belleforest, and as it is dramatized in Shakespeare's tragedy, there is a missing link, and that the action of the old saga had already been adapted to the conditions of the Elizabethan stage, and refashioned in accordance with the conventions of Elizabethan revenge tragedy, before Shakespeare took it in hand.

The selection of critical commentary contained in the present volume is designed to put before the reader at least the more significant of the multifarious opinions and attitudes to which the *Tragedy of Hamlet* has given rise over the past two and a half centuries. The play has never ceased to elicit and sustain critical attention, which is surely one measure of its greatness. A lesser work would have been exhausted long ago. For the early eighteenth century, the play posed no problem. The severest stricture that Dennis, writing in 1712, could level at it was its failure—which it shared with all Shakespeare's tragedies—to observe the law of poetic justice. For the anonymous auuthor of *Some Remarks on the Tragedy of Hamlet* (1736), the famous question of why the Prince delayed in avenging his father's murder, the answer was simple; if he had not delayed, there would have been no play. For the critics of the Romantic period, the play distinctly posed a problem; they isolated it in Hamlet's delay to action; and they found the explanation for his delay in the particular make-up of his nature. On these issues, critical discussion of the play has turned ever since, though the best recent criticism has stressed the need to look beyond the character of the Prince and to view the play in its totality.

Modern criticism of Shakespeare's plays has also drawn attention to the need to see them in the context of the moral and intellectual assumptions and attitudes that were current when they were composed. The selections from the writings of such figures as Lavater, Primaudaye, and Montaigne, included in the present volume, are designed to suggest something at least of the climate of late-Renaissance opinion as this would appear to have affected the conception of Shakespeare's treatment of the Hamlet story. The four subjects—melancholy, demonology, the nature of man, and death—on which I have focused attention here were, in their several ways, of absorbing interest to the late Renaissance, and each, in varying degrees, impinges on important issues raised by *The Tragedy of Hamlet*. The statements of Shakespeare's contemporaries on these matters warrant the attention of any serious student of the play. While it may be doubted whether or not knowledge of late sixteenth-century attitudes toward ghosts, or the physiological theory of the four

humors, will provide the key to the play's profoundest meanings, there
is no doubt at all that the failure to understand the opinions of Shakespeare's age concerning such matters as these (and one might include
the subject of revenge as well) can seriously impede the effort to deal
with the play on its own terms. The unquiet spirit that haunts the play
is, after all, the agent that sets the action in motion; and Hamlet's melancholy is both the cause and the effect of a pervasive sense of evil that
is the very ambiance of the tragedy.

Questions concerning the nature of man, and the nature of death,
carry us to the heart of the play. About the nature of man, the Renaissance was of two minds. The divergent views are recorded, among other
places, in Primaudaye's *French Academy* and Montaigne's *Apology of
Raymond Sebond*, selections from which are also reprinted below. They
have come together, in Shakespeare, in such a passage as Hamlet's speech
beginning "What a piece of work is a man" (II.ii.288ff.). Whether
Shakespeare had read Montaigne when he wrote *Hamlet* has been much
debated (Florio's translation appeared in the same year—1603—as the
first edition of the play, but Shakespeare could have seen it in manuscript). The parallels of thought and language between *Hamlet* and Florio's rendition of the *Essais* are very striking, but positive proof of a direct
influence at this point in Shakespeare's career is lacking. It does not
finally matter. The identity of feeling and thought evident again and
again in the essays and the tragedy is the important thing, however one
accounts for it. The great passage on death, time, and change, at the
end of the *Apology of Raymond Sebond*, might be spoken at any number
of points in *Hamlet*. In effect, it is. "And nothing remaineth or ever
continueth in one state," says Montaigne. "And nothing is at a like
goodness still," says Claudius at one of the most impressive moments in
the play (IV.vii.114). "If we should ever continue one and the same,
how is it then that now we rejoice at one thing, and now at another?"
asks Montaigne. "How comes it to pass we love things contrary, or we
hate them * * *?" This is as much as to ask what Hamlet is agonizingly
asking himself from the beginning of the play: how his mother could so
readily transfer her affections from her Hyperionlike first husband to his
satyrlike brother—a question that he puts to her directly in the course of
the scene in her chamber ("Could you on this fair mountain leave to
feed, / And batten on this moor?" [III.iv.67–68]). This is but a single
demonstration, in a play that abounds with like examples, of the contradictory nature of reality as Montaigne defines it. He does so in terms of
its most profound metaphysical implications—implications that take the
form of a series of bewildering paradoxes.

> How is it that we have different affections, holding no more the
> same sense in the same thought? For it is not likely that without

alteration we should take other passions, and *what admitteth alter-ations, continueth not the same*; and if it be not one selfsame, then is it not; but rather with being all one, the simple being doth also change, ever becoming other from other. And by consequence, nature's senses are deceived and lie falsely; taking what appeareth for what is; for want of truly knowing what it is that is.

The paradoxes are present in *Hamlet,* where they have been raised to the power of so many tragic truths: tragic because they point directly to as many appalling contradictions in the nature of things. Appearance contradicts reality, words contradict deeds, behavior contradicts purpose; nothing is what it appears to be, and nothing endures, least of all the high dedication of a passionate moment.

> What to ourselves in passion we purpose,
> The passion ending, doth the purpose lose.   (III.ii.176–77)

Thus the Player King to the Player Queen, in answer to her loud protes-tations of eternal fidelity. If, in the context, the words reflect most immediately upon Gertrude, they reflect as well upon her son, who has also proposed something to himself in a fit of passion, just after his first encounter with the ghost. Ironically enough, it is the other King, the one of shreds and patches, who has the final comment on this matter, which involves nothing less than the need, so urgently felt by the tragic protagonist throughout the play, for suiting the action to the word, the word to the action.

> That we would do,
> We should do when we would; for this "would" changes,
> And hath abatements and delays as many
> As there are tongues, are hands, are accidents,
> And then this "should" is like a spendthrift sigh
> That hurts by easing.   (IV.vii.116–21)

Any modern editor of a Shakespearean play is heavily indebted to the work that has been done in the field of textual bibliography over the past half century. My own indebtedness to the work of the late W. W. Greg will be evident to anyone familiar with the problems of Elizabethan textual criticism. I have also laid under heavy contribution studies of the second quarto of *Hamlet* by F. T. Bowers and J. R. Brown, and of the folio text by Charlton Hinman and Harold Jenkins. Professor Jenkins's account of actors' interpolations in the folio text, to which reference is made in the notes and Textual Commentary, has been a source of con-tinual enlightenment to me throughout the preparation of this edition. To him and it, I have a special obligation which I gratefully record. To the staffs of the Folger Shakespeare Library, Washington, D.C., where

work on this edition was begun, and the Bodleian Library, Oxford, where
it was completed, I wish to acknowledge my appreciation for many cour-
tesies.

CYRUS HOY

October 1962

Preface to the Second Edition

During the more than quarter of a century since this edition was first published, the text of *Hamlet* has continued to be a problem, and it always will be on the evidence that is currently available. Though the debate continues as to whether a modern edition of the play should be based on the second quarto (1604–5) or the first folio (1623), I persist in the belief that, all things considered, the second quarto provides the more authoritative text, and it remains the textual basis for this edition.

In preparing this revised Norton edition, I have been principally concerned with refining the punctuation and stage directions for the play, expanding the scope of the commentary notes on its language and action, and replacing certain of the critical pieces with materials that reflect some of the directions criticism of *Hamlet* has taken over the past three decades.

CYRUS HOY

May 1990

The Text of
HAMLET

THE
Tragicall Historie of
HAMLET,

Prince of Denmarke.

By William Shakespeare.

Newly imprinted and enlarged to almost as much
againe as it was, according to the true and perfect
Coppie.

AT LONDON,
Printed by I. R. for N. L. and are to be sold at his
shoppe vnder Saint Dunstons Church in
Fleetstreet. 1604.

[Dramatis Personae

CLAUDIUS, *King of Denmark.*
HAMLET, *son to the former and nephew to the present King.*
POLONIUS, *Lord Chamberlain.*
HORATIO, *friend to Hamlet.*
LAERTES, *son to Polonius.*
VOLTEMAND,
CORNELIUS,
ROSENCRANTZ,
GUILDENSTERN, } *courtiers.*
OSRIC,
A GENTLEMAN,
A PRIEST.

MARCELLUS,
BERNARDO, } *officers.*
FRANCISCO, *a soldier.*
REYNALDO, *servant to Polonius.*
PLAYERS.
TWO CLOWNS, *grave-diggers.*
FORTINBRAS, *Prince of Norway.*
A NORWEGIAN CAPTAIN.

ENGLISH AMBASSADORS.
GERTRUDE, *Queen of Denmark, and mother of Hamlet.*
OPHELIA, *daughter to Polonius.*

GHOST OF HAMLET'S FATHER.

LORDS, LADIES, OFFICERS, SOLDIERS, SAILORS, MESSENGERS, *and* ATTENDANTS.

SCENE: *Denmark.*]

Hamlet

Enter BERNARDO *and* FRANCISCO, *two sentinels.*

BER.   Who's there?

FRAN.   Nay, answer me. Stand and unfold yourself.

BER.   Long live the king!

FRAN.   Bernardo?

BER.   He.   5

FRAN.   You come most carefully upon your hour.

BER.   'Tis now struck twelve. Get thee to bed, Francisco.

FRAN.   For this relief much thanks. 'Tis bitter cold,
And I am sick at heart.

BER.   Have you had quiet guard?

FRAN.   Not a mouse stirring.   10

BER.   Well, good night.
If you do meet Horatio and Marcellus,
The rivals of my watch, bid them make haste.

Enter HORATIO *and* MARCELLUS.

FRAN.   I think I hear them. Stand, ho! Who is there?

HOR.   Friends to this ground.

MAR.   And liegemen to the Dane.   15

FRAN.   Give you good night.

MAR.   O, farewell, honest soldier!
Who hath relieved you?

FRAN.   Bernardo hath my place.
Give you good night.   *Exit* FRANCISCO.

MAR.   Holla, Bernardo!

BER.   Say—
What, is Horatio there?

HOR.   A piece of him.

BER.   Welcome, Horatio. Welcome, good Marcellus.   20

HOR.   What, has this thing appeared again to-night?

BER.   I have seen nothing.

MAR.   Horatio says 'tis but our fantasy,
And will not let belief take hold of him
Touching this dreaded sight twice seen of us.   25

[I.i] 13. *rivals* partners.   15. *Dane* King of Denmark.

Therefore I have entreated him along
With us to watch the minutes of this night,
That if again this apparition come,
He may approve our eyes and speak to it.

HOR.   Tush, tush, 'twill not appear.

BER.   Sit down awhile,   30
And let us once again assail your ears,
That are so fortified against our story,
What we have two nights seen.

HOR.   Well, sit we down,
And let us hear Bernardo speak of this.

BER.   Last night of all,   35
When yond same star that's westward from the pole
Had made his course t' illume that part of heaven
Where now it burns, Marcellus and myself,
The bell then beating one—

          Enter GHOST.

MAR.   Peace, break thee off. Look where it comes again.   40
BER.   In the same figure like the king that's dead.
MAR.   Thou art a scholar; speak to it, Horatio.
BER.   Looks 'a not like the king? Mark it, Horatio.
HOR.   Most like. It harrows me with fear and wonder.
BER.   It would be spoke to.
MAR.   Question it, Horatio.   45
HOR.   What art thou that usurp'st this time of night
Together with that fair and warlike form
In which the majesty of buried Denmark
Did sometimes march? By heaven I charge thee, speak.
MAR.   It is offended.
BER.   See, it stalks away.   50
HOR.   Stay. Speak, speak. I charge thee, speak.   *Exit* GHOST.
MAR.   'Tis gone and will not answer.
BER.   How now, Horatio! You tremble and look pale.
Is not this something more than fantasy?
What think you on't?   55
HOR.   Before my God, I might not this believe
Without the sensible and true avouch
Of mine own eyes.
MAR.   Is it not like the king?
HOR.   As thou art to thyself.
Such was the very armor he had on   60
When he the ambitious Norway combated.
So frowned he once when, in an angry parle,

29. *approve* confirm.   49. *sometimes* formerly.
36. *pole* polestar.   57. *sensible* confirmed by one of the senses.
44. *harrows* afflicts, distresses.   61. *Norway* King of Norway.
48. *buried Denmark* the buried King of Denmark.   62. *parle* parley.

He smote the sledded Polacks on the ice.
'Tis strange.
MAR.   Thus twice before, and jump at this dead hour,   65
  With martial stalk hath he gone by our watch.
HOR.   In what particular thought to work I know not,
  But in the gross and scope of mine opinion,
  This bodes some strange eruption to our state.
MAR.   Good now, sit down, and tell me he that knows,   70
  Why this same strict and most observant watch
  So nightly toils the subject of the land,
  And why such daily cast of brazen cannon
  And foreign mart for implements of war;
  Why such impress of shipwrights, whose sore task   75
  Does not divide the Sunday from the week.
  What might be toward that this sweaty haste
  Doth make the night joint-laborer with the day?
  Who is't that can inform me?
HOR.   That can I.
  At least, the whisper goes so. Our last king,   80
  Whose image even but now appeared to us,
  Was as you know by Fortinbras of Norway,
  Thereto pricked on by a most emulate pride,
  Dared to the combat; in which our valiant Hamlet
  (For so this side of our known world esteemed him)   85
  Did slay this Fortinbras; who by a sealed compact
  Well ratified by law and heraldry,
  Did forfeit, with his life, all those his lands
  Which he stood seized of, to the conqueror;
  Against the which a moiety competent   90
  Was gagéd by our king; which had returned
  To the inheritance of Fortinbras,
  Had he been vanquisher; as, by the same comart
  And carriage of the article designed,
  His fell to Hamlet. Now, sir, young Fortinbras,   95
  Of unimprovéd mettle hot and full,
  Hath in the skirts of Norway here and there
  Sharked up a list of lawless resolutes
  For food and diet to some enterprise
  That hath a stomach in't; which is no other,   100

---

63. *sledded Polacks* the Poles mounted on sleds or
sledges.
65. *jump* just, exactly.
68. *gross and scope* general drift.
72. *toils* causes to toil; *subject* people.
74. *mart* traffic, bargaining.
75. *impress* conscription.
77. *toward* imminent, impending.
83. *emulate* ambitious.
87. *heraldry* the law of arms, regulating tourna-

ments and state combats.
89. *seized* possessed.
90. *moiety competent* sufficient portion.
91. *gaged* pledged.
93. *comart* joint bargain.
94. *carriage* import.
96. *unimproved* unrestrained.
98. *Sharked up* picked up indiscriminately.
100. *stomach* spice of adventure.

As it doth well appear unto our state,
But to recover of us by strong hand
And terms compulsatory, those foresaid lands
So by his father lost; and this, I take it,
Is the main motive of our preparations,   105
The source of this our watch, and the chief head
Of this post-haste and romage in the land.
BER.   I think it be no other but e'en so.
Well may it sort that this portentous figure
Comes arméd through our watch so like the king   110
That was and is the question of these wars.
HOR.   A mote it is to trouble the mind's eye.
In the most high and palmy state of Rome,
A little ere the mightiest Julius fell,
The graves stood tenantless, and the sheeted dead   115
Did squeak and gibber in the Roman streets;
As stars with trains of fire, and dews of blood,
Disasters in the sun; and the moist star,
Upon whose influence Neptune's empire stands,
Was sick almost to doomsday with eclipse.   120
And even the like precurse of feared events,
As harbingers preceding still the fates
And prologue to the omen coming on,
Have heaven and earth together demonstrated
Unto our climatures and countrymen.   125

        Enter GHOST.
But soft, behold, lo where it comes again!
I'll cross it though it blast me.—Stay, illusion.
                    [GHOST] *spreads his arms.*
If thou hast any sound or use of voice,
Speak to me.
If there be any good thing to be done,   130
That may to thee do ease, and grace to me,
Speak to me.
If thou art privy to thy country's fate,
Which happily foreknowing may avoid,
O, speak!   135
Or if thou hast uphoarded in thy life
Extorted treasure in the womb of earth,
For which, they say, you spirits oft walk in death,
                        The cock crows.

106. *head* fountainhead.   121. *precurse* heralding, foreshadowing.
107. *romage* turmoil.   122. *harbingers* forerunners; *still* ever.
109. *sort* suit, be in accordance.   123. *omen* ominous event.
112. *mote* particle of dust.   125. *climatures* regions.
113. *palmy* flourishing.   127. *cross it* cross its path.
115. *sheeted* in shrouds.   134. *happily* haply, perchance.
118. *Disasters* ominous signs; *moist star* the moon.

Speak of it. Stay, and speak. Stop it, Marcellus.
MAR.   Shall I strike at it with my partisan?   140
HOR.   Do, if it will not stand.
BER.   'Tis here.
HOR.   'Tis here.
MAR.   'Tis gone.   [*Exit* GHOST.]
        We do it wrong, being so majestical,
        To offer it the show of violence;
        For it is as the air, invulnerable,   145
        And our vain blows malicious mockery.
BER.   It was about to speak when the cock crew.
HOR.   And then it started like a guilty thing
        Upon a fearful summons. I have heard
        The cock, that is the trumpet to the morn,   150
        Doth with his lofty and shrill-sounding throat
        Awake the god of day, and at his warning,
        Whether in sea or fire, in earth or air,
        Th' extravagant and erring spirit hies
        To his confine; and of the truth herein   155
        This present object made probation.
MAR.   It faded on the crowing of the cock.
        Some say that ever 'gainst that season comes
        Wherein our Savior's birth is celebrated,
        This bird of dawning singeth all night long,   160
        And then, they say, no spirit dare stir abroad,
        The nights are wholesome, then no planets strike,
        No fairy takes, nor witch hath power to charm,
        So hallowed and so gracious is that time.
HOR.   So have I heard and do in part believe it.   165
        But look, the morn in russet mantle clad
        Walks o'er the dew of yon high eastward hill.
        Break we our watch up, and by my advice
        Let us impart what we have seen to-night
        Unto young Hamlet, for upon my life   170
        This spirit, dumb to us, will speak to him.
        Do you consent we shall acquaint him with it,
        As needful in our loves, fitting our duty?
MAR.   Let's do't, I pray, and I this morning know
        Where we shall find him most convenient.   *Exeunt.*   175

---

140. *partisan* pike.
154. *extravagant* straying, vagrant; *erring* wander-
ing.
156. *probation* proof.

158. *'gainst* just before.
162. *strike* blast, destroy by malign influence.
163. *takes* bewitches.

[I.ii]
Flourish. Enter CLAUDIUS KING OF DENMARK, GERTRUDE THE
QUEEN, COUNCILLORS [*including*] POLONIUS, *and his son*
LAERTES, HAMLET, *cum aliis* [*including* VOLTEMAND
and CORNELIUS.]

KING.   Though yet of Hamlet our dear brother's death
        The memory be green, and that it us befitted
        To bear our hearts in grief, and our whole kingdom
        To be contracted in one brow of woe,
        Yet so far hath discretion fought with nature   5
        That we with wisest sorrow think on him,
        Together with remembrance of ourselves.
        Therefore our sometime sister, now our queen,
        Th' imperial jointress to this warlike state,
        Have we, as 'twere with a defeated joy,   10
        With an auspicious and a dropping eye,
        With mirth in funeral, and with dirge in marriage,
        In equal scale weighing delight and dole,
        Taken to wife; nor have we herein barred
        Your better wisdoms, which have freely gone   15
        With this affair along. For all, our thanks.
        Now follows that you know young Fortinbras,
        Holding a weak supposal of our worth,
        Or thinking by our late dear brother's death
        Our state to be disjoint and out of frame,   20
        Colleaguéd with this dream of his advantage,
        He hath not failed to pester us with message
        Importing the surrender of those lands
        Lost by his father, with all bands of law,
        To our most valiant brother. So much for him.   25
        Now for ourself, and for this time of meeting,
        Thus much the business is: we have here writ
        To Norway, uncle of young Fortinbras—
        Who, impotent and bedrid, scarcely hears
        Of this his nephew's purpose—to suppress   30
        His further gait herein, in that the levies,
        The lists, and full proportions are all made
        Out of his subject; and we here dispatch
        You, good Cornelius, and you, Voltemand,
        For bearers of this greeting to old Norway,   35
        Giving to you no further personal power
        To business with the king, more than the scope
        Of these delated articles allow.

[I.ii] 0.3 *cum aliis* with others
9. *jointress* a window who holds a jointure or life
interest in an estate.
14. *barred* excluded.

21. *Colleagued* united.
31. *gait* proceeding.
32. *proportions* forces or supplies for war.
38. *delated* expressly stated.

Farewell, and let your haste commend your duty.

COR. ⎱
VOL. ⎰ In that, and all things will we show our duty.   40

KING. We doubt it nothing, heartily farewell.

                         [*Exeunt* VOLTEMAND *and* CORNELIUS.]

And now, Laertes, what's the news with you?
You told us of some suit. What is't, Laertes?
You cannot speak of reason to the Dane
And lose your voice. What wouldst thou beg, Laertes,   45
That shall not be my offer, not thy asking?
The head is not more native to the heart,
The hand more instrumental to the mouth,
Than is the throne of Denmark to thy father.
What wouldst thou have, Laertes?

LAER.   My dread lord,   50
Your leave and favor to return to France,
From whence, though willingly, I came to Denmark
To show my duty in your coronation,
Yet now I must confess, that duty done,
My thoughts and wishes bend again toward France,   55
And bow them to your gracious leave and pardon.

KING. Have you your father's leave? What says Polonius?

POL. He hath, my lord, wrung from me my slow leave
By laborsome petition, and at last
Upon his will I sealed my hard consent.   60
I do beseech you give him leave to go.

KING. Take thy fair hour, Laertes. Time be thine,
And thy best graces spend it at thy will.
But now, my cousin Hamlet, and my son—

HAM. [*Aside.*] A little more than kin, and less than kind.   65

KING. How is it that the clouds still hang on you?

HAM. Not so, my lord. I am too much in the sun.

QUEEN. Good Hamlet, cast thy nighted color off,
And let thine eye look like a friend on Denmark.
Do not for ever with thy vailéd lids   70
Seek for thy noble father in the dust.
Thou know'st 'tis common—all that lives must die,
Passing through nature to eternity.

HAM. Ay, madam, it is common.

QUEEN.   If it be,
Why seems it so particular with thee?   75

HAM. Seems, madam? Nay, it is. I know not 'seems.'

---

44. *Dane* King of Denmark.
45. *lose your voice* speak in vain.
47. *native* joined by nature.
48. *instrumental* serviceable.
56. *pardon* indulgence.
60. *hard* reluctant.

64. *cousin* kinsman of any kind except parent, child, brother or sister.
65. *kin* related as nephew; *kind* (1) affectionate (2) natural, lawful.
70. *vailed* lowered.
75. *particular* personal, individual.

'Tis not alone my inky cloak, good mother,
Nor customary suits of solemn black,
Nor windy suspiration of forced breath,
No, nor the fruitful river in the eye,   80
Nor the dejected haviour of the visage,
Together with all forms, moods, shapes of grief,
That can denote me truly. These indeed seem,
For they are actions that a man might play,
But I have that within which passes show—   85
These but the trappings and the suits of woe.

KING.   'Tis sweet and commendable in your nature, Hamlet,
To give these mourning duties to your father,
But you must know your father lost a father,
That father lost, lost his, and the survivor bound   90
In filial obligation for some term
To do obsequious sorrow. But to persever
In obstinate condolement is a course
Of impious stubbornness. 'Tis unmanly grief.
It shows a will most incorrect to heaven,   95
A heart unfortified, a mind impatient,
An understanding simple and unschooled.
For what we know must be, and is as common
As any the most vulgar thing to sense,
Why should we in our peevish opposition   100
Take it to heart? Fie, 'tis a fault to heaven,
A fault against the dead, a fault to nature,
To reason most absurd, whose common theme
Is death of fathers, and who still hath cried,
From the first corse till he that died to-day,   105
'This must be so.' We pray you throw to earth
This unprevailing woe, and think of us
As of a father, for let the world take note
You are the most immediate to our throne,
And with no less nobility of love   110
Than that which dearest father bears his son
Do I impart toward you. For your intent
In going back to school in Wittenberg,
It is most retrograde to our desire,
And we beseech you, bend you to remain   115
Here in the cheer and comfort of our eye,
Our chiefest courtier, cousin, and our son.

QUEEN.   Let not thy mother lose her prayers, Hamlet.
I pray thee stay with us, go not to Wittenberg.

HAM.   I shall in all my best obey you, madam.   120

---

92. *obsequious* dutiful in performing funeral ob-   105. *corse* corpse.
sequies or manifesting regard for the dead; *persever*   114. *retrograde* contrary.
persevere.

KING. Why, 'tis a loving and a fair reply.
   Be as ourself in Denmark. Madam, come.
   This gentle and unforced accord of Hamlet
   Sits smiling to my heart, in grace whereof,
   No jocund health that Denmark drinks to-day   125
   But the great cannon to the clouds shall tell,
   And the king's rouse the heaven shall bruit again,
   Respeaking earthly thunder. Come away.
                 Flourish. Exeunt all but HAMLET.
HAM. O, that this too too sallied flesh would melt,
   Thaw, and resolve itself into a dew,   130
   Or that the Everlasting had not fixed
   His canon 'gainst self-slaughter. O God, God,
   How weary, stale, flat, and unprofitable
   Seem to me all the uses of this world!
   Fie on't, ah, fie, 'tis an unweeded garden   135
   That grows to seed. Things rank and gross in nature
   Possess it merely. That it should come to this,
   But two months dead, nay, not so much, not two.
   So excellent a king, that was to this
   Hyperion to a satyr, so loving to my mother,   140
   That he might not beteem the winds of heaven
   Visit her face too roughly. Heaven and earth,
   Must I remember? Why, she would hang on him
   As if increase of appetite had grown
   By what it fed on, and yet, within a month—   145
   Let me not think on't. Frailty, thy name is woman—
   A little month, or ere those shoes were old
   With which she followed my poor father's body
   Like Niobe, all tears, why she—
   O God, a beast that wants discourse of reason   150
   Would have mourned longer—married with my uncle,
   My father's brother, but no more like my father
   Than I to Hercules. Within a month,
   Ere yet the salt of most unrighteous tears
   Had left the flushing in her gallèd eyes,   155

127. *rouse* full draught of liquor; *bruit* echo.
129. *sallied* sullied. "Sallied" is the reading of Q2
(and Q1). F reads "solid." Since Hamlet's primary
concern is with the fact of the flesh's impurity, not
with its corporeality, the choice as between Q and
F clearly lies with Q. "Sally" is a legitimate sixteenth-century form of "sully"; it occurs in Dek-
ker's *Patient Grissil* (I.i.12), printed in 1603, as F.
T. Bowers has pointed out (in "Hamlet's 'Sullied'
or 'Solid' Flesh. A Bibliographical Case-History,"
Shakespeare Survey 9 [1956]: p. 44); and it occurs
as a noun at II.i.39 of *Hamlet*.
132. *canon* law.

137. *merely* entirely.
140. *Hyperion* the sun god.
141. *beteem* allowed.
149. *Niobe* wife of Amphion, King of Thebes, she
boasted of having more children than Leto and was
punished when her seven sons and seven daughters were slain by Apollo and Artemis, children of
Leto; in her grief she was changed by Zeus into a
stone, which continually dropped tears.
150. *wants* lacks; *discourse of reason* the reasoning
faculty.
155. *galled* sore from rubbing or chafing.

She married. O, most wicked speed, to post
With such dexterity to incestuous sheets!
It is not, nor it cannot come to good.
But break my heart, for I must hold my tongue.

Enter HORATIO, MARCELLUS, *and* BERNARDO.
HOR. Hail to your lordship!
HAM.   I am glad to see you well. 160
Horatio—or I do forget myself.
HOR. The same, my lord, and your poor servant ever.
HAM. Sir, my good friend, I'll change that name with you.
And what make you from Wittenberg, Horatio?
Marcellus? 165
MAR. My good lord!
HAM. I am very glad to see you. [*To* BERNARDO.] Good even, sir.—
But what, in faith, make you from Wittenberg?
HOR. A truant disposition, good my lord.
HAM. I would not hear your enemy say so, 170
Nor shall you do my ear that violence
To make it truster of your own report
Against yourself. I know you are no truant.
But what is your affair in Elsinore?
We'll teach you to drink deep ere you depart. 175
HOR. My lord, I came to see your father's funeral.
HAM. I prithee do not mock me, fellow-student,
I think it was to see my mother's wedding.
HOR. Indeed, my lord, it followed hard upon.
HAM. Thrift, thrift, Horatio. The funeral baked meats 180
Did coldly furnish forth the marriage tables.
Would I had met my dearest foe in heaven
Or ever I had seen that day, Horatio!
My father—methinks I see my father.
HOR. Where, my lord?
HAM.   In my mind's eye, Horatio. 185
HOR. I saw him once, 'a was a goodly king.
HAM. 'A was a man, take him for all in all,
I shall not look upon his like again.
HOR. My lord, I think I saw him yesternight.
HAM. Saw who? 190
HOR. My lord, the king your father.
HAM.   The king my father?
HOR. Season your admiration for a while
With an attent ear till I may deliver
Upon the witness of these gentlemen

163. *change* exchange.   192. *Season* temper, moderate; *admiration* won-
164. *make* do.   der, astonishment.
182. *dearest* direst.

This marvel to you.

HAM.   For God's love, let me hear!   195
HOR.   Two nights together had these gentlemen,
    Marcellus and Bernardo, on their watch
    In the dead waste and middle of the night
    Been thus encountered. A figure like your father,
    Armed at point exactly, cap-a-pe,   200
    Appears before them, and with solemn march
    Goes slow and stately by them. Thrice he walked
    By their oppressed and fear-surprisèd eyes
    Within his truncheon's length, whilst they, distilled
    Almost to jelly with the act of fear,   205
    Stand dumb and speak not to him. This to me
    In dreadful secrecy impart they did,
    And I with them the third night kept the watch,
    Where, as they had delivered, both in time,
    Form of the thing, each word made true and good,   210
    The apparition comes. I knew your father.
    These hands are not more like.
HAM.   But where was this?
MAR.   My lord, upon the platform where we watch.
HAM.   Did you not speak to it?
HOR.   My lord, I did,
    But answer made it none. Yet once methought   215
    It lifted up it head and did address
    Itself to motion, like as it would speak;
    But even then the morning cock crew loud,
    And at the sound it shrunk in haste away
    And vanished from our sight.
HAM.   'Tis very strange.   220
HOR.   As I do live, my honored lord, 'tis true,
    And we did think it writ down in our duty
    To let you know of it.
HAM.   Indeed, sirs, but
    This troubles me. Hold you the watch to-night?
ALL.   We do, my lord.
HAM.   Armed, say you?
ALL.   Armed, my lord.   225
HAM.   From top to toe?
ALL.   My lord, from head to foot.
HAM.   Then saw you not his face.
HOR.   O yes, my lord, he wore his beaver up.
HAM.   What, looked he frowningly?
HOR.   A countenance more in sorrow than in anger.   230

---

200. *at point exactly* in every particular; *cap-a-pe*
from head to foot.
204. *truncheon* military leader's baton.

216. *it* its.
228. *beaver* the part of the helmet that was drawn
down to cover the face.

HAM.   Pale or red?
HOR.   Nay, very pale.
HAM.   And fixed his eyes upon you?
HOR.   Most constantly.
HAM.   I would I had been there.
HOR.   It would have much amazed you.
HAM.   Very like.
    Stayed it long?
HOR.   While one with moderate haste might tell a hundred.   235
BOTH.   Longer, longer.
HOR.   Not when I saw't.
HAM.   His beard was grizzled, no?
HOR.   It was as I have seen it in his life,
    A sable silvered.
HAM.   I will watch to-night.
    Perchance 'twill walk again.
HOR.   I warr'nt it will.   240
HAM.   If it assume my noble father's person,
    I'll speak to it though hell itself should gape
    And bid me hold my peace. I pray you all,
    If you have hitherto concealed this sight,
    Let it be tenable in your silence still,   245
    And whatsomever else shall hap to-night,
    Give it an understanding but no tongue.
    I will requite your loves. So fare you well.
    Upon the platform 'twixt eleven and twelve
    I'll visit you.
ALL.   Our duty to your honor.   250
HAM.   Your loves, as mine to you. Farewell.
                              Exeunt [all but HAMLET].
    My father's spirit in arms? All is not well.
    I doubt some foul play. Would the night were come!
    Till then sit still, my soul. Foul deeds will rise,
    Though all the earth o'erwhelm them, to men's eyes.   *Exit.* 255

[I.iii]

                Enter LAERTES *and* OPHELIA *his sister.*
LAER.   My necessaries are embarked. Farewell.
    And, sister, as the winds give benefit
    And convoy is assistant, do not sleep,
    But let me hear from you.
OPH.   Do you doubt that?

---

235. *tell* count.   245. *tenable* retained.
237. *grizzled* grayish.   246. *whatsomever* whatsoever.
239. *sable silvered* black mixed with white.   253. *doubt* suspect.

LAER.   For Hamlet, and the trifling of his favor,   5
   Hold it a fashion and a toy in blood,
   A violet in the youth of primy nature,
   Forward, not permanent, sweet, not lasting,
   The perfume and suppliance of a minute,
   No more.
OPH.   No more but so?
LAER.   Think it no more.   10
   For nature crescent does not grow alone
   In thews and bulk, but as this temple waxes
   The inward service of the mind and soul
   Grows wide withal. Perhaps he loves you now,
   And now no soil nor cautel doth besmirch   15
   The virtue of his will, but you must fear,
   His greatness weighed, his will is not his own,
   For he himself is subject to his birth.
   He may not, as unvalued persons do,
   Carve for himself, for on his choice depends   20
   The safety and health of this whole state,
   And therefore must his choice be circumscribed
   Unto the voice and yielding of that body
   Whereof he is the head. Then if he says he loves you,
   It fits your wisdom so far to believe it   25
   As he in his particular act and place
   May give his saying deed, which is no further
   Than the main voice of Denmark goes withal.
   Then weigh what loss your honor may sustain
   If with too credent ear you list his songs,   30
   Or lose your heart, or your chaste treasure open
   To his unmastered importunity.
   Fear it, Ophelia, fear it, my dear sister,
   And keep you in the rear of your affection,
   Out of the shot and danger of desire.   35
   The chariest maid is prodigal enough
   If she unmask her beauty to the moon.
   Virtue itself scapes not calumnious strokes.
   The canker galls the infants of the spring
   Too oft before their buttons be disclosed,   40

[I.iii] 6. *fashion* the creation of a season only; *toy in blood* passing fancy.
7. *primy* of the springtime.
11. *crescent* growing.
12. *thews* sinews, strength; *this temple* the body.
15. *cautel* deceit.
16. *will* desire.
17. *greatness weighed* high position considered.
19. *unvalued persons* persons of no social importance.

20. *Carve for himself* act according to his own inclination.
23. *yielding* assent.
30. *credent* trusting.
34. *affection* feeling.
39. *canker* canker-worm (which feeds on roses); *galls* injures.
40. *buttons* buds.

And in the morn and liquid dew of youth
Contagious blastments are most imminent.
Be wary then; best safety lies in fear.
Youth to itself rebels, though none else near.
OPH.   I shall the effect of this good lesson keep   45
As watchman to my heart. But, good my brother,
Do not as some ungracious pastors do,
Show me the steep and thorny way to heaven,
Whiles like a puffed and reckless libertine
Himself the primrose path of dalliance treads   50
And recks not his own rede.
LAER.   O, fear me not.

    Enter POLONIUS.

I stay too long. But here my father comes.
A double blessing is a double grace;
Occasion smiles upon a second leave.
POL.   Yet here, Laertes? Aboard, aboard, for shame!   55
The wind sits in the shoulder of your sail,
And you are stayed for. There, my blessing with thee,
And these few precepts in thy memory
Look thou character. Give thy thoughts no tongue,
Nor any unproportioned thought his act.   60
Be thou familiar, but by no means vulgar.
Those friends thou hast, and their adoption tried,
Grapple them unto thy soul with hoops of steel,
But do not dull thy palm with entertainment
Of each new-hatched, unfledged courage. Beware   65
Of entrance to a quarrel, but being in,
Bear't that th' opposéd may beware of thee.
Give every man thy ear, but few thy voice;
Take each man's censure, but reserve thy judgment.
Costly thy habit as thy purse can buy,   70
But not expressed in fancy; rich not gaudy,
For the apparel oft proclaims the man,
And they in France of the best rank and station
Are of a most select and generous chief in that.
Neither a borrower nor a lender be,   75
For loan oft loses both itself and friend,
And borrowing dulls th' edge of husbandry.
This above all, to thine own self be true,
And it must follow as the night the day

---

42. *blastments* blights.
51. *recks* regards; *rede* counsel.
59. *character* engrave.
60. *unproportioned* inordinate.

61. *vulgar* common.
65. *courage* young blood, man of spirit.
74. *chief* eminence.
77. *husbandry* thriftiness.

Thou canst not then be false to any man.   80
Farewell. My blessing season this in thee!
LAER.   Most humbly do I take my leave, my lord.
POL.   The time invites you. Go, your servants tend.
LAER.   Farewell, Ophelia, and remember well
   What I have said to you.
OPH.   'Tis in my memory locked,   85
   And you yourself shall keep the key of it.
LAER.   Farewell.   *Exit* LAERTES.
POL.   What is't, Ophelia, he hath said to you?
OPH.   So please you, something touching the Lord Hamlet.
POL.   Marry, well bethought.   90
   'Tis told me he hath very oft of late
   Given private time to you, and you yourself
   Have of your audience been most free and bounteous.
   If it be so—as so 'tis put on me,
   And that in way of caution—I must tell you,   95
   You do not understand yourself so clearly
   As it behooves my daughter and your honor.
   What is between you? Give me up the truth.
OPH.   He hath, my lord, of late made many tenders
   Of his affection to me.   100
POL.   Affection? Pooh! You speak like a green girl,
   Unsifted in such perilous circumstance.
   Do you believe his tenders, as you call them?
OPH.   I do not know, my lord, what I should think.
POL.   Marry, I will teach you. Think yourself a baby   105
   That you have ta'en these tenders for true pay
   Which are not sterling. Tender yourself more dearly,
   Or (not to crack the wind of the poor phrase,
   Running it thus) you'll tender me a fool.
OPH.   My lord, he hath importuned me with love   110
   In honorable fashion.
POL.   Ay, fashion you may call it. Go to, go to.
OPH.   And hath given countenance to his speech, my lord,
   With almost all the holy vows of heaven.
POL.   Ay, springes to catch woodcocks. I do know,   115
   When the blood burns, how prodigal the soul
   Lends the tongue vows. These blazes, daughter,
   Giving more light than heat, extinct in both
   Even in their promise, as it is a-making,
   You must not take for fire. From this time   120
   Be something scanter of your maiden presence.

81. *season* ripen.   99. *tenders* offers.
83. *tend* attend, wait.   102. *Unsifted* untried.
90. *Marry* by Mary.   115. *springes* snares.

Set your entreatments at a higher rate
Than a command to parle. For Lord Hamlet,
Believe so much in him that he is young,
And with a larger tether may he walk   125
Than may be given you. In few, Ophelia,
Do not believe his vows, for they are brokers,
Not of that dye which their investments show,
But mere implorators of unholy suits,
Breathing like sanctified and pious bawds,   130
The better to beguile. This is for all:
I would not, in plain terms, from this time forth
Have you so slander any moment leisure
As to give words or talk with the Lord Hamlet.
Look to't, I charge you. Come your ways.   135
OPH.   I shall obey, my lord.   *Exeunt.*

[I.iv]

      Enter HAMLET, HORATIO *and* MARCELLUS.
HAM.   The air bites shrewdly; it is very cold.
HOR.   It is a nipping and an eager air.
HAM.   What hour now?
HOR.   I think it lacks of twelve.
MAR.   No, it is struck.
HOR.   Indeed? I heard it not. It then draws near the season   5
  Wherein the spirit held his wont to walk.
                A flourish of trumpets, and two pieces go off.
  What does this mean, my lord?
HAM.   The king doth wake to-night and takes his rouse,
  Keeps wassail, and the swagg'ring up-spring reels,
  And as he drains his draughts of Rhenish down,   10
  The kettledrum and trumpet thus bray out
  The triumph of his pledge.
HOR.   Is it a custom?
HAM.   Ay, marry, is't,
  But to my mind, though I am native here
  And to the manner born, it is a custom   15
  More honored in the breach than the observance.
  This heavy-headed revel east and west
  Makes us traduced and taxed of other nations.
  They clepe us drunkards, and with swinish phrase
  Soil our addition, and indeed it takes   20

---

122. *entreatments* military negotiations for a surrender.
127. *brokers* go-betweens.
128. *investments* clothes.
129. *implorators* solicitors.

[I.iv] 2. *eager* sharp.
9. *wassail* carousal; *up-spring* a German dance.
18. *taxed of* censured by.
19. *clepe* call.
20. *addition* title added to a man's name to denote
his rank.

From our achievements, though performed at height,
The pith and marrow of our attribute.
So oft it chances in particular men,
That for some vicious mole of nature in them,
As in their birth, wherein they are not guilty   25
(Since nature cannot choose his origin),
By the o'ergrowth of some complexion,
Oft breaking down the pales and forts of reason,
Or by some habit that too much o'er-leavens
The form of plausive manners—that these men,   30
Carrying, I say, the stamp of one defect,
Being nature's livery or fortune's star,
His virtues else, be they as pure as grace,
As infinite as man may undergo,
Shall in the general censure take corruption   35
From that particular fault. The dram of evil
Doth all the noble substance often doubt
To his own scandal.

    Enter GHOST.
HOR.   Look, my lord, it comes.
HAM.   Angels and ministers of grace defend us!
Be thou a spirit of health or goblin damned,   40
Bring with thee airs from heaven or blasts from hell,
Be thy intents wicked or charitable,
Thou com'st in such a questionable shape
That I will speak to thee. I'll call thee Hamlet,
King, father, royal Dane. O, answer me!   45
Let me not burst in ignorance, but tell
Why thy canonized bones, hearsèd in death,
Have burst their cerements; why the sepulchre
Wherein we saw thee quietly interred
Hath oped his ponderous and marble jaws   50
To cast thee up again. What may this mean
That thou, dead corse, again in complete steel
Revisits thus the glimpses of the moon,
Making night hideous, and we fools of nature
So horridly to shake our disposition   55
With thoughts beyond the reaches of our souls?
Say, why is this? wherefore? What should we do?
                     [GHOST] *beckons.*
HOR.   It beckons you to go away with it,

---

22. *attribute* reputation.
26. *his* its.
27. *complexion* one of the four temperaments
(sanguine, melancholy, choleric and phlegmatic).
29. *o'er-leavens* works change throughout.
30. *plausive* pleasing.

32. *livery* badge; *star* a person's fortune, rank, or
destiny, viewed as determined by the stars.
37. *doubt* put out, obliterate.
38. *his* its.
47. *canonized* buried according to the church's rule;
hearsed coffined, buried.

As if it some impartment did desire
To you alone.
MAR.   Look with what courteous action   60
It waves you to a more removéd ground.
But do not go with it.
HOR.   No, by no means.
HAM.   It will not speak; then I will follow it.
HOR.   Do not, my lord.
HAM.   Why, what should be the fear?
I do not set my life at a pin's fee,   65
And for my soul, what can it do to that,
Being a thing immortal as itself?
It waves me forth again. I'll follow it.
HOR.   What if it tempt you toward the flood, my lord,
Or to the dreadful summit of the cliff   70
That beetles o'er his base into the sea,
And there assume some other horrible form,
Which might deprive your sovereignty of reason
And draw you into madness? Think of it.
The very place puts toys of desperation,   75
Without more motive, into every brain
That looks so many fathoms to the sea
And hears it roar beneath.
HAM.   It waves me still.
Go on. I'll follow thee.
MAR.   You shall not go, my lord.
HAM.   Hold off your hands.   80
HOR.   Be ruled, You shall not go.
HAM.   My fate cries out
And makes each petty artere in this body
As hardy as the Nemean lion's nerve.
Still am I called. Unhand me, gentlemen.
By heaven, I'll make a ghost of him that lets me.   85
I say, away!—Go on. I'll follow thee.
                         [*Exeunt*] GHOST *and* HAMLET.
HOR.   He waxes desperate with imagination.
MAR.   Let's follow. 'Tis not fit thus to obey him.
HOR.   Have after. To what issue will this come?
MAR.   Something is rotten in the state of Denmark.   90
HOR.   Heaven will direct it.
MAR.   Nay, let's follow him.   *Exeunt.*

---

59. *impartment* communication.
71. *beetles* juts out.
73. *sovereignty of reason* state of being ruled by
reason.
75. *toys* fancies, impules.

82. *artere* artery.
83. *Nemean lion* slain by Hercules in the performance of one of his twelve labors.
85. *lets* hinders.

[I.v]

    Enter GHOST *and* HAMLET.
HAM.   Whither wilt thou lead me? Speak. I'll go no further.
GHOST.   Mark me.
HAM.   I will.
GHOST.   My hour is almost come
  When I to sulph'rous and tormenting flames
  Must render up myself.
HAM.   Alas, poor ghost!
GHOST.   Pity me not, but lend thy serious hearing   5
  To what I shall unfold.
HAM.   Speak. I am bound to hear.
GHOST.   So art thou to revenge, when thou shalt hear.
HAM.   What?
GHOST.   I am thy father's spirit,
  Doomed for a certain term to walk the night,   10
  And for the day confined to fast in fires,
  Till the foul crimes done in my days of nature
  Are burnt and purged away. But that I am forbid
  To tell the secrets of my prison house,
  I could a tale unfold whose lightest word   15
  Would harrow up thy soul, freeze thy young blood,
  Make thy two eyes like stars start from their spheres,
  Thy knotted and combinéd locks to part,
  And each particular hair to stand an end,
  Like quills upon the fretful porpentine.   20
  But this eternal blazon must not be
  To ears of flesh and blood. List, list, O, list!
  If thou didst ever thy dear father love—
HAM.   O God!
GHOST.   Revenge his foul and most unnatural murder.   25
HAM.   Murder!
GHOST.   Murder most foul, as in the best it is,
  But this most foul, strange, and unnatural.
HAM.   Haste me to know't, that I, with wings as swift
  As meditation or the thoughts of love,   30
  May sweep to my revenge.
GHOST.   I find thee apt,
  And duller shouldst thou be than the fat weed
  That roots itself in ease on Lethe wharf,
  Wouldst thou not stir in this. Now, Hamlet, hear.
  'Tis given out that, sleeping in my orchard,   35
  A serpent stung me. So the whole ear of Denmark

[I.v] 19. *an* on.
20. *porpentine* porcupine.
21. *eternal blazon* proclamation of the secrets of
eternity.
33. *Lethe* the river in Hades that brings forgetfulness.

Is by a forgéd process of my death
Rankly abused. But know, thou noble youth,
The serpent that did sting thy father's life
Now wears his crown.

HAM.   O my prophetic soul!   40
    My uncle!

GHOST.   Ay, that incestuous, that adulterate beast,
    With witchcraft of his wits, with traitorous gifts—
    O wicked wit and gifts that have the power
    So to seduce!—won to his shameful lust   45
    The will of my most seeming virtuous queen.
    O Hamlet, what a falling off was there,
    From me, whose love was of that dignity
    That it went hand in hand even with the vow
    I made to her in marriage, and to decline   50
    Upon a wretch whose natural gifts were poor
    To those of mine!
    But virtue, as it never will be moved,
    Though lewdness court it in a shape of heaven,
    So lust, though to a radiant angel linked,   55
    Will sate itself in a celestial bed
    And prey on garbage.
    But soft, methinks I scent the morning air.
    Brief let me be. Sleeping within my orchard,
    My custom always of the afternoon,   60
    Upon my secure hour thy uncle stole,
    With juice of cursed hebona in a vial,
    And in the porches of my ears did pour
    The leperous distilment, whose effect
    Holds such an enmity with blood of man   65
    That swift as quicksilver it courses through
    The natural gates and alleys of the body,
    And with a sudden vigor it doth posset
    And curd, like eager droppings into milk,
    The thin and wholesome blood. So did it mine,   70
    And a most instant tetter barked about
    Most lazar-like with vile and loathsome crust
    All my smooth body.
    Thus was I sleeping by a brother's hand
    Of life, of crown, of queen at once dispatched,   75
    Cut off even in the blossoms of my sin,
    Unhouseled, disappointed, unaneled,

---

37. *process* account.
61. *secure* free from suspicion.
62. *hebona* an imaginary poison, associated with
henbane.
68. *posset* curdle.
69. *eager* acid.

71. *tetter* a skin eruption; *barked* covered as with
bark.
77. *Unhouseled* without having received the sac-
rament; *disappointed* unprepared; *unaneled* without extreme unction.

No reck'ning made, but sent to my account
With all my imperfections on my head.
O, horrible! O, horrible! most horrible!   80
If thou hast nature in thee, bear it not.
Let not the royal bed of Denmark be
A couch for luxury and damnéd incest.
But howsomever thou pursues this act,
Taint not thy mind, nor let thy soul contrive   85
Against thy mother aught. Leave her to heaven,
And to those thorns that in her bosom lodge
To prick and sting her. Fare thee well at once.
The glowworm shows the matin to be near,
And gins to pale his uneffectual fire.   90
Adieu, adieu, adieu. Remember me.   [*Exit.*]

HAM.   O all you host of heaven! O earth! What else?
And shall I couple hell? O, fie! Hold, hold, my heart,
And you, my sinews, grow not instant old,
But bear me stiffly up. Remember thee?   95
Ay, thou poor ghost, whiles memory holds a seat
In this distracted globe. Remember thee?
Yea, from the table of my memory
I'll wipe away all trivial fond records,
All saws of books, all forms, all pressures past   100
That youth and observation copied there,
And thy commandment all alone shall live
Within the book and volume of my brain,
Unmixed with baser matter. Yes, by heaven!
O most pernicious woman!   105
O villain, villain, smiling, damnéd villain!
My tables—meet it is I set it down
That one may smile, and smile, and be a villain.
At least I am sure it may be so in Denmark.   [*Writing.*]
So, uncle, there you are. Now to my word: 110
It is 'Adieu, adieu. Remember me.'
I have sworn't.

          Enter HORATIO *and* MARCELLUS.

HOR.   My lord, my lord!
MAR.   Lord Hamlet!
HOR.   Heavens secure him!
HAM.   So be it!
MAR.   Illo, ho, ho, my lord!   115
HAM.   Hillo, ho, ho, boy! Come, bird, come.

---

83. *luxury* lust.
89. *matin* morning.
97. *globe* head.
98. *table* writing tablet, memorandum book (as at
line 107, below; here metaphorically of the mind).

99. *fond* foolish.
100. *saws* sayings; *forms* concepts; *pressures*
impressions.
115. *Illo, ho, ho* cry of the falconer to summon
his hawk.

MAR.   How is't, my noble lord?
HOR.   What news, my lord?
HAM.   O, wonderful!
HOR.   Good my lord, tell it.
HAM.   No, you will reveal it.
HOR.   Not I, my lord, by heaven.
MAR.   Nor I, my lord.   120
HAM.   How say you then, would heart of man once think it?
   But you'll be secret?
BOTH.   Ay, by heaven, my lord.
HAM.   There's never a villain dwelling in all Denmark
   But he's an arrant knave.
HOR.   There needs no ghost, my lord, come from the grave   125
   To tell us this.
HAM.   Why, right, you are in the right,
   And so without more circumstance at all
   I hold it fit that we shake hands and part,
   You, as your business and desire shall point you,
   For every man hath business and desire   130
   Such as it is, and for my own poor part,
   I will go pray.
HOR.   These are but wild and whirling words, my lord.
HAM.   I am sorry they offend you, heartily;
   Yes, faith, heartily.
HOR.   There's no offence, my lord.   135
HAM.   Yes, by Saint Patrick, but there is, Horatio,
   And much offence too. Touching this vision here,
   It is an honest ghost, that let me tell you.
   For your desire to know what is between us,
   O'ermaster't as you may. And now, good friends,   140
   As you are friends, scholars, and soldiers,
   Give me one poor request.
HOR.   What is't, my lord? We will.
HAM.   Never make known what you have seen to-night.
BOTH.   My lord, we will not.
HAM.   Nay, but swear't.
HOR.   In faith,   145
   My lord, not I.
MAR.   Nor I, my lord, in faith.
HAM.   Upon my sword.
MAR.   We have sworn, my lord, already.
HAM.   Indeed, upon my sword, indeed.
                           Ghost cries under the stage.
GHOST.   Swear.
HAM.   Ha, ha, boy, say'st thou so? Art thou there, truepenny?

---

136. *Saint Patrick* associated, in the late middle   sumably come.
ages, with purgatory, whence the ghost has pre-   149. *truepenny* honest fellow.

Come on. You hear this fellow in the cellarage.   150
Consent to swear.
HOR.   Propose the oath, my lord.
HAM.   Never to speak of this that you have seen,
Swear by my sword.
GHOST.   [*Beneath.*] Swear.
HAM.   Hic et ubique? Then we'll shift our ground.   155
Come hither, gentlemen,
And lay your hands again upon my sword.
Swear by my sword
Never to speak of this that you have heard.
GHOST.   [*Beneath.*] Swear by his sword.   160
HAM.   Well said, old mole! Canst work i' th' earth so fast?
A worthy pioneer! Once more remove, good friends.
HOR.   O day and night, but this is wondrous strange!
HAM.   And therefore as a stranger give it welcome.
There are more things in heaven and earth, Horatio,   165
Than are dreamt of in your philosophy.
But come.
Here as before, never, so help you mercy,
How strange or odd some'er I bear myself
(As I perchance hereafter shall think meet   170
To put an antic disposition on),
That you, at such times, seeing me, never shall,
With arms encumbered thus, or this head-shake,
Or by pronouncing of some doubtful phrase,
As 'Well, well, we know', or 'We could, and if we would'   175
Or 'If we list to speak', or 'There be, and if they might'
Or such ambiguous giving out, to note
That you know aught of me—this do swear,
So grace and mercy at your most need help you.
GHOST.   [*Beneath.*] Swear.   180
HAM.   Rest, rest, perturbèd spirit! So, gentlemen,
With all my love I do commend me to you,
And what so poor a man as Hamlet is
May do t'express his love and friending to you,
God willing, shall not lack. Let us go in together,   185
And still your fingers on your lips, I pray.
The time is out of joint. O cursèd spite
That ever I was born to set it right!
Nay, come, let's go together.   *Exeunt.*

---

155. *Hic et ubique* here and everywhere.   171. *antic* mad.
162. *pioneer* miner.   173. *encumbered* folded.

[II.i]

Enter old POLONIUS, *with his man* [REYNALDO].
POL.   Give him this money and these notes, Reynaldo.
REY.   I will, my lord.
POL.   You shall do marvellous wisely, good Reynaldo,
    Before you visit him, to make inquire
    Of his behavior.
REY.   My lord, I did intend it.   5
POL.   Marry, well said, very well said. Look you, sir,
    Enquire me first what Danskers are in Paris,
    And how, and who, what means, and where they keep,
    What company, at what expense; and finding
    By this encompassment and drift of question   10
    That they do know my son, come you more nearer
    Than your particular demands will touch it.
    Take you as 'twere some distant knowledge of him,
    As thus, 'I know his father and his friends,
    And in part him'. Do you mark this, Reynaldo?   15
REY.   Ay, very well, my lord.
POL.   'And in part him, but', you may say, 'not well,
    But if't be he I mean, he's very wild,
    Addicted so and so'. And there put on him
    What forgeries you please; marry, none so rank   20
    As may dishonour him. Take heed of that.
    But, sir, such wanton, wild, and usual slips
    As are companions noted and most known
    To youth and liberty.
REY.   As gaming, my lord?
POL.   Ay, or drinking, fencing, swearing, quarrelling,   25
    Drabbing—you may go so far.
REY.   My lord, that would dishonor him.
POL.   Faith, no, as you may season it in the charge.
    You must not put another scandal on him,
    That he is open to incontinency.   30
    That's not my meaning. But breathe his faults so quaintly
    That they may seem the taints of liberty,
    The flash and outbreak of a fiery mind,
    A savageness in unreclaiméd blood,
    Of general assault.
REY.   But, my good lord—   35
POL.   Wherefore should you do this?

[II.i] 7. *Danskers* Danes.   26. *Drabbing* whoring.
8. *means* wealth.   28. *season* moderate.
10. *encompassment* talking round the matter.   31. *quaintly* delicately.
20. *forgeries* invented wrongdoings.   34. *unreclaimed* untamed.
24. *liberty* license.   35. *Of general assault* assailing all.

REY.   Ay, my lord,
  I would know that.
POL.   Marry, sir, here's my drift,
  And I believe it is a fetch of warrant.
  You laying these slight sallies on my son,
  As 'twere a thing a little soiled i' th' working,   40
  Mark you,
  Your party in converse, him you would sound,
  Having ever seen in the prenominate crimes
  The youth you breathe of guilty, be assured
  He closes with you in this consequence,   45
  'Good sir', or so, or 'friend', or 'gentleman',
  According to the phrase or the addition
  Of man and country.
REY.   Very good, my lord.
POL. And then, sir, does 'a this—'a does—What was I about to
  say?
  By the mass, I was about to say something.   50
  Where did I leave?
REY. At 'closes in the consequence'.
POL. At 'closes in the consequence'—ay, marry,
  He closes thus: 'I know the gentleman.
  I saw him yesterday, or th' other day,   55
  Or then, or then, with such, or such, and as you say,
  There was 'a gaming, there o'ertook in's rouse,
  There falling out at tennis', or perchance
  'I saw him enter such a house of sale',
  Videlicet, a brothel, or so forth.   60
  See you, now—
  Your bait of falsehood takes this carp of truth,
  And thus do we of wisdom and of reach,
  With windlasses and with assays of bias,
  By indirections find directions out;   65
  So by my former lecture and advice
  Shall you my son. You have me, have you not?
REY. My lord, I have.
POL.   God buy ye; fare ye well.
REY. Good my lord.
POL. Observe his inclination in yourself.   70
REY. I shall, my lord.
POL. And let him ply his music.
REY.   Well, my lord.
POL. Farewell.   *Exit* REYNALDO.

---

38. *fetch of warrant* allowable device.
43. *prenominate* before-named.
45. *closes* agrees; *in this consequence* as follows.
47. *addition* title.
60. V*idelicet* namely.

63. *reach* ability.
64. *windlasses* roundabout approaches; *assays of bias* indirect attempts.
68. *God buy ye* God be with you.

Enter OPHELIA.

　　　　　　　How now, Ophelia, what's the matter?

OPH.　O my lord, my lord, I have been so affrighted!

POL.　With what, i' th' name of God?　　　　　　　　　　　　75

OPH.　My lord, as I was sewing in my closet,
Lord Hamlet with his doublet all unbraced,
No hat upon his head, his stockings fouled,
Ungartered and down-gyvéd to his ankle,
Pale as his shirt, his knees knocking each other,　　　　　80
And with a look so piteous in purport
As if he had been looséd out of hell
To speak of horrors—he comes before me.

POL.　Mad for thy love?

OPH.　　　　　　　　　　My lord, I do not know,
But truly I do fear it.

POL.　　　　　　　　　　What said he?　　　　　　　　　85

OPH.　He took me by the wrist, and held me hard,
Then goes he to the length of all his arm,
And with his other hand thus o'er his brow,
He falls to such perusal of my face
As 'a would draw it. Long stayed he so.　　　　　　　　90
At last, a little shaking of mine arm,
And thrice his head thus waving up and down,
He raised a sigh so piteous and profound
As it did seem to shatter all his bulk,
And end his being. That done, he lets me go,　　　　　95
And with his head over his shoulder turned
He seemed to find his way without his eyes,
For out adoors he went without their helps,
And to the last bended their light on me.

POL.　Come, go with me. I will go seek the king.　　　　100
This is the very ecstasy of love,
Whose violent property fordoes itself,
And leads the will to desperate undertakings
As oft as any passion under heaven
That does afflict our natures. I am sorry.　　　　　　105
What, have you given him any hard words of late?

OPH.　No, my good lord, but as you did command
I did repel his letters, and denied
His access to me.

POL.　　　　　　　　That hath made him mad.
I am sorry that with better heed and judgment　　　　110
I had not quoted him. I feared he did but trifle,

---

76. *closet* private room.
77. *unbraced* unlaced.
79. *down-gyved* hanging down, like gyves or fetters on a prisoner's ankles.

101. *ecstasy* madness.
102. *fordoes* detroys.
111. *quoted* observed.

And meant to wrack thee; but beshrew my jealousy.
By heaven, it is as proper to our age
To cast beyond ourselves in our opinions
As it is common for the younger sort   115
To lack discretion. Come, go we to the king.
This must be known, which being kept close, might move
More grief to hide than hate to utter love.
Come.   *Exeunt.*

[II.ii]

Flourish. Enter KING *and* QUEEN, ROSENCRANTZ *and* GUIL-
DENSTERN [*and* ATTENDANTS].

KING.   Welcome, dear Rosencrantz and Guildenstern.
Moreover that we much did long to see you,
The need we have to use you did provoke
Our hasty sending. Something have you heard
Of Hamlet's transformation—so call it,   5
Sith nor th' exterior nor the inward man
Resembles that it was. What it should be,
More than his father's death, that thus hath put him
So much from th' understanding of himself,
I cannot dream of. I entreat you both   10
That, being of so young days brought up with him,
And sith so neighboured to his youth and havior,
That you vouchsafe your rest here in our court
Some little time, so by your companies
To draw him on to pleasures, and to gather   15
So much as from occasion you may glean,
Whether aught to us unknown afflicts him thus,
That opened lies within our remedy.
QUEEN.   Good gentlemen, he hath much talked of you,
And sure I am two men there is not living   20
To whom he more adheres. If it will please you
To show us so much gentry and good will
As to expend your time with us awhile
For the supply and profit of our hope,
Your visitation shall receive such thanks   25
As fits a king's remembrance.
ROS.   Both your majesties
Might, by the sovereign power you have of us,
Put your dread pleasures more into command
Than to entreaty.
GUIL.   But we both obey,

---

112. *wrack* ruin.   [II.ii] 6. *Sith* since.
113. *proper to* characteristic of.   18. *opened* disclosed.
117. *close* secret; *move* cause.   22. *gentry* courtesy.

And here give up ourselves in the full bent   30
　To lay our service freely at your feet,
　To be commanded.
KING.　Thanks, Rosencrantz and gentle Guildenstern.
QUEEN.　Thanks, Guildenstern and gentle Rosencrantz.
　And I beseech you instantly to visit   35
　My too much changed son. Go, some of you,
　And bring these gentlemen where Hamlet is.
GUIL.　Heavens make our presence and our practices
　Pleasant and helpful to him!
QUEEN.　　　　　　　　　　　Ay, amen!
　　　　Exeunt ROSENCRANTZ *and* GUILDENSTERN [*with some* ATTEN-
　　　　DANTS].

　　　　Enter POLONIUS.
POL.　Th' ambassadors from Norway, my good lord,   40
　Are joyfully returned.
KING.　Thou still hast been the father of good news.
POL.　Have I, my lord? I assure my good liege,
　I hold my duty as I hold my soul,
　Both to my God and to my gracious king;   45
　And I do think—or else this brain of mine
　Hunts not the trail of policy so sure
　As it hath used to do—that I have found
　The very cause of Hamlet's lunacy.
KING.　O, speak of that, that do I long to hear.   50
POL.　Give first admittance to th' ambassadors.
　My news shall be the fruit to that great feast.
KING.　Thyself do grace to them, and bring them in.
　　　　　　　　　　　　　　　　　[*Exit* POLONIUS.]
　He tells me, my dear Gertrude, he hath found
　The head and source of all your son's distemper.   55
QUEEN.　I doubt it is no other but the main,
　His father's death and our o'erhasty marriage.
KING.　Well, we shall sift him.

　　　　Enter Ambassadors [(VOLTEMAND *and* CORNELIUS), *with* PO-
　　　　LONIUS].
　　　　　　　　　　　　Welcome, my good friends,
　Say, Voltemand, what from our brother Norway?
VOL.　Most fair return of greetings and desires.   60
　Upon our first, he sent out to suppress
　His nephew's levies, which to him appeared
　To be a preparation 'gainst the Polack,
　But better looked into, he truly found
　It was against your highness, whereat grieved,   65

42. *still* ever.　　　　　　　　　　63. *the Polack* the Polish nation.
56. *doubt* suspect.

That so his sickness, age, and impotence
Was falsely borne in hand, sends out arrests
On Fortinbras, which he in brief obeys,
Receives rebuke from Norway, and in fine,
Makes vow before his uncle never more   70
To give th' assay of arms against your majesty.
Whereon old Norway, overcome with joy,
Gives him threescore thousand crowns in annual fee,
And his commission to employ those soldiers,
So levied as before, against the Polack,   75
With an entreaty, herein further shown,   [*Gives a paper.*]
That it might please you to give quiet pass
Through your dominions for this enterprise,
On such regards of safety and allowance
As therein are set down.

KING.   It likes us well,   80
And at our more considered time we'll read,
Answer, and think upon this business.
Meantime we thank you for your well-took labor.
Go to your rest; at night we'll feast together.
Most welcome home!   *Exeunt* AMBASSADORS.

POL.   This business is well ended.   85
My liege and madam, to expostulate
What majesty should be, what duty is,
Why day is day, night night, and time is time,
Were nothing but to waste night, day, and time.
Therefore, since brevity is the soul of wit,   90
And tediousness the limbs and outward flourishes,
I will be brief. Your noble son is mad.
Mad call I it, for to define true madness,
What is't but to be nothing else but mad?
But let that go.

QUEEN.   More matter with less art.   95
POL.   Madam, I swear I use no art at all.
That he is mad, 'tis true: 'tis true 'tis pity,
And pity 'tis 'tis true. A foolish figure,
But farewell it, for I will use no art.
Mad let us grant him, then, and now remains   100
That we find out the cause of this effect,
Or rather say the cause of this defect,
For this effect defective comes by cause.
Thus it remains, and the remainder thus.
Perpend.   105

67. *borne in hand* deceived.
69. *in fine* in the end.
71. *assay* trial.
79. *regards* considerations.

90. *wit* understanding.
95. *matter* meaning, sense.
105. *Perpend* consider.

I have a daughter—have while she is mine—
Who in her duty and obedience, mark,
Hath given me this. Now gather, and surmise.   [*Reads.*]
      'To the celestial, and my soul's idol, the most beautified
Ophelia.'—That's an ill phrase, a vile phrase, 'beautified' is a 110
vile phrase. But you shall hear. Thus: [*Reads.*]
      'In her excellent white bosom, these, etc.'
QUEEN.   Came this from Hamlet to her?
POL.   Good madam, stay awhile. I will be faithful.

[*Reads Letter.*]

            'Doubt thou the stars are fire,   115
                  Doubt that the sun doth move;
            Doubt truth to be a liar;
                  But never doubt I love.

      O dear Ophelia, I am ill at these numbers. I have not art
to reckon my groans, but that I love thee best, O most best, be- 120
lieve it. Adieu.
                        Thine evermore, most dear lady, whilst
                              this machine is to him, HAMLET.'
This in obedience hath my daughter shown me,
And more above, hath his solicitings,   125
As they fell out by time, by means, and place,
All given to mine ear.
KING.   But how hath she
Received his love?
POL.   What do you think of me?
KING.   As of a man faithful and honorable.
POL.   I would fain prove so. But what might you think,   130
When I had seen this hot love on the wing,
(As I perceived it, I must tell you that,
Before my daughter told me), what might you,
Or my dear majesty your queen here, think,
If I had played the desk or table-book,   135
Or given my heart a winking, mute and dumb,
Or looked upon this love with idle sight,
What might you think? No, I went round to work,
And my young mistress thus I did bespeak:
'Lord Hamlet is a prince out of thy star.   140
This must not be'. And then I prescripts gave her,
That she should lock herself from his resort,
Admit no messengers, receive no tokens.
Which done, she took the fruits of my advice;
And he repelled, a short tale to make,   145

119. *numbers* verses.   between.
123. *machine* body.   138. *round* directly.
135. *played . . . table-book* acted as silent go-

Fell into a sadness, then into a fast,
Thence to a watch, thence into a weakness,
Thence to a lightness, and by this declension,
Into the madness wherein now he raves,
And all we mourn for.
KING.   Do you think 'tis this?   150
QUEEN.   It may be, very like.
POL.   Hath there been such a time—I would fain know that—
    That I have positively said ''Tis so',
    When it proved otherwise?
KING.   Not that I know.
POL.   [*Pointing to his head and shoulder.*] Take this from this,
    if this be otherwise.   155
    If circumstances lead me, I will find
    Where truth is hid, though it were hid indeed
    Within the centre.
KING.   How may we try it further?
POL.   You know sometimes he walks four hours together
    Here in the lobby.
QUEEN.   So he does, indeed.   160
POL.   At such a time I'll loose my daughter to him.
    Be you and I behind an arras then.
    Mark the encounter. If he love her not,
    And be not from his reason fall'n thereon,
    Let me be no assistant for a state,   165
    But keep a farm and carters.
KING.   We will try it.

                 Enter HAMLET [*reading on a book*].
QUEEN.   But look where sadly the poor wretch comes reading.
POL.   Away, I do beseech you both away,
    I'll board him presently.
                 [*Exeunt*] KING *and* QUEEN [*with* ATTENDANTS].
                 O, give me leave,
    How does my good Lord Hamlet?   170
HAM.   Well, God-a-mercy.
POL.   Do you know me, my lord?
HAM.   Excellent well, you are a fishmonger.
POL.   Not I, my lord.
HAM.   Then I would you were so honest a man.   175
POL.   Honest, my lord?
HAM.   Ay, sir, to be honest as this world goes, is to be one man
    picked out of ten thousand.
POL.   That's very true, my lord.

147. *watch* sleeplessness.   maic universe.
148. *lightness* lightheadedness.   169. *board* accost; *presently* immediately.
158. *centre* centre of the earth and of the Ptole-

HAM.   For if the sun breed maggots in a dead dog, being a good 180
kissing carrion—Have you a daughter?

POL.   I have, my lord.

HAM.   Let her not walk i' th' sun. Conception is a blessing, but as
your daughter may conceive—friend, look to't.

POL.   [*Aside.*] How say you by that? Still harping on my daughter. 185
Yet he knew me not at first. 'A said I was a fishmonger. 'A is far
gone. And truly in my youth I suffered much extremity for love,
very near this. I'll speak to him again.—What do you read, my
lord?

HAM.   Words, words, words. 190

POL.   What is the matter, my lord?

HAM.   Between who?

POL.   I mean the matter that you read, my lord.

HAM.   Slanders, sir; for the satirical rogue says here that old men
have grey beards, that their faces are wrinkled, their eyes purging 195
thick amber and plum-tree gum, and that they have a plentiful
lack of wit, together with most weak hams—all which, sir, though
I most powerfully and potently believe, yet I hold it not honesty to
have it thus set down, for yourself, sir, shall grow old as I am, if
like a crab you could go backward. 200

POL.   [*Aside.*] Though this be madness, yet there is method in't.—
Will you walk out of the air, my lord?

HAM.   Into my grave?

POL.   [*Aside.*] Indeed, that's out of the air. How pregnant sometimes his replies are! a happiness that often madness hits on, which 205
reason and sanity could not so prosperously be delivered of. I will
leave him, and suddenly contrive the means of meeting between
him and my daughter.—My lord, I will take my leave of you.

HAM.   You cannot take from me anything that I will not more
willingly part withal—except my life, except my life, except my 210
life.

Enter GUILDENSTERN *and* ROSENCRANTZ.

POL.   Fare you well, my lord.

HAM.   These tedious old fools!

POL.   You go to seek the Lord Hamlet. There he is.

ROS.   [*To* POLONIUS.] God save you, sir!   [*Exit* POLONIUS.] 215

GUIL.   My honored lord!

ROS.   My most dear lord!

HAM.   My excellent good friends! How dost thou, Guildenstern?
Ah, Rosencrantz! Good lads, how do you both?

ROS.   As the indifferent children of the earth. 220

GUIL.   Happy in that we are not over-happy;
On Fortune's cap we are not the very button.

---

204. *pregnant* full of meaning.
205. *happiness* aptness.

220. *indifferent* average.
222. *button* knob on the top of a cap.

HAM.   Nor the soles of her shoe?

ROS.   Neither, my lord.

HAM.   Then you live about her waist, or in the middle of her 225
favors.

GUIL.   Faith, her privates we.

HAM.   In the secret parts of Fortune? O, most true, she is a strumpet.
What news?

ROS.   None, my lord, but that the world's grown honest.   230

HAM.   Then is doomsday near. But your news is not true. Let me
question more in particular. What have you, my good friends,
deserved at the hands of Fortune, that she sends you to prison
hither?

GUIL.   Prison, my lord?   235

HAM.   Denmark's a prison.

ROS.   Then is the world one.

HAM.   A goodly one, in which there are many confines, wards, and
dungeons, Denmark being one o' th' worst.

ROS.   We think not so, my lord.   240

HAM.   Why then 'tis none to you; for there is nothing either good or
bad, but thinking makes it so. To me it is a prison.

ROS.   Why then your ambition makes it one. 'Tis too narrow for
your mind.

HAM.   O God, I could be bounded in a nutshell and count myself 245
a king of infinite space, were it not that I have bad dreams.

GUIL.   Which dreams indeed are ambition; for the very substance of
the ambitious is merely the shadow of a dream.

HAM.   A dream itself is but a shadow.

ROS.   Truly, and I hold ambition of so airy and light a quality that it 250
is but a shadow's shadow.

HAM.   Then are our beggars bodies, and our monarchs and out-
stretched heroes the beggars' shadows. Shall we to th' court? for,
by my fay, I cannot reason.

BOTH.   We'll wait upon you.   255

HAM.   No such matter. I will not sort you with the rest of my servants; for to speak to you like an honest man, I am most dreadfully
attended. But in the beaten way of friendship, what make you at
Elsinore?

ROS.   To visit you, my lord; no other occasion.   260

HAM.   Beggar that I am, I am even poor in thanks, but I thank you;
and sure, dear friends, my thanks are too dear a halfpenny. Were
you not sent for? Is it your own inclining? Is it a free visitation?
Come, come, deal justly with me. Come, come, nay speak.

GUIL.   What should we say, my lord?   265

HAM.   Anything but to th' purpose. You were sent for, and there is
a kind of confession in your looks, which your modesties have not

254. *fay* faith.   256. *sort you with* put you in the same class with.

craft enough to color. I know the good king and queen have sent
for you.

ROS.   To what end, my lord?   270

HAM.   That you must teach me. But let me conjure you by the rights
of our fellowship, by the consonancy of our youth, by the obligation of our ever-preserved love, and by what more dear a better
proposer can charge you withal, be even and direct with me whether
you were sent for or no.   275

ROS.   [*Aside to* GUILDENSTERN.] What say you?

HAM.   [*Aside.*] Nay, then, I have an eye of you.—If you love me,
hold not off.

GUIL.   My lord, we were sent for.

HAM.   I will tell you why; so shall my anticipation prevent your   280
discovery, and your secrecy to the king and queen moult no feather.
I have of late—but wherefore I know not—lost all my mirth, for-
gone all custom of exercises; and indeed it goes so heavily with my
disposition, that this goodly frame the earth seems to me a sterile
promontory, this most excellent canopy the air, look you, this brave   285
o'er-hanging firmament, this majestical roof fretted with golden
fire, why it appeareth nothing to me but a foul and pestilent congregation of vapors. What a piece of work is a man, how noble in
reason, how infinite in faculties, in form and moving, how express
and admirable in action, how like an angel in apprehension, how   290
like a god: the beauty of the world, the paragon of animals. And
yet to me, what is this quintessence of dust? Man delights not me,
nor woman neither, though by your smiling you seem to say so.

ROS.   My lord, there was no such stuff in my thoughts.

HAM.   Why did ye laugh, then, when I said 'Man delights not   295
me'?

ROS.   To think, my lord, if you delight not in man, what lenten
entertainment the players shall receive from you. We coted them
on the way, and hither are they coming to offer you service.

HAM.   He that plays the king shall be welcome—his majesty shall   300
have tribute on me; the adventurous knight shall use his foil and
target; the lover shall not sigh gratis; the humorous man shall end
his part in peace; the clown shall make those laugh whose lungs
are tickle o' th' sere; and the lady shall say her mind freely, or the
blank verse shall halt for't. What players are they?   305

ROS.   Even those you were wont to take such delight in, the trage-
dians of the city.

HAM.   How chances it they travel? Their residence, both in reputation and profit, was better both ways.

---

280. *prevent* forestall.
281. *discovery* disclosure.
286. *fretted* decorated with fretwork.
297. *lenten* scanty
298. *coted* passed.
301–2. *foil and target* spear and shield.
302. *humorous man* the actor who plays the ec-

centric character dominated by one of the four humors.
304. *tickle o' th' sere* easily set off (*sere* is that part
of a gunlock which keeps the hammar at full or
half cock).
305. *halt* limp.

ROS.   I think their inhibition comes by the means of the late in- 310
       novation.
HAM.   Do they hold the same estimation they did when I was in the
       city? Are they so followed?
ROS.   No, indeed, are they not.
HAM.   How comes it? Do they grow rusty?   315
ROS.   Nay, their endeavor keeps in the wonted pace; but there
       is, sir, an eyrie of children, little eyases, that cry out on the top of
       question, and are most tyrannically clapped for't. These are now
       the fashion, and so berattle the common stages (so they call them)
       that many wearing rapiers are afraid of goose quills and dare 320
       scarce come thither.
HAM.   What, are they children? Who maintains 'em? How are
       they escoted? Will they pursue the quality no longer than they can
       sing? Will they not say afterwards, if they should grow themselves
       to common players (as it is most like, if their means are no better), 325
       their writers do them wrong to make them exclaim against their
       own succession?
ROS.   Faith, there has been much to do on both sides; and the na-
       tion holds it no sin to tarre them to controversy. There was for a
       while no money bid for argument, unless the poet and the 330
       player went to cuffs in the question.
HAM.   Is't possible?
GUIL. O, there has been much throwing about of brains.
HAM.   Do the boys carry it away?
ROS.   Ay, that they do, my lord, Hercules and his load too.   335
HAM.   It is not very strange, for my uncle is King of Denmark, and
       those that would make mouths at him while my father lived give
       twenty, forty, fifty, a hundred ducats apiece for his picture in little.
       'Sblood, there is something in this more than natural, if philoso-
       phy could find it out.   A flourish. 340
GUIL. There are the players.
HAM.   Gentlemen, you are welcome to Elsinore. Your hands. Come
       then, th' appurtenance of welcome is fashion and ceremony.

---

310. *inhibition* prohibition of plays by authority
(possibly with reference to decree of the Privy
Council of 22 June 1600, limiting the number of
London theater companies to two, and stipulating
that the two were to perform only twice a week);
innovation meaning uncertain (sometimes taken
to refer to the re-introduction, ca. 1600, on the
London theatrical scene of companies of boy actors performing in private theaters; sometimes interpreted as "political upheaval," with special reference to Essex's rebellion, February, 1601).
317. *eyrie* nest; *eyases* nestling hawks (here, the
boys in the children's companies training as actors).
317–18. *on the top of question* louder than all
others on matter of dispute.

319. *common stages* public theaters (of the common *players* (below, line 325), organized in companies composed mainly of adult actors.
320. *goose quills* pens (of the satiric dramatists
writing for the private theaters).
323. *escoted* maintained; *pursue the quality* continue in the profession of acting.
324. *sing* i.e., until their voices change.
329. *tarre* incite.
330. *argument* plot of a play.
335. *load* i.e., the world (the sign of the Globe
Theatre represented Hercules bearing the world on
his shoulders).
337. *mouths* grimaces.
338. *in little* in miniature.
343. *appurtenance* adjuncts.

Let me comply with you in this garb, lest my extent to the players, which I tell you must show fairly outwards, should more ap- 345
pear like entertainment than yours. You are welcome. But my
uncle-father and aunt-mother are deceived.

GUIL.   In what, my dear lord?

HAM.   I am but mad north-north-west; when the wind is southerly
I know a hawk from a handsaw.   350

Enter POLONIUS.

POL.   Well be with you, gentlemen.

HAM.   Hark you, Guildenstern—and you too—at each ear a hearer.
That great baby you see there is not yet out of his swaddling clouts.

ROS.   Happily he is the second time come to them, for they say an
old man is twice a child.   355

HAM.   I will prophesy he comes to tell me of the players. Mark it.
—You say right, sir, a Monday morning, 'twas then indeed.

POL.   My lord, I have news to tell you.

HAM.   My lord, I have news to tell you.
When Roscius was an actor in Rome—   360

POL.   The actors are come hither, my lord.

HAM.   Buzz, buzz.

POL.   Upon my honor—

HAM.   Then came each actor on his ass—

POL.   The best actors in the world, either for tragedy, comedy, his- 365
tory, pastoral, pastoral-comical, historical-pastoral, tragical-histor-
ical, tragical-comical-historical-pastoral, scene individable, or poem
unlimited. Seneca cannot be too heavy nor Plautus too light. For
the law of writ and the liberty, these are the only men.

HAM.   O Jephthah, judge of Israel, what a treasure hadst thou!   370

POL.   What a treasure had he, my lord?

HAM.   Why—

'One fair daughter, and no more,
The which he loved passing well'.

POL.   [*Aside.*] Still on my daughter.   375

HAM.   Am I not i' th' right, old Jephthah?

POL.   If you call me Jephthah, my lord, I have a daughter that I love
passing well.

344. *extent* welcome.
350. *hawk* mattock or pickaxe (also called "hack,"
here used with a play on *hawk* as a bird); *handsaw*
a saw managed with one hand (here used with a
play on some corrupt form of *hernshaw*, "heron").
354. *Happily* perhaps.
360. *Roscius* the greatest of Roman comic actors,
though regarded by the Elizabethans as a tragic
one.
367. *scene individable* i.e., a play that observes the
unities of time and place.

367–68. *poem unlimited* a play that does not observe the unities; *Seneca* Roman writer of tragedies; *Plautus* Roman comic dramatist.
369. *law of writ and the liberty* i.e., plays according to strict classical rules, and those that ignored
the unities of time and place.
370. *Jephthah* was compelled to sacrifice a beloved daughter (Judges 11). Hamlet quotes from a
contemporary ballad titled *Jephthah, Judge of Israel* at lines 373–74, 382, and 384.

HAM.   Nay, that follows not.
POL.   What follows then, my lord?   380
HAM.   Why—

'As by lot, God wot'

and then, you know,

'It came to pass, as most like it was.'

The first row of the pious chanson will show you more, for look 385
where my abridgement comes.

Enter the PLAYERS.

You are welcome, masters; welcome, all.—I am glad to see thee
well.—Welcome, good friends.—O, old friend! Why thy face is
valanced since I saw thee last. Com'st thou to beard me in Denmark?—What, my young lady and mistress? By'r lady, your lady- 390
ship is nearer to heaven than when I saw you last by the altitude
of a chopine. Pray God your voice, like a piece of uncurrent gold,
be not cracked within the ring.—Masters, you are all welcome.
We'll e'en to't like French falconers, fly at anything we see. We'll
have a speech straight. Come give us a taste of your quality, come 395
a passionate speech.
1 PLAY.   What speech, my good lord?
HAM.   I heard thee speak me a speech once, but it was never
acted, or if it was, not above once, for the play, I remember, pleased
not the million; 'twas caviary to the general. But it was—as I re- 400
ceived it, and others whose judgments in such matters cried in the
top of mine—an excellent play, well digested in the scenes, set
down with as much modesty as cunning. I remember one said
there were no sallets in the lines to make the matter savory, nor no
matter in the phrase that might indict the author of affectation, but 405
called it an honest method, as wholesome as sweet, and by very
much more handsome than fine. One speech in't I chiefly loved.
'Twas Æneas' tale to Dido, and thereabout of it especially when
he speaks of Priam's slaughter. If it live in your memory, begin at
this line—let me see, let me see: 410

'The rugged Pyrrhus, like th' Hyrcanian beast'—

'tis not so; it begins with Pyrrhus—

---

385. *row* stanza.
389. *valanced* bearded.
390. *young lady* i.e., the boy who plays female roles.
392. *chopine* a shoe with high cork heel and sole.
393. *cracked within the ring* a coin cracked within the circle surrounding the head of the sovereign was no longer legal tender and so *uncurrent.*

395. *straight* immediately.
400. *caviary* caviare; *general* multitude.
402. *digested* arranged.
404. *sallets* salads, highly seasoned passages.
407. *more handsome than fine* admirable rather than appealing by mere cleverness.
411. *Hyrcanian beast* tiger.

'The rugged Pyrrhus, he whose sable arms,
Black as his purpose, did the night resemble
When he lay couchéd in th' ominous horse,   415
Hath now this dread and black complexion smeared
With heraldry more dismal; head to foot
Now is he total gules, horridly tricked
With blood of fathers, mothers, daughters, sons,
Baked and impasted with the parching streets,   420
That lend a tyrannous and a damnéd light
To their lord's murder. Roasted in wrath and fire,
And thus o'er-sizéd with coagulate gore,
With eyes like carbuncles, the hellish Pyrrhus
Old grandsire Priam seeks.'   425
  So proceed you.
POL.   Fore God, my lord, well spoken, with good accent and good
  discretion.
1 PLAY.   'Anon he finds him
  Striking too short at Greeks. His antique sword,   430
Rebellious to his arm, lies where it falls,
Repugnant to command. Unequal matched,
Pyrrhus at Priam drives, in rage strikes wide.
But with the whiff and wind of his fell sword
Th' unnervéd father falls. Then senseless Ilium,   435
Seeming to feel this blow, with flaming top
Stoops to his base, and with a hideous crash
Takes prisoner Pyrrhus' ear. For, lo! his sword,
Which was declining on the milky head
Of reverend Priam, seemed i' th' air to stick.   440
So as a painted tyrant Pyrrhus stood,
And like a neutral to his will and matter,
Did nothing.
But as we often see, against some storm,
A silence in the heavens, the rack stand still,   445
The bold winds speechless, and the orb below
As hush as death, anon the dreadful thunder
Doth rend the region; so, after Pyrrhus' pause,
A rouséd vengeance sets him new awork,
And never did the Cyclops' hammers fall   450
On Mars's armor, forged for proof eterne,
With less remorse than Pyrrhus' bleeding sword
Now falls on Priam.

---

415. *horse* i.e., the Trojan horse.
418. *gules* heraldic term for red; *tricked* delineated.
423. *o'er-sized* covered as with size; *coagulate*
clotted.
432. *Repugnant* refractory.
434. *fell* fierce, cruel.

444. *against* just before.
445. *rack* mass of cloud.
448. *region* air.
450. *Cyclops* giant workmen who made armor in
the smithy of Vulcan.
451. *proof eterne* to be forever impenetrable.

Out, out, thou strumpet, Fortune! All you gods,
In general synod take away her power,   455
Break all the spokes and fellies from her wheel,
And bowl the round nave down the hill of heaven
As low as to the fiends.'
POL.   This is too long.
HAM.   It shall to the barber's with your beard.—Prithee say on. 460
He's for a jig, or a tale of bawdry, or he sleeps. Say on; come to
Hecuba.
1 PLAY.   'But who, ah woe! had seen the mobled queen—'
HAM.   'The mobled queen'?
POL.   That's good.   465
1 PLAY.   'Run barefoot up and down, threat'ning the flames
With bisson rheum, a clout upon that head
Where late the diadem stood, and for a robe,
About her lank and all o'er-teeméd loins,
A blanket, in the alarm of fear caught up—   470
Who this had seen, with tongue in venom steeped,
'Gainst Fortune's state would treason have pronounced.
But if the gods themselves did see her then,
When she saw Pyrrhus make malicious sport
In mincing with his sword her husband's limbs,   475
The instant burst of clamor that she made,
Unless things mortal move them not at all,
Would have made milch the burning eyes of heaven,
And passion in the gods.'
POL.   Look whe'r he has not turned his color, and has tears in's 480
eyes. Prithee no more.
HAM.   'Tis well. I'll have thee speak out the rest of this soon.—
Good my lord, will you see the players well bestowed? Do you
hear, let them be well used, for they are the abstract and brief
chronicles of the time; after your death you were better have a bad 485
epitaph than their ill report while you live.
POL.   My lord, I will use them according to their desert.
HAM.   God's bodkin, man, much better. Use every man after his
desert, and who shall 'scape whipping? Use them after your own
honor and dignity. The less they deserve, the more merit is in your 490
bounty. Take them in.
POL.   Come, sirs.
HAM.   Follow him, friends. We'll hear a play tomorrow. [*Aside to
First Player.*] Dost thou hear me, old friend, can you play 'The
Murder of Gonzago'?   495

---

456. *fellies* the curved pieces forming the rim of a
wheel.
457. *nave* hub of a wheel.
463. *mobled* muffled.
467. *bisson rheum* blinding tears.

469. *o'er-teemed* exhausted by many births.
472. *state* government.
478. *milch* moist, tearful (lit., milk-giving).
484. *abstract* summary account.
488. *God's bodkin* by God's dear body.

1 PLAY.   Ay, my lord.
HAM.   We'll ha't tomorrow night. You could for a need study a speech
   of some dozen or sixteen lines which I would set down and insert
   in't, could you not?
1 PLAY.   Ay, my lord.   500
HAM.   Very well. Follow that lord, and look you mock him not.
                          Exeunt POLONIUS *and* PLAYERS.
   My good friends, I'll leave you till night. You are welcome to
   Elsinore.
ROS.   Good my lord. *Exeunt* [ROSENCRANTZ *and* GUILDENSTERN].
HAM.   Ay, so God buy to you. Now I am alone.   505
   O, what a rogue and peasant slave am I!
   Is it not monstrous that this player here,
   But in a fiction, in a dream of passion,
   Could force his soul so to his own conceit
   That from her working all his visage wanned;   510
   Tears in his eyes, distraction in his aspect,
   A broken voice, and his whole function suiting
   With forms to his conceit? And all for nothing,
   For Hecuba!
   What's Hecuba to him or he to her,   515
   That he should weep for her? What would he do
   Had he the motive and the cue for passion
   That I have? He would drown the stage with tears,
   And cleave the general ear with horrid speech,
   Make mad the guilty, and appal the free,   520
   Confound the ignorant, and amaze indeed
   The very faculties of eyes and ears.
   Yet I,
   A dull and muddy-mettled rascal, peak
   Like John-a-dreams, unpregnant of my cause,   525
   And can say nothing; no, not for a king
   Upon whose property and most dear life
   A damned defeat was made. Am I a coward?
   Who calls me villain, breaks my pate across,
   Plucks off my beard and blows it in my face,   530
   Tweaks me by the nose, gives me the lie i' th' throat
   As deep as to the lungs? Who does me this?
   Ha, 'swounds, I should take it; for it cannot be
   But I am pigeon-livered and lack gall
   To make oppression bitter, or ere this   535
   I should 'a fatted all the region kites
   With this slave's offal. Bloody, bawdy villain!

509. *conceit* imagination.   525. *unpregnant* not quickened to action.
519. *general* public.   536. *region kites* kites of the air.
524. *muddy-mettled* dull-spirited; *peak* mope.

Remorseless, treacherous, lecherous, kindless villain!
Why, what an ass am I! This is most brave,
That I, the son of a dear father murdered,   540
Prompted to my revenge by heaven and hell,
Must like a whore unpack my heart with words,
And fall a-cursing like a very drab,
A scullion! Fie upon't! foh!
About, my brains. Hum—I have heard   545
That guilty creatures sitting at a play,
Have by the very cunning of the scene
Been struck so to the soul that presently
They have proclaimed their malefactions;
For murder, though it have no tongue, will speak   550
With most miraculous organ. I'll have these players
Play something like the murder of my father
Before mine uncle. I'll observe his looks.
I'll tent him to the quick. If 'a do blench,
I know my course. The spirit that I have seen   555
May be a devil, and the devil hath power
T' assume a pleasing shape, yea, and perhaps
Out of my weakness and my melancholy,
As he is very potent with such spirits,
Abuses me to damn me. I'll have grounds   560
More relative than this. The play's the thing
Wherein I'll catch the conscience of the king.   *Exit.*

[III.i]

Enter KING, QUEEN, POLONIUS, OPHELIA, ROSENCRANTZ,
GUILDENSTERN, LORDS.

KING.   And can you by no drift of conference
Get from him why he puts on this confusion,
Grating so harshly all his days of quiet
With turbulent and dangerous lunacy?
ROS.   He does confess he feels himself distracted,   5
But from what cause 'a will by no means speak.
GUIL.   Nor do we find him forward to be sounded,
But with a crafty madness keeps aloof

---

538. *kindless* unnatural. Following this line, *F* adds the words "Oh Vengeance!" Their inappropriateness to the occasion is noted by Professor Harold Jenkins (in his "Playhouse Interpolations in the Folio Text of Hamlet," *Studies in Bibliography* 13 [1960]: 37). Professor Jenkins remarks that the folio text, by introducing Hamlet's "call for vengeance while he is still absorbed in self-reproaches, both anticipates and misconstrues" the crisis of his passion and of the speech, which comes in fact at line

545 ("About, my brains"), when "he abandons his self-reproaches and plans action."
544. *scullion* kitchen wench.
548. *presently* immediately.
554. *tent* probe; *blench* flinch.
560. *Abuses* deludes.
561. *relative* relevant.

[III.i] 7. *forward* willing.

When we would bring him on to some confession
Of his true state.
QUEEN.   Did he receive you well?   10
ROS.   Most like a gentleman.
GUIL.   But with much forcing of his disposition.
ROS.   Niggard of question, but of our demands
    Most free in his reply.
QUEEN.   Did you assay him
    To any pastime?   15
ROS.   Madam, it so fell out that certain players
    We o'er-raught on the way. Of these we told him,
    And there did seem in him a kind of joy
    To hear of it. They are here about the court,
    And as I think, they have already order   20
    This night to play before him.
POL.   'Tis most true,
    And he beseeched me to entreat your majesties
    To hear and see the matter.
KING.   With all my heart, and it doth much content me
    To hear him so inclined.   25
    Good gentlemen, give him a further edge,
    And drive his purpose into these delights.
ROS.   We shall, my lord. *Exeunt* ROSENCRANTZ *and* GUILDENSTERN.
KING.   Sweet Gertrude, leave us too,
    For we have closely sent for Hamlet hither,
    That he, as 'twere by accident, may here   30
    Affront Ophelia.
    Her father and myself (lawful espials)
    We'll so bestow ourselves that, seeing unseen,
    We may of their encounter frankly judge,
    And gather by him, as he is behaved,   35
    If't be th' affliction of his love or no
    That thus he suffers for.
QUEEN.   I shall obey you.—
    And for your part, Ophelia, I do wish
    That your good beauties be the happy cause
    Of Hamlet's wildness. So shall I hope your virtues   40
    Will bring him to his wonted way again,
    To both your honors.
OPH.   Madam, I wish it may.
                            [*Exit* QUEEN *with* LORDS.]
POL.   Ophelia, walk you here.—Gracious, so please you,
    We will bestow ourselves.—[*to* OPHELIA.] Read on this book,

---

14. *essay* try to win.   29. *closely* privately.
17. *o'er-raught* overtook.   31. *Affront* meet face to face.
26. *give him a further edge* sharpen his inclina-   32. *espials* spies.
tion.

That show of such an exercise may color   45
Your loneliness.—We are oft to blame in this,
'Tis too much proved, that with devotion's visage
And pious action we do sugar o'er
The devil himself.
KING.   [*Aside.*]   O, 'tis too true.
How smart a lash that speech doth give my conscience!   50
The harlot's cheek, beautied with plast'ring art,
Is not more ugly to the thing that helps it
Then is my deed to my most painted word.
O heavy burden!
POL.   I hear him coming. Let's withdraw, my lord.   55
                              [*Exeunt* KING *and* POLONIUS.]

        Enter HAMLET.
HAM.   To be, or not to be, that is the question:
    Whether 'tis nobler in the mind to suffer
    The slings and arrows of outrageous fortune,
    Or to take arms against a sea of troubles,
    And by opposing end them. To die, to sleep—   60
    No more; and by a sleep to say we end
    The heartache, and the thousand natural shocks
    That flesh is heir to: 'tis a consummation
    Devoutly to be wished. To die, to sleep—
    To sleep, perchance to dream, ay there's the rub;   65
    For in that sleep of death what dreams may come
    When we have shuffled off this mortal coil
    Must give us pause. There's the respect
    That makes calamity of so long life:
    For who would bear the whips and scorns of time,   70
    Th' oppressor's wrong, the proud man's contumely,
    The pangs of despised love, the law's delay,
    The insolence of office, and the spurns
    That patient merit of th' unworthy takes,
    When he himself might his quietus make   75
    With a bare bodkin? Who would fardels bear,
    To grunt and sweat under a weary life,
    But that the dread of something after death,
    The undiscovered country, from whose bourn
    No traveller returns, puzzles the will,   80
    And makes us rather bear those ills we have
    Than fly to others that we know not of?
    Thus conscience does make cowards of us all,

---

45. *exercise* act of devotion; *color* give an appearance of naturalness to.
52. *to* compared to.
65. *rub* obstacle (lit., obstruction encountered by
bowler's ball).

67. *coil* bustle, turmoil.
75. *quietus* settlement.
76. *bodkin* dagger; *fardels* burdens.
79. *bourn* realm.

And thus the native hue of resolution
Is sicklied o'er with the pale cast of thought,   85
And enterprises of great pitch and moment
With this regard their currents turn awry
And lose the name of action. Soft you now,
The fair Ophelia.—Nymph, in thy orisons
Be all my sins remembered.

OPH.   Good my lord,   90
How does your honor for this many a day?

HAM.   I humbly thank you, well.

OPH.   My lord, I have remembrances of yours
That I have longed long to re-deliver.
I pray you now receive them.

HAM.   No, not I,   95
I never gave you aught.

OPH.   My honored lord, you know right well you did,
And with them words of so sweet breath composed
As made the things more rich. Their perfume lost,
Take these again, for to the noble mind   100
Rich gifts wax poor when givers prove unkind.
There, my lord.

HAM.   Ha, ha! are you honest?

OPH.   My lord?

HAM.   Are you fair?   105

OPH.   What means your lordship?

HAM.   That if you be honest and fair, your honesty should admit no
discourse to your beauty.

OPH.   Could beauty, my lord, have better commerce than with honesty?   110

HAM.   Ay, truly, for the power of beauty will sooner transform honesty from what it is to a bawd than the force of honesty can translate beauty into his likeness. This was sometime a paradox, but
now the time gives it proof. I did love you once.

OPH.   Indeed, my lord, you made me believe so.   115

HAM.   You should not have believed me, for virtue cannot so inoculate our old stock but we shall relish of it. I loved you not.

OPH.   I was the more deceived.

HAM.   Get thee to a nunnery. Why wouldst thou be a breeder of
sinners? I am myself indifferent honest, but yet I could accuse me 120
of such things that it were better my mother had not borne me: I
am very proud, revengeful, ambitious, with more offences at my
beck than I have thoughts to put them in, imagination to give
them shape, or time to act them in. What should such fellows as
I do crawling between earth and heaven? We are arrant knaves all; 125

---

86. *pitch* height.
87. *regard* consideration.
89. *orisons* prayers.

103. *honest* chaste.
116–17. *inoculate* graft.
120. *indifferent honest* moderately respectable.

believe none of us. Go thy ways to a nunnery. Where's your father?

OPH.   At home, my lord.

HAM.   Let the doors be shut upon him, that he may play the fool
nowhere but in's own house. Farewell.   130

OPH.   O, help him, you sweet heavens!

HAM.   If thou dost marry, I'll give thee this plague for thy dowry:
be thou as chaste as ice, as pure as snow, thou shalt not escape
calumny. Get thee to a nunnery, farewell. Or if thou wilt needs
marry, marry a fool, for wise men know well enough what mon-   135
sters you make of them. To a nunnery, go, and quickly too. Farewell.

OPH.   Heavenly powers, restore him!

HAM.   I have heard of your paintings well enough. God hath given
you one face, and you make yourselves another. You jig and am-   140
ble, and you lisp; you nickname God's creatures, and make your
wantonness your ignorance. Go to, I'll no more on't, it hath made
me mad. I say we will have no moe marriage. Those that are married already, all but one, shall live. The rest shall keep as they are.
To a nunnery, go.   *Exit.* 145

OPH.   O, what a noble mind is here o'erthrown!
The courtier's, soldier's, scholar's, eye, tongue, sword,
Th' expectancy and rose of the fair state,
The glass of fashion and the mould of form,
Th' observed of all observers, quite quite down!   150
And I of ladies most deject and wretched,
That sucked the honey of his musiced vows,
Now see that noble and most sovereign reason
Like sweet bells jangled, out of time and harsh;
That unmatched form and feature of blown youth   155
Blasted with ecstasy. O, woe is me
T' have seen what I have seen, see what I see!

      Enter KING *and* POLONIUS.

KING.   Love? His affections do not that way tend,
Nor what he spake, though it lacked form a little,
Was not like madness. There's something in his soul   160
O'er which his melancholy sits on brood,
And I do doubt the hatch and the disclose
Will be some danger; which for to prevent,
I have in quick determination
Thus set it down: he shall with speed to England   165
For the demand of our neglected tribute.

141–42. *make your wantonness your ignorance*
excuse your wanton behavior with the plea that
you don't know any better.
143. *moe* more.
148. *expectancy* hope.

149. *glass* mirror.
155. *blown* blooming.
156. *ecstasy* madness.
158. *affections* emotions.
162. *doubt* fear.

Haply the seas and countries different,
With variable objects, shall expel
This something-settled matter in his heart
Whereon his brains still beating puts him thus   170
From fashion of himself. What think you on't?
POL.   It shall do well. But yet do I believe
The origin and commencement of his grief
Sprung from neglected love.—How now, Ophelia?
You need not tell us what Lord Hamlet said,   175
We heard it all.—My lord, do as you please,
But if you hold it fit, after the play
Let his queen-mother all alone entreat him
To show his grief. Let her be round with him,
And I'll be placed, so please you, in the ear   180
Of all their conference. If she find him not,
To England send him; or confine him where
Your wisdom best shall think.
KING.   It shall be so.
Madness in great ones must not unwatched go.   *Exeunt.*

[III.ii]

        Enter HAMLET *and three of the* PLAYERS.
HAM.   Speak the speech, I pray you, as I pronounced it to you,
trippingly on the tongue; but if you mouth it as many of our players
do, I had as lief the town-crier spoke my lines. Nor do not saw the
air too much with your hand thus, but use all gently, for in the
very torrent, tempest, and as I may say, whirlwind of your passion,   5
you must acquire and beget a temperance that may give it smooth-
ness. O, it offends me to the soul to hear a robustious periwig-
pated fellow tear a passion to tatters, to very rags, to split the ears
of the groundlings, who for the most part are capable of nothing
but inexplicable dumb shows and noise. I would have such a fel-   10
low whipped for o'erdoing Termagant. It out-Herods Herod. Pray
you avoid it.
1 PLAY.   I warrant your honour.
HAM.   Be not too tame neither, but let your own discretion be your
tutor. Suit the action to the word, the word to the action, with this 15
special observance, that you o'erstep not the modesty of nature; for
anything so o'erdone is from the purpose of playing, whose end
both at the first, and now, was and is, to hold as 'twere the mirror
up to nature, to show virtue her own feature, scorn her own image,
and the very age and body of the time his form and pressure. Now   20

---

179. *round* plain-spoken.

[III.ii] 9. *groundlings* spectators who paid least and
stood on the ground.

11. *Termagant* thought to be a Mohammedan de-
ity, and represented in medieval mystery plays as a
violent and ranting personage; *Herod* represented
in the mystery plays as a blustering tyrant.

this overdone, or come tardy off, though it makes the unskilful
laugh, cannot but make the judicious grieve, the censure of the
which one must in your allowance o'erweigh a whole theatre of
others. O, there be players that I have seen play—and heard others
praise, and that highly—not to speak it profanely, that neither hav-   25
ing th' accent of Christians, nor the gait of Christian, pagan, nor
man, have so strutted and bellowed that I have thought some of
nature's journeymen had made men, and not made them well,
they imitated humanity so abominably.

1 PLAY.   I hope we have reformed that indifferently with us.   30

HAM.   O, reform it altogether. And let those that play your clowns
speak no more than is set down for them, for there be of them that
will themselves laugh, to set on some quantity of barren spectators
to laugh too, though in the meantime some necessary question of
the play be then to be considered. That's villainous, and shows a   35
most pitiful ambition in the fool that uses it. Go, make you
ready.   [*Exeunt* PLAYERS.]

    Enter POLONIUS, GUILDENSTERN, *and* ROSENCRANTZ.
How now, my lord? Will the king hear this piece of work?

POL.   And the queen too, and that presently.

HAM.   Bid the players make haste.   [*Exit* POLONIUS.]   40
Will you two help to hasten them?

ROS.   Ay, my lord.   *Exeunt they two.*

HAM.   What, ho, Horatio!

    Enter HORATIO.

HOR.   Here, sweet lord, at your service.

HAM.   Horatio, thou art e'en as just a man   45
As e'er my conversation coped withal.

HOR.   O my dear lord!

HAM.   Nay, do not think I flatter,
For what advancement may I hope from thee,
That no revenue hast but thy good spirits
To feed and clothe thee? Why should the poor be flattered?   50
No, let the candied tongue lick absurd pomp,
And crook the pregnant hinges of the knee
Where thrift may follow fawning. Dost thou hear?
Since my dear soul was mistress of her choice
And could of men distinguish her election,   55
S'hath sealed thee for herself, for thou hast been
As one in suff'ring all that suffers nothing,
A man that Fortune's buffets and rewards
Hast ta'en with equal thanks; and blest are those

---

22. *censure* judgment, opinion.   52. *pregnant* ready.
30. *indifferently* fairly well.   53. *thrift* profit.
46. *coped* encountered.   55. *election* choice.

Whose blood and judgment are so well comeddled   60
That they are not a pipe for Fortune's finger
To sound what stop she please. Give me that man
That is not passion's slave, and I will wear him
In my heart's core, ay, in my heart of heart,
As I do thee. Something too much of this.   65
There is a play to-night before the king.
One scene of it comes near the circumstance
Which I have told thee of my father's death.
I prithee, when thou seest that act afoot,
Even with the very comment of thy soul   70
Observe my uncle. If his occulted guilt
Do not itself unkennel in one speech,
It is a damnéd ghost that we have seen,
And my imaginations are as foul
As Vulcan's stithy. Give him heedful note,   75
For I mine eyes will rivet to his face,
And after we will both our judgments join
In censure of his seeming.
HOR.   Well, my lord.
If 'a steal aught the whilst this play is playing,
And 'scape detecting, I will pay the theft.   80

    Enter Trumpets and Kettledrums, KING, QUEEN, POLONIUS,
    OPHELIA [ROSENCRANTZ, GUILDENSTERN, *and other* LORDS *at-*
    tendant].

HAM.   They are coming to the play. I must be idle.
  Get you a place.
KING.   How fares our cousin Hamlet?
HAM.   Excellent, i' faith, of the chameleon's dish. I eat the air,
  promise-crammed. You cannot feed capons so.   85
KING.   I have nothing with this answer, Hamlet. These words are not
  mine.
HAM.   No, nor mine now. [*To* POLONIUS.] My lord, you played once
  i' th' university, you say?
POL.   That did I, my lord, and was accounted a good actor.   90
HAM.   What did you enact?
POL.   I did enact Julius Cæsar. I was killed i' th' Capitol; Brutus
  killed me.
HAM.   It was a brute part of him to kill so capital a calf there. Be the
  players ready?   95
ROS.   Ay, my lord, they stay upon your patience.
QUEEN.   Come hither, my dear Hamlet, sit by me.

---

60. *comeddled* mingled.
70. *the very comment of thy soul* with a keenness
of observation that penetrates to the very being.
71. *occulted* hidden.
72. *unkennel* reveal.

75. *stithy* forge.
78. *censure* opinion.
81. *idle* crazy.
84. *chameleon's dish* the air, on which the chameleon was supposed to feed.

HAM.   No, good mother, here's metal more attractive.
POL.   [*To the* KING.] O, ho! do you mark that?
HAM.   Lady, shall I lie in your lap?   100
                        [*Lying down at* OPHELIA's *feet.*]
OPH.   No, my lord.
HAM.   I mean, my head upon your lap?
OPH.   Ay, my lord.
HAM.   Do you think I meant country matters?
OPH.   I think nothing, my lord.   105
HAM.   That's a fair thought to lie between maids' legs.
OPH.   What is, my lord?
HAM.   Nothing.
OPH.   You are merry, my lord.
HAM.   Who, I?   110
OPH.   Ay, my lord.
HAM.   O God, your only jig-maker! What should a man do but be
        merry? For look you how cheerfully my mother looks, and my
        father died within's two hours.
OPH.   Nay, 'tis twice two months, my lord.   115
HAM.   So long? Nay then, let the devil wear black, for I'll have a
        suit of sables. O heavens! die two months ago, and not forgotten
        yet? Then there's hope a great man's memory may outlive his life
        half a year, but by'r lady 'a must build churches then, or else shall
        'a suffer not thinking on, with the hobby-horse, whose epitaph is   120
        'For O, for O, the hobby-horse is forgot!'

             The trumpets sound. Dumb Show follows.
Enter a KING *and a* QUEEN [*very lovingly*]; *the* QUEEN *embracing him*
and he her. [*She kneels, and makes show of protestation unto him.*]
He takes her up, and declines his head upon her neck. He lies him
down upon a bank of flowers; she, seeing him asleep, leaves him.
Anon come in another man, takes off his crown, kisses it, pours
poison in the sleeper's ears, and leaves him. The QUEEN *returns,*
finds the KING *dead, makes passionate action. The* POISONER *with*
some three or four come in again, seem to condole with her. The
dead body is carried away. The POISONER *woos the* QUEEN *with gifts;*
she seems harsh awhile, but in the end accepts love.   [*Exeunt.*]
OPH.   What means this, my lord?
HAM.   Marry, this is miching mallecho; it means mischief.
OPH.   Belike this show imports the argument of the play.

             Enter PROLOGUE.
HAM.   We shall know by this fellow. The players cannot keep coun-   125
sel; they'll tell all.
OPH.   Will 'a tell us what this show meant?

---

120. *hobby-horse* the figure of a horse fastened
round the waist of a morris dancer. Puritan efforts
to suppress the country sports in which the hobby-
horse figured led to a popular ballad lamenting the
fact that "the hobby-horse is forgot."
123. *miching mallecho* skulking or crafty crime.

HAM.   Ay, or any show that you will show him. Be not you ashamed
to show, he'll not shame to tell you what it means.

OPH.   You are naught, you are naught. I'll mark the play.   130

PRO.

> *For us, and for our tragedy,*
> *Here stooping to your clemency,*
> *We beg your hearing patiently.*   [*Exit.*]

HAM.   Is this a prologue, or the posy of a ring?

OPH.   'Tis brief, my lord.   135

HAM.   As woman's love.

Enter [*the* PLAYER] KING *and* QUEEN.

P. KING.   *Full thirty times hath Phœbus' cart gone round*
Neptune's salt wash and Tellus' orbéd ground,
And thirty dozen moons with borrowed sheen
About the world have times twelve thirties been,   140
Since love our hearts and Hymen did our hands
Unite comutual in most sacred bands.

P. QUEEN.   *So many journeys may the sun and moon*
Make us again count o'er ere love be done!
But woe is me, you are so sick of late,   145
So far from cheer and from your former state,
That I distrust you. Yet though I distrust,
Discomfort you, my lord, it nothing must.
For women's fear and love hold quantity,
In neither aught, or in extremity.   150
Now what my love is proof hath made you know,
And as my love is sized, my fear is so.
Where love is great, the littlest doubts are fear;
Where little fears grow great, great love grows there.

P. KING.   *Faith, I must leave thee, love, and shortly too;*   155
My operant powers their functions leave to do.
And thou shalt live in this fair world behind,
Honored, beloved, and haply one as kind
For husband shalt thou—

P. QUEEN.   *O, confound the rest!*
Such love must needs be treason in my breast.   160
In second husband let me be accurst!
None wed the second but who killed the first.

HAM.   That's wormwood.

P. QUEEN.   *The instances that second marriage move*
Are base respects of thrift, but none of love.   165

---

130. *naught* naughty, lewd.
134. *posy* brief motto engraved on a finger-ring.
137. *Phœbus' cart* the sun's chariot.
138. *Tellus' orbed ground* the earth (Tellus was the Roman goddess of the earth).
141. *Hymen* god of marriage.

147. *distrust* fear for.
149. *hold quantity* are proportional, weigh alike.
152. *as my love is sized* according to the greatness of my love.
156. *operant* vital.
164. *instances* motives.

A second time I kill my husband dead,
When second husband kisses me in bed.
P. KING.   I do believe you think what now you speak,
But what we do determine oft we break.
Purpose is but the slave to memory,   170
Of violent birth, but poor validity;
Which now, the fruit unripe, sticks on the tree,
But fall unshaken when they mellow be.
Most necessary 'tis that we forget
To pay ourselves what to ourselves is debt.   175
What to ourselves in passion we propose,
The passion ending, doth the purpose lose.
The violence of either grief or joy
Their own enactures with themselves destroy.
Where joy most revels, grief doth most lament;   180
Grief joys, joy grieves, on slender accident.
This world is not for aye, nor 'tis not strange
That even our loves should with our fortunes change;
For 'tis a question left us yet to prove,
Whether love lead fortune, or else fortune love.   185
The great man down, you mark his favorite flies;
The poor advanced makes friends of enemies;
And hitherto doth love on fortune tend,
For who not needs shall never lack a friend,
And who in want a hollow friend doth try,   190
Directly seasons him his enemy.
But orderly to end where I begun,
Our wills and fates do so contrary run
That our devices still are overthrown;
Our thoughts are ours, their ends none of our own.   195
So think thou wilt no second husband wed,
But die thy thoughts when thy first lord is dead.
P. QUEEN.   Nor earth to me give food, nor heaven light,
Sport and repose lock from me day and night,
To desperation turn my trust and hope,   200
An anchor's cheer in prison be my scope,
Each opposite that blanks the face of joy
Meet what I would have well, and it destroy,
Both here and hence pursue me lasting strife,
If once a widow, ever I be wife!   205
HAM.   If she should break it now!
P. KING.   'Tis deeply sworn. Sweet, leave me here awhile.
My spirits grow dull, and fain I would beguile
The tedious day with sleep.   [Sleeps.]

171. *validity* endurance.   191. *seasons him* ripens him into.
179. *enactures* enactments.   201. *anchor's* anchorite's.
182. *aye* ever.

P. QUEEN   *Sleep rock thy brain,*
   And never come mischance between us twain!   *Exit.* 210
HAM.   Madam, how like you this play?
QUEEN.   The lady doth protest too much, methinks.
HAM.   O, but she'll keep her word.
KING.   Have you heard the argument? Is there no offence in't?
HAM.   No, no, they do but jest, poison in jest; no offence i' th' world. 215
KING.   What do you call the play?
HAM.   'The Mouse-trap.' Marry, how? Tropically. This play is the
image of a murder done in Vienna. Gonzago is the duke's name;
his wife, Baptista. You shall see anon. 'Tis a knavish piece of
work, but what of that? Your majesty, and we that have free 220
souls, it touches us not. Let the galled jade wince, our withers are
unwrung.

    Enter LUCIANUS.
This is one Lucianus, nephew to the king.
OPH.   You are as good as a chorus, my lord.
HAM.   I could interpret between you and your love, if I could see 225
the puppets dallying.
OPH.   You are keen, my lord, you are keen.
HAM.   It would cost you a groaning to take off mine edge.
OPH.   Still better, and worse.
HAM.   So you mis-take your husbands.—Begin, murderer. Leave 230
thy damnable faces and begin. Come, the croaking raven doth
bellow for revenge.
LUC.   *Thoughts black, hands apt, drugs fit, and time agreeing,*
   Confederate season, else no creature seeing,
   Thou mixture rank, of midnight weeds collected,   235
   With Hecate's ban thrice blasted, thrice infected,
   Thy natural magic and dire property
   On wholesome life usurps immediately.
                                    [Pours the poison in his ears.]
HAM.   'A poisons him i' th' garden for his estate. His name's Gon-
zago. The story is extant, and written in very choice Italian. You 240
shall see anon how the murderer gets the love of Gonzago's wife.
OPH.   The king rises.
HAM.   What, frighted with false fire?
QUEEN.   How fares my lord?
POL.   Give o'er the play.   245
KING.   Give me some light. Away!
POL.   Lights, lights, lights! *Exeunt all but* HAMLET *and* HORATIO.
HAM.   Why, let the strucken deer go weep,
            The hart ungalléd play.

221. *gallad jade* sorebacked horse.   under a blight.
236. *Hecate* goddess of witchcraft; *blasted* fallen

For some must watch while some must sleep;   250
          Thus runs the world away.

Would not this, sir, and a forest of feathers—if the rest of my
fortunes turn Turk with me—with two Provincial roses on my razed
shoes, get me a fellowship in a cry of players?
HOR.   Half a share.   255
HAM.   A whole one, I.

          For thou dost know, O Damon dear,
               This realm dismantled was
          Of Jove himself, and now reigns here
               A very, very—pajock.   260

HOR.   You might have rhymed.
HAM.   O good Horatio, I'll take the ghost's word for a thousand pound.
     Didst perceive?
HOR.   Very well, my lord.
HAM.   Upon the talk of the poisoning.   265
HOR.   I did very well note him.
HAM.   Ah, ha! Come, some music. Come, the recorders.

          For if the king like not the comedy,
          Why then, belike he likes it not, perdy.

Come, some music.   270

          Enter ROSENCRANTZ *and* GUILDENSTERN.
GUIL.   Good my lord, vouchsafe me a word with you.
HAM.   Sir, a whole history.
GUIL.   The king, sir—
HAM.   Ay, sir, what of him?
GUIL.   Is in his retirement marvellous distempered.   275
HAM.   With drink, sir?
GUIL.   No, my lord, with choler.
HAM.   Your wisdom should show itself more richer to signify this to
     the doctor, for for me to put him to his purgation would perhaps
     plunge him into more choler.   280
GUIL.   Good my lord, put your discourse into some frame, and start
     not so wildly from my affair.
HAM.   I am tame, sir. Pronounce.
GUIL.   The queen your mother, in most great affliction of spirit,
     hath sent me to you.   285
HAM.   You are welcome.

252. *feathers* plumes for actors' costumes.
253. *Provincial roses* i.e., Provençal roses. Ribbon
rosettes resembling these French roses were used
to decorate shoes; *razed* with ornamental slashing.
254. *cry* company.
260. *pajock* presumably a variant form of "patch-
cock," a despicable person. Cf. III.iv.104.

268. *For if . . . comedy* a seeming parody of *The
Spanish Tragedy*, IV.i. 197–98 ("And if the world
like not this tragedy,/Hard is the hap of old Hi-
eronimo"), where another revenger's dramatic entertainment is referred to.
277. *choler* one of the four bodily humors, an excess of which gave rise to anger.

GUIL.   Nay, good my lord, this courtesy is not of the right breed. If
it shall please you to make me a wholesome answer, I will do your
mother's commandment. If not, your pardon and my return shall
be the end of my business.   290

HAM.   Sir, I cannot.

ROS.   What, my lord?

HAM.   Make you a wholesome answer; my wit's diseased. But, sir,
such answer as I can make, you shall command, or rather, as you
say, my mother. Therefore no more, but to the matter. My mother, 295
you say—

ROS.   Then thus she says: your behavior hath struck her into amazement and admiration.

HAM.   O wonderful son, that can so stonish a mother! But is there
no sequel at the heels of this mother's admiration? Impart.   300

ROS.   She desires to speak with you in her closet ere you go to bed.

HAM.   We shall obey, were she ten times our mother. Have you any
further trade with us?

ROS.   My lord, you once did love me.

HAM.   And do still, by these pickers and stealers.   305

ROS.   Good my lord, what is your cause of distemper? You do surely
bar the door upon your own liberty, if you deny your griefs to your
friend.

HAM.   Sir, I lack advancement.

ROS.   How can that be, when you have the voice of the king himself 310
for your succession in Denmark?

HAM.   Ay, sir, but 'while the grass grows'—the proverb is something
musty.

                Enter the PLAYERS *with recorders.*

O, the recorders! Let me see one. To withdraw with you—why do
you go about to recover the wind of me, as if you would drive me 315
into a toil?

GUIL.   O my lord, if my duty be too bold, my love is too unman-
nerly.

HAM.   I do not well understand that. Will you play upon this
pipe?   320

GUIL.   My lord, I cannot.

HAM.   I pray you.

GUIL.   Believe me, I cannot.

HAM.   I do beseech you.

GUIL.   I know no touch of it, my lord.   325

HAM.   It is as easy as lying. Govern these ventages with your fingers
and thumb, give it breath with your mouth, and it will discourse
most eloquent music. Look you, these are the stops.

288. *wholesome* reasonable.
300. *admiration* wonder.
305. *pickers and stealers* hands.
312. *"while the grass grows"* a proverb ending "the

horse starves."
314. *withdraw* step aside for private conversation.
316. *toil* net, snare.
326. *ventages* holes or stops in the recorder.

GUIL.   But these cannot I command to any utt'rance of harmony.
        I have not the skill.   330
HAM.   Why, look you now, how unworthy a thing you make of
        me! You would play upon me, you would seem to know my stops,
        you would pluck out the heart of my mystery, you would sound
        me from my lowest note to the top of my compass; and there is
           much music, excellent voice, in this little organ, yet cannot you 335
make it speak. 'Sblood, do you think I am easier to be played on than
a pipe? Call me what instrument you will, though you can fret
me, you cannot play upon me.

            Enter POLONIUS.
        God bless you, sir!
POL.   My lord, the queen would speak with you, and presently.   340
HAM.   Do you see yonder cloud that's almost in shape of a camel?
POL.   By th' mass and 'tis, like a camel indeed.
HAM.   Methinks it is like a weasel.
POL.   It is backed like a weasel.
HAM.   Or like a whale.   345
POL.   Very like a whale.
HAM.   Then I will come to my mother by and by. [*Aside.*] They fool
        me to the top of my bent.—I will come by and by.
POL.   I will say so.   [*Exit* POLONIUS.]
HAM.   'By and by' is easily said. Leave me, friends.   350
                                        [*Exeunt all but* HAMLET.]
        'Tis now the very witching time of night,
        When churchyards yawn, and hell itself breathes out
        Contagion to this world. Now could I drink hot blood,
        And do such bitter business as the day
        Would quake to look on. Soft, now to my mother.   355
        O heart, lose not thy nature; let not ever
        The soul of Nero enter this firm bosom.
        Let me be cruel, not unnatural;
        I will speak daggers to her, but use none.
        My tongue and soul in this be hypocrites: 360
        How in my words somever she be shent,
        To give them seals never my soul consent!   *Exit.*

[III.iii]

            Enter KING, ROSENCRANTZ, *and* GUILDENSTERN.
KING.   I like him not, nor stands it safe with us
        To let his madness range. Therefore prepare you.
        I your commission will forthwith dispatch,

---

338. *fret* (1) a stop on the fingerboard of a guitar   mother.
(2) annoy.   361. *somever* soever; *shent* reproved, abused.
357. *Nero* Roman emperor who murdered his

And he to England shall along with you.
The terms of our estate may not endure   5
Hazard so near's as doth hourly grow
Out of his brows.
GUIL.   We will ourselves provide,
    Most holy and religious fear it is
    To keep those many many bodies safe
    That live and feed upon your majesty.   10
ROS.   The single and peculiar life is bound
    With all the strength and armor of the mind
    To keep itself from noyance, but much more
    That spirit upon whose weal depends and rests
    The lives of many. The cess of majesty   15
    Dies not alone, but like a gulf doth draw
    What's near it with it. It is a massy wheel
    Fixed on the summit of the highest mount,
    To whose huge spokes ten thousand lesser things
    Are mortised and adjoined, which when it falls,   20
    Each small annexment, petty consequence,
    Attends the boist'rous ruin. Never alone
    Did the king sigh, but with a general groan.
KING.   Arm you, I pray you, to this speedy voyage,
    For we will fetters put about this fear,   25
    Which now goes too free-footed.
ROS.   We will haste us.

                                    Exeunt Gentlemen.

    Enter POLONIUS.
POL.   My lord, he's going to his mother's closet.
    Behind the arras I'll convey myself
    To hear the process. I'll warrant she'll tax him home,
    And as you said, and wisely was it said,   30
    'Tis meet that some more audience than a mother,
    Since nature makes them partial, should o'erhear
    The speech of vantage. Fare you well, my liege.
    I'll call upon you ere you go to bed,
    And tell you what I know.
KING.   Thanks, dear my lord. *Exit* [POLONIUS]. 35
    O, my offence is rank, it smells to heaven;
    It hath the primal eldest curse upon't,
    A brother's murder. Pray can I not,
    Though inclination be as sharp as will.
    My stronger guilt defeats my strong intent,   40

[III.iii] 5. *terms of our estate* conditions required
for our rule as king.
7. *brows* threatning looks that suggest the dangerous plots Hamlet's brain is hatching.
11. *peculiar* private.
13. *noyance* harm.

15. *cess* cessation, extinction.
20. *mortised* jointed (as with mortise and tenon).
33. *of vantage* (1) in addition; (2) from a convenient place for listening.
39. *will* carnal desire.

And like a man to double business bound,
I stand in pause where I shall first begin,
And both neglect. What if this curséd hand
Were thicker than itself with brother's blood,
Is there not rain enough in the sweet heavens   45
To wash it white as snow? Whereto serves mercy
But to confront the visage of offence?
And what's in prayer but this twofold force,
To be forestalléd ere we come to fall,
Or pardoned being down? Then I'll look up.   50
My fault is past. But, O, what form of prayer
Can serve my turn? 'Forgive me my foul murder'?
That cannot be, since I am still possessed
Of those effects for which I did the murder—
My crown, mine own ambition, and my queen.   55
May one be pardoned and retain th' offence?
In the corrupted currents of this world
Offence's gilded hand may shove by justice,
And oft 'tis seen the wicked prize itself
Buys out the law. But 'tis not so above.   60
There is no shuffling; there the action lies
In his true nature, and we ourselves compelled,
Even to the teeth and forehead of our faults,
To give in evidence. What then? What rests?
Try what repentance can. What can it not?   65
Yet what can it when one can not repent?
O wretched state! O bosom black as death!
O liméd soul, that struggling to be free
Art more engaged! Help, angels! Make assay.
Bow, stubborn knees, and heart with strings of steel,   70
Be soft as sinews of the new-born babe.
All may be well.   [*He kneels.*]

        Enter HAMLET.
HAM.   Now might I do it pat, now 'a is a-praying,
And now I'll do't—and so 'a goes to heaven,
And so am I revenged. That would be scanned.   75
A villain kills my father, and for that,
I, his sole son, do this same villain send
To heaven.
Why, this is hire and salary, not revenge.
'A took my father grossly, full of bread,   80
With all his crimes broad blown, as flush as May;
And how his audit stands who knows save heaven?

61. *shuffling* doubledealing; *action* legal action.   80. *grossly* unprepared spiritually.
68. *limed soul* caught by sin as the bird by lime.   81. *as flush as May* in full flower.
69. *assay* an effort.

But in our circumstance and course of thought
'Tis heavy with him; and am I then revenged
To take him in the purging of his soul,   85
When he is fit and seasoned for his passage?
No.
Up, sword, and know thou a more horrid hent.
When he is drunk asleep, or in his rage,
Or in th' incestuous pleasure of his bed,   90
At game a-swearing, or about some act
That has no relish of salvation in't—
Then trip him, that his heels may kick at heaven,
And that his soul may be as damned and black
As hell, whereto it goes. My mother stays.   95
This physic but prolongs thy sickly days.   *Exit.*
KING.   [*Rising.*] My words fly up, my thoughts remain below.
Words without thoughts never to heaven go.   *Exit.*

[III.iv]

    Enter [QUEEN] GERTRUDE *and* POLONIUS.
POL.   'A will come straight. Look you lay home to him.
Tell him his pranks have been too broad to bear with,
And that your grace hath screen'd and stood between
Much heat and him. I'll silence me even here.
Pray you be round.
QUEEN.   I'll warrant you. Fear me not.   5
Withdraw, I hear him coming.

                    [POLONIUS *goes behind the arras.*]

    Enter HAMLET.
HAM.   Now, mother, what's the matter?
QUEEN.   Hamlet, thou hast thy father much offended.
HAM.   Mother, you have my father much offended.
QUEEN.   Come, come, you answer with an idle tongue.   10
HAM.   Go, go, you question with a wicked tongue.
QUEEN.   Why, how now, Hamlet?
HAM.   What's the matter now?
QUEEN.   Have you forgot me?
HAM.   No, by the rood, not so.
You are the queen, your husband's brother's wife,
And would it were not so, you are my mother.   15

---

83. *in our circumstance* considering all evidence;
course beaten way, habit.
88. *hent* occasion, opportunity.

[III.iv] 5. Following Polonius's "Pray you be round"
(which in *F* reads "Pray you be round with him"),
F adds the line: "*Ham. within.* Mother, mother,
mother." Of which Professor Jenkins remarks (*SB*,

13.35), "What sort of prince is this who cannot
come to his mother's chamber without announcing his arrival by calling 'Mother' three times in
the corridor?" A similar instance where the *F* text
supplies offstage calls in support of onstage references to a character's approach occurs at IV.ii.1.
13. *rood* cross.

QUEEN.   Nay, then I'll set those to you that can speak.
HAM.   Come, come, and sit you down. You shall not budge.
   You go not till I set you up a glass
   Where you may see the inmost part of you.
QUEEN.   What wilt thou do? Thou wilt not murder me?   20
   Help, ho!
POL.   [Behind.] What, ho! help!
HAM.   [Draws.] How now, a rat?
   Dead for a ducat, dead!
         [Thrusts his sword through the arras and kills POLONIUS.]
POL.   [Behind.] O, I am slain!   25
QUEEN.   O me, what hast thou done?
HAM.   Nay, I know not.
   Is it the king?
QUEEN.   O, what a rash and bloody deed is this!
HAM.   A bloody deed? Almost as bad, good mother,
   As kill a king and marry with his brother.   30
QUEEN.   As kill a king?
HAM.   Ay, lady, it was my word.
         [Lifts up the arras and sees the body of POLONIUS.]
   Thou wretched, rash, intruding fool, farewell!
   I took thee for thy better. Take thy fortune.
   Thou find'st to be too busy is some danger.—
   Leave wringing of your hands. Peace, sit you down   35
   And let me wring your heart, for so I shall
   If it be made of penetrable stuff,
   If damnéd custom have not brazed it so
   That it be proof and bulwark against sense.
QUEEN.   What have I done that thou dar'st wag thy tongue   40
   In noise so rude against me?
HAM.   Such an act
   That blurs the grace and blush of modesty,
   Calls virtue hypocrite, takes off the rose
   From the fair forehead of an innocent love,
   And sets a blister there, makes marriage-vows   45
   As false as dicers' oaths. O, such a deed
   As from the body of contraction plucks
   The very soul, and sweet religion makes
   A rhapsody of words. Heaven's face does glow
   O'er this solidity and compound mass   50
   With heated visage, as against the doom—
   Is thought-sick at the act.
QUEEN.   Ay me, what act,

---

38. *brazed* plated it as with brass.   50. *this solidity and compound mass* the earth, as
39. *proof* impenetrable, as of armor.   compounded of the four elements.
47. *contraction* the contract of marriage. 51. *doom* Judgment Day.

That roars so loud and thunders in the index?
HAM.   Look here upon this picture and on this,
     The counterfeit presentment of two brothers.   55
     See what a grace was seated on this brow:
     Hyperion's curls, the front of Jove himself,
     An eye like Mars, to threaten and command,
     A station like the herald Mercury
     New lighted on a heaven-kissing hill—   60
     A combination and a form indeed
     Where every god did seem to set his seal
     To give the world assurance of a man.
     This was your husband. Look you now what follows.
     Here is your husband, like a mildewed ear   65
     Blasting his wholesome brother. Have you eyes?
     Could you on this fair mountain leave to feed,
     And batten on this moor? Ha, have you eyes?
     You cannot call it love, for at your age
     The heyday in the blood is tame, it's humble,   70
     And waits upon the judgment, and what judgment
     Would step from this to this? Sense sure you have,
     Else could you not have motion, but sure that sense
     Is apoplexed, for madness would not err
     Nor sense to ecstasy was ne'er so thralled   75
     But it reserved some quantity of choice
     To serve in such a difference. What devil was't
     That thus hath cozened you at hoodman-blind?
     Eyes without feeling, feeling without sight,
     Ears without hands or eyes, smelling sans all,   80
     Or but a sickly part of one true sense
     Could not so mope. O shame, where is thy blush?
     Rebellious hell,
     If thou canst mutine in a matron's bones,
     To flaming youth let virtue be as wax   85
     And melt in her own fire. Proclaim no shame
     When the compulsive ardor gives the charge,
     Since frost itself as actively doth burn,
     And reason panders will.
QUEEN.   O Hamlet, speak no more!
     Thou turn'st my eyes into my very soul,   90

---

53. *index* table of contents; thus, indication of what
is to follow.
55. *counterfeit presentment* portrait.
57. *front* forehead.
59. *station* bearing, figure.
68. *batten* feed like an animal.
70. *heyday* ardor.
72. *Sense* the senses collectively, which according

to Aristotelian tradition are found in all creatures
that have the power of locomotion.
75. *ecstasy* madness.
78. *hoodman-blind* blindman's bluff.
80. *sans* without.
82. *mope* act without full use of one's wits.
89. *will* desire.

And there I see such black and grainéd spots
As will not leave their tinct.
HAM.   Nay, but to live
  In the rank sweat of an enseaméd bed,
  Stewed in curruption, honeying and making love
  Over the nasty sty—
QUEEN.   O, speak to me no more!   95
  These words like daggers enter in my ears.
  No more, sweet Hamlet.
HAM.   A murderer and a villain,
  A slave that is not twentieth part the tithe
  Of your precedent lord, a vice of kings,
  A cutpurse of the empire and the rule,   100
  That from a shelf the precious diadem stole
  And put it in his pocket—
QUEEN.   No more.

     Enter GHOST.
HAM.   A king of shreds and patches—
  Save me and hover o'er me with your wings,   105
  You heavenly guards! What would your gracious figure?
QUEEN.   Alas, he's mad.
HAM.   Do you not come your tardy son to chide,
  That lapsed in time and passion lets go by
  Th' important acting of your dread command?   110
  O, say!
GHOST.   Do not forget. This visitation
  Is but to whet thy almost blunted purpose.
  But look, amazement on thy mother sits.
  O, step between her and her fighting soul!   115
  Conceit in weakest bodies strongest works.
  Speak to her, Hamlet.
HAM.   How is it with you, lady?
QUEEN.   Alas, how is't with you,
  That you do bend your eye on vacancy,
  And with th' incorporal air do hold discourse?   120
  Forth at your eyes your spirits wildly peep,
  And as the sleeping soldiers in th' alarm,
  Your bedded hair like life in excrements
  Start up and stand an end. O gentle son,
  Upon the heat and flame of thy distemper   125
  Sprinkle cool patience. Whereon do you look?

91. *grainéd spots* indelible stains.
92. *tinct* color.
93. *enseaméd* greasy.
99. *vice* a character in the morality plays, presented often as a buffoon (here, a caricature).

116. *Conceit* imagination.
123. *excrements* nails, hair (whatever grows out of
the body).
124. *an* on.

HAM. On him, on him! Look you how pale he glares.
    His form and cause conjoined, preaching to stones,
    Would make them capable.—Do not look upon me,
    Lest with this piteous action you convert   130
    My stern effects. Then what I have to do
    Will want true color—tears perchance for blood.
QUEEN. To whom do you speak this?
HAM. Do you see nothing there?
QUEEN. Nothing at all, yet all that is I see.   135
HAM. Nor did you nothing hear?
QUEEN. No, nothing but ourselves.
HAM. Why, look you there. Look how it steals away.
    My father, in his habit as he lived!
    Look where he goes even now out at the portal. *Exit* GHOST. 140
QUEEN. This is the very coinage of your brain.
    This bodiless creation ecstasy
    Is very cunning in.
HAM. My pulse as yours doth temperately keep time,
    And makes as healthful music. It is not madness   145
    That I have uttered. Bring me to the test,
    And I the matter will re-word, which madness
    Would gambol from. Mother, for love of grace,
    Lay not that flattering unction to your soul,
    That not your trespass but my madness speaks.   150
    It will but skin and film the ulcerous place
    Whiles rank corruption, mining all within,
    Infects unseen. Confess yourself to heaven,
    Repent what's past, avoid what is to come,
    And do not spread the compost on the weeds,   155
    To make them ranker. Forgive me this my virtue,
    For in the fatness of these pursy times
    Virtue itself of vice must pardon beg,
    Yea, curb and woo for leave to do him good.
QUEEN. O Hamlet, thou hast cleft my heart in twain.   160
HAM. O, throw away the worser part of it,
    And live the purer with the other half.
    Good night—but go not to my uncle's bed.
    Assume a virtue, if you have it not.
    That monster custom, who all sense doth eat,   165
    Of habits devil, is angel yet in this,

---

129. *capable* able to respond.
132. *want* lack.
148. *gambol* leap or start, as a shying horse.
149. *unction* ointment; hence, soothing notion.
152. *mining* undermining.
157. *fatness* grossness, slackness; *pursy* corpulent.
165. *who all sense doth eat* who consumes all human sense, both bodily and spiritual.

166. *Of habits devil* being a devil in, or in respect of, habits (with a play on "habits," as meaning both settled practices and garments, whereby devilish practices contrast with "actions fair and good," line 167, and devilish garments contrast with the "frock or livery" of line 168, which custom in its angelic aspect provides).

That to the use of actions fair and good
He likewise gives a frock or livery
That aptly is put on. Refrain to-night,
And that shall lend a kind of easiness   170
To the next abstinence; the next more easy;
For use almost can change the stamp of nature,
And either curb the devil, or throw him out
With wondrous potency. Once more, good night,
And when you are desirous to be blest,   175
I'll blessing beg of you. For this same lord
I do repent; but heaven hath pleased it so,
To punish me with this, and this with me,
That I must be their scourge and minister.
I will bestow him and will answer well   180
The death I gave him. So, again, good night.
I must be cruel only to be kind.
This bad begins and worse remains behind.
One word more, good lady.
QUEEN.   What shall I do?
HAM.   Not this, by no means, that I bid you do: 185
Let the bloat king tempt you again to bed,
Pinch wanton on your cheek, call you his mouse,
And let him, for a pair of reechy kisses,
Or paddling in your neck with his damned fingers,
Make you to ravel all this matter out,   190
That I essentially am not in madness,
But mad in craft. 'Twere good you let him know,
For who that's but a queen, fair, sober, wise,
Would from a paddock, from a bat, a gib,
Such dear concernings hide? Who would so do?   195
No, in despite of sense and secrecy,
Unpeg the basket on the house's top,
Let the birds fly, and like the famous ape,
To try conclusions, in the basket creep
And break your own neck down.   200
QUEEN.   Be thou assured, if words be made of breath
And breath of life, I have no life to breathe
What thou hast said to me.
HAM.   I must to England; you know that?
QUEEN.   Alack,
I had forgot. 'Tis so concluded on.   205

183. *This* i.e., the death of Polonius (cf. line 178);
remains behind is yet to come.
188. *reechy* dirty.
191. *essentially* in fact.
194. *paddock* toad; *gib* tom-cat.
197–200. *Unpeg the basket * * * neck down* the
story is lost (in it, apparently, the ape carries a cage
of birds to the top of a house, releases them by
accident, and, surprised at their flight, imagines
he can imitate it by first creeping into the basket
and then leaping out. The moral of the story, for
the queen, is not to expose herself to destruction
by making public what good sense decrees should
be kept secret.).

HAM.   There's letters sealed, and my two school-fellows,
Whom I will trust as I will adders fanged,
They bear the mandate; they must sweep my way
And marshal me to knavery. Let it work,
For 'tis the sport to have the engineer   210
Hoist with his own petar; and't shall go hard
But I will delve one yard below their mines
And blow them at the moon. O, 'tis most sweet
When in one line two crafts directly meet.
This man shall set me packing.   215
I'll lug the guts into the neighbour room.
Mother, good night indeed. This counsellor
Is now most still, most secret, and most grave,
Who was in life a foolish prating knave.
Come sir, to draw toward an end with you.   220
Good night, mother.

Exit [HAMLET *tugging in* POLONIUS].

[IV.i]

Enter KING [TO THE] QUEEN, *with* ROSENCRANTZ *and* GUIL-
DENSTERN.

KING.   There's matter in these sighs, these profound heaves,
You must translate; 'tis fit we understand them.
Where is your son?
QUEEN.   Bestow this place on us a little while.

[*Exeunt* ROSENCRANTZ *and* GUILDENSTERN.]
Ah, mine own lord, what have I seen to-night!   5
KING.   What, Gertrude, how does Hamlet?
QUEEN.   Mad as the sea and wind when both contend
Which is the mightier. In his lawless fit,
Behind the arras hearing something stir,
Whips out his rapier, cries 'A rat, a rat!'   10
And in this brainish apprehension kills
The unseen good old man.
KING.   O heavy deed!
It had been so with us had we been there.
His liberty is full of threats to all—
To your yourself, to us, to every one.   15
Alas, how shall this bloody deed be answered?
It will be laid to us, whose providence
Should have kept short, restrained, and out of haunt,
This mad young man. But so much was our love,

211. *petar* a bomb or charge for blowing in gates.
217. *indeed* in earnest (cf. lines 163, 174, 181)

[IV.i] The action is continuous with that of the
preceding scene. The Queen does not leave the
stage. Concerning the traditional editorial division

of Acts III and IV, see Granville-Barker, below,
pp. 192–93, 194–95.
2. *translate* explain.
11. *brainish apprehension* frenzied delusion.
18. *out of haunt* away from society.

We would not understand what was most fit,   20
But like the owner of a foul disease,
To keep it from divulging, let it feed
Even on the pith of life. Where is he gone?
QUEEN.   To draw apart the body he hath killed,
O'er whom his very madness, like some ore   25
Among a mineral of metals base,
Shows itself pure: 'a weeps for what is done.
KING.   O Gertrude, come away!
The sun no sooner shall the mountains touch
But we will ship him hence, and this vile deed   30
We must with all our majesty and skill
Both countenance and excuse. Ho, Guildenstern!

> *Enter* ROSENCRANTZ *and* GUILDENSTERN.
Friends both, go join you with some further aid.
Hamlet in madness hath Polonius slain,
And from his mother's closet hath he dragged him.   35
Go seek him out; speak fair, and bring the body
Into the chapel. I pray you haste in this.
> [*Exeunt* ROSENCRANTZ *and* GUILDENSTERN.]
Come, Gertrude, we'll call up our wisest friends
And let them know both what we mean to do
And what's untimely done; so haply slander—   40
Whose whisper o'er the world's diameter,
As level as the cannon to his blank,
Transports his poisoned shot—may miss our name,
And hit the woundless air. O, come away!
My soul is full of discord and dismay.   *Exeunt.* 45

[IV.ii]

> *Enter* HAMLET.
HAM.   Safely stowed.—But soft, what noise? Who calls on Hamlet?
O, here they come.

> [*Enter*] ROSENCRANTZ, [GUILDENSTERN,] *and* OTHERS.
ROS.   What have you done, my lord, with the dead body?
HAM.   Compounded it with dust, whereto 'tis kin.
ROS.   Tell us where 'tis, that we may take it thence   5
And bear it to the chapel.
HAM.   Do not believe it.
ROS.   Believe what?
HAM.   That I can keep your counsel and not mine own. Besides,

---

26. *mineral* mine.
42. *As level* as sure of aim; *blank* target.

[IV.ii] 1. After the words "Safely stowed," F adds the line: "*Gentlemen within. Hamlet, Lord Ham-*

let." Here, as at III.iv.5, "when a character speaks of hearing someone coming, F provides, though Q does not, for the audience to hear it too" (Jenkins, *SB*, 13.35).

to be demanded of a sponge—what replication should be made by   10
the son of a king?

ROS.   Take you me for a sponge, my lord?

HAM.   Ay, sir, that soaks up the king's countenance, his rewards,
his authorities. But such officers do the king best service in the
end. He keeps them like an apple in the corner of his jaw, first   15
mouthed to be last swallowed. When he needs what you have
gleaned, it is but squeezing you and, sponge, you shall be dry
again.

ROS.   I understand you not, my lord.

HAM.   I am glad of it. A knavish speech sleeps in a foolish ear.   20

ROS.   My lord, you must tell us where the body is, and go with us
to the king.

HAM.   The body is with the king, but the king is not with the body.
The king is a thing—

GUIL.   A thing, my lord!   25

HAM.   Of nothing. Bring me to him. Hide fox, and all after.

Exeunt.

[IV.iii]

    Enter KING, *and two or three.*

KING.   I have sent to seek him, and to find the body.
How dangerous is it that this man goes loose!
Yet must not we put the strong law on him.
He's loved of the distracted multitude,
Who like not in their judgment but their eyes,   5
And where 'tis so, th' offender's scourge is weighed,
But never the offence. To bear all smooth and even,
This sudden sending him away must seem
Deliberate pause. Diseases desperate grown
By desperate appliance are relieved,   10
Or not at all.

    Enter ROSENCRANTZ, [GUILDENSTERN,] *and all the rest.*
    How now! what hath befall'n?

ROS.   Where the dead body is bestowed, my lord,
We cannot get from him.

KING.   But where is he?

ROS.   Without, my lord; guarded, to know your pleasure.

KING.   Bring him before us.

ROS.   Ho! bring in the lord.   15

    They enter [*with* HAMLET].

KING.   Now, Hamlet, where's Polonius?

---

10. *replication* reply.
26. *Hide fox, and all after* presumably a cry in
some game such as hide-and-seek. The words,
which do not occur in Q2, may be an actor's addition.

[IV.iii] 9. *Deliberate pause* carefully considered.

HAM.   At supper.
KING.   At supper? Where?
HAM.   Not where he eats, but where 'a is eaten. A certain convo-
cation of politic worms are e'en at him. Your worm is your only   20
emperor for diet. We fat all creatures else to fat us, and we fat
ourselves for maggots. Your fat king and your lean beggar is but
variable service—two dishes, but to one table. That's the end.
KING.   Alas, alas!
HAM.   A man may fish with the worm that hath eat of a king, and   25
eat of the fish that hath fed of that worm.
KING.   What dost thou mean by this?
HAM.   Nothing but to show you how a king may go a progress through
the guts of a beggar.
KING.   Where is Polonius?   30
HAM.   In heaven. Send thither to see. If your messenger find him
not there, seek him i' th' other place yourself. But if, indeed, you
find him not within this month, you shall nose him as you go up
the stairs into the lobby.
KING.   [To ATTENDANTS.] Go seek him there.   35
HAM.   'A will stay till you come.   [Exeunt ATTENDANTS.]
KING.   Hamlet, this deed, for thine especial safety—
Which we do tender, as we dearly grieve
For that which thou hast done—must send thee hence
With fiery quickness. Therefore prepare thyself.   40
The bark is ready, and the wind at help,
Th' associates tend, and everything is bent
For England.
HAM.   For England?
KING.   Ay, Hamlet.
HAM.   Good.
KING.   So is it, if thou knew'st our purposes.
HAM.   I see a cherub that sees them. But come, for England!   45
Farewell, dear mother.
KING.   Thy loving father, Hamlet.
HAM.   My mother. Father and mother is man and wife, man and
wife is one flesh. So, my mother. Come, for England.   Exit.
KING.   Follow him at foot; tempt him with speed aboard.   50
Delay it not; I'll have him hence to-night.
Away! for everything is sealed and done
That else leans on th' affair. Pray you make haste.
                          [Exeunt all but the KING.]
And, England, if my love thou hold'st at aught—
As my great power thereof may give thee sense,   55

28. progress the state journey of a ruler.
38. tender value.
45. cherub one of the cherubim, the watchmen or

sentinels of heaven, and thus endowed with the
keenest vision.

Since yet thy cicatrice looks raw and red
After the Danish sword, and thy free awe
Pays homage to us—thou mayst not coldly set
Our sovereign process, which imports at full
By letters congruing to that effect   60
The present death of Hamlet. Do it, England,
For like the hectic in my blood he rages,
And thou must cure me. Till I know 'tis done,
Howe'er my haps, my joys were ne'er begun.   *Exit.*

[IV.iv]

    Enter FORTINBRAS *with his* ARMY *over the stage.*
FORT.   Go, captain, from me greet the Danish king.
Tell him that by his licence Fortinbras
Craves the conveyance of a promised march
Over his kingdom. You know the rendezvous.
If that his majesty would aught with us,   5
We shall express our duty in his eye,
And let him know so.
CAP.   I will do't, my lord.
FORT.   Go softly on.   *[Exeunt all but the* CAPTAIN.]

    Enter HAMLET, ROSENCRANTZ, [GUILDENSTERN,] *and* OTHERS.
HAM.   Good sir, whose powers are these?
CAP.   They are of Norway, sir.   10
HAM.   How purposed, sir, I pray you?
CAP.   Against some part of Poland.
HAM.   Who commands them, sir?
CAP.   The nephew to old Norway, Fortinbras.
HAM.   Goes it against the main of Poland, sir,   15
Or for some frontier?
CAP.   Truly to speak, and with no addition,
We go to gain a little patch of ground
That hath in it no profit but the name.
To pay five ducats, five, I would not farm it;   20
Nor will it yield to Norway or the Pole
A ranker rate should it be sold in fee.
HAM.   Why, then the Polack never will defend it.
CAP.   Yes, it is already garrisoned.
HAM.   Two thousand souls and twenty thousand ducats   25

---

56. *cicatrice* scar, used here of memory of a defeat.
58. *coldly set* regard with indifference.
59. *process* mandate.
60. *congruing to* in accordance with.
62. *hectic* consumptive fever.
64. *haps* fortunes.

[IV.iv] 3. *conveyance* conduct.
6. *eye* presence.
15. *main* chief part.
17. *addition* exaggeration.
20. *To pay* i.e., for a yearly rental.
22. *a ranker rate* a greater price; *sold in fee* sold with absolute and perpetual possession.

Will not debate the question of this straw.
This is th' imposthume of much wealth and peace,
That inward breaks, and shows no cause without
Why the man dies. I humbly thank you, sir.
CAP.   God buy you, sir.   [*Exit.*]
ROS.   Will't please you go, my lord?   30
HAM.   I'll be with you straight. Go a little before.
                                    [*Exeunt all but* HAMLET.]
How all occasions do inform against me,
And spur my dull revenge! What is a man,
If his chief good and market of his time
Be but to sleep and feed? A beast, no more.   35
Sure he that made us with such large discourse,
Looking before and after, gave us not
That capability and godlike reason
To fust in us unused. Now, whether it be
Bestial oblivion, or some craven scruple   40
Of thinking too precisely on th' event—
A thought which, quartered, hath but one part wisdom
And ever three parts coward—I do not know
Why yet I live to say 'This thing's to do',
Sith I have cause, and will, and strength, and means,   45
To do't. Examples gross as earth exhort me:
Witness this army of such mass and charge,
Led by a delicate and tender prince,
Whose spirit, with divine ambition puffed,
Makes mouths at the invisible event,   50
Exposing what is mortal and unsure
To all that fortune, death, and danger dare,
Even for an eggshell. Rightly to be great
Is not to stir without great argument,
But greatly to find quarrel in a straw   55
When honor's at the stake. How stand I then,
That have a father killed, a mother stained,
Excitements of my reason and my blood,
And let all sleep, while to my shame I see
The imminent death of twenty thousand men   60
That for a fantasy and trick of fame
Go to their graves like beds, fight for a plot
Whereon the numbers cannot try the cause,

27. *imposthume* abscess.
32. *inform* take shape.
34. *market* profit.
36. *discourse* power of reasoning.
39. *fust* grow musty.
50. *Makes mouths at* makes scornful faces at, derides.

53–56. *Rightly to be great . . . honor's at the stake* i.e., to be rightly great is *not* to refuse to act ("stir") in a dispute ("argument") because the grounds are insufficient, but to be moved to action even in trivial circumstances where a question of honor is involved.
63. *try the cause* settle by combat.

Which is not tomb enough and continent
To hide the slain? O, from this time forth,   65
My thoughts be bloody, or be nothing worth!   *Exit.*

[IV.v]

     Enter HORATIO, [QUEEN] GERTRUDE, *and a* GENTLEMAN.

QUEEN.   I will not speak with her.
GENT.   She is importunate, indeed distract.
   Her mood will needs be pitied.
QUEEN.   What would she have?
GENT.   She speaks much of her father, says she hears
   There's tricks i' th' world, and hems, and beats her heart,   5
   Spurns enviously at straws, speaks things in doubt
   That carry but half sense. Her speech is nothing,
   Yet the unshaped use of it doth move
   The hearers to collection; they aim at it,
   And botch the words up fit to their own thoughts,   10
   Which, as her winks and nods and gestures yield them,
   Indeed would make one think there might be thought,
   Though nothing sure, yet much unhappily.
HOR.   'Twere good she were spoken with, for she may strew
   Dangerous conjectures in ill-breeding minds.   15
QUEEN.   Let her come in.   [*Exit* GENTLEMAN.]
   [*Aside.*] To my sick soul, as sin's true nature is,
   Each toy seems prologue to some great amiss.
   So full of artless jealousy is guilt,
   It spills itself in fearing to be spilt.   20

     Enter OPHELIA [*distracted*].

OPH.   Where is the beauteous majesty of Denmark?
QUEEN.   How now, Ophelia?
OPH.   How should I your true love know   *She sings.*
               From another one?
               By his cockle hat and staff,   25
                 And his sandal shoon.
QUEEN.   Alas, sweet lady, what imports this song?
OPH.   Say you? Nay, pray you mark.

       He is dead and gone, lady,   (*Song.*)
       He is dead and gone;   30

---

64. *continent* receptacle.

[IV.v] 6. *Spurns enviously at straws* takes exception, spitefully, to trifles.
7. *nothing* nonsense.
8. *unshaped use* disordered manner.
9. *collection* attempts at shaping meaning; *aim*
guess.

13. *sure* certain.
18. *toy* trifle.
19. *artless jealousy* ill-concealed suspicion.
20. *spills* destroys.
25. *cockle hat* hat bearing a cockle shell, worn by
a pilgrim who had been to the shrine of St. James
of Compostella, in Spain.
26. *shoon* shoes.

At his head a grass-green turf,
At his heels a stone.

O, ho!
QUEEN: Nay, but Ophelia—
OPH.   Pray you mark.
       [*Sings.*] White his shroud as the mountain snow—   35

       Enter KING.
QUEEN.   Alas, look here, my lord.
OPH.   Larded all with sweet flowers;   (*Song.*)
                 Which bewept to the grave did not go
                 With true-love showers.
KING.   How do you, pretty lady?   40
OPH.   Well, good dild you! They say the owl was a baker's daughter.
   Lord, we know what we are, but know not what we may be. God
   be at your table!
KING.   Conceit upon her father.
OPH.   Pray let's have no words of this, but when they ask you what 45
   it means, say you this:

                 To-morrow is Saint Valentine's day,   (*Song.*)
                 All in the morning betime,
                 And I a maid at your window,
                 To be your Valentine.   50
                 Then up he rose, and donn'd his clo'es,
                 And dupped the chamber-door,
                 Let in the maid, that out a maid
                 Never departed more.
KING.   Pretty Ophelia—   55
OPH.   Indeed, without an oath, I'll make an end on't.

[*Sings.*]   By Gis and by Saint Charity,
                 Alack, and fie for shame!
                 Young men will do't, if they come to't;
                 By Cock, they are to blame.   60
                 Quoth she 'Before you tumbled me,
                 You promised me to wed'.

He answers:

                 'So would I 'a done, by yonder sun,
                 An thou hadst not come to my bed'.   65

---

37. *Larded* garnished, strewn.
41. *good dild you* God yield (requite) you.
41. *They say the owl was a baker's daughter* allusion to a folktale in which a baker's daughter was
transformed into an owl because of her ungener-
ous behavior (giving short measure) when Christ
asked for bread in the baker's shop.

44. *Conceit upon her father* i.e., obsessed with her
father's death.
48. *betime* early.
52. *dupped* opened.
57. *Gis* Jesus.
60. *Cock* corruption of *God*.

KING.   How long hath she been thus?

OPH.   I hope all will be well. We must be patient, but I cannot
choose but weep to think they would lay him i' th' cold ground.
My brother shall know of it, and so I thank you for your good
counsel. Come, my coach! Good night, ladies, good night. Sweet 70
ladies, good night, good night.   [Exit.]

KING.   Follow her close; give her good watch, I pray you.

                    [Exeunt HORATIO and GENTLEMAN.]
O, this is the poison of deep grief; it springs
All from her father's death, and now behold!
O Gertrude, Gertrude!   75
When sorrows come, they come not single spies,
But in battalions: first, her father slain;
Next, your son gone, and he most violent author
Of his own just remove; the people muddied,
Thick and unwholesome in their thoughts and whispers   80
For good Polonius' death; and we have done but greenly
In hugger-mugger to inter him; poor Ophelia
Divided from herself and her fair judgment,
Without the which we are pictures, or mere beasts;
Last, and as much containing as all these,   85
Her brother is in secret come from France,
Feeds on his wonder, keeps himself in clouds,
And wants not buzzers to infect his ear
With pestilent speeches of his father's death,
Wherein necessity, of matter beggared,   90
Will nothing stick our person to arraign
In ear and ear. O my dear Gertrude, this,
Like to a murd'ring piece, in many places
Gives me superfluous death. Attend,   A noise within.

        Enter a MESSENGER.
Where are my Switzers? Let them guard the door.   95
What is the matter?

MESS.   Save yourself, my lord.
The ocean, overpeering of his list,
Eats not the flats with more impiteous haste
Then young Laertes, in a riotous head,
O'erbears your officers. The rabble call him lord,   100
And as the world were now but to begin,

79. *remove* banishment, departure; *muddied* stirred
up and confused.
81. *greenly* without judgment.
82. *hugger-mugger* secrecy and disorder.
87. *in clouds* i.e., of suspicion and rumor.
88. *wants* lacks.
90. *of matter beggared* lacking facts.
91. *nothing stick* in no way hesitate.
93. *murd'ring piece* cannon loaded with shot meant

to scatter.
94. *F* omits the King's "Attend," but substitutes,
by way of drawing attention to the "noise within,"
what Jenkins (SB 13.36) terms "a more obvious
exclamation from the Queen: 'Alacke, what noyse
is this?' "
95. *Switzers* Swiss bodyguard.
97. *list* boundary.
99. *riotous head* turbulent mob.

Antiquity forgot, custom not known,
The ratifiers and props of every word,
They cry 'Choose we, Laertes shall be king'.
Caps, hands, and tongues, applaud it to the clouds,   105
'Laertes shall be king, Laertes king'.
QUEEN.   How cheerfully on the false trail they cry!   *A noise within.*
O, this is counter, you false Danish dogs!
KING.   The doors are broke.

      Enter LAERTES, *with* OTHERS.
LAER.   Where is this king?—Sirs, stand you all without.   110
ALL.   No, let's come in.
LAER.   I pray you give me leave.
ALL.   We will, we will.   [*Exeunt his followers.*]
LAER.   I thank you. Keep the door.—O thou vile king,
Give me my father!
QUEEN.   Calmly, good Laertes.
LAER.   That drop of blood that's calm proclaims me bastard,   115
Cries cuckold to my father, brands the harlot
Even here between the chaste unsmirchéd brow
Of my true mother.
KING.   What is the cause, Laertes,
That thy rebellion looks so giant-like?
Let him go, Gertrude. Do not fear our person.   120
There's such divinity doth hedge a king
That treason can but peep to what it would,
Acts little of his will. Tell me, Laertes.
Why thou art thus incensed. Let him go, Gertrude.
Speak, man.   125
LAER.   Where is my father?
KING.   Dead.
QUEEN.   But not by him.
KING.   Let him demand his fill.
LAER.   How came he dead? I'll not be juggled with.
To hell allegiance, vows to the blackest devil,
Conscience and grace to the profoundest pit!   130
I dare damnation. To this point I stand,
That both the worlds I give to negligence,
Let come what comes, only I'll be revenged
Most throughly for my father.
KING.   Who shall stay you?
LAER.   My will, not all the world's.   135
And for my means, I'll husband them so well
They shall go far with little.
KING.   Good Laertes,

---

108. *counter* hunting backward on the trail.   134. *throughly* thoroughly.
120. *fear* fear for.

If you desire to know the certainty
Of your dear father, is't writ in your revenge
That, swoopstake, you will draw both friend and foe,   140
Winner and loser?
LAER.   None but his enemies.
KING.   Will you know them, then?
LAER.   To his good friends thus wide I'll ope my arms,
And like the kind life-rend'ring pelican,
Repast them with my blood.
KING.   Why, now you speak   145
Like a good child and a true gentleman.
That I am guiltless of your father's death,
And am most sensibly in grief for it,
It shall as level to your judgment 'pear
As day does to your eye.
                    A noise within: 'Let her come in.'   150
LAER.   How now? What noise is that?

          Enter OPHELIA.
O, heat dry up my brains! tears seven times salt
Burn out the sense and virtue of mine eye!
By heaven, thy madness shall be paid with weight
Till our scale turn the beam. O rose of May,   155
Dear maid, kind sister, sweet Ophelia!
O heavens! is't possible a young maid's wits
Should be as mortal as an old man's life?
Nature is fine in love, and where 'tis fine
It sends some precious instance of itself   160
After the thing it loves.
OPH.   They bore him barefac'd on the bier;   (*Song.*)
                    Hey non nonny, nonny, hey nonny;
                    And in his grave rain'd many a tear—

Fare you well, my dove!   165
LAER.   Hadst thou thy wits, and didst persuade revenge,
It could not move thus.
OPH.   You must sing 'A-down, a-down,' and you 'Call him a-down-
a.' O, how the wheel becomes it! It is the false steward, that stole
his master's daughter.   170
LAER.   This nothing's more than matter.
OPH.   There's rosemary, that's for remembrance. Pray you, love, re-
member. And there is pansies, that's for thoughts.

---

140. *swoopstake* sweepstake, taking all the stakes
on the gambling table.
144. *pelican* supposed to feed her young with her
own blood.
149. *level* plain.

153. *virtue* power.
159. *fine* refined to purity.
169. *wheel* burden, refrain.
172–78. Harold Jenkins in his Arden edition of
Hamlet (London and New York, 1982) 536–42,

LAER.   A document in madness, thoughts and remembrance fitted.

OPH.   There's fennel for you, and columbines. There's rue for you, 175
and here's some for me. We may call it herb of grace a Sundays.
O, you must wear your rue with a difference. There's a daisy. I
would give you some violets, but they withered all when my father
died. They say 'a made a good end.

[*Sings.*]   For bonny sweet Robin is all my joy.   180
LAER.   Thought and affliction, passion, hell itself,
    She turns to favor and to prettiness.
OPH.   And will 'a not come again?   (*Song.*)
                    And will 'a not come again?
                        No, no, he is dead,   185
                        Go to thy death-bed,
                    He never will come again.

                    His beard was as white as snow,
                    All flaxen was his poll;
                        He is gone, he is gone,   190
                        And we cast away moan:
                    God-a-mercy on his soul!

And of all Christian souls, I pray God. God buy you.   [*Exit.*]
LAER.   Do you see this, O God?
KING.   Laertes, I must commune with your grief,   195
    Or you deny me right. Go but apart,
    Make choice of whom your wisest friends you will,
    And they shall hear and judge 'twixt you and me.
    If by direct or by collateral hand
    They find us touched, we will our kingdom give,   200
    Our crown, our life, and all that we call ours,
    To you in satisfaction; but if not,
    Be you content to lend your patience to us,
    And we shall jointly labor with your soul
    To give it due content.
LAER.   Let this be so.   205

---

suggests that Ophelia gives rosemary (emblematic
of remembrance) and pansies (of thoughts) to
Laertes; that she gives fennel and columbines (both
signifying marital infidelity) to the Queen; she gives
rue (for repentance) to the King (keeping some for
herself as a sign of her sorrow, but noting that the
King is to wear his rue with *a difference*, an heraldic term designating a mark for distinguishing one
branch of a family from another in a coat-of-arms).

The daisy, an emblem of love's victims, is given to
the King as substitute for the absent Hamlet, whose
absence he has caused. The King would also be
given the violets (emblems of faithfulness, associated both with Ophelia's love for Hamlet, and Polonius's service to the state, both now lost) were
these still available. Each gift of flowers represents
a symbolic reproach to the recipient.
189. *poll* head.

His means of death, his obscure funeral—
No trophy, sword, nor hatchment, o'er his bones,
No noble rite nor formal ostentation—
Cry to be heard, as 'twere from heaven to earth,
That I must call't in question.
KING.   So you shall;   210
And where th' offence is, let the great axe fall.
I pray you go with me.   *Exeunt.*

[IV.vi]

    Enter HORATIO *and* OTHERS.
HOR.   What are they that would speak with me?
GENTLEMEN.   Sea-faring men, sir. They say they have letters for you.
HOR.   Let them come in.   [*Exit* GENTLEMAN.]
    I do not know from what part of the world
    I should be greeted, if not from Lord Hamlet.   5

    Enter SAILORS.
SAIL.   God bless you, sir.
HOR.   Let him bless thee too.
SAIL.   'A shall, sir, an't please him. There's a letter for you, sir—it
came from th' ambassador that was bound for England—if your
name be Horatio, as I am let to know it is.   10
HOR.   [*Reads*]. 'Horatio, when thou shalt have overlooked this, give
these fellows some means to the king. They have letters for him.
Ere we were two days old at sea, a pirate of very warlike appointment gave us chase. Finding ourselves too slow of sail, we put on
a compelled valor, and in the grapple I boarded them. On the   15
instant they got clear of our ship, so I alone became their prisoner.
They have dealt with me like thieves of mercy, but they knew what
they did; I am to do a good turn for them. Let the king have the
letters I have sent, and repair thou to me with as much speed as
thou wouldest fly death. I have words to speak in thine ear will   20
make thee dumb; yet are they much too light for the bore of the
matter. These good fellows will bring thee where I am. Rosencrantz and Guildenstern hold their course for England. Of them I
have much to tell thee. Farewell.
                     He that thou knowest thine, HAMLET.'   25
Come, I will give you way for these your letters,
And do't the speedier that you may direct me
To him from whom you brought them.   *Exeunt.*

---

207. *hatchment* coat of arms.   [IV.vi] 21. *bore* literally, caliber of a gun; hence,
size, importance.

[IV.vii]

Enter KING *and* LAERTES.

KING.   Now must your conscience my acquittance seal,
And you must put me in your heart for friend,
Sith you have heard, and with a knowing ear,
That he which hath your noble father slain
Pursued my life.

LAER.   It well appears. But tell me   5
Why you proceeded not against these feats,
So criminal and so capital in nature,
As by your safety, greatness, wisdom, all things else,
You mainly were stirred up.

KING.   O, for two special reasons,
Which may to you, perhaps, seem much unsinewed,   10
But yet to me th' are strong. The queen his mother
Lives almost by his looks, and for myself—
My virtue or my plague, be it either which—
She is so conjunctive to my life and soul
That, as the star moves not but in his sphere,   15
I could not but by her. The other motive,
Why to a public count I might not go,
Is the great love the general gender bear him,
Who, dipping all his faults in their affection,
Work like the spring that turneth wood to stone,   20
Convert his gyves to graces; so that my arrows,
Too slightly timbered for so loud a wind,
Would have reverted to my bow again,
But not where I had aimed them.

LAER.   And so have I a noble father lost,   25
A sister driven into desp'rate terms,
Whose worth, if praises may go back again,
Stood challenger on mount of all the age
For her perfections. But my revenge will come.

KING.   Break not your sleeps for that. You must not think   30
That we are made of stuff so flat and dull
That we can let our beard be shook with danger,
And think it pastime. You shortly shall hear more.
I loved you father, and we love our self,
And that, I hope, will teach you to imagine—   35

Enter a MESSENGER *with letters.*

MESS.   These to your majesty; this to the queen.

[IV.vii] 7. *capital* punishable by death.
10. *unsinewed* weak.
14. *conjunctive* closely joined.
17. *count* reckoning.

18. *general gender* common people.
21. *gyves* fetters.
35. Following the entrance of the Messenger, the
King says in F "How now? What Newes?" and the

KING.   From Hamlet! Who brought them?
MESS.   Sailors, my lord, they say. I saw them not.
  They were given me by Claudio; he received them
  Of him that brought them.
KING.   Laertes, you shall hear them.—   40
  Leave us.   [*Exit* MESSENGER.]
    [*Reads.*] 'High and mighty, you shall know I am set naked on
  your kingdom. To-morrow shall I beg leave to see your kingly eyes,
  when I shall, first asking your pardon, thereunto recount the oc-
  casion of my sudden and more strange return.

                                                   HAMLET.'   45

  What should this mean? Are all the rest come back?
  Or is it some abuse, and no such thing?
LAER.   Know you the hand?
KING.   'Tis Hamlet's character. 'Naked'!
  And in a postscript here, he says 'alone'.   50
  Can you devise me?
LAER.   I am lost in it, my lord. But let him come.
  It warms the very sickness in my heart
  That I shall live and tell him to his teeth
  'Thus didest thou.'
KING.   If it be so, Laertes—   55
  As how should it be so, how otherwise?—
  Will you be ruled by me?
LAER.   Ay, my lord,
  So you will not o'errule me to a peace.
KING.   To thine own peace. If he be now returned,
  As checking at his voyage, and that he means   60
  No more to undertake it, I will work him
  To an exploit now ripe in my device,
  Under the which he shall not choose but fall;
  And for his death no wind of blame shall breathe
  But even his mother shall uncharge the practice   65
  And call it accident.
LAER.   My lord, I will be ruled;
  The rather if you could devise it so
  That I might be the organ.
KING.   It falls right.
  You have been talked of since your travel much,

Messenger replies, "Letters my Lord from *Hamlet.*" Jenkins comments (*SB* 13.36): "In *Q* the King
is not told the letters come from Hamlet; he is left
to find this out as he reads, and his cry 'From
Hamlet' betokens his astonishment on doing so. I
think Hamlet would not have approved of the *F*
messenger who robs his bomb of the full force of
its explosion. Shakespeare's messenger did not even
know he carried such a bomb, for the letters had
reached him via sailors who were ignorant of their

sender. They took him for 'th' Embassador that
was bound for *England*' (IV.vi.9). *F*, with its too
knowledgeable messenger, by seeking to enhance
the effect, destroys it."
51. *devise* explain to.
60. *checking at* turning aside from (like a falcon
turning from its quarry for other prey).
65. *uncharge the practice* regard the deed as free
from villainy.
68. *organ* instrument.

And that in Hamlet's hearing, for a quality   70
Wherein they say you shine. Your sum of parts
Did not together pluck such envy from him
As did that one, and that, in my regard,
Of the unworthiest siege.
LAER.   What part is that, my lord?
KING.   A very riband in the cap of youth,   75
    Yet needful too, for youth no less becomes
    The light and careless livery that it wears
    Than settled age his sables and his weeds,
    Importing health and graveness. Two months since
    Here was a gentleman of Normandy.   80
    I have seen myself, and served against, the French,
    And they can well on horseback, but this gallant
    Had witchcraft in't. He grew unto his seat,
    And to such wondrous doing brought his horse,
    As had he been incorpsed and demi-natured   85
    With the brave beast. So far he topped my thought
    That I, in forgery of shapes and tricks,
    Come short of what he did.
LAER.   A Norman was't?
KING.   A Norman.
LAER.   Upon my life, Lamord.
KING.   The very same.   90
LAER.   I know him well. He is the brooch indeed
    And gem of all the nation.
KING.   He made confession of you,
    And gave you such a masterly report
    For art and exercise in your defence,   95
    And for your rapier most especial,
    That he cried out 'twould be a sight indeed
    If one could match you. The scrimers of their nation
    He swore had neither motion, guard, nor eye,
    If you opposed them. Sir, this report of his   100
    Did Hamlet so envenom with his envy
    That he could nothing do but wish and beg
    Your sudden coming o'er, to play with you.
    Now out of this—
LAER.   What out of this, my lord?
KING.   Laertes, was your father dear to you?   105
    Or are you like the painting of a sorrow,
    A face without a heart?
LAER.   Why ask you this?

---

74. *siege* rank.   86. *topped* excelled.
78. *weeds* garments.   87. *forgery* invention.
85. *incorpsed* made one body; *demi-natured* like a   98. *scrimers* fencers (French *escrimeurs*).
centaur, half man half horse.

KING.   Not that I think you did not love your father,
But that I know love is begun by time,
And that I see in passages of proof,   110
Time qualifies the spark and fire of it.
There lives within the very flame of love
A kind of wick or snuff that will abate it,
And nothing is at a like goodness still,
For goodness, growing to a plurisy,   115
Dies in his own too much. That we would do,
We should do when we would; for this 'would' changes,
And hath abatements and delays as many
As there are tongues, are hands, are accidents,
And then this 'should' is like a spendthrift's sigh   120
That hurts by easing. But to the quick of th' ulcer—
Hamlet comes back; what would you undertake
To show yourself in deed your father's son
More than in words?
LAER.   To cut his throat i' th' church.
KING.   No place indeed should murder sanctuarize;   125
Revenge should have no bounds. But good Laertes,
Will you do this, keep close within your chamber;
Hamlet returned shall know you are come home;
We'll put on those shall praise your excellence,
And set a double varnish on the fame   130
The Frenchman gave you, bring you in fine together,
And wager on your heads. He, being remiss,
Most generous, and free from all contriving,
Will not peruse the foils, so that with ease,
Or with a little shuffling, you may choose   135
A sword unbated, and in a pass of practice
Requite him for your father.
LAER.   I will do't,
And for that purpose I'll anoint my sword.
I bought an unction of a mountebank
So mortal that but dip a knife in it,   140
Where it draws blood no cataplasm so rare,
Collected from all simples that have virtue
Under the moon, can save the thing from death
That is but scratched withal. I'll touch my point
With this contagion, that if I gall him slightly,   145
It may be death.
KING.   Let's further think of this,

110. *passages of proof* incidents of experience.
111. *qualifies* weakens.
115. *plurisy* excess.
121. *quick* sensitive flesh.
125. *sanctuarize* give sanctuary to.
132. *remiss* careless.

134. *peruse* inspect.
136. *unbated* not blunted; *pass of practice* treacherous thrust.
141. *cataplasm* poultice.
142. *simples* medicinal herbs.

Weigh what convenience both of time and means
May fit us to our shape. If this should fail,
And that our drift look through our bad performance,
'Twere better not assayed. Therefore this project   150
Should have a back or second that might hold
If this did blast in proof. Soft, let me see.
We'll make a solemn wager on your cunnings—
I ha't.
When in your motion you are hot and dry—   155
As make your bouts more violent to that end—
And that he calls for drink, I'll have preferred him
A chalice for the nonce, whereon but sipping,
If he by chance escape your venomed stuck,
Our purpose may hold there.—But stay, what noise?   160

    Enter QUEEN.

QUEEN.   One woe doth tread upon another's heel,
  So fast they follow. Your sister's drowned, Laertes.
LAER.   Drowned? O, where?
QUEEN.   There is a willow grows askant the brook
  That shows his hoar leaves in the glassy stream.   165
  Therewith fantastic garlands did she make
  Of crowflowers, nettles, daisies, and long purples
  That liberal shepherds give a grosser name,
  But our cold maids do dead men's fingers call them.
  There on the pendent boughs her crownet weeds   170
  Clamb'ring to hang, an envious sliver broke,
  When down her weedy trophies and herself
  Fell in the weeping brook. Her clothes spread wide,
  And mermaid-like awhile they bore her up,
  Which time she chanted snatches of old lauds,   175
  As one incapable of her own distress,
  Or like a creature native and indued
  Unto that element. But long it could not be
  Till that her garments, heavy with their drink,
  Pulled the poor wretch from her melodious lay   180
  To muddy death.
LAER.   Alas, then she is drowned?
QUEEN.   Drowned, drowned.
LAER.   Too much of water hast thou, poor Ophelia,

---

148. *shape* plan.
149. *drift* scheme.
151. *back or second* something in support.
152. *blast in proof* burst during trial (like a faulty cannon).
155. *motion* exertion.
157. *preferred* offered to.
158. *nonce* occasion.
159. *stuck* thrust.

164. *askant* alongside.
165. *hoar* gray.
168. *liberal* free-spoken, licentious.
169. *cold* chaste.
170. *crownet* coronet.
171. *envious* malicious.
175. *lauds* hymns.
176. *incapable of* insensible to.
177. *indued* endowed.

And therefore I forbid my tears; but yet
It is our trick; nature her custom holds,   185
Let shame say what it will. When these are gone,
The woman will be out. Adieu, my lord.
I have a speech o' fire that fain would blaze
But that this folly drowns it.   *Exit.*

KING.   Let's follow, Gertrude.
How much I had to do to calm his rage!   190
Now fear I this will give it start again;
Therefore let's follow.   *Exeunt.*

[V.i]

Enter two CLOWNS.

CLOWN. Is she to be buried in Christian burial when she wilfully
   seeks her own salvation?

OTHER. I tell thee she is, therefore make her grave straight. The
   crowner hath sat on her, and finds it Christian burial.

CLOWN. How can that be, unless she drowned herself in her own   5
   defence?

OTHER. Why, 'tis found so.

CLOWN. It must be 'se offendendo', it cannot be else. For here lies
   the point: if I drown myself wittingly, it argues an act, and an act
   hath three branches—it is to act, to do, to perform; argal, she   10
   drowned herself wittingly.

OTHER. Nay, but hear you, Goodman Delver.

CLOWN. Give me leave. Here lies the water; good. Here stands the
   man; good. If the man go to this water and drown himself, it is,
   will he, nill he, he goes—mark you that. But if the water come to   15
   him and drown him, he drowns not himself. Argal, he that is not
   guilty of his own death shortens not his own life.

OTHER. But is this law?

CLOWN. Ay, marry, is't; crowner's quest law.

OTHER. Will you ha' the truth on't? If this had not been a gentle-   20
   woman, she should have been buried out o' Christian burial.

CLOWN. Why, there thou say'st. And the more pity that great folk
   should have count'nance in this world to drown or hang themselves more than their even-Christen. Come, my spade. There is
   no ancient gentlemen but gard'ners, ditchers, and grave-makers.   25
   They hold up Adam's profession.

OTHER. Was he a gentleman?

CLOWN. 'A was the first that ever bore arms.

OTHER. Why, he had none.

---

187. *woman* unmanly part of nature.

[V.i] 0.1 CLOWNS rustics.
4. *crowner* coroner.
8. *se offendendo* the Clown's blunder for *se defen-*

dendo ("in self-defense").
10. *argal* therefore (corrupt form of *ergo*).
19. *quest* inquest.
24. *even-Christen* fellow Christian.

CLOWN. What, art a heathen? How dost thou understand the Scrip- 30
ture? The Scripture says Adam digged. Could he dig without arms?
I'll put another question to thee. If thou answerest me not to the
purpose, confess thyself—

OTHER. Go to.

CLOWN. What is he that builds stronger than either the mason, the 35
shipwright, or the carpenter?

OTHER. The gallows-maker, for that frame outlives a thousand ten-
ants.

CLOWN. I like thy wit well, in good faith. The gallows does well. But
how does it well? It does well to those that do ill. Now thou dost 40
ill to say the gallows is built stronger than the church. Argal, the
gallows may do well to thee. To't again, come.

OTHER. Who builds stronger than a mason, a shipwright, or a carpenter?

CLOWN. Ay tell me that, and unyoke.   45

OTHER. Marry, now I can tell.

CLOWN. To't.

OTHER. Mass, I cannot tell.

Enter HAMLET *and* HORATIO *afar off.*

CLOWN. Cudgel thy brains no more about it, for your dull ass will
not mend his pace with beating. And when you are asked this 50
question next, say 'a grave-maker.' The houses he makes lasts till
doomsday. Go, get thee in, and fetch me a stoup of liquor.

[*Exit* OTHER CLOWN.]

[HAMLET *and* HORATIO *come forward as* CLOWN *digs and sings.*]

  In youth, when I did love, did love,   (*Song.*)
   Methought it was very sweet,
  To contract-O-the time for-a-my behove, 55
   O, methought there-a-was nothing-a-meet.

HAM. Has this fellow no feeling of his business, that 'a sings in grave-
making?

HOR. Custom hath made it in him a property of easiness.

HAM. 'Tis e'en so. The hand of little employment hath the daintier 60
sense.

CLOWN. But age, with his stealing steps, (*Song.*)
   Hath clawed me in his clutch,
   And hath shipped me into the land,
   As if I had never been such. 65

[*Throws up a skull.*]

---

45. *tell me that, and unyoke* answer the question
and then you can relax.
52. *stoup* tankard.
55. *behove* benefit.
55–56. The repeated *a* and *o* may represent the
Clown's vocal embellishments, but more probably
they represent his grunting as he takes breath in
the course of his digging.
59. *a property of easiness* a habit that comes easily
to him.

HAM.   That skull had a tongue in it, and could sing once. How the
knave jowls it to the ground, as if 'twere Cain's jawbone, that
did the first murder! This might be the pate of a politician, which
this ass now o'erreaches; one that would circumvent God, might it
not?   70
HOR.   It might, my lord.
HAM.   Or of a courtier, which could say, 'Good morrow, sweet lord!
How does thou, sweet lord?' This might be my Lord Such-a-one,
that praised my Lord Such-a-one's horse, when 'a went to beg it,
might it not?   75
HOR.   Ay, my lord.
HAM.   Why, e'en so, and now my Lady Worm's, chopless, and
knock'd abut the mazzard with a sexton's spade. Here's fine revo-
lution, an we had the trick to see't. Did these bones cost no more
the breeding but to play at loggats with them? Mine ache to think   80
on't.
CLOWN.   A pick-axe and a spade, a spade,   (*Song.*)
                 For and a shrouding sheet:
                 O, a pit of clay for to be made
                 For such a guest is meet.   85
                      [*Throws up another skull.*]
HAM.   There's another. Why may not that be the skull of a lawyer?
Where be his quiddities now, his quillets, his cases, his tenures,
and his tricks? Why does he suffer this mad knave now to knock
him about the sconce with a dirty shovel, and will not tell him of
his action of battery? Hum! This fellow might be in's time a great   90
buyer of land, with his statutes, his recognizances, his fines, his
double vouchers, his recoveries. Is this the fine of his fines, and
the recovery of his recoveries, to have his fine pate full of fine dirt?
Will his vouchers vouch him no more of his purchases, and double ones too, than the length and breadth of a pair of indentures?   95
The very conveyances of his lands will scarcely lie in this box, and
must th' inheritor himself have no more, ha?
HOR.   Not a jot more, my lord.
HAM.   Is not parchment made of sheepskins?
HOR.   Ay, my lord, and of calves' skins too.   100
HAM.   They are sheep and calves which seek out assurance in that.
   I will speak to this fellow. Whose grave's this, sirrah?
CLOWN.   Mine, sir.

---

67. *jowls* hurls.
69. *circumvent* cheat.
77. *chopless* with lower jaw missing.
78. *mazzard* head.
80. *loggats* small logs of wood for throwing at a
mark.
87. *quiddities* subtle distinctions; *quillets* quibbles.

91. *recognizances* legal bonds, defining debts
92. *vouchers* persons vouched or called on to warrant a title.
92. *recoveries* legal processes to break an entail.
95. *pair of indentures* deed or legal agreement in
duplicate.
96. *conveyances* deeds by which property is transferred.

[*Sings.*] O, a pit of clay for to be made—

HAM.   I think it be thine indeed, for thou liest in't.   105

CLOWN.   You lie out on't, sir, and therefore 'tis not yours. For my
part, I do not lie in't, yet it is mine.

HAM.   Thou dost lie in't, to be in't and say it is thine. 'Tis for the
dead, not for the quick; therefore thou liest.

CLOWN.   'Tis a quick lie, sir; 'twill away again from me to you.   110

HAM.   What man dost thou dig it for?

CLOWN.   For no man, sir.

HAM.   What woman, then?

CLOWN.   For none neither.

HAM.   Who is to be buried in't?   115

CLOWN.   One that was a woman, sir; but, rest her soul, she's dead.

HAM.   How absolute the knave is! We must speak by the card, or
equivocation will undo us. By the Lord, Horatio, this three years
I have took note of it, the age is grown so picked that the toe of the
peasant comes so near the heel of the courtier, he galls his kibe.   120
How long hast thou been grave-maker?

CLOWN.   Of all the days i' th' year, I came to't that day that our last
King Hamlet overcame Fortinbras.

HAM.   How long is that since?

CLOWN.   Cannot you tell that? Every fool can tell that. It was that   125
very day that young Hamlet was born—he that is mad, and sent
into England.

HAM.   Ay, marry, why was he sent into England?

CLOWN.   Why, because 'a was mad. 'A shall recover his wits there;
or, if 'a do not, 'tis no great matter there.   130

HAM.   Why?

CLOWN.   'Twill not be seen in him there. There the men are as mad
as he.

HAM.   How came he mad?

CLOWN.   Very strangely, they say.   135

HAM.   How strangely?

CLOWN.   Faith, e'en with losing his wits.

HAM.   Upon what ground?

CLOWN.   Why, here in Denmark. I have been sexton here, man and
boy, thirty years.   140

HAM.   How long will a man lie i' th' earth ere he rot?

CLOWN.   Faith, if 'a be not rotten before 'a die—as we have many
pocky corses now-a-days that will scarce hold the laying in—'a will
last you some eight year or nine year. A tanner will last you nine
year.   145

HAM.   Why he more than another?

---

117. *absolute* positive; *card* card on which the
points of the mariner's compass are marked (i.e.,
absolutely to the point).

119. *picked* fastidious.
120. *kibe* chilblain.
143. *pocky* infected with pox (syphillis).

CLOWN. Why, sir, his hide is so tanned with his trade that 'a will
keep out water a great while; and your water is a sore decayer of
your whoreson dead body. Here's a skull now hath lien you i' th'
earth three and twenty years.   150
HAM. Whose was it?
CLOWN. A whoreson mad fellow's it was. Whose do you think it
was?
HAM. Nay, I know not.
CLOWN. A pestilence on him for a mad rogue! 'A poured a flagon of
Rhenish on my head once. This same skull, sir, was, sir, Yorick's   155
skull, the king's jester.
HAM. [Takes the skull.] This?
CLOWN. E'en that.
HAM. Alas, poor Yorick! I knew him, Horatio—a fellow of infinite
jest, of most excellent fancy. He hath bore me on his back a thou-   160
sand times, and now how abhorred in my imagination it is! My
gorge rises at it. Here hung those lips that I have kissed I know not
how oft. Where be your gibes now, your gambols, your songs,
your flashes of merriment that were wont to set the table on a roar?
Not one now to mock your own grinning? Quite chop-fall'n? Now   165
get you to my lady's chamber, and tell her, let her paint an inch
thick, to this favor she must come. Make her laugh at that. Prithee, Horatio, tell me one thing.
HOR. What's that, my lord?
HAM. Dost thou think Alexander looked o' this fashion i' th' earth?   170
HOR. E'en so.
HAM. And smelt so? Pah!   [Throws down the skull.]
HOR. E'en so, my lord.
HAM. To what base uses we may return, Horatio! Why may not
imagination trace the noble dust of Alexander till 'a find it stopping   175
a bung-hole?
HOR. 'Twere to consider too curiously to consider so.
HAM. No, faith, not a jot, but to follow him thither with modesty
enough, and likelihood to lead it. Alexander died, Alexander was
buried, Alexander returneth to dust; the dust is earth; of earth we   180
make loam; and why of that loam whereto he was converted might
they not stop a beer-barrel?

> Imperious Cæsar, dead and turned to clay,
> Might stop a hole to keep the wind away.
> O, that that earth which kept the world in awe   185
> Should patch a wall t'expel the winter's flaw!

---

155. *Rhenish* Rhine wine.   186. *flaw* gust.
177. *too curiously* over ingeniously.

But soft, but soft awhile! Here comes the king,
The queen, the courtiers.

> *Enter* KING, QUEEN, LAERTES, *and the Corse* [*with a Doctor
> of Divinity as* PRIEST *and* LORDS *attendant*].
>   Who is this they follow?
And with such maiméd rites? This doth betoken
The corse they follow did with desperate hand   190
Fordo it own life. 'Twas of some estate.
Couch we awhile and mark.   [*Retires with* HORATIO.]
LAER.   What ceremony else?
HAM.   That is Laertes, a very noble youth. Mark.
LAER.   What ceremony else?   195
DOCTOR.   Her obsequies have been as far enlarged
  As we have warranty. Her death was doubtful,
  And but that great command o'ersways the order,
  She should in ground unsanctified been lodged
  Till the last trumpet. For charitable prayers,   200
  Shards, flints, and pebbles, should be thrown on her.
  Yet here she is allowed her virgin crants,
  Her maiden strewments, and the bringing home
  Of bell and burial.
LAER.   Must there no more be done?
DOCTOR.   No more be done.   205
  We should profane the service of the dead
  To sing a requiem and such rest to her
  As to peace-parted souls.
LAER.   Lay her i' th' earth,
  And from her fair and unpolluted flesh
  May violets spring! I tell thee, churlish priest,   210
  A minist'ring angel shall my sister be
  When thou liest howling.
HAM.   What, the fair Ophelia!
QUEEN.   Sweets to the sweet. Farewell!   [*Scatters flowers.*]
  I hoped thou shouldst have been my Hamlet's wife.
  I thought thy bride-bed to have decked, sweet maid,   215
  And not have strewed thy grave.
LAER.   O, treble woe
  Fall ten times treble on that curséd head
  Whose wicked deed thy most ingenious sense
  Deprived thee of! Hold off the earth awhile,
  Till I have caught her once more in mine arms.   220
                            [*Leaps into the grave.*]

---

191. *Fordo* destroy; *it* its.
201. *Shards* bits of broken pottery.

202. *crants* garland.
218. *most ingenious* of quickest apprehension.

Now pile your dust upon the quick and dead,
Till of this flat a mountain you have made
T' o'er-top old Pelion or the skyish head
Of blue Olympus.

HAM.   [*Coming forward.*] What is he whose grief
Bears such an emphasis, whose phrase of sorrow   225
Conjures the wand'ring stars, and makes them stand
Like wonder-wounded hearers? This is I,
Hamlet the Dane.

[LAERTES *climbs out of the grave.*]

LAER.   The devil take thy soul!   [*Grappling with him.*]

HAM.   Thou pray'st not well.
I prithee take thy fingers from my throat,   230
For though I am not splenitive and rash,
Yet have I in me something dangerous,
Which let thy wisdom fear. Hold off thy hand.

KING.   Pluck them asunder.

QUEEN.   Hamlet! Hamlet!   235

ALL.   Gentlemen!

HOR.   Good my lord, be quiet.

[*The* ATTENDANTS *part them.*]

HAM.   Why, I will fight with him upon this theme
Until my eyelids will no longer wag.

QUEEN.   O my son, what theme?   240

HAM.   I loved Ophelia. Forty thousand brothers
Could not with all their quantity of love
Make up my sum. What wilt thou do for her?

KING.   O, he is mad, Laertes.

QUEEN.   For love of God, forbear him.   245

HAM.   'Swounds, show me what thou't do.
Woo't weep, woo't fight, woo't fast, woo't tear thyself,
Woo't drink up eisel, eat a crocodile?
I'll do't. Dost come here to whine?
To outface me with leaping in her grave?   250
Be buried quick with her, and so will I.
And if thou prate of mountains, let them throw
Millions of acres on us, till our ground,
Singeing his pate against the burning zone,
Make Ossa like a wart! Nay, an thou'lt mouth,   255
I'll rant as well as thou.

QUEEN.   This is mere madness;

---

223. *Pelion* a mountain in Thessaly, like Olympus, line 224, and Ossa, line 255 (the allusion is to the war in which the Titans fought the gods and, in their attempt to scale heaven, heaped Ossa and Olympus on Pelion, or Pelion and Ossa on Olympus).

225. *such an emphasis* so vehement an expression or display.
231. *splenitive* fiery-tempered (from the spleen, seat of anger).
247. *Woo't* wilt (thou).
248. *eisel* vinegar.

And thus awhile the fit will work on him.
Anon, as patient as the female dove
When that her golden couplets are disclosed,
His silence will sit drooping.
HAM.   Hear you, sir.   260
  What is the reason that you use me thus?
  I loved you ever. But it is no matter.
  Let Hercules himself do what he may,
  The cat will mew, and dog will have his day.
KING.   I pray thee, good Horatio, wait upon him.   265
                                         Exit Hamlet and Horatio.
  [*To* LAERTES.] Strengthen your patience in our last night's speech.
  We'll put the matter to the present push.—
  Good Gertrude, set some watch over your son.—
  This grave shall have a living monument.
  An hour of quiet shortly shall we see;   270
  Till then in patience our proceeding be.   *Exeunt.*

[V.ii]

                         Enter HAMLET *and* HORATIO.
HAM.   So much for this, sir; now shall you see the other.
  You do remember all the circumstance?
HOR.   Remember it, my lord!
HAM.   Sir, in my heart there was a kind of fighting
  That would not let me sleep. Methought I lay   5
  Worse than the mutines in the bilboes. Rashly,
  And praised be rashness for it—let us know,
  Our indiscretion sometime serves us well,
  When our deep plots do pall; and that should learn us
  There's a divinity that shapes our ends,   10
  Rough-hew them how we will—
HOR.   That is most certain.
HAM.   Up from my cabin,
  My sea-gown scarfed about me, in the dark
  Groped I to find out them, had my desire,
  Fingered their packet, and in fine withdrew   15
  To mine own room again, making so bold,
  My fears forgetting manners, to unseal
  Their grand commission; where I found, Horatio—
  Ah, royal knavery!—an exact command,
  Larded with many several sorts of reasons,   20
  Importing Denmark's health, and England's too,

---

259. *couplets* newly-hatched pair.

[V.ii] 6. *mutines* mutineers; *bilboes* fetters.

9. *pall* fail.
15. *Fingered* filched.
20. *Larded* garnished.

With, ho! such bugs and goblins in my life,
That on the supervise, no leisure bated,
No, not to stay the grinding of the axe,
My head should be struck off.
HOR.   Is't possible?   25
HAM.   Here's the commission; read it at more leisure.
   But wilt thou hear now how I did proceed?
HOR.   I beseech you.
HAM.   Being thus benetted round with villainies,
   Or I could make a prologue to my brains,   30
   They had begun the play. I sat me down,
   Devised a new commission, wrote it fair.
   I once did hold it, as our statists do,
   A baseness to write fair, and labored much
   How to forget that learning; but sir, now   35
   It did me yeoman's service. Wilt thou know
   Th' effect of what I wrote?
HOR.   Ay, good my lord.
HAM.   An earnest conjuration from the king,
   As England was his faithful tributary,
   As love between them like the palm might flourish,   40
   As peace should still her wheaten garland wear
   And stand a comma 'tween their amities,
   And many such like as's of great charge,
   That on the view and knowing of these contents,
   Without debatement further more or less,   45
   He should those bearers put to sudden death,
   Not shriving-time allowed.
HOR.   How was this sealed?
HAM.   Why, even in that was heaven ordinant,
   I had my father's signet in my purse,
   Which was the model of that Danish seal,   50
   Folded the writ up in the form of th' other,
   Subscribed it, gave't th' impression, placed it safely,
   The changeling never known. Now, the next day
   Was our sea-fight, and what to this was sequent
   Thou knowest already.   55
HOR.   So Guildenstern and Rosencrantz go to't.
HAM.   Why, man, they did make love to this employment.
   They are not near my conscience; their defeat
   Does by their own insinuation grow.

---

22. *bugs and goblins* imaginary horrors (here, horrendous crimes attributed to Hamlet, and represented as dangers should he be allowed to live).
23. *supervise* perusal; *bated* deducted, allowed.
24. *stay* await.
30. *Or* ere.
33. *statists* statesmen.

42. *comma* a connective that also acknowledges separateness.
43. *charge* (1) importance (2) burden (the double meaning fits the play that makes "as's" into "asses").
48. *ordinant* guiding.
52. *Subscribed* signed.
59. *insinuation* intrusion.

'Tis dangerous when the baser nature comes   60
Between the pass and fell incenséd points
Of mighty opposites.
HOR.   Why, what a king is this!
HAM.   Does it not, think thee, stand me now upon—
He that hath killed my king and whored my mother,
Popped in between th' election and my hopes,   65
Thrown out his angle for my proper life,
And with such coz'nage—is't not perfect conscience
To quit him with this arm? And is't not to be damned
To let this canker of our nature come
In further evil?   70
HOR.   It must be shortly known to him from England
What is the issue of the business there.
HAM.   It will be short; the interim is mine.
And a man's life's no more than to say 'one'.
But I am very sorry, good Horatio,   75
That to Laertes I forgot myself;
For by the image of my cause I see
The portraiture of his. I'll court his favours.
But sure the bravery of his grief did put me
Into a tow'ring passion.
HOR.   Peace; who comes here?   80

        Enter [OSRIC] a courtier.
OSR.   Your lordship is right welcome back to Denmark.
HAM.   I humbly thank you, sir. [Aside to HORATIO.] Dost know this
water-fly?
HOR.   [Aside to HAMLET.] No, my good lord.
HAM.   [Aside to HORATIO.] Thy state is the more gracious, for 'tis a   85
vice to know him. He hath much land, and fertile. Let a beast be
lord of beasts, and his crib shall stand at the king's mess. 'Tis a
chough, but as I say, spacious in the possession of dirt.
OSR.   Sweet lord, if your lordship were at leisure, I should impart a
thing to you from his majesty.   90
HAM.   I will receive it, sir, with all diligence of spirit. Put your bon-
net to his right use. 'Tis for the head.
OSR.   I thank your lordship, it is very hot.
HAM.   No, believe me, 'tis very cold; the wind is northerly.
OSR.   It is indifferent cold, my lord, indeed.   95
HAM.   But yet methinks it is very sultry and hot for my complexion.
OSR.   Exceedingly, my lord; it is very sultry, as 'twere—I cannot tell

---

61. *pass* thrust; *fell* fierce.
63. *Does it not* * * * *stand me now upon* is it not
incumbent upon me.
65. *election* i.e., to the kingship, Denmark being
an elective monarchy.
66. *angle* fishing line; *proper* own.

68. *quit* repay.
79. *bravery* ostentatious display.
87. *mess* table.
88. *chough* jackdaw; thus, a chatterer.
95. *indifferent* somewhat.
96. *complexion* temperament.

how. My lord, his majesty bade me signify to you that 'a has laid
a great wager on your head. Sir, this is the matter—

HAM.   I beseech you, remember. 100

[HAMLET *moves him to put on his hat.*]

OSR.   Nay, good my lord; for my ease, in good faith. Sir, here is
newly come to court Laertes; believe me, an absolute gentleman,
full of most excellent differences, of very soft society and great
showing. Indeed, to speak feelingly of him, he is the card or cal-
endar of gentry, for you shall find in him the continent of what 105
part a gentleman would see.

HAM.   Sir, his definement suffers no perdition in you, though I know
to divide him inventorially would dozy th' arithmetic of memory,
and yet but yaw neither in respect of his quick sail. But in the
verity of extolment, I take him to be a soul of great article, and 110
his infusion of such dearth and rareness as, to make true diction
of him, his semblable is his mirror, and who else would trace him,
his umbrage, nothing more.

OSR.   Your lordship speaks most infallibly of him.

HAM.   The concernancy, sir? Why do we wrap the gentleman in our 115
more rawer breath?

OSR.   Sir?

HOR.   Is't not possible to understand in another tongue? You will
to't, sir, really.

HAM.   What imports the nomination of this gentleman? 120

OSR.   Of Laertes?

HOR.   [*Aside.*] His purse is empty already. All's golden words are
spent.

HAM.   Of him, sir.

OSR.   I know you are not ignorant— 125

HAM.   I would you did, sir; yet, in faith, if you did, it would not
much approve me. Well, sir.

OSR.   You are not ignorant of what excellence Laertes is—

HAM.   I dare not confess that, lest I should compare with him in
excellence; but to know a man well were to know himself. 130

OSR.   I mean, sir, for his weapon; but in the imputation laid on him
by them in his meed, he's unfellowed.

HAM.   What's his weapon?

OSR.   Rapier and dagger.

HAM.   That's two of his weapons—but well. 135

---

103. *differences* distinguishing qualities.
103–4. *great showing* distinguished appearance.
104. *card* map.
105. *continent* all-containing embodiment.
107. *definement* definition.
108. *divide him inventorially* classify him in detail; *dozy* dizzy.
109. *yaw* hold to a course unsteadily like a ship
that steers wild.
110. *article* scope, importance.

111. *infusion* essence; *dearth* scarcity.
112. *semblable* likeness; *trace* (1) draw (2) follow.
113. *umbrage* shadow.
115. *concernancy* import, relevance.
119. *to't* i.e., get to an understanding.
120. *nomination* mention.
127. *approve* commend.
129. *compare* compete.
132. *meed* pay; *unfellowed* unequaled.

OSR.   The king, sir, hath wagered with him six Barbary horses, against
the which he has impawned, as I take it, six French rapiers and
poniards, with their assigns, as girdle, hangers, and so. Three of
the carriages, in faith, are very dear to fancy, very responsive to the
hilts, most delicate carriages, and of very liberal conceit.   140

HAM.   What call you the carriages?

HOR.   [*Aside to* HAMLET.] I knew you must be edified by the margent
ere you had done.

OSR.   The carriages, sir, are the hangers.

HAM.   The phrase would be more germane to the matter if we could   145
carry a cannon by our sides. I would it might be hangers till then.
But on! Six Barbary horses against six French swords, their assigns,
and three liberal conceited carriages; that's the French bet against
the Danish. Why is this all impawned, as you call it?

OSR.   The king, sir, hath laid, sir, that in a dozen passes between   150
yourself and him he shall not exceed you three hits; he hath laid
on twelve for nine, and it would come to immediate trial if your
lordship would vouchsafe the answer.

HAM.   How if I answer no?

OSR.   I mean, my lord, the opposition of your person in trial.   155

HAM.   Sir, I will walk here in the hall. If it please his majesty, it is
the breathing time of day with me. Let the foils be brought, the
gentleman willing, and the king hold his purpose; I will win for
him an I can. If not, I will gain nothing but my shame and the
odd hits.   160

OSR.   Shall I deliver you so?

HAM.   To this effect, sir, after what flourish your nature will.

OSR.   I commend my duty to your lordship.

HAM.   Yours. [*Exit* OSRIC.] He does well to commend it himself;
there are no tongues else for's turn.   165

HOR.   This lapwing runs away with the shell on his head.

HAM.   'A did comply, sir, with his dug before 'a sucked it. Thus has
he, and many more of the same bevy that I know the drossy age
dotes on, only got the tune of the time; and out of an habit of
encounter, a kind of yesty collection which carries them through   170

---

137. *impawned* staked.
138. *assigns* appendages.
140. *carriages* an affected word for *hangers*, i.e.,
straps from which the weapon was hung; *liberal
conceit* elaborate design.
142. *margent* margin (where explanatory notes were
printed).
150–51. *in a dozen passes . . . he shall not exceed
you three hits* the odds the King proposes seem to
be that in a match of twelve bouts, Hamlet will
win at least five. Laertes would need to win by at
least eight to four.
151–52. *he hath laid on twelve for nine* "he" apparently is Laertes, who has seemingly raised the

odds against himself by wagering that out of twelve
bouts he will win nine.
157. *breathing time* time for taking exercise.
159. *an* if.
166. *lapwing* a bird reputedly so precocious as to
run as soon as hatched.
167. *comply* observe the formalities of courtesy; *dug*
mother's nipple.
168. *bevy* a covey of quails or lapwings.
168. *drossy* frivolous.
170. *encounter* manner of address or accosting;
yesty collection a frothy and superficial patchwork
of terms from the conversation of others.

and through the most fanned and winnowed opinions; and do but
blow them to their trial, the bubbles are out.

    Enter a LORD.

LORD.   My lord, his majesty commended him to you by young Osric,
who brings back to him that you attend him in the hall. He sends
to know if your pleasure hold to play with Laertes, or that you will 175
take longer time.

HAM.   I am constant to my purposes; they follow the king's pleasure.
If his fitness speaks, mine is ready; now or whensoever, provided I
be so able as now.

LORD.   The king and queen and all are coming down.   180

HAM.   In happy time.

LORD.   The queen desires you to use some gentle entertainment to
Laertes before you fall to play.

HAM.   She well instructs me.   *[Exit* LORD.]

HOR.   You will lose, my lord.   185

HAM.   I do not think so. Since he went into France I have been in
continual practice. I shall win at the odds. But thou wouldst not
think how ill all's here about my heart. But it is no matter.

HOR.   Nay, good my lord—

HAM.   It is but foolery, but it is such a kind of gaingiving as would 190
perhaps trouble a woman.

HOR.   If your mind dislike anything, obey it. I will forestall their
repair hither, and say you are not fit.

HAM.   Not a whit, we defy augury. There is special providence in
the fall of a sparrow. If it be now, 'tis not to come; if it be not to 195
come, it will be now; if it be not now, yet it will come. The readiness is all. Since no man of aught he leaves knows, what is't to
leave betimes? Let be.

A table prepared. *[Enter]* TRUMPETS, DRUMS, *and* OFFICERS *with*
cushions; KING, QUEEN, [OSRIC] *and all the* STATE, *[with] foils, dag-*
gers, *and* LAERTES.

KING.   Come, Hamlet, come, and take this hand from me.
              [The KING *puts* LAERTES' *hand into* HAMLET's.]

HAM.   Give me your pardon, sir. I have done you wrong,   200
But pardon 't as you are a gentleman.
This presence knows, and you must needs have heard,
How I am punished with a sore distraction.
What I have done
That might your nature, honor, and exception,   205
Roughly awake, I here proclaim was madness.
Was 't Hamlet wronged Laertes? Never Hamlet.
If Hamlet from himself be ta'en away,

---

171. *winnowed* tested, freed from inferior elements.

178. *fitness* convenience, inclination.
190. *gaingiving* misgiving.

And when he's not himself does wrong Laertes,
Then Hamlet does it not, Hamlet denies it.   210
Who does it then? His madness. If't be so,
Hamlet is of the faction that is wronged;
His madness is poor Hamlet's enemy.
Sir, in this audience,
Let my disclaiming from a purposed evil   215
Free me so far in your most generous thoughts
That I have shot my arrow o'er the house
And hurt my brother.
LAER.   I am satisfied in nature,
Whose motive in this case should stir me most
To my revenge. But in my terms of honor   220
I stand aloof, and will no reconcilement
Till by some elder masters of known honor
I have a voice and precedent of peace
To keep my name ungored. But till that time
I do receive your offered love like love,   225
And will not wrong it.
HAM.   I embrace it freely,
And will this brother's wager frankly play.
Give us the foils.
LAER.   Come, one for me.
HAM.   I'll be your foil, Laertes. In mine ignorance
Your skill shall, like a star i' th' darkest night,   230
Stick fiery off indeed.
LAER.   You mock me, sir.
HAM.   No, by this hand.
KING.   Give them the foils, young Osric. Cousin Hamlet,
You know the wager?
HAM.   Very well, my lord;
Your Grace has laid the odds o' th' weaker side.   235
KING.   I do not fear it, I have seen you both;
But since he is bettered, we have therefore odds.
LAER.   This is too heavy; let me see another.
HAM.   This likes me well. These foils have all a length?
                                      [*They prepare to play.*]
OSR.   Ay, my good lord.   240
KING.   Set me the stoups of wine upon that table.
If Hamlet give the first or second hit,
Or quit in answer of the third exchange,
Let all the battlements their ordnance fire.
The king shall drink to Hamlet's better breath,   245
And in the cup an union shall he throw,

---

223. *voice and precedent* authoritative statement justified by precedent.
229. *foil* (1) setting for gem (2) weapon.
237. *bettered* perfected through training.

239. *have all a langth* are all of the same length.
243. *quit in answer* literally, give as good as he gets (i.e., if the third bout is a draw).
246. *union* pearl.

Richer than that which four successive kings
In Denmark's crown have worn. Give me the cups,
And let the kettle to the trumpet speak,
The trumpet to the cannoneer without,   250
The cannons to the heavens, the heaven to earth,
'Now the king drinks to Hamlet'. Come, begin—
                                    Trumpets the while.
And you, the judges, bear a wary eye.
HAM.   Come on, sir.
LAER.   Come, my lord.   [*They play.*]
HAM.   One.
LAER.   No.
HAM.   Judgment.
OSR.   A hit, a very palpable hit.   255
            Drums, trumpets, and shot. Flourish; a piece goes off.
LAER.   Well, again.
KING.   Stay, give me drink. Hamlet, this pearl is thine.
    Here's to thy health. Give him the cup.
HAM.   I'll play this bout first; set it by awhile.
    Come.   [*They play.*] 260
    Another hit; what say you?
LAER.   I do confess't.
KING.   Our son shall win.
QUEEN.   He's fat, and scant of breath.
    Here, Hamlet, take my napkin, rub thy brows.
    The queen carouses to thy fortune, Hamlet.   265
HAM.   Good madam!
KING.   Gertrude, do not drink.
QUEEN.   I will, my lord; I pray you pardon me.
KING.   [*Aside.*] It is the poisoned cup; it is too late.
HAM.   I dare not drink yet, madam; by and by.   270
QUEEN.   Come, let me wipe thy face.
LAER.   My lord, I'll hit him now.
KING.   I do not think't.
LAER.   [*Aside.*] And yet it is almost against my conscience.
HAM.   Come, for the third, Laertes. You do but dally.
    I pray you pass with your best violence;   275
    I am afeard you make a wanton of me.
LAER.   Say you so? Come on.   [*They play.*]
OSR.   Nothing, neither way.
LAER.   Have at you now! [LAERTES *wounds* HAMLET; *then, in scuf-
    fling, they change rapiers.*]
KING.   Part them. They are incensed.   280
HAM.   Nay, come again.
            [HAMLET *wounds* LAERTES. *The* QUEEN *falls.*]

---

263. *fat* out of training.   276. *make a wanton of me* trifle with me.

OSR. Look to the queen there, ho!
HOR. They bleed on both sides. How is it, my lord?
OSR. How is't, Laertes?
LAER. Why, as a woodcock to mine own springe, Osric.   285
  I am justly killed with mine own treachery.
HAM. How does the queen?
KING.   She swoons to see them bleed.
QUEEN. No, no, the drink, the drink! O my dear Hamlet!
  The drink, the drink! I am poisoned.   [*Dies.*]
HAM. O, villainy! Ho! let the door be locked.   290
  Treachery! seek it out.   [LAERTES falls. *Exit* OSRIC.]
LAER. It is here, Hamlet. Hamlet, thou art slain;
  No med'cine in the world can do thee good.
  In thee there is not half an hour's life.
  The treacherous instrument is in thy hand,   295
  Unbated and envenomed. The foul practice
  Hath turned itself on me. Lo, here I lie,
  Never to rise again. Thy mother's poisoned.
  I can no more. The king, the king's to blame.
HAM. The point envenomed too?   300
  Then, venom, to thy work.   [*Wounds the* KING.]
ALL. Treason! treason!
KING. O, yet defend me, friends. I am but hurt.
HAM. Here, thou incestuous, murd'rous, damnéd Dane,
  Drink off this potion. Is thy union here?   305
  Follow my mother.   [KING *dies.*]
LAER.   He is justly served.
  It is a poison tempered by himself.
  Exchange forgiveness with me, noble Hamlet.
  Mine and my father's death come not upon thee,
  Nor thine on me!   [*Dies.*] 310
HAM. Heaven make thee free of it! I follow thee.
  I am dead, Horatio. Wretched queen, adieu!
  You that look pale and tremble at this chance,
  That are but mutes or audience to this act,
  Had I but time, as this fell sergeant Death   315
  Is strict in his arrest, O, I could tell you—
  But let it be. Horatio, I am dead:
  Thou livest; report me and my cause aright
  To the unsatisfied.
HOR.   Never believe it.
  I am more an antique Roman than a Dane.   320
  Here's yet some liquor left.
HAM.   As th'art a man,
  Give me the cup. Let go. By heaven, I'll ha't.

285. *springe* trap.   315. *fell* cruel; *sergeant* an officer whose duty is to
296. *Unbated* unblunted; *practice* plot.   summon persons to appear before a court.

O God, Horatio, what a wounded name,
Things standing thus unknown, shall I leave behind me!
If thou didst ever hold me in thy heart,   325
Absent thee from felicity awhile,
And in this harsh world draw thy breath in pain,
To tell my story.   *A march afar off.*
          What warlike noise is this?
      Enter OSRIC.
OSR.   Young Fortinbras, with conquest come from Poland,
To th' ambassadors of England gives   330
This warlike volley.
HAM.   O, I die, Horatio!
The potent poison quite o'er-crows my spirit.
I cannot live to hear the news from England,
But I do prophesy th' election lights
On Fortinbras. He has my dying voice.   335
So tell him, with th' occurrents, more and less,
Which have solicited—the rest is silence.   [*Dies.*]
HOR.   Now cracks a noble heart. Good night, sweet prince,
And flights of angels sing thee to thy rest!   [*March within.*]
Why does the drum come hither?   340

      Enter FORTINBRAS, *with the* AMBASSADORS [*and with drum,*
      colors, and ATTENDANTS].
FORT.   Where is this sight?
HOR.   What is it you would see?
If aught of woe or wonder, cease your search.
FORT.   This quarry cries on havoc. O proud death,
What feast is toward in thine eternal cell
That thou so many princes at a shot   345
So bloodily hast struck?
AMB.   The sight is dismal;
And our affairs from England come too late.
The ears are senseless that should give us hearing
To tell him his commandment is fulfilled,
That Rosencrantz and Guildenstern are dead.   350
Where should we have our thanks?
HOR.   Not from his mouth,
Had it th' ability of life to thank you.
He never gave commandment for their death.
But since, so jump upon this bloody question,
You from the Polack wars, and you from England,   355
Are here arrived, give order that these bodies

---

332. *o'er-crows* triumphs over.   343. *quarry* pile of dead.
335. *voice* vote.   344. *toward* impending.
336. *more and less* great and small.   354. *jump* exactly.
337. *solicited* incited, prompted.

High on a stage be placéd to the view,
And let me speak to th' yet unknowing world
How these things came about. So shall you hear
Of carnal, bloody, and unnatural acts;   360
Of accidental judgments, casual slaughters;
Of deaths put on by cunning and forced cause;
And, in this upshot, purposes mistook
Fall'n on th' inventors' heads. All this can I
Truly deliver.
FORT.   Let us haste to hear it,   365
And call the noblest to the audience.
For me, with sorrow I embrace my fortune.
I have some rights of memory in this kingdom,
Which now to claim my vantage doth invite me.
HOR.   Of that I shall have also cause to speak,   370
And from his mouth whose voice will draw on more.
But let this same be presently performed,
Even while men's minds are wild, lest more mischance
On plots and errors happen.
FORT.   Let four captains
Bear Hamlet like a soldier to the stage,   375
For he was likely, had he been put on,
To have proved most royal; and for his passage
The soldier's music and the rite of war
Speak loudly for him.
Take up the bodies. Such a sight as this   380
Becomes the field, but here shows much amiss.
Go, bid the soldiers shoot.
               Exeunt [*marching. A peal of ordnance shot off*].

---

362. *put on* instigated; *forced cause* by reason of   376. *put on* set to perform in office.
compulsion.   377. *passage* death.

Textual Commentary

The first edition of *Hamlet* was printed in quarto in 1603. It was published apparently without authorization—not surprisingly in view of the fact that it presents a pirated text of the play. This so-called "bad" quarto (Q1) is a reported text, put together from memory by a group of actors who had either seen the play performed, or who had themselves performed in it, on the London stage. Their purpose, presumably, was to furnish themselves with an acting version of the play to take on tour in the provinces. Most of their memories seem to have been drawn from the Shakespearean version of the tragedy, though it appears likely that memories of the pre-Shakespearean *Hamlet* have been incorporated at several points into the Q1 text. In it, Polonius is named Corambis (he is called Corambus in *Der Bestrafte Brudermord*). Reynaldo is Montano, and the nunnery scene occurs in Act II, immediately after Polonius/Corambis has made his suggestion to "loose" his daughter to Hamlet. In the Q1 version of the scene in Gertrude's chamber, the Queen explicitly denies having been a party to her husband's murder (thereby clearing up a point that is not clear in the more authoritative editions, and which Coleridge and other critics have wondered about), and she pledges herself to assist her son in his revenge. Q1 presents just the sort of garbled text that memorial reconstructions regularly do. The line of the action as we know it from the later editions is roughly preserved, though it is greatly simplified and vulgarized; and the Shakespearean language is thoroughly dissipated.

An authorized version of the play was duly published in the following year (the title pages of some copies of the second quarto bear the date 1604, others are dated 1605). All the evidence—especially that of the stage directions—suggests that this second quarto (Q2) was printed from Shakespeare's own manuscript. It is the fullest text of the play that survives (almost 3800 lines, as opposed to the 2220 type-lines of Q1), and the most authoritative, though its authority is somewhat diminished as a result of the many compositorial errors and omissions made in the process of printing, and also as a result of the fact that the bad first quarto was frequently consulted, for whatever reason, during the early stages of the printing of Q2, so that what should be, and in most respects is, the most authoritative text of the play has been contaminated at sundry points throughout the first act from the reported text of Q1.

A third quarto (Q3), printed from Q2, was published in 1611; and sometime between then and 1623 a fourth quarto (Q4, undated), printed from Q3, appeared. Neither Q3 nor Q4 has any independent textual authority.

The text of *Hamlet* that appeared in the folio collection (F) of Shakespeare's complete works in 1623 is generally supposed to have been printed from—or at least to have had behind it, if it were not directly printed from—the official theatrical promptbook. Thus it presumably represents the play as it had come to be acted by the King's Men some twenty years after its original production. It omits some 230 lines found in Q2, though it contains some 80 lines that are missing from Q2. There are numerous verbal differences between the two texts. Many of these are compositorial errors, occasioned when either the Q2 or the F workmen misread their manuscript. Examples are such variants as "cap" (F), "lap" (Q2), at II.ii.222; "loneliness" (F), "lowliness" (Q2), at III.i.46; "feature" (F), "stature" (Q2), at III.i.155; "so loud a wind" (F), "so loved Arm'd" (Q2), at IV.vii.22; "argal" (F), "or all" (Q2), at V.i.10, where in each case, F gives a correct reading for what is a literal misprint in Q2. But the folio has its share of compositorial misreadings as well. The "time" (Q2), "tune" (F) variant at III.i.154 is an example of one that has long been received into editions of the play. The famous case of the "sallied" (Q2) vs. the "solid" (F) flesh that Hamlet wishes, at I.ii.129, would melt, is almost certainly another.[1]

Not all the instances where F displays a word or phrase different from the corresponding reading in Q2 are due, however, to compositorial misreadings. There is no decisive evidence for supposing that the folio text represents a Shakespearean revision of the play as it appears in Q2, though this is sometimes argued. And assuming that the folio text derives from the official promptbook, and thus reflects theatrical practices, there is good reason to suppose that, where F departs from Q2 and a compositor is not responsible, the F variants represent verbal changes that had come to be made in the text by the actors themselves, over the years during which the play was performed. The folio text of *Hamlet* exhibits, in fact, just the sort of changes that one might expect to take place in the language of a play that had been in an active theatrical repertory for two decades. By comparison with the text of Q2, the actors can be seen taking certain liberties with their lines. Verbal substitutions have been made, catch words and phrases are repeated, and most troublesome of all perhaps, as Professor Harold Jenkins has pointed out in an important article,[2] the actors have interpolated a number of "gag lines" into their parts, of which the "Oh Vengeance" that F (but not Q2) interjects midway through Hamlet's soliloquy at the close of the second act is the most egregious.

For all its typographical imperfections, the second quarto gives us a text of *Hamlet* that must be regarded as superior to that of the folio, not only because it is fuller, but because it is closer to a Shakespearean manuscript source. It is the basis of the present edition. The folio text has been regularly consulted, and readings from it have been received into the present edition to supply Q2 omissions of words and phrases, to correct Q2 misprints, and to emend other corruptions in the Q2 text. The folio is, of course, the authority for the longer passages omitted from Q2 (as, for instance, at II.ii.231–58; II.ii.315–35; V.ii.68–80). The precise extent of my use of the folio text,

---

1. For persuasive arguments that both Q2 readings here are the right ones, see G. W. Williams, "Hamlet's Reason, Jangled out of Time: III.i.166," *Notes and Queries* 205 (1960): 329–31; and F. T. Bowers, "Hamlet's 'Sullied' or 'Solid' Flesh. A Bibliographical Case-History," *Shakespeare Survey* 9 (1956): 44–47.

2. "Playhouse Interpolations in the Folio Text of *Hamlet*," *Studies in Bibliography* 13 (1960): 31–47.

and of all other editions of the play apart from Q2, is shown in the Textual Notes, where all substantive departures from the text of the second quarto are recorded. The Q2 spelling has been modernized for the present edition, and the punctuation has been silently emended where intelligibility has seemed to require it. I have sought, however, to retain wherever possible the relatively light Q2 system of pointing, which is often highly revealing, chiefly, one would like to suppose, because it reflects at a not too distant remove Shakespeare's own intentions. The stage directions of this edition are those of the second quarto. Editorial additions to them are enclosed in square brackets. Strong preterit verb endings are marked with an acute accent (´) in verse passages where the meter requires that they be stressed.

TEXTUAL NOTES

Emendations of the second quarto text received into the present edition are printed inside the square bracket with—to the right of the bracket—an abbreviated reference to the edition in which the emendation first appears. The rejected Q2 reading follows. *om.* means *omitted*. Editions are referred to by the following abbreviations:

Q1	Quarto, 1603
Q2	Quarto, 1604–5
Q3	Quarto, 1611
Q4	Quarto, Undated
Q5	Quarto, 1637
F	Folio, 1623
F2	Folio, 1632

The following later editions also cited in the notes, by name: Rowe (1709); Pope (1723–25); Theobald (1733); Hanmer (1744); Warburton (1747); Johnson (1765); Capell (1767–68); Malone (1790); Collier (1842–44); Keightley (1867); Furness (1877); New Cambridge (1934).

[I.i] 16. soldier] *F*; souldiers *Q2*. 44. harrows] *F*; horrowes *Q2*. 45. Question it] *F*; Speak to it *Q2*. 73. why] *F*; with *Q2*. 73. cast] *F*; cost *Q1–2*. 88. those] *F*; these *Q2*. 91. returned]*F*; returne *Q2*. 94. designed] *Pope*; desseigne *Q2*; designe *F*. 112. mote] *Q4*; moth *Q2*; *om. F*. 121. feared] *Collier*; feare *Q2*; *om. F*. 138. you] *Q1, F*; your *Q2*. 140. at] *F*; *om. Q2*.
[I.ii] s.d. Councillors] Counsaile: as *Q2*. 58. He]*Q1,3,F*; *om. Q2*. 67. Not so, my] *F*; Not so much my *Q2*. 77. good] *F*; coold *Q2*. 82. shapes] *Q3*; chapes *Q2*; shewes *F*. 96. a mind] *F*; or minde *Q2*. 132. self] *F*; seale *Q2*. 133. weary] *F*; wary *Q2*. 137. come to this] *F*; come thus *Q2*. 143. would] *Q1,F*; should *Q2*. 175. you to drink deep ere] *Q1,F*; you for to drink ere *Q2*. 178. see] *Q1,F*; *om. Q2*. 235. hundred] *Q1,F*; hundreth *Q2*. 254. Foul] *Q1,F*; fonde *Q2*.

[I.iii] 3. is] *F*; in *Q2*. 12. bulk] *F*; bulkes *Q2*. 18. For he * * * birth] *F*; *om. Q2*. 49. like] *F*; *om. Q2*. 74. Are]*Q1,F*; Or *Q2*. 75. be] *F*; boy *Q2*. 76. loan] *F*; loue *Q2*. 77. dulls th'] *F7*; dulleth *Q2*. 83. invites] *F*; inuests *Q2*. 109. Running] *Collier*; tendring *Q1*; Wrong *Q2*; Roaming *F*. 115. springes] *Q1,F*; springs *Q2*. 125. tether] *F*; tider *Q2*. 130. bawds] *Theobald*; bonds *Q2,F*. 131. beguile] *Q3,F*; beguide *Q2*.
[I.iv] 2 a] *F*; *om. Q2*. 19. clepe]*Q5*;clip *Q2*; *om. F*. 27. the]*Pope*; their *Q2*; *om. F*. 36. evil] *Keightley*; eale *Q2*; *om. F*. 37. often doubt] *Collier*; of a doubt *Q2*; *om. F*.
[I.v] 20. fretful] *Q1,F*; fearefull *Q2*. 47. a] *F*; *om. Q2*. 55. lust] *Q1,F*; but *Q2*. 56. sate] *Q1,F*; sort *Q2*. 68. posset] *F*; possesse *Q2*. 95. stiffly] *F*; swiftly *Q2*. 116. bird] *F*; and *Q2*. 122. my lord] *Q1,F*; *om. Q2*.
[II.i] s.d. with his man] with his man or two

Q2. 28. no] *F; om. Q2.* 38. warrant] *F;* wit
Q2. 40. i' th'] *F;* with *Q2.* 62. takes] *F;* take
Q2. 104. passion] *F;* passions *Q2.*
[II.ii] 57. o'erhasty]*F;* hastie *Q2.* 90. since]*F;*
om. Q2. 97. he is] *F;* hee's *Q2.* 125. above]
F; about *Q2.* 136. winking] *F;* working *Q2.*
142. his] *Q3,F;* her *Q2.* 148. a] *F; om. Q2.*
150. 'tis] *F; om. Q2.* 206. sanity] *F;* sanctity
Q2. 207–8. suddenly * * * between him and]
F; om. Q2. 218. excellent] *Q3,F;* extent *Q2.*
221. over-happy] *F;* euer happy *Q2.* 222. cap]
F; lap *Q2.* 230. that] *F; om. Q2.* 231–58.
Let me question * * * dreadfully attended]
F; om. Q2. 288. What a piece] *F;* What peece
Q2. 303–4. the clown * * * sere] *F,* where
"tickle" reads "tickled"; *om. Q2.* 315–35.
How comes it * * * load too] *F; om. Q2.*
319. berattle] *F2;* be-rattled *F.* 325. most like]
Pope; like most *F.* 344. lest] *F;* let *Q2.* 344.
my] *Q3,F;* me *Q2.* 366–67. tragical-histor-
ical . . . pastoral] *F; om. Q2.* 390. By'r] *F;*
by *Q2.* 394. French falconers] *Q1,F;* friendly
Fankners *Q2.* 405. affectation] *F;* affection
Q2. 408. tale] *F;* talke *Q2.* 435. Then * * *
Ilium] *F; om. Q2.* 442. And like] *F;* Like
Q2. 456. fellies] *Furness;* follies *Q2;* fallies
F. 497. for a need] *Q1,F;* for need *Q2.* 498.
dozen or] *Q1,F;* dosen lines, or *Q2.* 510.
his] *F;* the *Q2.* 517. the cue for] *F;* that for
Q2. 540. father] *Q3; om. Q2,F.* 544. scul-
lion] *F;* stallyon *Q2;* scalion *Q1.* 556. devil
. . . devil] *F;* deale . . . deale *Q2.*
[III.i] 32. lawful espials] *F; om. Q2.* 33. We'll]
F; wee'le *Q2.* 46. loneliness] *F;* lowlines *Q2.*
55. Let's] *F; om. Q2.* 83. of us all] *F; om.
Q2.* 99. the] *F;* these *Q2.* 107. your honesty
should] *F;* you should *Q2.* 119. to] *F; om.
Q2.* 125. all] *F; om. Q2.* 141. lisp] *F;* list
Q2. 142. your ignorance] *F;* ignorance *Q2.*
148. expectancy] *F;* expectation *Q2.* 153.
that] *F;* what *Q2.* 155. feature] *F;* stature *Q2.*
184. unwatched] *F;* unmatcht *Q2.*
[III.ii] 8. tatters] *F;* totters *Q2.* 19. own feature]
F; feature *Q2.* 23. the which] *F;* which *Q2.*
25. praise] *F;* praysd *Q2.* 80. detecting] *F;*
detected *Q2.* 102–3. I mean * * * lord] *F;*
om. Q2. 123. this is miching mallecho] *F;*
this munching *Mallico Q2.* 125. counsel] *F;*
om. Q2. 138. orbed ground] *F;* orb'd the
ground *Q2.* 146. your] *F;* our *Q2.* 148–49.
must. / For women's] *F;* must. / For women
feare too much, euen as they loue, / And
womens *Q2.* 150. In neither aught] *F;* Eyther
none, in neither ought *Q2.* 151. love] *F;* Lord
Q2. 181. joys] *F;* joy *Q2.* 201. An] *Theobald;* And *Q2; om. F.* 205. once a widow]
F; once I be a widdow *Q2.* 205. be wife]
Q4,F; be a wife *Q2.* 234. Confederate] *Q1,F;*
Considerat *Q2.* 236. infected] *Q1,F;* inuected
Q2. 243. What * * * fire] *Q1,F; om. Q2.*
253. two] *F; om. Q2.* 281. start] *F;* stare *Q2.*
290. my] *F; om. Q2.* 327. thumb] *F;* the
vmber *Q2.* 334. the top of] *F; om. Q2.* 337–
38, can fret me] *F;* fret me not *Q2.* 349–50.
Pol. I will say so. / *Ham.* 'By and by' is easily
said. Leave me, friends.] *F; Ham.* * * *

/ Leaue me friends. / I will, say so. By and
by is easily said, *Q2.* 352. breathes] *F;* breakes
Q2. 354. bitter business as the day] *F;* business as the bitter day *Q2.* 359. daggers] *F;*
dagger *Q2.*
[III.iii] 17. It is] *F;* or it is *Q2.* 19. huge] *F;*
hough *Q2.* 22. ruin] *F;* raine *Q2.* 23. with]
F; om. Q2. 50. pardoned] *F;* pardon *Q2.*
58. shove] *F;* showe *Q2.* 73. pat] *F;* but *Q2.*
79. hire and salary] *F;* base and silly *Q2.*
[III.iv] 5. warrant] *F;* wait *Q2.* 19. inmost] *F;*
most *Q2.* 53. That roars * * * index] *F;* line
assigned to Hamlet in *Q2.* 60. a heaven-
kissing] *F;* a-heaue, a kissing *Q2.* 89. pan-
ders] *F;* pardons *Q2.* 90. eyes into my very
soul] *F;* very eyes into my soule *Q2.* 91.
grained] *F;* greeued *Q2.* 92. will not leave
their tinct] *F;* will leaue there their tinct *Q2.*
98. tithe] *F;* kyth *Q2.* 147. I] *F; om. Q2.*
162. live]*F;* leaue *Q2.* 169. Refrain to-night]
F; to refraine night *Q2.* 173. curb] *Malone;*
om. Q2,F. 219. a foolish] *F;* a most foolish
Q2.
[IV.i] 40. so * * * slander] *Capell; om. Q2,F.*
[IV,ii] 4. Compounded] *Q3,F;* Compound *Q2.*
26. Hide * * * after] *F; om. Q2.*
[IV.iii] 40. With * * * quickness] *F; om. Q2.*
64. were ne'er begun] *F;* will nere begin *Q2.*
[IV.v] 9. aim] *F;* yawn *Q2.* 16. *Queen.* Let her
come in.]*F;* speech assigned to Horatio in
Q2. 38. grave] *F;* ground *Q2.* 80. their] *F;*
om. Q2. 87. his] *F;* this *Q2.* 95. are] *Q3,F;*
is *Q2.* 104. They] *F;* The *Q2.* 140. swoop-
stake] *Q1;* soopstake *Q2,F.* 150. Let her come
in] *F;* assigned to Laertes in *Q2.* 155. Till]
F; Tell *Q2.* 158. an old] *F;* a poor *Q2.* 159–
61. Nature * * * it loves] *F; om. Q2.* 163.
Hey * * * hey nonny] *F; om. Q2.* 177. O,
you must] *F;* you may *Q2.* 181. affliction]
F; afflictions *Q2.* 189. All] *F; om. Q2.* 193.
I pray God] *F; om. Q2.* 194. see] *F; om. Q2.*
[IV.vi] 18. good] *F; om. Q2.* 21. bore] *F;* bord
Q2. 25. He] *F;* So *Q2.* 26. give] *F; om. Q2.*
[IV.vii] 6. proceeded] *F;* proceede *Q2.* 14,
conjunctive] *F;* concliue *Q2.* 22. so loud a
wind] *F;* so loued Arm'd *Q2.* 24. had] *F;*
have *Q2.* 44. and more strange] *F; om. Q2.*
54. shall] *F; om. Q2.* 60. As checking] *F;* As
the King *Q2.* 86. my] *F;* me *Q2.* 113. wick]
Rowe; weeke *Q2.* 132. on] *F;* ore *Q2.* 138.
that] *F; om. Q2.* 165. hoar] *F;* horry *Q2.*
169. cold] *F;* cull-cold *Q2.*
[V.i] 8. "se offendendo"] *F;* so offended *Q2.*
10. argal] *F;* or all *Q2.* 29–31. *Other.* Why,
he had none. / *Clown.* What, * * * without
arms?] *F; om. Q2.* 37. frame] *F; om. Q2.*
48.1. *afar off]* *F; om. Q2.* 52. stoup] *F;* soope
Q2. 57. that] *F; om. Q2.* 78. mazzard] *F;*
massene *Q2.* 92–93. Is this the fine of his
fines, and the recovery of his recoveries] *F;*
om. Q2. 94. Will his vouchers] *F;* will
vouchers *Q2.* 94–95. double ones too] *F;*
doubles *Q2.* 104. O] *F;* or *Q2.* 122 all] *F;*
om. Q2. 143; now-a-days] *F; om. Q2.* 150.
three and twenty years] *F;* 23 years *Q2.* 166.
chamber] *F;* table *Q2.* 186. winter's] *F;* waters

Q2. 201. Shards] *F*; *om*. Q2. 217. times tre-
ble] *F*; times double Q2. 231. and] *F*; *om*.
Q2. 261. thus] *F*; this Q2. 270. shortly] *F*;
thereby Q2.
[V.ii] 5. Methought]*F*; my thought Q2. 9. pall]
F; fall Q2. 17. unseal] *F*; unfold Q2. 43.
as's] *F* (Assis); as sir Q2. 57. Why, man * * *
employment] *F*; *om*. Q2. 68–80. To quit
* * * comes here] *F*; *om*. Q2. 73. interim
is] *Hanmer*; interim's *F*. 78. court] *Rowe*;
count *F*; *om*. Q2. 82. humbly] *F*; humble
Q2.91. Put] *F*; *om*. Q2. 96. sultry] Q3,*F*;
sully Q2. 96. for] *F*; or Q2. 131. his] Q5;
this Q2. 138. hangers] *F*; hanger Q2. 146.
might be] Q3,*F*; be might Q2. 149.

impawned] *New Cambridge*; *om*. Q2;
impon'd *F*. 149. as] *F*; *om* Q2. 164 He] *F*;
om. Q2. 167. comply]*F*; so Q2. 168. bevy]
F; breede Q2. 170. yesty] *F*; histy Q2. 171.
fanned] *Warburton*; prophane Q2; fond *F*.
171. winnowed] *F*; trennowed Q2. 195. be
now, 'tis] *F*; be, tis Q2. 214. Sir, in this
audience] *F*; *om*. Q2. 224. keep] *F*; *om*. Q2.
224. till] *F*; all Q2. 237. bettered] *F*; better
Q2. 246. union] *F*; Onixe Q2. 276. afeard]
F; sure Q2. 292. Hamlet, thou] *F*;thou Q2.
295. thy] *F*; my Q2. 304. murd'rous] *F*; *om*.
Q2. 305. thy union] *F*; the Onixe Q2. 358.
th' yet] Q3, *F*; yet Q2. 362. forced] *F*; for no
Q2. 371. on] *F*; no Q2.

INTELLECTUAL
BACKGROUNDS

MELANCHOLY

PETER DE LA PRIMAUDAYE: The French Academy †

Of the blood and of other humors in the body . . .

We understand by a *Humor*, a liquid and running body into which the food is converted in the liver, to this end: that bodies might be nourished and preserved by them. And as there are four elements of which our bodies are compounded, so there are four sorts of humors answerable to their natures, being all mingled together with the blood, as we may see by experience in blood let out of one's body. For uppermost we see as it were a little skim like to the flower or working of new wine, or of other wine when it is poured forth. Next, we may see as it were small streams of water mingled with the blood. And in the bottom is seen a black and thicker humor, like to the lees of wine in a wine vessel. So that if we know how to consider wisely of these things, it will be easy for us to understand the distinction of these sundry humors, and their nature. Now, concerning the first of them, we are to know that the proper nature of blood is to be hot and moist, wherein it answereth to the nature of air. It is temperate, sweet, and fatty, as also the best and chiefest part of nourishment. For albeit all the other humors do nourish likewise, and are carried of the blood, nevertheless that humor which is properly called blood is the chiefest part of nourishment. * * * Next, that thin skim which is seen on the top of it, resembling the flower of wine, is that humor that is called yellow choler, or the choleric humor, which is hot and dry, of a bitter taste, and answerable to the nature of fire. * * * Moreover, those small streams of water which we see mingled in the blood proceed of the phlegmatic humor that is cold and moist, like to water of whose nature it holdeth * * * and without taste, or as some affirm, it is somewhat brackish, but not fatty. Lastly, the black humor and most earthy, which looketh like the very bottom of a deep, red, and thick wine, or like the lees in a vessel full of wine or oil, is the melancholic humor, or as some term it, black choler, being cold and dry like to the earth, with which it hath some agreement, and of taste somewhat sharp.

Of the diverse temperatures and complexions of men, according to the humors that bear most sway in them . . .

* * * But we account those natures to be well tempered which approach nearest to the perfect temperature. And as every humor ruleth more or

---

†. Translated by "T. B. C.," London, 1594. The first extract is from 2.64 (pp. 358–59); the second from 2.68 (pp. 380–82).

less in every one, so he is called either sanguine, or phlegmatic, or choleric, or melancholic. Again, as the other humors bear sway next unto the principal, so is a man said to be either phlegmatic-sanguine, choleric-sanguine, or melancholic-sanguine. The like may be said of the other humors according to their temperature, as also of the affections which have some agreement with them. Hereof it is that, when there is excess of the phlegmatic humor in men, their natures are commonly slothful, they shun labor and give themselves to bodily pleasures, they love dainties, and delicate meats and drinks, they are tender and effeminate, and clean contrary to stout and valiant men. And if there be excess of the choleric humor, their natures are easily provoked and stirred up to wrath, but their anger is as a fire of thorns that, being soon kindled and making a great noise, is by and by quenched again. Their gestures also are more quick and vehement, and their hastiness is commonly foolish and turbulent. They babble much, and are like to vessels full of holes, unable to hold in and keep any secret matter. They are fierce in assailing, but inconstant in sustaining the assault, in some sort resembling the nature of dogs, which bark and bite if they can, and afterward fly away. And if there be excess of the melancholic humor, the natures of such are sad, still hard to please, suspicious, conceited,[1] obstinate, some more and some less. And if the choleric and melancholic humors be corrupt and mingled together, their natures become monstrous, proud, full of envy, fraud, subtilities, venemous and poisonful, hateful and diabolical. And when the malignant spirits know men's nature thus disposed, no doubt but they take occasion thereby to intermingle themselves, if God permit them, and propose to use them for the punishing of men: I say they will join themselves unto them, and make them their instruments, as God on the other side useth those natures that are most moderate and best tempered, making them instruments of his glory.

Now, we may call to mind what we learned before almost to the same end, touching the means whereby evil spirits might trouble the imagination, fantasy and minds of men. We may say as much of the humors of the body, whose motions and nature they know very well. Whereby they can so much the more easily abuse them in their damnable work— and will, as we may judge by the example of him that was possessed and lunatic, of whom the Evangelists make mention.[2] * * * And by that which they wrote of him, it seemeth that he was subject to the falling sickness, that returneth oftentimes according to the course of the moon, which naturally hath great affinity with the humors, and great power over them. And therefore it is very likely that the evil spirit which tormented this poor lunatic watched the occasions of his disease to afflict him the more, and to cause him to fall either in the fire or in the water, as he did indeed, thereby to work his death. * * * Which example show-

1. Ingenious.
2. See Matthew 17.14–18, Mark 9.14–29, Luke 9.37–42.

eth unto us what is the malice of the devil, what pleasure he taketh in hurting of men, what means and what occasions he seeketh for and maketh choice of, and what access unto us we may offer him through our corrupt nature, through our vices and sins, and through our inclinations and manners that are naturally evil and perverse, if God letteth him loose the bridle by his just judgment. * * * For this cause, we ought to take good heed that we give not our common enemy those occasions that he seeketh to have from us, to the end that he abuse us not, nor anything that is ours, and which God hath bestowed upon us. This is the reason why the consideration of our temperature, complexion, and natural inclination is very necessary for us: because the knowledge hereof affordeth unto us many good instruments that may stand us in great stead throughout our whole life, as well for the preservation of the health of our bodies, as for the rule and government of our affections and manners, as also in regard of the familiarity and acquaintance which we have one with another. For through the contemplation hereof, we may know, not only the causes of health and sickness, of the life and death of the body, but also of that of the soul. For as the good humors corrupt in our bodies according as we have heard, and breed in them sundry diseases, which finally lead them unto death; even so by means of sin all those good and natural affections, which ought to be the seeds of virtue in us, are corrupted and turn into vices, that are the diseases of the soul, and bring unto it the second and eternal death: as, contrariwise, virtues are the health and life thereof.

TIMOTHY BRIGHT: A Treatise of Melancholy †

How melancholy altereth those actions which rise out of the brain.

Touching actions which rise from the brain, melancholy causeth dullness of conceit,[1] both by reason the substance of the brain in such persons is more gross, and their spirit not so prompt and subtle as is requisite for ready understanding. Again, almost all the senses standing in a kind of passive nature, a substance cold and dry—and by consequent hard—is not so meet thereto; which, as it serveth well to retain that which is once engraven, so like adamant it keepeth, in comparison of other tempers, that which once it hath received: whereby as they are unfit to commit readily to memory, so retain they that is committed in surer custody. Sometime it falleth out that melancholy men are found very witty, and quickly discern, either because the humor of melancholy with some

† London, 1586. This extract is from chapter 22,   1. Apprehension.
pp. 129–31.

heat is so made subtle that, as from the driest wood riseth the clearest flame, and from the lees of wine is distilled a strong and burning aqua vitae, in like sort their spirits, both from the dryness of the matter, and straining of the gross substance from which they pass, receiving a pureness, are instruments of such sharpness, which is the dry light that Heraclitus approved. To this, other reasons may be added, as: exercise of their wits, wherein they be indefatigable, which maketh them seem to have that of a natural readiness which custom of exercise, and use hath found in them. Moreover, while their passions be not yet vehement, whereby they might be overcarried, melancholy breedeth a jealousy of doubt in that they take in deliberation, and causeth them to be the more exact and curious in pondering the very moments of things. To these reasons may be added the vehemancy of their affections once raised: which carrieth them, with all their faculties thereto belonging, into the depth of that they take pleasure to inter-meddle in. For though the melancholy man be not so easily affected with any other passion as with those of fear, sadness, and jealousy, yet being once thoroughly heat with a contrary passion, retaineth the fervency thereof far longer time than any other complexion, and more fervently boileth therewith, by reason his heart and spirit hath more solidity of substance to entertain deeply the passion, which in a more rare and thin sooner vanisheth away. Thus greediness of desire in those things which they affect maketh them diligent and painful, wary and circumspect, and so in actions of brain and sense not inferior to the best tempers; as also it maketh them stiff in opinion. Their resolution riseth of long deliberation, because of doubt and distrust which, as it is not easily bred, so it is also hard to remove. Such persons are doubtful, suspicious, and thereby long in deliberation, because those domestical fears, or that internal obscurity, causeth an opinion of danger in outward affairs where there is no cause of doubt. Their dreams are fearful, partly by reason of their fancy, waking, is most occupied about fears and terrors, which retaineth the impression in sleep; and partly through black and dark fumes of melancholy rising up to the brain, whereof the fantasy forgeth objects, and disturbeth the sleep of melancholy persons. * * *

DEMONOLOGY

LEWES LAVATER: Of Ghosts and Spirits Walking by
Night †

*Melancholic persons and mad men imagine many things which in very
deed are not.*

There have been very many in all ages which have utterly denied that
there be any spirits or strange sights. The philosophers of Epicurus's sect
did jest and laugh at all those things which were reported of them, and
counted them as feigned and counterfeit, by the which only children
and fools and plain simple men were made afraid. * * * True it is that
many men do sadly[1] persuade themselves that they see or hear ghosts:
for that which they imagine they see or hear proceedeth either of melancholy, madness, weakness of the senses, fear, or of some other perturbation; or else when they see or hear beasts, vapors, or some other natural
things, then they vainly suppose they have seen sights I wot not what.
* * *

There is no doubt but that almost all those things which the common
people judge to be wonderful sights are nothing less than so.[2] But in the
mean season it can not be denied but that strange sights, and many other
such like things, are sometimes heard and also seen.

And first it can not be denied but that some men which, either by
dispositions of nature or for that[3] they have sustained great misery, are
now become heavy and full of melancholy, imagine many times with
themselves, being alone, miraculous and strange things. Sometimes they
affirm in great sooth that they verily hear and see this or that thing,
which not withstanding neither they nor yet any other man did once see
or hear: which thing we sometimes see by experience to be true in those
men which be troubled with great headaches or subject to other diseases
of the body, or cannot take rest in the night, or are distraughted of their
wits. Those which dwell with such kind of men, when they hear them
tell such absurd tales, such strange things, and such marvelous visions,
albeit they pity their unfortunate estate, yet can they not many times
contain themselves from laughing. * * *

†Translated into English by "R. H.," London,
1572. The extracts here printed are from 1.2 (pp.
9–10), 2.2 (pp. 102–9), 2.4 (p. 114), 2.13 (pp.
159–61), and 2.15 (p. 163).

1. Seriously.
2. I.e., delusions.
3. Because.

The Papists' doctrine touching the souls of dead men, and the appearing of them.

The papists in former times have publicly both taught and written that those spirits which men sometime see and hear be either good or bad angels, or else the souls of those which either live in everlasting bliss, or in purgatory, or in the place of damned persons; and that divers of them are those souls that crave aid and deliverance of men. * * *

Of this place, to wit, purgatory, popish writers teach marvelous things. Some of them say that purgatory is also under the earth as hell is. Some say that hell and purgatory are both one place, albeit the pains be divers according to the deserts of souls. * * * Some of them say that the pain of purgatory is all one with the punishment of hell, and that they differ only in this, that the one hath an end, the other no end: and that it is far more easy to endure all the pains of this world which all men since Adam's time have sustained, even unto the day of the last judgment, than to bear one day's space the least of those two punishments. * * *

Hereunto they add that the spirits, as well of the good as the ill, do come and are sent unto men living, from hell; and that by the common law of justice, all men at the day of judgment shall come to their trial from hell; and that none before that time can come from thence. Farther they teach that by God's license and dispensation, certain, yea before the day of judgment, are permitted to come out of hell, and that not forever, but only for a season, for the instructing and terrifying of the living. * * *

But as concerning the time and place when and where spirits do proffer themselves to be seen, they say no certain rule can be given, for this standeth wholly in God's pleasure, who if he list to deliver any, suffereth him to make his appearance forthwith even in such places as he may be well heard in. And that spirits do not always appear under a visible shape, but sometimes invisibly, insomuch that sometimes nothing else is heard of them but sneezing, spitting, sighing, and clapping of hands. etc. * * * And wheresoever these spirits be, they say that they endure punishment. Besides that souls do not appear nor answer unto every man's interrogatories, but that of a great number they scantly appear unto one. And therefore they teach whensoever such visions of spirits are showed, men should use fasting and prayer or ever they demand any question of them. * * * Besides this, shrift and massing[4] should be used ere we question with them: farther, that we should not give credit as soon as we hear but one sign, but await to hear the same thrice repeated, which in the first book of Samuel and third chapter is read to have been done by Samuel being yet a child: for otherwise the divel may delude and deceive us, as he doth very often. * * *

---

4. Saying of masses.

* * * This [the use of some form of prayer] done, we should, as they teach, fall to questioning with them, and say: "Thou spirit, we beseech thee by Christ Jesus, tell us what thou art, and if there be any amongst us to whom thou wouldst gladly make answer, name him, or by some sign declare so much." After this, the question is to be moved, each man there present being recited,[5] whether he would answer unto this or that man. And if at the name of any he speak, or make a noise, all other demands remaining should be made unto him, as these and such like: What man's soul he is? For what cause he is come, and what he doth desire? Whether he require any aid by prayers and suffrages? Whether by massing or alms-giving he may be released? * * *

Moreover, popish writers teach us to discern good spirits from evil by four means. First, they say that if he be a good spirit, he will at the beginning somewhat terrify men, but again soon revive and comfort them. * * * Their second note is to descry them by their outward and visible shape. For if they appear under the form of a lion, bear, dog, toad, serpent, cat, or black ghost, it may easily be gathered that it is an evil spirit. And that, on the other side, good spirits do appear under the shape of a dove, a man, a lamb, or in the brightness and clear light of the sun.

We must also consider whether the voice which we hear be sweet, lowly, sober, and sorrowful, or otherwise terrible and full of reproach, for so they term it.

Thirdly, we must note whether the spirit teach ought that doth vary from the doctrine of the apostles, and other doctors approved by the church's censure; or whether he utter anything that doth dissent from the faith, good manners, and ceremonies of the church, according to the cannonical rites or decrees of councils, and against the laws of the holy Church of Rome.

Fourthly, we must take diligent heed whether in his words, deeds, and gestures, he do show forth any humility, acknowledging or confessing of his sins and punishments, or whether we hear of him any groaning, weeping, complaint, boasting, threatening, slander or blasphemy. For as the beggar doth rehearse his own misery, so likewise do good spirits that desire any help or deliverance. * * *

Testimonies out of the word of God that neither the souls of the faithful nor of infidels do walk upon the earth after they are once parted from their bodies.

Now, that the souls neither of the faithful nor of infidels do wander any longer on the earth when they be once severed from the bodies, I will make it plain and evident unto you by these reasons following. First,

5. Called by name.

certain it is that such as depart hence either die in faith or in unbelief. Touching those that go hence in a right belief, their souls are by and by in possession of life everlasting; and they that depart in unbelief do straightway become partakers of eternal damnation. The souls do not vanish away and die with the body, as the Epicures' opinion is, neither yet be in every place, as some do imagine. * * *

What those things are which men see and hear: and first, that good angels do sometimes appear.

But thou wilt say, "I do not yet clearly and plainly understand what manner of things those are whereof * * * historiographers, holy fathers, and others make mention: as that holy apostles, bishops, martyrs, confessors, virgins, and many other which died long ago, appeared unto certain men lying at the point of death, gave them warning, answered unto certain questions, commanded them to do this or that thing. * * *" You will say, "I hear and understand very well that these things are not men's souls, which continually remain in their appointed places. I pray you, then, what are they?" To conclude in few words: If it be not a vain persuasion proceeding through weakness of the senses, through fear, or some such like cause, or if it be not deceit of men, or some natural thing * * * it is either a good or evil angel, or some other forewarning sent by God. * * * For as servants stand before their masters to fulfill their commandments, even so are the angels pressed and ready to serve God. Isaiah the 63[:9]: "The angel of his face," that is, which standeth ready in his sight, "preserved them." And further, they which often stand in presence of their lords are acceptable unto them, and privy to their secrets. Out of this place of Matthew [18:10], Saint Jerome in his commentaries, and other fathers do conclude that God doth assign unto every soul as soon as he createth him his peculiar angel, which taketh care of him. But whether that everyone of the elect have his proper angel, or many angels be appointed unto him, it is not expressly set forth, yet this is most sure and certain, that God hath given his angels in charge to have regard and care over us.

That sometimes, yea and for the most part, evil angels do appear.

Contrariwise, evil angels are hurtful and enemies unto men; they follow them everywhere, to the end they may withdraw them from true worshipping of God, and from faith in his only son, Jesus Christ, unto sundry other things. These appear in divers shapes: for if the devil, as Paul doth witness, transformed himself into an angel of light, no less may he take the shape of a prophet, an apostle, evangelist, bishop, and martyr, and appear in their likeness; or so bewitch us, that we verily suppose we hear or see them in very deed. He taketh on him to tell of things to come, whether he hit them right or wrong. He affirmeth that he is this or that soul, that he may be delivered by this or that means, that by these means he may purchase credit and authority unto those things which have no ground of scripture.

G. GIFFORD: A Discourse of the Subtle Practices of Devils by Witches and Sorcerers †

Devils have no power to hurt men's bodies or goods, but upon special leave given unto them.

The reprobate angels are mighty, fierce and subtle. * * * They be instruments of God's vengeance, and executioners of his wrath. They do not exercise power and authority which is absolute, and at their own will and appointment, but so far as God leteth forth the chain to give them scope. Touching the reprobate,[1] which despise the ways of God and are disobedient, we are taught that God in righteous vengeance giveth them over into their[2] hands, for they would not love his laws, nor honor him as their God. Therefore they come under the tyranny of wicked devils, which work in them with power; their hearts do they harden; their eyes, even the eyes of their minds, do they blind; they kindle and stir up in them all filthy lusts, and carry them headlong into foul and abominable sins.

THE NATURE OF MAN

PETER DE LA PRIMAUDAYE: The French Academy ‡

Of Man

ASER. When I direct my flight now and then, my companions, even unto the heavens, and with the wings of contemplation behold their wonderful greatness; their terrible motions, being contrary and without ceasing; the living brightness, rare beauty, and incomparable force of the sun and moon; their unchangeable course, one while cause of light, and by and by after of darkness; the infinite number of goodly stars, and of so many other celestial signs: and from this excellent and constant order of all these things, as one ravished and amazed, when I withdraw my spirit lower into the elementary region, to admire and wonder at the

---

† London, 1587; this extract appears on sig. D2.
1. I.e., reprobate humans.
2. I.e., of the reprobate angels.

‡ Translated by "T. B. C.," London, 1594. This extract is from 1.1 (pp. 9–17).

situation and spreading of the earth amidst the waters, both of them
making one round mass or lump, which in the midst of this great firmament occupieth the room but of a prick or tittle in respect thereof:
besides, when I acknowledge in this earth and water as many sundry and
most beautiful plants, and kinds of earthy and watery creatures, as there
are grains of sand on the sea banks: and when I delight myself in the
variety of minerals and precious stones, considering the form, quality,
and virtue of each of these things: briefly, when I admire the diversity of
times and seasons, the continual spring of fountains, the certain course
of rivers, and generally, so many wonderful works under the cope of
heaven, I cannot marvel enough at the excellency of Man, for whom
all these things were created, and are maintained and preserved in their
being and moving, by one and the same divine providence always like
unto itself.

AMANA. There is nothing more certain than this, that all things whatsoever either the eye can behold, or the ear hear, were created for the
benefit, profit, and use of man, and that he was made excellent above
all things to rule over them: yea, the very angels are sent to minister for
their sakes, which shall receive the inheritance of salvation.

ARAM. Oh unspeakable and heavenly goodness, which hast created man
little lower than thyself, and crowned him with glory and worship! But
tell us, I pray thee, Achitob, more particularly, what this great and principal work of nature—Man—is, to what end his being was given him,
and how he hath showed forth the fruits thereof. For it must needs be
that there is something in him greatly to be wondered at, seeing all
things were created to serve and obey him.

ACHITOB. Truly ye have reason, companions, to begin our happy assem-
bly with that knowledge which we ought to have of ourselves, as being
the storehouse of all wisdom, and beginning of salvation: whereof we
may have an assured testimony from that father of philosophy, Socrates,
who beholding the first precept written at Delphos in that temple of
Apollo, which was so renowned throughout Graecia, namely, *Know thy
self*, was forthwith driven into a very deep cogitation, and being rapt with
contemplation of spirit, he began from that time forward to doubt and
to inquire of himself. * * * Ignorance of a man's self, saith Lactantius,
and the want[1] of knowledge wherefore and to what end he is born, is
the cause of error, of evil * * * of forsaking the light to walk in darkness.
Now if we account it a shameful thing to be ignorant of those things
which belong to the life of man, surely the not knowing of ourselves is
much more dishonest. Let us then consider what man is, according to
that mean knowledge, which by the grace of God we are endued withal.
* * * Man is a creature made of God after his own image, just, holy,
good and right by nature, and compounded of soul and body. I say of

---

1. Lack.

soul, which was inspired of God with spirit and life, and of a perfect natural body, framed of the earth by the same power of God. In this sort man had his being of the eternal workmaster of the whole world, of whom he was created by his incomprehensible goodness, to be made partaker of his immortality and permanent felicity, for this only end: to set forth the glory of his Creator, and to speak and do those things that are agreeable unto him, through the acknowledgment of his benefits. From which end man, being fallen of his own free will through ingratitude and disobedience, was bereaved of all those ornaments, which he had received before of God, and instead of righteousness and holiness, all iniquity, filthiness and uncleanness entered into him: whereby he was made the slave of sin and death, from whence all those miseries had their beginnings, wherewith the life of man is overwhelmed. His soul also was wrapped with infinite hurtful passions and perturbations, which work in it a continual disquietness, and his body became subject to innumerable travails, and violent untowardness. * * * Notwithstanding, God, whose goodness and mercy are endless, reestablished and assured the succession of his immortal inheritance unto those whom it pleased him by grace to make dead to sin and alive to himself, through the satisfaction of his wrath made by the innocency of his eternal son, purging them in his blood, and opening unto them by him the gates of heaven, after he hath renewed them in righteousness, holiness and innocency, that they may follow after godliness and religion. * * * Furthermore, the same heavenly grace blessing this holy desire of the man regenerate, causeth him to draw out of the doctrine of holy scriptures that wherewithal he may, if not heal perfectly his wicked inclinations, yet at the least contain and repress them in such sort that they break not out into any damnable execution. He teacheth him also to receive the infirmities of his flesh as fatherly chastisements for his sin, and as necessary means to exercise him, and to keep him in awe. And lastly, for the upshot and perfection of all happiness and felicity in this world, he instructeth him how he may lead a quiet and peaceful life in beholding the wonderful works of the divinity, which he is to adore and honor, and in the amendment and correction of his manners naturally corrupted, by squaring them after the pattern of virtue, that so he may be made worthy and fit to govern human affairs, for the profit of many: and at length attain to the perfection of a wise man, by joining together the active life with the contemplative in the certain hope and expectation of a second, immortal and most blessed life. * * *

MICHEL DE MONTAIGNE: An Apology of Raymond Sebond †

Let us now but consider man alone, without other help, armed but with his own weapons, and unprovided of the grace and knowledge of God, which is all his honor, all his strength, and all the ground of his being. Let us see what holdfast, or freehold, he hath in this gorgeous and goodly equipage. Let him with the utmost power of his discourse make me understand upon what foundation he hath built those great advantages and odds he supposeth to have over other creatures. Who hath persuaded him that this admirable moving of heaven's vaults; that the eternal light of these lamps so fiercely rolling over his head; that the horror-moving and continual motion of this infinite vast ocean, were established, and continue so many ages, for his commodity and service? Is it possible to imagine anything so ridiculous as this miserable and wretched creature, which is not so much as master of himself, exposed and subject to the offenses of all things, and yet dareth call himself master and emperor of this universe? In whose power it is not to know the least part of it, much less to command the same. And the privilege, which he so fondly[1] challengeth, to be the only absolute creature in this huge world's frame, perfectly able to know the absolute beauty and several parts thereof, and that he is only of power[2] to yield the great Architect thereof due thanks for it, and to keep account both of the receipts and layings out of the world. Who hath sealed him this patent? Let him show us his letters of privilege for so noble and so great a charge.

DEATH

HIERONYMOUS CARDANUS: Comfort ‡

Therefore Socrates was wont to say that death might be resembled either to sound sleep, a long journey, or destruction, as is the death of brute beasts. If the soul doth live, and after death feeleth nothing, then is it like unto a sound sleep, because therein we rest without either feeling or understanding, and after a while return to the same exercises. Most assured it is that such sleeps are most sweet as be most sound. For those are the best wherein, like unto dead men, we dream nothing. The broken sleeps, the slumber and dreams full of visions, are commonly in them that have weak and sickly bodies. * * *

---

†*Essays*, in John Florio's translation, London, 1603; from 2.12 (p. 258).
1. Foolishly.

2. I.e., he alone has the power.
‡Translated by Thomas Bedingfield, London, 1576. This extract is from book 2 (sigs. Dii^r–Diii^v).

* * * But if thou compare death to long travel, and that the soul—being let loose from prison of the body—seeth all things and walketh everywhere, then what can be considered more happy. For the soul, being burdened with the body, is neither free nor rightly knoweth anything, but being overladen with cares, doth behold only the figure of things, and as it were through a web, or cloth, guesseth a sight, and certainly knoweth nothing; but being free, doth not only cast off all hindrance, but also beholdeth all things without interruption, which being true, who is he that willingly would eschew death? * * *

For there is nothing that doth better or more truly prophesy the end of life than when a man dreameth that he doth travel and wander into far countries, and chiefly if he imagineth himself to ride upon a white horse, that is swift; and that he traveleth in countries unknown without hope of return, in such sort naturally divining of that shortly will come to pass indeed. But if death be resembled to destruction—which, as is already proved, is most impossible—yet can it no ways be accompted [1] evil. Because whatsoever is not, cannot be evil, else we should lament for them that never were born, nor never were at all; and they that are not, can nothing suffer.

MICHEL DE MONTAIGNE: An Apology of Raymond Sebond †

* * * In few, *there is no constant existence, neither of our being, nor of the objects.* [1] And we, and our judgment, and all mortal things else, do uncessantly roll, turn and pass away. Thus can nothing be certainly established, nor of the one, nor of the other; both the judging and the judged being in continual alteration and motion. We have no communication with being; for every human nature is ever in the middle between being born and dying; giving nothing of itself but an obscure appearance and shadow, and an uncertain and weak opinion. And if perhaps you fix your thought to take its being, it would be even as if one should go about to poison the water: for, how much the more he shall close and press that which by its own nature is ever gliding, so much the more he shall lose what he would hold and fasten. Thus, seeing all things are subject to pass from one change to another, reason, which therein seeketh a real subsistence, finds herself deceived, as unable to apprehend anything subsistent and permanent: forsomuch as each thing either cometh to a being, and is not yet altogether; or beginneth to die before it be born. * * *

---

1. Accounted.
†*Essays*, in John Florio's translation, London, 1603; from 2.12 (pp. 350 and 351).

1. I.e., the material objects of the external world; "in few": in short.

And * * * we others do foolishly fear a kind of death whenas we have already passed, and daily pass, so many others. For not only, as Heraclitus said, the death of fire is a generation of air, and the death of air a generation of water; but also we may most evidently see it in ourselves. The flower of age dieth, fadeth and fleeteth, when age comes upon us; and youth endeth in the flower of a full grown man's age; childhood in youth, and the first age dieth in infancy; and yesterday endeth in this day, and today shall die in tomorrow. And *nothing remaineth or ever continueth in one state.* For to prove it, if we should ever continue one and the same, how is it then that now we rejoice at one thing, and now at another? How comes it to pass we love things contrary, or we hate them * * * or we blame them? How is it that we have different affections, holding no more the same sense in the same thought? For it is not likely that without alteration we should take other passions, and *what admitteth alterations, continueth not the same;* and if it be not one selfsame, then is it not; but rather with being all one, the simple being doth also change, ever becoming other from other. And by consequence, nature's senses are deceived and lie falsely; taking what appeareth for what is; for want of truly knowing what it is that is. But then what is it, that is indeed? That which is eternal, that is to say, that which never had birth, nor ever shall have end; and to which no time can bring change or cause alteration. * * *

MICHEL DE MONTAIGNE: Of Physiognomy †

We trouble death with the care of life, and life with the care of death. The one annoyeth, the other affrights us. It is not against death we prepare ourselves; it is a thing too momentary. A quarter of an hour of passion without consequence and without annoyance deserves not particular precepts. To say truth, we prepare ourselves against the preparations of death. *Philosophy teacheth us ever to have death before our eyes, to foresee and consider it before it come;* then giveth us rules and precautions so to provide that such foresight and thought hurt us not. So do physicians, who cast us into diseases that they may employ their drugs and skill about them. If we have not known how to live, it is injustice to teach us how to die, and deform the end from all the rest. Have we known how to live constantly and quietly, we shall know how to die resolutely and reposedly. They may brag as much as they please * * * *The whole life of a philosopher is the meditation of his death.* But, methinks, it is indeed the end, yet not the scope of life. It is her last, it is her extremity; yet not her object. Herself must be unto herself, her aim, her drift and her design. Her direct study is to order, to direct and to

† *Essays*, in John Florio's translation, London, 1603; from 3.12 (pp. 626–27).

suffer herself. In the number of many other offices which the general and principal chapter, "To Know how to Live," containeth, is this special article, "To Know how to Die." And of the easiest, did not our own fear weigh it down. To judge them by their profit and by the naked truth, the lessons of simplicity yield not much to those which doctrine preacheth to the contrary unto us. Men are different in feeling, and diverse in force; they must be directed to their good according to themselves, and by divers ways. * * *

I never saw mean peasant of my neighbor's enter into cogitation, or care, with what assurance or countenance he should pass this last hour. Nature teacheth him never to muse on death but when he dieth. And then hath he a better grace in it than Aristotle, whom death perplexeth doubly, both by herself and by so long a premeditation. Therefore was it Caesar's opinion that *the least premeditated death was the happiest and the easiest * * * He grieves more than he need, that grieves before he need.* The sharpness of this imagination proceeds from our curiosity. Thus we ever hinder ourselves, desiring to forerun and sway natural prescriptions. It is but for doctors, being in health, to fare the worse by it, and to frown and startle at the image of death. The vulgar sort have neither need of remedy nor comfort but when the shock or stroke cometh, and justly considers no more of it than he feeleth. And is it not as we say, that the vulgars' stupidity and want of apprehension afford them this patience in present evils, and this deep carelessness of sinister future accidents? That their mind—being more gross, dull and blockish—is less penetrable and agitable? In God's name, if it be so, let us henceforth keep a school of brutality. It is the utmost fruit that sciences promise unto us, to which she so gently bringeth her disciples.

EXTRACTS FROM THE SOURCES

SAXO GRAMMATICUS

Amleth †

At this time Horwendil and Feng, whose father Gerwendil had been governor of the Jutes, were appointed in his place by Rorik to defend Jutland. But Horwendil held the monarchy for three years, and then, to win the height of glory, devoted himself to roving.[1] Then Koll, King of Norway, in rivalry of his great deeds and renown, deemed it would be a handsome deed if by his greater strength in arms he could bedim the far-famed glory of the rover; and, cruising about the sea, he watched for Horwendil's fleet and came up with it. There was an island lying in the middle of the sea, which each of the rovers, bringing his ships up on either side, was holding. The captains were tempted by the pleasant look of the beach, and the comeliness of the shores led them to look through the interior of the spring-tide woods, to go through the glades, and roam over the sequestered forests. It was here that the advance of Koll and Horwendil brought them face to face without any witness. Then Horwendil endeavoured to address the king first, asking him in what way it was his pleasure to fight, and declaring that one best which needed the courage of as few as possible. For, said he, the duel was the surest of all modes of combat for winning the meed of bravery, because it relied only upon native courage, and excluded all help from the hand of another. Koll marvelled at so brave a judgment in a youth, and said: "Since thou hast granted me the choice of battle, I think it is best to employ that kind which needs only the endeavours of two, and is free from all the tumult. Certainly it is more venturesome, and allows of a speedier award of the victory. * * * But since the issue remains doubtful, we must pay some regard to gentle dealing, and must not give way so far to our inclinations as to leave the last offices undone. * * * Let us, therefore, have this pious stipulation, that the conqueror shall give funeral rites to the conquered. For all allow that these are the last duties of human kind, from which no righteous man shrinks. Let each army lay aside its sternness and perform this function in harmony. Let jealousy depart at death, let the feud be buried in the tomb. * * *"

After mutually pledging their faiths to these terms, they began the battle. * * * Horwendil, in his too great ardour, became keener to attack his enemy than to defend his own body; and, heedless of his shield, had grasped his sword with both hands; and his boldness did not fail. For by his rain of blows he destroyed Koll's shield and deprived him of it, and at last hewed off his foot and drove him lifeless to the ground. Then,

---

† Translated by Oliver Elton. From *The Sources of Hamlet*, edited by Israel Gollancz (London: Oxford UP, 1926; reissued by Frank Cass & Company, Ltd.) 95–131.

1. Literally, piracy ("piraticae incubuerat" in the Latin original).

not to fail of his compact, he buried him royally, gave him a howe of lordly make and pompous obsequies. Then he pursued and slew Koll's sister Sela, who was a skilled warrior and experienced in roving.

He had now passed three years in valiant deeds of war; and, in order to win higher rank in Rorik's favour, he assigned to him the best trophies and the pick of the plunder. His friendship with Rorik enabled him to woo and win in marriage his daughter Gerutha, who bore him a son Amleth.

Such great good fortune stung Feng with jealousy, so that he resolved treacherously to waylay his brother, thus showing that goodness is not safe even from those of a man's own house. And behold, when a chance came to murder him, his bloody hand sated the deadly passion of his soul. Then he took the wife of the brother he had butchered, capping unnatural murder with incest. For whoso yields to one iniquity, speedily falls an easier victim to the next, the first being an incentive to the second. Also the man veiled the monstrosity of his deed with such hardihood of cunning, that he made up a mock pretence of goodwill to excuse his crime, and glossed over fratricide with a show of righteousness. Gerutha, said he, though so gentle that she would do no man the slightest hurt, had been visited with her husband's extremest hate; and it was all to save her that he had slain his brother; for he thought it shameful that a lady so meek and unrancorous should suffer the heavy disdain of her husband. Nor did his smooth words fail in their intent; for at courts, where fools are sometimes favoured and backbiters preferred, a lie lacks not credit. Nor did Feng keep from shameful embraces the hands that had slain a brother; pursuing with equal guilt both of his wicked and impious deeds.

Amleth beheld all this, but feared lest too shrewd a behaviour might make his uncle suspect him. So he chose to feign dulness, and pretend an utter lack of wits. This cunning course not only concealed his intelligence but ensured his safety. Every day he remained in his mother's house utterly listless and unclean, flinging himself on the ground, and bespattering his person with foul and filthy dirt. His discoloured face and visage smutched with slime denoted foolish and grotesque madness. All he said was of a piece with these follies; all he did savoured of utter lethargy. In a word, you would not have thought him a man at all, but some absurd abortion due to a mad fit of destiny. He used at times to sit over the fire, and, raking up the embers with his hands, to fashion wooden crooks, and harden them in the fire, shaping at their tips certain barbs, to make them hold more tightly to their fastenings. When asked what he was about, he said that he was preparing sharp javelins to avenge his father. This answer was not a little scoffed at, all men deriding his idle and ridiculous pursuit; but the thing helped his purpose afterwards. Now it was his craft in this matter that first awakened in the deeper observers a suspicion of his cunning. For his skill in a trifling art betokened the hidden talent of the craftsman; nor could they believe the spirit dull where the hand had acquired so cunning a workmanship. Lastly, he always watched with the most punctual care over his pile of stakes that he had pointed in the fire. Some people, therefore, declared that his mind was quick enough, and fancied that he only played the simpleton in order to hide his understanding, and veiled some deep purpose under a cunning feint. His wiliness (said these) would be most readily detected, if a fair woman were put in his way in some secluded place, who should provoke his mind to the temptations of love; all men's natural temper being too blindly amorous to be artfully dissembled, and this passion being also too impetuous to be checked by cunning. Therefore, if his lethargy were feigned, he would seize the opportunity, and yield straightway to violent delights. So men were commissioned to draw the young man in his rides into a remote part of the forest, and there assail him with a temptation of this nature. Among these chanced to be a foster-brother of Amleth, who had not ceased to have regard to their common nurture; and who esteemed his present orders less than the memory of their past fellowship. He attended Amleth among his appointed train, being anxious not to entrap, but to warn him; and was persuaded that he would suffer the worst if he showed the slightest glimpse of sound reason, and above all if he did the act of love openly. This was also plain enough to Amleth himself. For when he was bidden mount his horse, he deliberately set himself in such a fashion that he turned his back to the neck and faced about, fronting the tail; which he proceeded to encompass with the reins, just as if on that side he would check the horse in its furious pace. By this cunning thought he eluded the trick, and overcame the treachery of his uncle. The reinless steed galloping on, with the rider directing its tail, was ludicrous enough to behold.

Amleth went on, and a wolf crossed his path amid the thicket. When his companions told him that a young colt had met him, he retorted, that in Feng's stud there were too few of that kind fighting. This was a gentle but witty fashion of invoking a curse upon his uncle's riches. When they averred that he had given a cunning answer, he answered that he had spoken deliberately: for he was loth to be thought prone to lying about any matter, and wished to be held a stranger to falsehood; and accordingly he mingled craft and candour in such wise that, though his words did not lack truth, yet their was nothing to betoken the truth and betray how far his keenness went.

Again, as he passed along the beach, his companions found the rudder of a ship which had been wrecked, and said they had discovered a huge knife. "This," said he, "was the right thing to carve such a huge ham;" by which he really meant the sea, to whose infinitude, he thought, this enormous rudder matched. Also, as they passed the sandhills, and bade him look at the meal, meaning the sand, he replied that it had been ground small by the hoary tempests of the ocean. His companions praising his answer, he said that he had spoken it wittingly. Then they purposely left him, that he might pluck up more courage to practise wantonness. The woman whom his uncle had dispatched met him in a dark spot, as though she had crossed him by chance; and he took her and would have ravished her, had not his foster-brother, by a secret device, given him an inkling of the trap. For this man, while pondering the fittest way to play privily the prompter's part, and forestall the young man's hazardous lewdness, found a straw on the ground and fastened it underneath the tail of a gadfly that was flying past; which he then drove towards the particular quarter where he knew Amleth to be: an act which served the unwary prince exceedingly well. The token was interpreted as shrewdly as it had been sent. For Amleth saw the gadfly, espied with curiosity the straw which it wore embedded in its tail, and perceived that it was a secret warning to beware of treachery. Alarmed, scenting a trap, and fain to possess his desire in greater safety, he caught up the woman in his arms and dragged her off to a distant and impenetrable fen. Moreover, when they had lain together, he conjured her earnestly to disclose the matter to none, and the promise of silence was accorded as heartily as it was asked. For both of them had been under the same fostering in their childhood; and this early rearing in common had brought Amleth and the girl into great intimacy.

So, when he had returned home, they all jeeringly asked him whether he had given way to love, and he avowed that he had ravished the maid. When he was next asked where he did it, and what had been his pillow, he said that he had rested upon the hoof of a beast of burden, upon a cockscomb, and also upon a ceiling. For, when he was starting into temptation, he had gathered fragments of all these things, in order to avoid lying. And though his jest did not take aught of the truth out of the story, the answer was greeted with shouts of merriment from the bystanders. The maiden, too, when questioned on the matter, declared that he had done no such thing; and her denial was the more readily credited when it was found that the escort had not witnessed the deed. Then he who had marked the gadfly in order to give a hint, wishing to show Amleth that to his trick he owed his salvation, observed that latterly he had been singly devoted to Amleth. The young man's reply was apt. Not to seem forgetful of his informant's service, he said that he had seen a certain thing bearing a straw flit by suddenly, wearing a stalk of chaff fixed on its hinder parts. The cleverness of this speech, which made the rest split with laughter, rejoiced the heart of Amleth's friend.

Thus all were worsted, and none could open the secret lock of the young man's wisdom. But a friend of Feng, gifted more with assurance than judgment, declared that the unfathomable cunning of such a mind could not be detected by any vulgar plot, for the man's obstinacy was so great that it ought not to be assailed with any mild measures; there were many sides to his wiliness, and it ought not to be entrapped by any one

method. Accordingly, said he, his own profounder acuteness had hit on
a more delicate way, which was well fitted to be put in practice, and
would effectually discover what they desired to know. Feng was purposely to absent himself, pretending affairs of great import. Amleth should
be closeted alone with his mother in her chamber; but a man should
first be commissioned to place himself in a concealed part of the room
and listen heedfully to what they talked about. For if the son had any
wits at all he would not hesitate to speak out in the hearing of his mother,
or fear to trust himself to the fidelity of her who bore him. The speaker,
loth to seem readier to devise than to carry out the plot, zealously prof-
fered himself as the agent of the eavesdropping. Feng rejoiced at the
scheme, and departed on pretence of a long journey. Now he who had
given this counsel repaired privily to the room where Amleth was shut
up with his mother, and lay down skulking in the straw. But Amleth
had his antidote for the treachery. Afraid of being overheard by some
eavesdropper, he at first resorted to his usual imbecile ways, and crowed
like a noisy cock, beating his arms together to mimic the flapping of
wings. Then he mounted the straw and began to swing his body and
jump again and again, wishing to try if aught lurked there in hiding.
Feeling a lump beneath his feet, he drove his sword into the spot, and
impaled him who lay hid. Then he dragged him from his concealment
and slew him. Then, cutting his body into morsels, he seethed it in
boiling water, and flung it through the mouth of an open sewer for the
swine to eat, bestrewing the stinking mire with his hapless limbs. Having
in this wise eluded the snare, he went back to the room. Then his mother
set up a great wailing, and began to lament her son's folly to his face;
but he said: "Most infamous of women! dost thou seek with such lying
lamentations to hide thy most heavy guilt? Wantoning like a harlot,
thou has entered a wicked and abominable state of wedlock, embracing
with incestuous bosom thy husband's slayer, and wheedling with filthy
lures of blandishment him who had slain the father of thy son. This,
forsooth, is the way that the mares couple with the vanquishers of their
mates; for brute beasts are naturally incited to pair indiscriminately; and
it would seem that thou, like them, hast clean forgot thy first husband.
As for me, not idly do I wear the mask of folly; for I doubt not that he
who destroyed his brother will riot as ruthlessly in the blood of his kindred.
Therefore it is better to choose the garb of dulness than that of sense,
and to borrow some protection from a show of utter frenzy. Yet the
passion to avenge my father still burns in my heart; but I am watching
the chances, I await the fitting hour. There is a place for all things;
against so merciless and dark a spirit must be used the deeper devices of
the mind. And thou, who hadst been better employed in lamenting
thine own disgrace, know it is superfluity to bewail my witlessness; thou
shouldst weep for the blemish in thine own mind, not for that in another's. On the rest see thou keep silence." With such reproaches he rent

the heart of his mother and redeemed her to walk in the ways of virtue; teaching her to set the fires of the past above the seductions of the present.

When Feng returned, nowhere could he find the man who had suggested the treacherous espial; he searched for him long and carefully, but none said they had seen him anywhere. Amleth, among others, was asked in jest if he had come on any trace of him, and replied that the man had gone to the sewer, but had fallen through its bottom and been stifled by the floods of filth, and that he had been devoured by the swine that came up all about that place. This speech was flouted by those who heard; for it seemed senseless, though really it expressly avowed the truth.

Feng now suspected that his stepson was certainly full of guile, and desired to make away with him, but durst not do the deed for fear of the displeasure, not only of Amleth's grandsire Rorik, but also of his own wife. So he thought that the King of Britain should be employed to slay him, so that another could do the deed, and he be able to feign innocence. Thus, desirous to hide his cruelty, he chose rather to besmirch his friend than to bring disgrace on his own head. Amleth, on departing, gave secret orders to his mother to hang the hall with woven knots, and to perform pretended obsequies for him a year thence; promising that he would then return. Two retainers of Feng then accompanied him, bearing a letter graven on wood—a kind of writing material frequent in old times; this letter enjoined the king of the Britons to put to death the youth who was sent over to him. While they were reposing, Amleth searched their coffers, found the letter, and read the instructions therein. Whereupon he erased all the writing on the surface, substituted fresh characters, and so, changing the purport of the instructions, shifted his own doom upon his companions. Nor was he satisfied with removing from himself the sentence of death and passing the peril on to others, but added an entreaty that the King of Britain would grant his daughter in marriage to a youth of great judgment whom he was sending to him. Under this was falsely marked the signature of Feng.

*   *   *

[*In Britain, Amleth gains the confidence of the King, and is given his daughter as wife. When the King executes Amleth's companions, Amleth feigns indignation and receives from the King, as compensation, gold which he later melts in the fire, and conceals in some hollow sticks.*]

When he has passed a whole year with the king he obtained leave to make a journey, and returned to his own land, carrying away of all his princely wealth and state only the sticks which held the gold. On reaching Jutland, he exchanged his present attire for his ancient demeanour, which he had adopted for righteous ends, purposely assuming an aspect of absurdity. Covered with filth, he entered the banquet-room where his own obsequies were being held, and struck all men utterly aghast, rumour having falsely noised abroad his death. At last terror melted into mirth, and the guests jeered and taunted one another, that he whose last rites they were celebrating as though he were dead, should appear in the flesh. When he was asked concerning his comrades, he pointed to the sticks he was carrying, and said, "Here is both the one and the other." This he observed with equal truth and pleasantry; for his speech, though most thought it idle, yet departed not from the truth; for it pointed at the weregild of the slain as though it were themselves. Thereon, wishing to bring the company into a gayer mood, he joined the cupbearers, and diligently did the office of plying the drink. Then, to prevent his loose dress hampering his walk, he girded his sword upon his side, and purposely drawing it several times, pricked his fingers with its point. The bystanders accordingly had both sword and scabbard riveted across with an iron nail. Then, to smooth the way more safely to his plot, he went to the lords and plied them heavily with draught upon draught, and drenched them all so deep in wine, that their feet were made feeble with drunkenness, and they turned to rest within the palace, making their bed where they had revelled. Then he saw they were in a fit state for his plots, and thought that here was a chance offered to do his purpose. So he took out of his bosom the stakes he had long ago prepared, and went into the building, where the ground lay covered with the bodies of the nobles wheezing off their sleep and their debauch. Then, cutting away its supports, he brought down the hanging his mother had knitted, which covered the inner as well as the outer walls of the hall. This he flung upon the snorers, and then applying the crooked stakes, he knotted and bound them up in such insoluble intricacy, that not one of the men beneath, however hard he might struggle, could contrive to rise. After this he set fire to the palace. The flames spread, scattering the conflagration far and wide. It enveloped the whole dwelling, destroyed the palace, and burnt them all while they were either buried in deep sleep or vainly striving to arise. Then he went to the chamber of Feng, who had before this been conducted by his train into his pavilion; plucked up a sword that chanced to be hanging to the bed, and planted his own in its place. Then, awakening his uncle, he told him that his nobles were perishing in the flames, and that Amleth was here, armed with his old crooks to help him, and thirsting to exact the vengeance, now long overdue, for his father's murder. Feng, on hearing this, leapt from his couch, but was cut down while, deprived of his own sword, he strove in vain to draw the strange one. O valiant Amleth, and worthy of immortal fame, who being shrewdly armed with a feint of folly, covered a wisdom too high for human wit under a marvellous disguise of silliness! and not only found in his subtlety means to protect his own safety, but also by its guidance found opportunity to avenge his father. By this skilful defence of himself, and strenuous revenge for his parent, he has left it doubtful whether we are to think more of his wit or his bravery. * * *

BELLEFOREST

The Hystorie of Hamblet, Prince of Denmarke. †

Chapter I. How Horuendile and Fengon were made Gouernours of the Prouince of Ditmarse, and how Horuendile marryed Geruth, daughter to Roderick chief K. of Denmark: by whom he had Hamblet: and how after his marriage his brother Fengon slewe him trayterously, and marryed his brothers wife, and what followed.

* * * King Rodericke as then raigning in Denmarke, after hee had appeased the troubles in the countrey, and driuen the Sweathlanders and Slaueans from thence; he diuided the kingdom into diuers Prouinces, placing Gouernours therein, * * * giuing the gouernment of Iutie (at this present called Ditmarsse) * * * [to] two valiant & warlike Lords, Horuendile and Fengon, sonnes to Geruendile, who likewise had beene Gouernour of that Prouince. Now the greatest honor that men of noble birth could at that time win and obtaine, was in exercising the art of Piracie vpon the seas; assayling their neighbours, & the countries bordering vpon them: and how much the more they vsed to rob, pill, and spoyle other Prouinces, and Ilands farre adiacent, so much the more their honours and reputation increased and augmented: wherein Horuendile obtained the highest place in his time, beeing the most renouned Pirate that in those dayes scoured the seas, & hauens of the North parts: whose great fame, so mooued the heart of Collere king of Norway, that he was much grieued to heare that Horuendile surmounting him in feates of armes, thereby obscuring the glorie by him alreadie obtained vpon the seas * * * This valiant and hardy king, hauing chalenged Horuendile to fight with him body to body, the combate was by him accepted, with conditions, that hee which should be vanquished, should loose all the riches he had in his ship, and that the vanquisher should cause the body of the vanquished (that should bee slaine in the combate) to be honourably buried, death being the prise and reward of him that should loose the battaile: and to conclude, Collere king of Norway (although a valiant, hardy and couragious prince) was in the end vanquished and slaine by Horuendile: who presently caused a Tombe to be erected, and therein (with all honorable obseques fit for a prince) buried the body of king Collere, according to their auncient manner, and superstitions in those dayes, and the conditions of the combate,

† Translated anonymously from *Le Cinquiesme Tome des Histoires Tragiques* of F. de Belleforest (Paris, 1582), and published in London in 1608. The following extracts are taken from the unique copy of the translation preserved in the Library of Trinity College, Cambridge, and are reproduced here by kind permission of the Master and Fellows of Trinity College. The punctuation of the original has been slightly modified. The spelling of the original has been preserved. In the French text, the hero's name is Amleth.

bereauing the Kings shippes of all their riches, and hauing slaine the kings sister, a very braue and valiant warriour, and ouer runne all the coast of Norway, and the Northren Ilands, returned home againe layden with much treasure, sending the most part thereof to his soueraigne king Rodericke, thereby to procure his good liking, and so to be accounted one of the greatest fauorites about his maiestie.

The King allured by those presents, and esteeming himselfe happy to haue so valiant a subiect, sought by a great fauour and courtesie, to make him become bounden vnto him perpetually, giuing him Geruth his daughter to his wife, of whom he knew Horuendile to bee already much inamored: and the more to honor him, determined himselfe in person to conduct her into Iutie, where the marriage was celebrated according to the ancient manner: and to be briefe, of this marriage proceeded Hamblet, of whom I intend to speake, and for his cause haue chosen to renew this present Hystorie.

Fengon, brother to this Prince Horuendile, who onely fretting and despighting in his heart at the great honor and reputation wonne by his brother in warlike affaires, but solicited and prouoked (by a foolish ielousie) to see him honored with royall aliance, and fearing thereby to bee deposed from his part of the gouernment: or rather desiring to be onely Gouernour: thereby to obscure the memorie of the victories and conquests of his brother Horuendile; determined (whatsoeuer happened) to kill him, which hee effected in such sort, that no man once so much as suspected him, euery man esteeming that from such and so firme a knot of alliance and consanguinitie, there could proceed no other issue then the full effects of vertue and courtesie * * * Was not this a craftie and subtile Counsellor: but he might haue thought that the mother, knowing her husbands case, would not cast her sonne into the danger of death. But Fengon hauing secretly assembled certain men, & perceiuing himself strong enough to execute his interprise, Horuendile his brother being at a banquet with his friends, sodainely set vpon him, where he slewe him as traiterously, as cunningly he purged himselfe of so detestable a murther to his subiects: for that before he had any violent or bloody handes, or once committed parricide vpon his brother, hee had incestuously abused his wife, whose honour he ought as well to haue sought and procured, as traiterously he pursued and effected his destruction: and it is most certaine, that the man that abandoneth himselfe to any notorious and wicked action, whereby he becommeth a great sinner, hee careth not to commit much more haynous and abhominable offences, & couered his boldnesse and wicked practise with so great subtiltie and policie, and vnder a vaile of meere simplicitie, that beeing fauoured for the honest loue that he bare to his sister in lawe, for whose sake hee affirmed, hee had in that sort murthered his brother, that his sinne found excuse among the common people, & of the Nobilitie was esteemed for iustice: for that Geruth being as courteous a Princesse, as any then liuing

in the North parts, and one that had neuer once so much as offended
any of her subiects, either commons, or Courtyers; this adulterer and
infamous murtherer, slaundered his dead brother, that hee would haue
slaine his wife, and that hee by chance finding him vpon the point ready
to doe it, in defence of the Lady had slaine him, bearing off the blows
which as then hee strooke at the innocent Princesse, without any other
cause of malice whatsoeuer: wherein hee wanted no false witnesses to
approoue his act, which deposed in like sort, as the wicked calumniator
himselfe protested, being the same persons that had born him company,
& were participants of his treason, so that instead of pursuing him as a
parricide, & an incestuous person, al the Courtyers admired and flattered him in his good fortune: making more account of false witnesses
and detestable wicked reporters, and more honouring the callumniators,
then they esteemed of those that seeking to call the matter in question,
and admiring the vertues of the murthered Prince would haue punished
the massacrers and bereauers of his life. Which was the cause that Fengon, boldned and incouraged by such impunitie, durst venture to couple
himselfe in marriage with her, whom hee vsed as his Concubine, during
good Horuendiles life, in that sort spotting his name with a double vice,
and charging his conscience with abhominable guilt, and twofold impi-
etie, as incestuous adulterie, and parricide murther: and that the vnfor-
tunate and wicked woman, that had receaued the honour to bee the wife
of one of the valiantest and wisest Princes in the North, imbased her
selfe in such vile sort, as to falsifie her faith vnto him, and which is
worse, to marrie him, that had bin the tyranous murtherer of her lawfull
husband: which made diuers men thinke, that she had been the causer
of the murther, thereby to liue in her adultery without controle. * * *

Chapter II. How Hamblet counterfeited the mad man, to escape the tyr-
annie of his vncle, and how he was tempted by a woman (through his
vncles procurement) who thereby thought to vnderminde the Prince, and
by that meanes to finde out whether he counterfeited madnesse or not:
and how Hamblet would by no meanes bee brought to consent vnto her;
and what followed.

Geruth hauing (as I sayd before) so much forgotten herselfe, the prince
Hamblet perceiuing himselfe to bee in danger of his life, as beeing abandoned of his owne mother, and forsaken of all men; and assuring himselfe that Fengon would not detract[1] the time, to send him the same way
his father Horuendile was gone: to begiule the tyrant in his subtilties
(that esteemed him to bee of such a minde, that if he once attained to
mans estate, he wold not long delay the time to reuenge the death of his
father) counterfeiting the mad man with such craft & subtill practises,

1. Delay.

that hee made shewe as if hee had vtterly lost his wittes: and vnder that vayle hee couered his pretence, and defended his life from the treasons and practises of the tyrant his vncle. * * *

Hamblet in this sorte counterfeiting the madde man, many times did diuers actions of great and deepe consideration, and often made such and so fitte answeres, that a wise man would soone haue iudged from what spirite so fine an inuention mighte proceede, for that standing by the fire and sharpning sticks like poynards and prickes, one in smiling manner asked him wherefore he made those little staues so sharpe at the points, I prepare (saith he) piersing dartes, and sharpe arrowes, to reuenge my fathers death, fooles as I said before, esteemed those his words as nothing, but men of quicke spirits, and such as hadde a deeper reache began to suspect somewhat, esteeming that vnder that kinde of folly there lay hidden a greate & rare subtilty, such as one day might bee preiudiciall to their prince, saying that vnder colour of such rudenes he shadowed a crafty pollicy, and by his deuised simplicitye, he concealed a sharp and pregnant spirit, for which cause they counselled the king to try, & know if it were possible, how to discouer the intent & meaning of the young prince, & they could find no better, nor more fit inuention to intrap him then to set some faire, and beawtifull woman in a secret place, that with flattering speeches and all the craftiest meanes she could vse, should purposely seek to allure his mind to haue his pleasure of her. * * * To this end certaine courtiers were appointed to leade Hamblet into a solitary place within the woods, whether they brought the woman, inciting him to take their pleasures together, and to imbrace one another * * * and surely the poore prince at this assault had bin in great danger, if a gentleman (that in Horuendiles time had bin nourished with him) had not showne himselfe more affectioned to the bringing vp he had receiued with Hamblet, then desirous to please the Tirant, who by all meanes sought to intangle the sonne in the same nets wherein the father had ended his dayes. This Gentleman bare the courtiers (appointed as aforesaide of this treason) company, more desiring to giue the prince instructions what he should do, then to intrap him making full account that the least showe of perfect sence and wisdome that Hamblet should make, would be sufficient to cause him to loose his life: and therefore by certain signes, he gaue Hamblet intelligence, in what danger hee was like to fall if by any meanes hee seemed to obaye, or once like the wanton toyes, & vicious prouocations of the gentlewoman, sent thither by his Uncle: which much abashed the prince, as then wholy beeing in affection to the Lady, but by her he was likewise informed of the treason, as being one that from her infancy loued and fauoured him, and would haue been exceeding sorrowfull for his misfortune, and much more to leaue his companie without inioying the pleasure of his body, whome shee loued more than her selfe. The Prince in this sort hauing both deceiued the courtiers, and the Ladyes expectation, that affirmed and swoore that hee neuer once offered to haue his pleasure of the woman, although in subtilty hee affirmed the contrary: euery man there vpon assured themselues that without all doubt hee was distraught of his sences, that his braynes were as then wholly void of force and incapable of reasonable apprehension so that as then Fengons practise took no effect: but for al that he left not off: still seeking by al meanes to finde out Hamblets subtilty: as in the next chapter you shall perceiue.

Chapter III. How Fengon Vncle to Hamblet a second time to intrap him in his pollitick madnes: caused one of his counsellors to be secretly hidden in the Queenes chamber: behind the arras, to heare what speeches past between Hamblet and the Queen and how Hamblet killed him, and escaped that danger and what followed.

Among the friends of Fengon, ther was one that aboue al the rest, doubted of Hamblets practises, in counterfeiting the madman, who for that cause said, that it was impossible that so craftie a gallant as Hamblet that counterfeited the foole, should be discouered with so common & vnskilfull practises, which might easily bee perceiued, and that to finde out his politique pretence it were necessary to inuent some subtill and craftie meanes, more atractiue: wherby the gallant might not haue the leysure to vse his accustomed dissimulation, which to effect he said he knewe a fit waie and a most conuenient meane to effect the kings desire, and thereby to intrap Hamblet in his subtilties, and cause him of his owne accord to fall into the net prepared for him, and thereby euidently shewe his secret meaning: his deuise was thus, that King Fengon should make as though he were to goe some long voyage, concerning affayres of great importance and that in the meane time Hamblet should be shut vp alone in a chamber with his mother, wherein some other should secretly be hidden behind the hangings, vnknowne either to him or his mother, there to stand and heere their speeches, and the complots by them to bee taken, concerning the accomplishments of the dissembling fooles pretence, assuring the king that if there were any point of wisedome and perfect sence in the gallants spirit that without all doubte he would easily discouer it to his mother as being deuoid of all feare that she would vtter or make knowne his secret intent, beeing the woman that had borne him in her bodie, and nourished him so carefully, and withall offered himselfe to be the man, that should stand to harken, and beare witnesse of Hamblets speeches with his mother, that hee might not be esteemed a counsellor in such a case, wherein he refused to be the executioner, for the behoofe and seruice of his prince. This inuention pleased the King exceeding well, esteeming it as the onelie, and soueraigne remedie to heale the prince of his lunacie, and to that ende making a long voyage issued out of his pallace, and road to hunt in the forrest, meane time the counsellor entred secretly into the Queenes chamber, and there hid himselfe behind the arras,[2] not long before the Queen and Hamblet came thither, who beeing craftie and pollitique, as soone as hee was within the chamber doubting some treason, and fearing if he should speake seuerely and wisely to his mother touching his secret practises he would be vnderstood, and by that meanes intercepted, vsed his ordinary manner of dissimulation, and began to come like a cocke beating with his armes, in such manner as cockes vse to strike with their wings, vpon the hangings of the chamber, whereby feeling something stirring vnder them, hee cried a rat a rat, and presently drawing his sworde thrust it into the hangings, which done, pulled the counsellour (halfe dead) out by the heeles, made an end of killing him, and beeing slaine, cut his bodie in peeces, which he caused to be boyled and then cast it into an open vaulte or priuie, that so it mighte serue for foode to the hogges, by which meanes hauing discouered the ambushe, and giuen the inuenter thereof his iust rewarde, hee came againe to his mother, who in the meane time wepte and tormented her selfe, to see all her hopes frustrate, for that what fault soeuer she had committed, yet was shee sore grieued, to see her onely child made a meere mockery, euery man reproaching her with his folly, one point whereof she had as then seene before her eyes, which was no small pricke to her conscience, esteeming that the Gods sent her that punishment, for ioyning incestuously in marriage with the tyrannous murtherer of her husband * * * and while in this sort she sate tormenting her selfe, Hamlet entred into the chamber, who hauing once againe searched euery corner of the same, distrusting his mother as well as the rest, and perceiuing himselfe to bee alone, began in sober and discreet manner to speak vnto her saying.

What treason is this, O most infamous woman! of all that euer prostrated themselues to the will of an abhominable whoremonger who vnder the vail of a dissembling creature couereth the most wicked and detestable crime that man could euer imagine, or was committed. How may I be assured to trust you, that like a vile wanton adulteresse, altogether impudent & giuen ouer to her pleasure, runnes spreading forth her armes ioyfully to imbrace the trayterous villanous tyrant, that murthered my father, and most incestuously receiuest the villain into the lawfull bed of your loyall spouse, impudently entertaining him in steede of the deare father of your miserable and discomforted sonne, if the gods graunt him not the grace speedilie to escape from a captiuity so vnworthie the degree he holdeth, and the race & noble familie of his ancestors. Is this the part of a queene, and daughter to a king? to liue like a bruite beast, (and like

<hr/>

2. Here, and in what follows, Shakespeare's play has obviously influenced the translation. There is no mention of "hangings" or of an arras in the original. Israel Gollancz, in *The Sources of Hamlet* (Oxford 1926, 319–20), notes: "In Belleforest (as in Saxo) the counsellor hides under a quilt (F. *lou-* *dier, lodier;* L. *stramentum*): Hamlet jumps on this quilt (*sauta sur ce lodier*); in *The Hystorie* the quilt becomes a curtain or tapestry—'hanging' and 'arras,' from Shakespeare. And, further, the English translator adds what is not found in Belleforest or Saxo, the very words of the play, 'A rat! a rat!' "

a mare that yeeldeth her bodie to the horse that hath beaten hir companion awaye,) to followe the pleasure of an abhominable king, that hath murthered a farre more honester and better man than himself in massacring Horuendile, the honor, and glory of the Danes, who are now esteemed of no force nor valour at all, since the shining splendure of knighthood, was brought to an end by the most wickedest, and cruellest villaine liuing vpon earth: I for my part will neuer account him for my kinsman, nor once knowe him for mine vncle, nor you my deer mother for not hauing respect to the blud that ought to haue vnited vs so straightly together & who neither with your honor nor without suspition of consent to the death of your husband could euer haue agreed to haue marryed with his cruell enemie: O Queene Geruthe, it is the part of a bitch, to couple with many, and desire acquaintance of diuers mastiffes: it is licentiousnes only that hath made you deface out of your minde the memory of the valor & vertues of the good King your husband and my father: it was an vnbrideled desire that guided the daughter of Roderick to imbrace the Tirant Fengon, & not to remember Horuendile (vnworthy of so strange intertainment), neither that he killed his brother traiterously, and that shee being his fathers wife betrayed him, although he so well fauoured and loued her, that for her sake he vtterly bereaued Norway of her riches and valiant souldiers, to augment the treasures of Roderick, and make Geruthe wife to the hardyest prince in Europe. It is not the parte of a woman, much lesse of a princesse, in whome all modesty, curtesie, compassion and loue ought to abound, thus to leaue her deare child to fortune in the bloody & murtherous hands of a villain and traytor, bruite beasts do not so: for Lyons, Tygers, ounces, and leopards fight for the safety and defence of their whelpes, and birds that haue beakes, claws and wings, resist such as would rauish them of their yong ones, but you to the contrary expose and deliuer mee to death, whereas ye should defend me. Is not this as much as if you should betray me, when you knowing the peruersenes of the tyrant and his intents, ful of deadly counsell as touching the race & image of his brother, haue not once sought nor desired to finde the meanes to saue your child (& only son) by sending him into Swethland, Norway or England, rather then to leaue him as a pray to youre infamous adulterer? bee not offended I praye you Madame, if transported with dolour and griefe I speake so boldely vnto you, and that I respect you lesse then duetie requireth, for you hauing forgotten mee, and wholy reiected the memorye of the deceased K. my father, must not bee abashed if I also surpasse the bounds and limits of due consideration. Beholde into what distresse I am now fallen, and to what mischiefe my fortune, and your ouer great lightnesse, and want of wisedome haue induced mee, that I am constrained to playe the madde man to saue my life in steed of vsing and practising armes, following aduentures, and seeking all meanes to make my selfe knowne to bee the true and vndoubted heire of the valiant and vertuous

King Horuendile, it was not without cause, and iuste occasion, that my
gestures, countenances and words seeme all to proceed from a madman,
and that I desire to haue all men esteeme me wholy depriued of sence
and reasonable vnderstanding, by cause I am well assured, that he that
hath made no conscience to kill his owne brother, (accustomed to
murthers, & allured with desire of gouernement without controll in his
treasons) will not spare to saue himselfe with the like crueltie, in the
blood, & flesh of the loyns of his brother, by him massacred: & therefore
it is better for me to fayne madnesse then to vse my right sences as nature
hath bestowed them vpon me. The bright shining clearnes therof I am
forced to hide vnder this shadow of dissimulation, as the sun doth hir
beams vnder some great cloud, when the wether in sommertime ouer-
casteth: the face of a mad man, serueth to couer my gallant countenance, & the gestures of a fool are fit for me, to the end that guiding my
self wisely therein I may preserue my life for the Danes & the memory
of my late deceased father, for that the desire of reuenging his death is
so ingrauen in my heart that if I dye not shortly, I hope to take such and
so great vengeance, that these Countryes shall foreuer speake thereof.
Neuerthelesse I must stay the time, meanes, and occasion, lest by making ouer great hast, I be now the cause of mine owne sodaine ruine and
ouerthrow, and by that meanes, end, before I beginne to effect my hearts
desire: hee that hath to doe with a wicked, disloyall, cruell, and discour-
teous man, must vse craft, and politike inuentions, such as a fine witte
can best imagine, not to discouer his interprise: for seeing that by force
I cannot effect my desire, reason alloweth me by dissimulation, subtiltie,
and secret practises to proceed therein. To conclude, weepe not (Madame)
to see my folly, but rather sigh and lament your owne offence, tormenting your conscience in regard of the infamie that hath so defiled the
ancient renowne and glorie that (in times past) honoured Queene Geruth: for wee are not to sorrowe and grieue at other mens vices, but for
our owne misdeedes, and great follyes. Desiring you, for the surplus of
my proceedings, aboue all things (as you loue your owne life and welfare) that neither the king, nor any other may by any meanes know mine
intent, and let me alone with the rest, for I hope in the ende to bring
my purpose to effect. Although the Queene perceiued herselfe neerly
touched, and that Hamlet mooued her to the quicke, where she felt
herselfe interested: neuertheless shee forgot all disdaine & wrath, which
thereby she might as then haue had, hearing herselfe so sharply chiden
& reprooued, for the joy she then conceaued, to behold the gallant spirit
of her sonne, and to thinke what she might hope, & the easier expect of
his so great policie and wisdome. But on the one side she durst not lift
vp her eyes to behold him, remembring her offence, & on the other side
she would gladly haue imbraced her son, in regard of the wise admonitions by him giuen vnto her, which as then quenched the flames of
vnbridled desire, and before had moued her to affect K. Fengon: to

ingraff in her heart the vertuous actions of her lawfull spouse, whom inwardly she much lamented, when she beheld the liuely image and portraiture of his vertue & great wisedome in her childe, representing his fathers haughtie and valiant heart: and so ouercome and vanquished with this honest passion, and weeping most bitterly, hauing long time fixed her eyes vpon Hamlet, as beeing rauished into some great and deepe contemplation, & as it were wholy amazed; at the last imbracing him in her armes (with the like loue that a vertuous mother may or can vse, to kisse and entertaine her owne childe) shee spake vnto him in this manner.

I know well (my Sonne) that I haue done thee great wrong in marrying with Fengon, the cruell tyrant and murtherer of thy father, and my loyal spouse: but when thou shalt consider the small meanes of resistance, and the treason of the Palace, with the little cause of confidence we are to expect or hope for of the Courtiers, all wrought to his will: as also the power hee made ready, if I should haue refused to like of him, thou wouldest rather excuse, then accuse me of lasciuiousnes or inconstancy, much lesse offer me that wrong, to suspect that euer they mother Geruthe once consented to the death & murther of her husband: swearing vnto thee (by the maiestie of the Gods) that if it had layne in my power to haue resisted the Tyrant, although it had beene with the losse of my blood, yea and of my life, I would surely haue saued the life of my Lord and husband, with as good a will & desire, as since that time, I haue often beene a meanes to hinder and impeach the shortning of thy life, which being taken away, I will no longer liue here vpon earth: for seeing that thy sences are whole and sound, I am in hope to see an easie meanes inuented, for the reuenging of thy fathers death. Neuerthelesse, mine owne sweet sonne, if thou hast pittie of thyselfe, or care of the memorie of thy father (although thou wilt do nothing for her, that deserueth not the name of a mother in this respect) I pray thee carie thine affayres wisely, bee not hastie, nor ouer furious in thy interprises, neither yet aduance thyselfe more then reason shall mooue thee to effect thy purpose. Thou seest there is not almost any man wherein thou mayest put thy trust, nor any woman to whom I dare vtter the least part of my secrets, that would not presently report it to thine aduersarie, who although in outward shew he dissembleth to loue thee, the better to inioy his pleasures of me, yet hee distrusteth and feareth mee for thy sake, and is not so simple to be easily perswaded, that thou are a foole or mad, so that if thou chance to doe any thing that seemeth to proceed of wisedome or policie (how secretly soeuer it be done) he will presently be informed thereof, and I am greatly afraide that the deuils haue shewed him, what hath past at this present betweene vs: (Fortune so much pursueth and contrarieth our ease and welfare) or that this murther that now thou hast committed, be not the cause of both our destructions, which I by no meanes will seeme to know, but will keepe secret both thy wisedone & hardy interprise. Beseeching the Gods (my good sonne) that they guiding thy heart, directing thy counsels and prospering thy interprise, I may see thee possesse and inioy that which is thy right, and weare the crowne of Denmarke, by the Tyrant taken from thee: that I may reioyce in thy prosperitie, and therewith content my self, seeing with what courage and boldnesse thou shalt take vengeance vpon the murtherer of thy father, as also vpon all those that haue assisted and fauoured him, in his murtherous and bloody enterprise.

Madame (sayd Hamlet) I will put my trust in you, and from hence-foorth meane not to meddle further with your affayres, beseeching you (as you loue your owne flesh and blood) that you will from hence foorth no more esteeme of the adulterer mine enemie, whom I will surely kill, or cause to be put to death, in despite of all the deuils in hel: and haue he neuer so manie flattering courtezans to defend him yet will I bring him to his death, & they themselues also shall beare him company therein: as they haue bin his peruerse counsellors in the action of killing my father, and his companions in his treason, massacre, and cruell enter-prise. And reason requireth, that euen as trayterously they then caused their prince to bee put to death, that with the like (nay well much more) iustice they should pay the interest of their fellonious actions. * * *

After this Fengon (as if hee had beene out some long iourney) came to the Court againe, and asked for him that had receiued the charge to play the intillegencer, to entrap Hamlet, in his dissembled wisedome, was abashed to heare neither newes nor tydings of him, and for that cause asked Hamlet what was become of him: naming the man. The Prince that neuer vsed lying, and who in all the answers that euer he made (during his counterfeit madnesse) neuer strayed from the trueth (as a generous minde is a mortal enemie to vntruth) answered and sayd, that the counsellor he sought for, was gone downe through the priuie, where beeing choaked by the filthynesse of the place, the Hogs meeting him had filled their bellyes.[3]

3. What follows in Belleforest—the account of Hamlet's voyage to England, his sojourn there, his return to Denmark and the manner of his revenge— parallels in all important details the narration of those events as given in Saxo.

ESSAYS IN
CRITICISM

JOHN DENNIS

From An Essay on the Genius and Writings of Shakespeare†

* * * But indeed Shakespeare has been wanting in the exact distribution of poetical justice not only in his *Coriolanus*, but in most of his best tragedies, in which the guilty and the innocent perish promiscuously; as Duncan and Banquo in *Macbeth*, as likewise Lady Macduff and her children; Desdemona in *Othello*; Cordelia, Kent, and King Lear, in the tragedy that bears his name; Brutus and Portia in *Julius Caesar*, and young Hamlet in the *Tragedy of Hamlet*. For though it may be said in defense of the last, that Hamlet had a design to kill his uncle who then reigned; yet this is justified by no less than a call from heaven, and raising up one from the dead to urge him to it. The good and the bad then perishing promiscuously in the best of Shakespeare's tragedies, there can be either none or very weak instruction in them: for such promiscuous events call the government of providence into question, and by sceptics and libertines are resolved into chance.

ANONYMOUS

From Some Remarks on the Tragedy of Hamlet Prince of Denmark‡

Now I am come to mention Hamlet's madness, I must speak my opinion of our poet's conduct in this particular. To conform to the ground-work of his plot, Shakespeare makes the young prince feign himself mad. I cannot but think this to be injudicious; for so far from securing himself from any violence which he feared from the usurper, which was his design in so doing, it seems to have been the most likely way of getting himself confined, and consequently, debarred from an opportunity of revenging his father's death, which now seemed to be his only aim; and accordingly it was the occasion of his being sent away to England. Which design, had it taken effect upon his life, he never could have revenged his father's murder. To speak truth, our poet, by keeping too close to the ground-work of his plot, has fallen into an absurdity; for there appears no reason at all in nature, why the young prince did not put the usurper

† London, 1712, 9–10.

‡ London, 1736. This has often been attributed to Sir Thomas Hanmer, but the attribution has been challenged. For the argument against it, see

Clarence D. Thorpe, "Thomas Hanmer and the Anonymous Essay on *Hamlet*," *Modern Language Notes* 49 (1934): 493–98. This extract is from 33–34.

to death as soon as possible, especially as Hamlet is represented as a youth so brave, and so careless of his own life.

The case indeed is this: Had Hamlet gone naturally to work, as we could suppose such a prince to do in parallel circumstances, there would have been an end of our play. The poet therefore was obliged to delay his hero's revenge; but then he should have contrived some good reason for it.

SAMUEL JOHNSON

[The Praise of Variety]†

If the dramas of Shakespeare were to be characterized, each by the particular excellence which distinguishes it from the rest, we must allow to the tragedy of *Hamlet* the praise of variety. The incidents are so numerous, that the argument of the play would make a long tale. The scenes are interchangeably diversified with merriment and solemnity; with merriment that includes judicious and instructive observations, and solemnity, not strained by poetical violence above the natural sentiments of man. New characters appear from time to time in continual succession, exhibiting various forms of life and particular modes of conversation. The pretended madness of Hamlet causes much mirth, the mournful distraction of Ophelia fills the heart with tenderness, and every personage produces the effect intended, from the apparition that in the first act chills the blood with horror, to the fop in the last, that exposes affectation to just contempt.

The conduct is perhaps not wholly secure against objections. The action is indeed for the most part in continual progression, but there are some scenes which neither forward nor retard it. Of the feigned madness of Hamlet there appears no adequate cause, for he does nothing which he might not have done with the reputation of sanity. He plays the madman most, when he treats Ophelia with so much rudeness, which seems to be useless and wanton cruelty.

Hamlet is, through the whole play, rather an instrument than an agent. After he has, by the strategem of the play, convicted the King, he makes no attempt to punish him, and his death is at last effected by an incident which Hamlet has no part in producing.

The catastrophe is not very happily produced; the exchange of weapons is rather an expedient of necessity, than a stroke of art. A scheme might easily have been formed, to kill Hamlet with the dagger, and Laertes with the bowl.

† From *The Plays of William Shakespeare* (London, 1765) 8.311.

The poet is accused of having shown little regard to poetical justice, and may be charged with equal neglect of poetical probability. The apparition left the regions of the dead to little purpose; the revenge which he demands is not obtained but by the death of him that was required to take it; and the gratification which would arise from the destruction of an usurper and a murderer, is abated by the untimely death of Ophelia, the young, the beautiful, the harmless, and the pious.

WILLIAM RICHARDSON

The Character of Hamlet†

* * * The death of his father was a natural evil, and as such he endures it. That he is excluded from succeeding immediately to the royalty that belongs to him, seems to affect him slightly; for to vehement and vain ambition he appears superior. He is moved by finer principles, by an exquisite sense of virtue, of moral beauty and turpitude. The impropriety of Gertrude's behavior, her ingratitude to the memory of her former husband, and the depravity she discovers in the choice of a successor, afflict his soul, and cast him into utter agony. Here then is the principle and spring of all his actions. * * *

The man whose sense of moral excellence is uncommonly exquisite, will find it a source of pleasure and of pain in his commerce with mankind. Susceptible of every moral impression, the display of virtuous actions will yield him delight, and the contrary excite uneasiness. * * * The triumph and inward joy of a son, on account of the fame and the high desert of a parent, is of a nature very sublime and tender. His sorrow is no less acute and overwhelming, if those, united to him by a connection so intimate, have acted unbecomingly, and have incurred disgrace. Such is the condition of Hamlet. Exquisitely sensible of moral beauty and deformity, he discerns turpitude in a parent. Surprise, on a discovery so painful and unexpected, adds bitterness to his sorrow; and led, by the same moral principle to admire and glory in the high desert of his father, even this admiration contributes to his uneasiness. Aversion to his uncle, arising from the same origin, has a similar tendency, and augments his anguish. All these feelings and emotions uniting together, are rendered still more violent, exasperated by his recent interview with the Queen, struggling for utterance, but restrained. Agitated and overwhelmed with afflicting images, no soothing, no exhilarating affection can have admission into his heart. His imagination is visited by no vision of happiness;

† From A *Philosophical Analysis and Illustration of some of Shakespeare's Remarkable Characters* (London, 1774) 97–98, 100–104.

and he wishes for deliverance from his afflictions, by being delivered from a painful existence.

HENRY MACKENZIE

Criticism on the Character and Tragedy of Hamlet†

*   *   *

Of all the characters of Shakspeare, that of Hamlet has been generally thought the most difficult to be reduced to any fixed or settled principle. With the strongest purposes of revenge, he is irresolute and inactive; amidst the gloom of the deepest melancholy, he is gay and jocular; and while he is described as a passionate lover, he seems indifferent about the object of his affections. It may be worth while to inquire whether any leading idea can be found, upon which these apparent contradictions may be reconciled, and a character so pleasing in the closet, and so much applauded on the stage, rendered as unambiguous in the general as it is striking in detail. I will venture to lay before my readers some observations on this subject, though with the diffidence due to a question of which the public has doubted, and much abler critics have already written.

The basis of Hamlet's character seems to be an extreme sensibility of mind, apt to be strongly impressed by its situation, and overpowered by the feelings which that situation excites. Naturally of the most virtuous and most amiable dispositions, the circumstances in which he was placed unhinged those principles of action, which, in another situation, would have delighted mankind, and made himself happy. That kind of distress which he suffered was, beyond all others, calculated to produce this effect. His misfortunes were not the misfortunes of accident, which, though they may overwhelm at first, the mind will soon call up reflections to alleviate, and hopes to cheer: they were such as reflection only serves to irritate, such as rankle in the soul's tenderest part, her sense of virtue, and feelings of natural affection; they arose from an uncle's villainy, a mother's guilt, a father's murder!—Yet, amidst the gloom of melancholy, and the agitation of passion, in which his calamities involve him, there are occasional breakings-out of a mind richly endowed by nature, and cultivated by education. We perceive gentleness in his demeanour, wit in his conversation, taste in his amusements, and wisdom in his reflections.

That Hamlet's character, thus formed by nature, and thus modelled by situation, is often variable and uncertain, I am not disposed to deny.

† From *The Mirror* 99 (April 18, 1770). Reprinted in *Memorials of Shakespeare*, ed. Nathan Drake (London, 1828) 371–78.

I will content myself with the supposition that this is the very character which Shakspeare meant to allot him. Finding such a character in real life, of a person endowed with feelings so delicate as to border on weakness, with sensibility too exquisite to allow of determined action, he has placed it where it could be best exhibited, in scenes of wonder, of terror, and of indignation, where its varying emotions might be most strongly marked amidst the workings of imagination, and the war of the passions.

This is the very management of the character by which, above all others, we could be interested in its behalf. Had Shakspeare made Hamlet pursue his vengeance with a steady determined purpose, had he led him through difficulties arising from accidental causes, and not from the doubts and hesitation of his own mind, the anxiety of the spectator might have been highly raised; but it would have been anxiety for the event, not for the person. As it is, we feel not only the virtues, but the weaknesses of Hamlet, as our own; we see a man who, in other circumstances, would have exercised all the moral and social virtues, one whom nature had formed to be

> Th' expectancy and rose of the fair state,
> The glass of fashion, and the mould of form,
> Th' observ'd of all observers,

placed in a situation in which even the amiable qualities of his mind serve but to aggravate his distress, and to perplex his conduct. Our compassion for the first, and our anxiety for the latter, are excited in the strongest manner; and hence arises that indescribable charm in Hamlet, which attracts every reader and every spectator, which the more perfect characters of the tragedies never dispose us to feel.

The Orestes of the Greek poet, who, at his first appearance, lays down a plan of vengeance which he resolutely pursues, interests us for the accomplishment of his purpose; but of him we think only as the instrument of that justice which we wish to overtake the murderers of Agamemnon. We feel with Orestes, (or rather with Sophocles, for in such passages we always hear the poet in his hero,) that 'it is fit that such gross infringements of the moral law should be punished with death, in order to render wickedness less frequent;' but when Horatio exclaims on the death of his friend,

Now crack'd a noble heart!

we forget the murder of the king, the villainy of Claudius, the guilt of Gertrude; our recollection dwells only on the memory of that 'sweet prince,' the delicacy of whose feelings a milder planet should have ruled, whose gentle virtues should have bloomed through a life of felicity and usefulness.

Hamlet, from the very opening of the piece, is delineated as one under the dominion of melancholy, whose spirits were overborne by his feelings. Grief for his father's death, and displeasure at his mother's marriage, prey on his mind; and he seems, with the weakness natural to such a disposition, to yield to their controul. He does not attempt to resist or combat these impressions, but is willing to fly from the contest, though it were into the grave.

> Oh! that this too too solid flesh would melt, &c.

Even after his father's ghost has informed him of his murder, and commissioned him to avenge it, we find him complaining of that situation in which his fate had placed him:

> The time is out of joint; oh! cursed spight,
> That ever I was born to set it right!

And afterwards, in the perplexity of his condition, meditating on the expediency of suicide:

> To be, or not to be, that is the question.

The account he gives of his own feelings to Rosencrantz and Guildenstern, which is evidently spoken in earnest, though somewhat covered with the mist of his affected distraction, is exactly descriptive of a mind full of that weariness of life which is characteristic of low spirits: 'This goodly frame, the earth, seems to me a sterile promontory,' &c. And, indeed, he expressly delineates his own character as of the kind abovementioned, when, hesitating on the evidence of his uncle's villainy, he says,

> The spirit that I have seen
> May be the devil, and the devil hath power
> T' assume a pleasing shape; yea, and perhaps,
> *Out of my weakness and my melancholy,*
> Abuses me to damn me.

This doubt of the grounds on which our purpose is founded, is as often the effect as the cause of irresolution, which first hesitates, and then seeks out an excuse for its hesitation.

It may, perhaps, be doing Shakspeare no injustice to suppose that he sometimes began a play without having fixed in his mind, in any determined manner, the plan or conduct of his piece. The character of some principal person of the drama might strike his imagination strongly in the opening scenes; as he went on, this character would continue to impress itself on the conduct as well as the discourse of that person, and, it is possible, might affect the situations and incidents, especially in those romantic or legendary subjects, where history did not confine him to certain unchangeable events. In the story of Amleth, the son of Horwondil, told by Saxo-Grammaticus, from which the tragedy of Hamlet is taken, the young prince, who is to revenge the death of his father, murdered by his uncle Fengo, counterfeits madness, that he may be allowed to remain about the court in safety and without suspicion. He never forgets his purposed vengeance, and acts with much more cunning towards its accomplishment than the Hamlet of Shakspeare. But Shakspeare, wishing to elevate the hero of his tragedy, and at the same time to interest the audience in his behalf, throws around him, from the beginning, the majesty of melancholy, along with that sort of weakness and irresolution which frequently attends it. The incident of the Ghost, which is entirely the poet's own, and not to be found in the Danish legend, not only produces the happiest stage effect, but is also of the greatest advantage in unfolding that character which is stamped on the young prince at the opening of the play. In the communications of such a visionary being, there is an uncertain kind of belief, and a dark unlimited horror, which are aptly suited to display the wavering purpose and varied emotions of a mind endowed with a delicacy of feeling that often shakes its fortitude, with sensibility that overpowers its strength.

JOHANN WOLFGANG VON GOETHE

[A Soul Unfit]†

* * * "Conceive a prince such as I have painted him, and that his father suddenly dies. Ambition and the love of rule are not the passions that inspire him. As a king's son, he would have been contented; but now he is first constrained to consider the difference which separates a sovereign from a subject. The crown was not hereditary; yet a longer possession of it by his father would have strengthened the pretensions of an only son, and secured his hopes of the succession. In place of this, he now beholds himself excluded by his uncle, in spite of specious promises, most probably forever. He is now poor in goods and favor, and a stranger in the scene which from youth he had looked upon as his inheritance. His temper here assumes its first mournful tinge. He feels that now he is not more, that he is less, than a private nobleman; he offers himself as the servant of every one; he is not courteous and condescending, he is needy and degraded.

"His past condition he remembers as a vanished dream. It is in vain that his uncle strives to cheer him, to present his situation in another point of view. The feeling of his nothingness will not leave him.

"The second stroke that came upon him wounded deeper, bowed still more. It was the marriage of his mother. The faithful tender son had yet

---

† From *Wilhelm Meister's Apprenticeship* (1795), translated by Thomas Carlyle. This selection is drawn from book 4, chapter 13.

a mother, when his father passed away. He hoped, in the company of his surviving noble-minded parent, to reverence the heroic form of the departed; but his mother too he loses, and it is something worse than death that robs him of her. The trustful image, which a good child loves to form of its parents, is gone. With the dead there is no help, on the living no hold. She also is a woman, and her name is Frailty, like that of all her sex.

"Now first does he feel himself completely bent and orphaned; and no happiness of life can repay what he has lost. Not reflective or sorrowful by nature, reflection and sorrow have become for him a heavy obligation. It is thus that we see him first enter on the scene. * * *

"Figure to yourselves this youth, * * * this son of princes; conceive him vividly, bring his state before your eyes, and then observe him when he learns that his father's spirit walks; stand by him in the terrors of the night, when the venerable ghost itself appears before him. A horrid shudder passes over him; he speaks to the mysterious form; he sees it beckon him; he follows it, and hears. The fearful accusation of his uncle rings in his ears; the summons to revenge, and the piercing oft-repeated prayer, Remember me!

"And when the ghost has vanished, who is it that stands before us? A young hero panting for vengeance? A prince by birth, rejoicing to be called to punish the usurper of his crown? No! trouble and astonishment take hold of the solitary young man: he grows bitter against smiling villains, swears that he will not forget the spirit, and concludes with the significant ejaculation:—

'The time is out of joint: O cursed spite,
That ever I was born to set it right!'

"In these words, I imagine, will be found the key to Hamlet's whole procedure. To me it is clear that Shakespeare meant, in the present case, to represent the effects of a great action laid upon a soul unfit for the performance of it. In this view the whole piece seems to me to be composed. There is an oak-tree planted in a costly jar, which should have borne only pleasant flowers in its bosom; the roots expand, the jar is shivered.

"A lovely, pure, noble, and most moral nature, without the strength of nerve which forms a hero, sinks beneath a burden which it cannot bear and must not cast away. All duties are holy for him; the present is too hard. Impossibilities have been required of him; not in themselves impossibilities, but such for him. He winds, and turns, and torments himself; he advances and recoils; is ever put in mind, ever puts himself in mind; at last does all but lose his purpose from his thoughts; yet still without recovering his peace of mind."

* * *

AUGUSTUS WILLIAM SCHLEGEL

Criticisms on Shakespeare's Tragedies: *Hamlet*†

* * * *Hamlet* is singular in its kind: a tragedy of thought inspired by continual and never-satisfied meditation on human destiny and the dark perplexity of the events of this world, and calculated to call forth the very same meditation in the minds of the spectators. This enigmatical work resembles those irrational equations in which a fraction of unknown magnitude always remains, that will in no way admit of solution. Much has been said, much written, on this piece, and yet no thinking head who anew expresses himself on it, will (in his view of the connexion and the signification of all the parts) entirely coincide with his predecessors. What naturally most astonishes us, is the fact that with such hidden purposes, with a foundation laid in such unfathomable depth, the whole should, at a first view, exhibit an extremely popular appearance. The dread appearance of the Ghost takes possession of the mind and the imagination almost at the very commencement; then the play within the play, in which, as in a glass, we see reflected the crime, whose fruitlessly attempted punishment constitutes the subject-matter of the piece; the alarm with which it fills the King; Hamlet's pretended and Ophelia's real madness; her death and burial; the meeting of Hamlet and Laertes at her grave; their combat, and the grand determination; lastly, the appearance of the young hero Fortinbras, who, with warlike pomp, pays the last honours to an extinct family of kings; the interspersion of comic characteristic scenes with Polonius, the courtiers, and the grave-diggers, which have all of them their signification,—all this fills the stage with an animated and varied movement. The only circumstance from which this piece might be judged to be less theatrical than other tragedies of Shakspeare is, that in the last scenes the main action either stands still or appears to retrograde. This, however, was inevitable, and lay in the nature of the subject. The whole is intended to show that a calculating consideration, which exhausts all the relations and possible consequences of a deed, must cripple the power of acting; as Hamlet himself expresses it:—

> And thus the native hue of resolution
> Is sicklied o'er with the pale cast of thought;
> And enterprises of great pith and moment,
> With this regard, their currents turn awry,
> And lose the name of action.

With respect to Hamlet's character: I cannot, as I understand the poet's views, pronounce altogether so favourable a sentence upon it as Goethe

---

† From *Lectures on Dramatic Art and Literature* (1808), translated by John Black (London, 1846) 404–6.

does. He is, it is true, of a highly cultivated mind, a prince of royal manners, endowed with the finest sense of propriety, susceptible of noble ambition, and open in the highest degree to an enthusiastic admiration of that excellence in others of which he himself is deficient. He acts the part of madness with unrivalled power, convincing the persons who are sent to examine into his supposed loss of reason, merely by telling them unwelcome truths, and rallying them with the most caustic wit. But in the resolutions which he so often embraces and always leaves unexecuted, his weakness is too apparent: he does himself only justice when he implies that there is no greater dissimilarity than between himself and Hercules. He is not solely impelled by necessity to artifice and dissimulation, he has a natural inclination for crooked ways; he is a hypocrite towards himself; his far-fetched scruples are often mere pretexts to cover his want of determination: thoughts, as he says on a different occasion, which have

> —— but one part wisdom
> And ever three parts coward. ——

He has been chiefly condemned both for his harshness in repulsing the love of Ophelia, which he himself had cherished, and for his insensibility at her death. But he is too much overwhelmed with his own sorrow to have any compassion to spare for others; besides his outward indifference gives us by no means the measure of his internal perturbation. On the other hand, we evidently perceive in him a malicious joy, when he has succeeded in getting rid of his enemies, more through necessity and accident, which alone are able to impel him to quick and decisive measures, than by the merit of his own courage, as he himself confesses after the murder of Polonius, and with respect to Rosencrantz and Guildenstern. Hamlet has no firm belief either in himself or in anything else: from expressions of religious confidence he passes over to sceptical doubts; he believes in the Ghost of his father as long as he sees it, but as soon as it has disappeared, it appears to him almost in the light of a deception.[1] He has even gone so far as to say, "there is nothing either good or bad, but thinking makes it so;" with him the poet loses himself here in labyrinths of thought, in which neither end nor beginning is discoverable. The stars themselves, from the course of events, afford no answer to the question so urgently proposed to them. A voice from another world, commissioned it would appear, by heaven, demands vengeance for a monstrous enormity, and the demand remains without effect; the criminals are at last punished, but, as it were, by an accidental blow, and not in the solemn way requisite to convey to the world a warning example

---

1. It has been censured as a contradiction, that Hamlet in the soliloquy on self-murder should say, The undiscover'd country, from whose bourn No traveller returns—— For was not the Ghost a returned traveller? Shakspeare, however, purposely wished to show, that Hamlet could not fix himself in any conviction of any kind whatever.

of justice; irresolute foresight, cunning treachery, and impetuous rage, hurry on to a common destruction; the less guilty and the innocent are equally involved in the general ruin. The destiny of humanity is there exhibited as a gigantic Sphinx, which threatens to precipitate into the abyss of scepticism all who are unable to solve her dreadful enigmas.

*   *   *

SAMUEL TAYLOR COLERIDGE

Notes on the Tragedies: *Hamlet*†

* * * The preparation *informative* of the audience [is] just as much as was precisely necessary: how gradual first, and with the uncertainty appertaining to a question—

> What, has *this thing* appeared *again* to-night. (3)

Even the word "again" has it *credibilizing* effect. Then the representative of the ignorance of the audience, Horatio (not himself but [quoted by] Marcellus to Bernardo) anticipates the common solution, " 'tis but our phantasy." But Marcellus rises secondly into "[this] dreaded sight." Then this "thing" becomes at once an "apparition," and that too an intelligent spirit that is to be *spoken* to.

> Tush, tush! 'twill not appear. (4)

Then the shivery feeling, at such a time, with two eye-witnesses, of sitting down to hear a story of a ghost, and this, too, a ghost that had appeared two nights before [at] about this very time. The effort of the narrator to master his own imaginative terrors; the consequent elevation of the style, itself a continuation of this effort; the turning off to an *outward* object, "yon same star." O heaven! words are wasted to those that feel and to those who do not feel the exquisite judgement of Shakespeare. * * *

> [I.i.70–72.
>   *Mar.* Good now, sit down, and tell me, he that knows,
> Why this same strict and most observant watch
> So nightly toils the subject of the land.] (5)

† From *Coleridge's Shakespearean Criticism*, ed. Thomas M. Raysor (Cambridge: Harvard UP) 20–37. Copyright © 1930 by the President and Fellows of Harvard College, 1958 by Thomas M. Raysor. Reprinted by permission of the editor. The footnotes are Raysor's. Page numbers given in parentheses refer to the text of this Norton Critical Edition of *Hamlet*.

The exquisitely natural transit into the narration retrospective. [When the Ghost re-appears, note] Horatio's increased courage from having translated the late individual spectre into thought and past experience, and Marcellus' and Bernardo's sympathy with it [Horatio's courage] in daring to strike, while yet the former feeling returns in

> We do it wrong [being so majestical,
> To offer it the show of violence.] (7)

*   *   *

[I.i.169–71.
Let us impart what we have seen to-night
Unto young Hamlet; for, upon my life,
This spirit, dumb to us, will speak to him.] (7)

The unobtrusive and yet fully adequate mode of introducing the main character, *young* Hamlet, upon whom transfers itself all the interest excited for the acts and concerns of the king, his father.

[I.ii.] Relief by change of scene to the royal court. This [relief is desirable] on any occasion; but how judicious that Hamlet should not have to take up the leavings of exhaustion. The set, pedantically antithetic form of the king's speech—tho' in the concerns that galled the heels of conscience, rhetorical below a king, yet in what follows, not without majesty. Was he not a royal brother?

*   *   *

[I.iii.] This scene must be regarded as one of Shakespeare's lyric movements in the play, and the skill with which it is interwoven with the dramatic parts is peculiarly an excellence of our poet. You experience the sensation of a pause without the sense of a stop. You will observe in Ophelia's short and general answer to the long speech of Laertes the natural carelessness of innocence, which cannot think such a code of cautions and prudences necessary to its own preservation.

*   *   *

[I.iv.] In addition to the other excellencies of Hamlet's speech concerning the wassail music, so finely revealing the predominant idealism, the ratiocinative meditativeness of his character, it has the advantage of giving nature and probability to the impassioned continuity of the speech instantly directed to the Ghost. The momentum had been given to his mental activity, the full current of the thoughts and words had set in, and the very forgetfulness, in the fervor of his argumentation, of the purpose for which he was there, aided in preventing the appearance from benumbing the mind. Consequently, it acted as a new impulse, a sudden stroke which increased the velocity of the body already in motion, while it altered the direction. The co-presence of Horatio, Marcellus, and Bernardo is most judiciously contrived, for it renders the courage of Hamlet and his impetuous eloquence perfectly intelligible. The knowledge, the *unthought* of consciousness, the *sensation*, of human auditors, of flesh and blood sympathists, acts as a support, a stimulation *a tergo*, while the *front* of the mind, the whole consciousness of the speaker, is filled by the solemn apparition. Add, too, that the apparition itself has by its frequent previous appearances been brought nearer to a thing of this world. This accrescence of objectivity in a ghost that yet retains all its ghostly attributes and fearful subjectivity, is truly wonderful.

[I.v.92–112. The speech of Hamlet as the Ghost vanishes.
Ham. O all you host of heaven! O earth! what else?
And shall I couple hell? O, fie! Hold, hold, my heart; etc.] (23)

I remember nothing equal to this burst unless it be the first speech of Prometheus,[1] after the exit of Vulcan and the two Afrites, in Aeschylus. But Shakespeare alone could have produced the vow of Hamlet to make his memory a blank of all maxims and generalized truths that "observation had copied there," followed by the immediate noting down the generalized fact,

That one may smile, and smile, and be a villain. (23)

[II.i. Polonius and Reynaldo. Polonius and Ophelia.]

In all things dependent on, or rather made up of, fine address, the *manner* is no more or otherwise rememberable than the light motions, steps, and gestures of youth and health. But this is almost everything; no wonder, therefore, if that which can be *put down by rule* in the memory should appear mere poring, maudlin-eyed cunning, slyness blinking thro' the watery eye of superannuation. So in this admirable scene, Polonius, who is throughout the skeleton of his own former skill and statecraft, hunts the trail of policy at a dead scent, supplied by the weak fever-smell in his own nostrils.

*   *   *

[II.ii.172–73.
Pol. Do you know me, my lord?
Ham. Excellent well; you are fishmonger.] (33)

["Fishmonger";] *i.e.* you are sent to *fish* out the secret. This is Hamlet's meaning. The purposely obscure lines—

For if the sun [breed maggots in a dead dog, being a god kissing carrion—Have you a daughter?] (34)

---

1. *Prometheus Bound*, 88–127. The following reference to the 'two Afrites' seems curious, for Afrites are evil demons of Mohammedan mythology; but it is clear that Coleridge refers to the two attendants of Vulcan, Power and Force ($\beta\iota\alpha$ and $K\rho\acute{\alpha}\tau o\varsigma$).

I rather think refer to some thought in Hamlet's mind contrasting the lovely daughter with such a tedious old fool, her father, as *he* represents Polonius to himself. "Why, fool as he is, he is some degrees in rank above a dead dog's carcase; and if the sun, being a god that kisses carrion, can raise life out of a dead dog, why may [not] good fortune, that favors fools, have raised a lovely girl out of this dead-alive old fool."

*   *   *

[II.ii.423–89.
'The rugged Pyrrhus, he whose sable arms,' etc.] (40)

This admirable substitution of the epic for the dramatic, giving such a *reality* to the impassioned dramatic diction of Shakespeare's own dialogue,[2] and authorized too by the actual style of the tragedies before Shakespeare *(Porrex and Ferrex, Titus Andronicus,* etc.) is worthy of notice. The fancy that a burlesque was intended, sinks below criticism. The lines, as *epic* narrative, are superb.

*   *   *

[III.i.103.
Ham. Ha, ha! are you honest?] (46)

Here it is evident that the penetrating Hamlet perceived, from the strange and forced manner of Ophelia, that the sweet girl was not acting a part of her own—in short, saw into the strategem—and his after speeches are not directed to Ophelia, but to the listeners and spies.

Hamlet here discovers that he is watched, and Ophelia a decoy. Even this in a mood so anxious and irritable accounts for a certain harshness in him; and yet a wild upworking of love, sporting with opposites with a wilful self-tormenting irony, is perceptible throughout: *ex. gr.* "I did love you"[3] and [his reference to] the faults of the sex from which Ophelia is so characteristically free that the freedom therefrom constitutes her character. Here again Shakespeare's charm of constituting female character by absence of characters, [of] outjuttings.[4]

[III.i.143–45, Hamlet to Ophelia.
. . . . I say, we will have no more marriages: those that are married already, all but one, shall live; the rest shall keep as they are.] (47)

2. For this fine observation Coleridge is indebted to Schlegel, though with alterations. Schlegel's excellent treatment of this problem is worth reading in its entirety, but space forbids quotation of more than two sentences which Coleridge used. "They [Shakespeare's commentators] have not considered that this speech must not be judged by itself but in the place where it stands. That which is meant to appear as dramatic invention in the play itself, must contrast with the play's dignified poetry in the same degree as theatrical elevation with simple nature." *Werke,* vi.251.
3. "I did love you once."
4. Cf. i.133, 233; ii.353–54.

The dallying with the inward purpose that of one who had not brought his mind to the steady acting point, would fain *sting* the uncle's mind,—but to stab the body!

The soliloquy of Ophelia is the perfection of love—so exquisitely unselfish!

[III.ii. The dialogue of Hamlet with the players.] (48–49)

One and among the happiest [instances] of Shakespeare's power of diversifying the scene while he is carrying on the plot.

[III.ii.93–95.
     Pol. I did enact Julius Caesar: I was killed i' the Capitol; Brutus killed me.
     Ham. It was a brute part of him to kill so capital a calf there.] (50)

In any direct form to have kept Hamlet's love for Ophelia before the audience, would have made a breach in the unity of the interest; but yet to the thoughtful reader it is suggested by his spite to poor Polonius, whom he cannot let rest.

[III.ii. The play.]

As in the first interview with the players by *epic* verse, so here [the style of the play performed before the court is distinguished] by rhyme.

* * *

[III.ii.358–60. Hamlet's soliloquy.
     . . . . now could I drink hot blood,
     And do such bitter business as the day
     Would quake to look on.] (57)

The utmost Hamlet arrives to is a disposition, a mood, to do *something*. *What* is still left undecided, while every word he utters tends to betray his disguise.

The perfect equal to any call of the moment is Hamlet, let it only not be for a future.

* * *

[III.iii.27–29.
     Pol. My lord, he's going to his mother's closet:
     Behind the arras I'll convey myself,
     To hear the process.] (58)

Polonius's volunteer obtrusion of himself into this business, while it is appropriate to his character, still letching after former importance, removes all likelihood that Hamlet should suspect his presence, and prevents us from making his death injure Hamlet in our opinion.

[III.iii.36–72. The king's remorse.
O, my offence is rank, it smells to heaven.] (58–59)

The king's speech well marks the difference between crime and guilt of habit. The conscience is still admitted to audience. Nay, even as an audible soliloquy, it is far less improbable than is supposed by such as have watched men only in the beaten road of their feelings. But it deserves to be dealt on, that final "All may be well"; a degree of merit [is] attributed by the self-flattering soul to its own struggle, tho' baffled, and to the indefinite half-promise, half-command, to persevere in religious duties. The divine medium of the Christian doctrine of expiation [is] in this: not what you have done, but what you *are*, must determine. Metanoia.[5]

*   *   *

[III.iv.29–31.
Ham. A bloody deed! almost as bad, good mother,
As kill a king, and marry with his brother.
Queen. As kill a king!] (61)

I confess that Shakespeare has left the character of the queen in an unpleasant perplexity. Was she or was she not conscious of the fratricide?

[IV.ii.12–14.
Ros. Take you me for a sponge, my lord?
Ham. Ay, sir; that soaks up the king's countenance, his rewards, his authorities.] (68)

Hamlet's madness is made to consist in the full utterance of all the thoughts that had past thro' his mind before—in telling home truths.

[IV.v. Ophelia's singing.] The conjunction here of these two thoughts that had never subsisted in disjunction, the love for Hamlet and her filial love, and the guileless floating on the surface of her pure imagination of the cautions so lately expressed and the fears not too delicately avowed by her father and brother concerning the danger to which her honor lay exposed.

Thought and affliction, passion, murder[6] itself,
She turns to favor and to prettiness.
[IV.v.181–82.] (77)

This play of association is sweetly instanced in the close—

. . . . My brother shall know of it: and [so] I thank you for your good *counsel*.   [IV.v.69–70.] (74)

---

5. Μετάνοια, repentance.   6. Read '*hell*.'

*   *   *

[IV. vi. Hamlet's capture by the pirates, as explained in his letter.]

Almost the only play of Shakespeare, in which mere accidents, inde-pendent of all will, form an essential part of the plot; but here how judiciously in keeping with the character of the over-meditative Hamlet, ever at last determined by accident or by a fit of passion.

[IV.vii.81–106. The king] first awakens Laertes' vanity by the praises of the report[er], then gratifies it by the report itself, and then [comes to the point—

> . . . . Sir, this report of his]
> Did Hamlet so envenom with his envy
> [That he could nothing do but wish and beg
> Your sudden coming o'er, to play with him.] (81)

And that Laertes might be excused in some degree for not cooling, the act concludes with the affecting death of Ophelia. Who does not see [her], like a little projection of land into a lake or stream, covered with spring-flowers, lying quietly reflected in the great waters, but at length [being] undermined and loosened, becomes a floating faery isle, and after a brief vagrancy sinks almost without an eddy!

*   *   *

[V. i.] The contrast between the clowns and Hamlet as two extremes— the [clowns'] mockery of logic, the traditional wit valued like truth for its antiquity, and treasured up, like a tune, for use.

The Character of Hamlet.

1. Shakespeare's mode of conceiving characters out of his own intel-lectual and moral faculties, by conceiving any one intellectual or moral faculty in morbid excess and then placing himself, thus mutilated and diseased, under given circumstances. This we shall have repeated occa-sion to re-state and enforce. In Hamlet I conceive him to have wished to exemplify the moral necessity of a due balance between our attention to outward objects and our meditation on inward thoughts—a due bal-ance between the real and the imaginary world. In Hamlet this balance does not exist—his thoughts, images, and fancy [being] far more vivid than his perceptions, and his very perceptions instantly passing thro' the medium of his contemplations, and acquiring as they pass a form and color not naturally their own. Hence great, enormous, intellectual activ-

ity, and a consequent proportionate aversion to real action, with all its symptoms and accompanying qualities.

Action is transitory, a step, a blow,[7] etc.

WILLIAM HAZLITT

Characters of Shakespear's Plays: *Hamlet*†

This is that Hamlet the Dane, whom we read of in our youth, and whom we may be said almost to remember in our after-years; he who made that famous soliloquy on life, who gave the advice to the players, who thought 'this goodly frame, the earth, a steril promontory, and this brave o'er-hanging firmament, the air, this majestical roof fretted with golden fire, a foul and pestilent congregation of vapours'; whom 'man delighted not, nor woman neither'; he who talked with the grave-diggers, and moralised on Yorick's skull; the school-fellow of Rosencraus and Guildenstern at Wittenberg; the friend of Horatio; the lover of Ophelia; he that was mad and sent to England; the slow avenger of his father's death; who lived at the court of Horwendillus five hundred years before we were born, but all whose thoughts we seem to know as well as we do our own, because we have read them in Shakespear.

Hamlet is a name; his speeches and sayings but the idle coinage of the poet's brain. What then, are they not real? They are as real as our own thoughts. Their reality is in the reader's mind. It is *we* who are Hamlet. This play has a prophetic truth, which is above that of history. Whoever has become thoughtful and melancholy through his own mishaps or those of others; whoever has borne about with him the clouded brow of reflection, and thought himself 'too much i' th' sun'; whoever has seen the golden lamp of day dimmed by envious mists rising in his own breast, and could find in the world before him only a dull blank with nothing left remarkable in it; whoever has known 'the pangs of despised love, the insolence of office, or the spurns which patient merit of the unworthy takes'; he who has felt his mind sink within him, and sadness cling to his heart like a malady, who has had his hopes blighted and his youth staggered by the apparitions of strange things; who cannot be well at ease, while he sees evil hovering near him like a spectre; whose powers of action have been eaten up by thought, he to whom the universe seems infinite, and himself nothing; whose bitterness of soul makes him careless of consequences, and who goes to a play as his best resource

7. "Action is transitory—a step, a blow,
      ·   ·   ·   ·   ·

Suffering is permanent, obscure and dark,
And shares the nature of infinity."
                Wordsworth, *The Borders*, III.v.
† From *Characters of Shakespear's Plays* (1817).

to shove off, to a second remove, the evils of life by a mock representation of them—this is the true Hamlet.

We have been so used to this tragedy that we hardly know how to criticise it any more than we should know how to describe our own faces. But we must make such observations as we can. It is the one of Shakespear's plays that we think of the oftenest, because it abounds most in striking reflections on human life, and because the distresses of Hamlet are transferred, by the turn of his mind, to the general account of humanity. Whatever happens to him we apply to ourselves, because he applies it so himself as a means of general reasoning. He is a great moraliser; and what makes him worth attending to is, that he moralises on his own feelings and experience. He is not a common-place pedant. If *Lear* is distinguished by the greatest depth of passion, HAMLET is the most remarkable for the ingenuity, originality, and unstudied development of character. Shakespear had more magnanimity than any other poet, and he has shewn more of it in this play than in any other. There is no attempt to force an interest: every thing is left for time and circumstances to unfold. The attention is excited without effort, the incidents succeed each other as matters of course, the characters think and speak and act just as they might do, if left entirely to themselves. There is no set purpose, no straining at a point. The observations are suggested by the passing scene—the gusts of passion come and go like sounds of music borne on the wind. The whole play is an exact transcript of what might be supposed to have taken place at the court of Denmark, at the remote period of time fixed upon, before the modern refinements in morals and manners were heard of. It would have been interesting enough to have been admitted as a by-stander in such a scene, at such a time, to have heard and witnessed something of what was going on. But here we are more than spectators. We have not only 'the outward pageants and the signs of grief'; but 'we have that within which passes shew.' We read the thoughts of the heart, we catch the passions living as they rise. Other dramatic writers give us very fine versions and paraphrases of nature; but Shakespear, together with his own comments, gives us the original text, that we may judge for ourselves. This is a very great advantage.

The character of Hamlet stands quite by itself. It is not a character marked by strength of will or even of passion, but by refinement of thought and sentiment. Hamlet is as little of the hero as a man can well be: but he is a young and princely novice, full of high enthusiasm and quick sensibility—the sport of circumstances, questioning with fortune and refining on his own feelings, and forced from the natural bias of his disposition by the strangeness of his situation. He seems incapable of deliberate action, and is only hurried into extremities on the spur of the occasion, when he has no time to reflect, as in the scene where he kills Polonius, and again, where he alters the letters which Rosencraus and Guildenstern are taking with them to England, purporting his death. At

other times, when he is most bound to act, he remains puzzled, undecided, and sceptical, dallies with his purposes, till the occasion is lost,
and finds out some pretence to relapse into indolence and thoughtful-
ness again. For this reason he refuses to kill the King when he is at his
prayers, and by a refinement in malice, which is in truth only an excuse
for his own want of resolution, defers his revenge to a more fatal opportunity, when he shall be engaged in some act 'that has no relish of
salvation in it.'

> 'He kneels and prays,
> And now I'll do't, and so he goes to heaven,
> And so am I reveng'd: *that would be scann'd.*
> He kill'd my father, and for that,
> I, his sole son, send him to heaven.
> Why this is reward, not revenge.
> Up sword and know thou a more horrid time,
>   When he is drunk, asleep, or in a rage.'

He is the prince of philosophical speculators; and because he cannot
have his revenge perfect, according to the most refined idea his wish can
form, he declines it altogether. So he scruples to trust the suggestions of
the ghost, contrives the scene of the play to have surer proof of his uncle's
guilt, and then rests satisfied with this confirmation of his suspicions,
and the success of his experiment, instead of acting upon it. Yet he is
sensible of his own weakness, taxes himself with it, and tries to reason
himself out of it.

> 'How all occasions do inform against me,
> And spur my dull revenge! What is a man,
> If his chief good and market of his time
> Be but to sleep and feed? A beast; no more.
> Sure he that made us with such large discourse,
> Looking before and after, gave us not
> That capability and god-like reason
> To rust in us unus'd. Now whether it be
> Bestial oblivion, or some craven scruple
> Of thinking too precisely on th' event,—
> A thought which quarter'd, hath but one part wisdom,
> And ever three parts coward;—I do not know
> Why yet I live to say, this thing's to do;
> Sith I have cause, and will, and strength, and means
> To do it. Examples gross as earth exhort me:
> Witness this army of such mass and charge,
> Led by a delicate and tender prince,
> Whose spirit with divine ambition puff'd,
> Makes mouths at the invisible event,
> Exposing what is mortal and unsure

To all that torture, death, and danger dare,
Even for an egg-shell. 'Tis not to be great
Never to stir without great argument;
But greatly to find quarrel in a straw,
When honour's at the stake. How stand I then,
That have a father kill'd, a mother stain'd,
Excitements of my reason and my blood,
And let all sleep, while to my shame I see
The imminent death of twenty thousand men,
That for a fantasy and trick of fame,
Go to their graves like beds, fight for a plot
Whereon the numbers cannot try the cause,
Which is not tomb enough and continent
To hide the slain?—O, from this time forth,
My thoughts be bloody or be nothing worth.'

Still he does nothing; and this very speculation on his own infirmity only affords him another occasion for indulging it. It is not from any want of attachment to his father or of abhorrence of his murder that Hamlet is thus dilatory, but it is more to his taste to indulge his imagination in reflecting upon the enormity of the crime and refining on his schemes of vengeance, than to put them into immediate practice. His ruling passion is to think, not to act: and any vague pretext that flatters this propensity instantly diverts him from his previous purposes.

The moral perfection of this character has been called in question, we think, by those who did not understand it. It is more interesting than according to rules; amiable, though not faultless. The ethical delineations of 'that noble and liberal casuist' (as Shakespear has been well called) do not exhibit the drab-coloured quakerism of morality. His plays are not copied either from The Whole Duty of Man, or from The Academy of Compliments! We confess we are a little shocked at the want of refinement in those who are shocked at the want of refinement in Hamlet. The neglect of punctilious exactness in his behavior either partakes of the 'licence of the time,' or else belongs to the very excess of intellectual refinement in the character, which makes the common rules of life, as well as his own purpose, sit loose upon him. He may be said to be amenable only to the tribunal of his own thoughts, and is too much taken up with the airy world of contemplation to lay as much stress as he ought on the practical consequences of things. His habitual principles of action are unhinged and out of joint with the time. His conduct to Ophelia is quite natural in his circumstances. It is that of assumed severity only. It is the effect of disappointed hope, of bitter regrets, of affection suspended, not obliterated, by the distractions of the scene around him! Amidst the natural and preternatural horrors of his situation, he might be excused in delicacy from carrying on a regular courtship. When 'his father's spirit was in arms,' it was not a time for the son to make love

in. He could neither marry Ophelia, nor wound her mind by explaining
the cause of his alienation, which he durst hardly trust himself to think
of. It would have taken him years to have come to a direct explanation
on the point. In the harassed state of his mind, he could not have done
much otherwise than he did. His conduct does not contradict what he
says when he sees her funeral,

> 'I loved Ophelia: forty thousand brothers
> Could not with all their quantity of love
> Make up my sum.'

Nothing can be more affecting or beautiful than the Queen's apos-
trophe to Ophelia on throwing the flowers into the grave.

> —'Sweets to the sweet, farewell.
> I hop'd thou should'st have been my Hamlet's wife:
> I thought thy bride-bed to have deck'd, sweet maid,
> And not have strew'd thy grave.'

Shakespear was thoroughly a master of the mixed motives of human
character, and he here shews us the Queen, who was so criminal in
some respects, not without sensibility and affection in other relations of
life.—Ophelia is a character almost too exquisitely touching to be dwelt
upon. Oh rose of May, oh flower too soon faded! Her love, her madness,
her death, are described with the truest touches of tenderness and pathos.
It is a character which nobody but Shakespear could have drawn in the
way that he has done, and to the conception of which there is not even
the smallest approach, except in some of the old romantic ballads.[1] Her
brother, Laertes, is a character we do not like so well: he is too hot and
choleric, and somewhat rhodomontade. Polonius is a perfect character
in its kind; nor is there any foundation for the objections which have
been made to the consistency of this part. It is said that he acts very
foolishly and talks very sensibly. There is no inconsistency in that. Again,
that he talks wisely at one time and foolishly at another; that his advice
to Laertes is very excellent, and his advice to the King and Queen on
the subject of Hamlet's madness very ridiculous. But he gives the one as
a father, and is sincere in it; he gives the other as a mere courtier, a
busy-body, and is accordingly officious, garrulous, and impertinent. In
short, Shakespear has been accused of inconsistency in this and other
characters, only because he has kept up the distinction which there is in
nature, between the understandings and the moral habits of men, between
the absurdity of their ideas and the absurdity of their motives. Polonius
is not a fool, but he makes himself so. His folly, whether in his actions
or speeches, comes under the head of impropriety of intention.

1. In the account of her death, a friend has pointed
out an instance of the poet's exact observation of
nature:—'There is a willow growing o'er a brook.
That shews its hoary leaves i' the' glassy stream'
The inside of the leaves of the willow, next the
water, is of a whitish colour, and the reflection
would therefore be 'hoary.'

We do not like to see our author's plays acted, and least of all, HAM-LET. There is no play that suffers so much in being transferred to the stage. Hamlet himself seems hardly capable of being acted. Mr. Kemble[2] unavoidably fails in this character from a want of ease and variety. The character of Hamlet is made up of undulating lines; it has the yielding flexibility of 'a wave o' th' sea.' Mr. Kemble plays it like a man in armour, with a determined inveteracy of purpose, in one undeviating straight line, which is as remote from the natural grace and refined susceptibility of the character, as the sharp angles and abrupt starts which Mr. Kean[3] introduces into the part. Mr. Kean's Hamlet is as much too splenetic and rash as Mr. Kemble's is too deliberate and formal. His manner is too strong and pointed. He throws a severity, approaching to virulence, into the common observations and answers. There is nothing of this in Hamlet. He is, as it were, wrapped up in his reflections, and only *thinks aloud*. There should therefore be no attempt to impress what he says upon others by a studied exaggeration of emphasis or manner; no *talking at* his hearers. There should be as much of the gentleman and scholar as possible infused into the part, and as little of the actor. A pensive air of sadness should sit reluctantly upon his brow, but no appearance of fixed and sullen gloom. He is full of weakness and melancholy, but there is no harshness in his nature. He is the most amiable of misanthropes.

A. C. BRADLEY

[What Actually Happens in the Play]†

* * * Turn to the first words Hamlet utters when he is alone; turn, that is to say, to the place where the author is likely to indicate his meaning most plainly. What do you hear?

> *O, that this too too solid flesh would melt,*
> *Thaw and resolve itself into a dew!*
> *Or that the Everlasting had not fix'd*
> *His canon 'gainst self-slaughter! Oh God! God!*
> *How weary, stale, flat and unprofitable,*
> *Seem to me all the uses of this world!*
> *Fie on't! ah fie! 'tis an unweeded garden,*
> *That grows to seed; things rank and gross in nature*
> *Possess it merely.*

2. John Philip Kemble, English actor (1757–1823) [Editor].

3. Edmund Kean, English actor (1787–1833)

[Editor].

† From *Shakespearean Tragedy* (London, 1903). Bradley's footnotes have been omitted.

Here are a sickness of life, and even a longing for death, so intense that nothing stands between Hamlet and suicide except religious awe. And what has caused them? The rest of the soliloquy so thrusts the answer upon us that it might seem impossible to miss it. It was not his father's death; that doubtless brought deep grief, but mere grief for some one loved and lost does not make a noble spirit loathe the world as a place full only of things rank and gross. It was not the vague suspicion that we know Hamlet felt. Still less was it the loss of the crown; for though the subserviency of the electors might well disgust him, there is not a reference to the subject in the soliloquy, nor any sign elsewhere that it greatly occupied his mind. It was the moral shock of the sudden ghastly disclosure of his mother's true nature, falling on him when his heart was aching with love, and his body doubtless was weakened by sorrow. And it is essential, however disagreeable, to realise the nature of this shock. It matters little here whether Hamlet's age was twenty or thirty: in either case his mother was a matron of mature years. All his life he had believed in her, we may be sure, as such a son would. He had seen her not merely devoted to his father, but hanging on him like a newly-wedded bride, hanging on him

> As if increase of appetite had grown
> By what it fed on.

He had seen her following his body 'like Niobe, all tears.' And then within a month—'O God! a beast would have mourned longer'—she married again, and married Hamlet's uncle, a man utterly contemptible and loathsome in his eyes; married him in what to Hamlet was incestuous wedlock; married him not for any reason of state, nor even out of old family affection, but in such a way that her son was forced to see in her action not only an astounding shallowness of feeling but an eruption of coarse sensuality, 'rank and gross,' speeding post-haste to its horrible delight. Is it possible to conceive an experience more desolating to a man such as we have seen Hamlet to be; and is its result anything but perfectly natural? It brings bewildered horror, then loathing, then despair of human nature. His whole mind is poisoned. He can never see Ophelia in the same light again: she is a woman, and his mother is a woman: if she mentions the word 'brief' to him, the answer drops from his lips like venom, 'as woman's love.' The last words of the soliloquy, which is *wholly* concerned with this subject, are,

> But break, my heart, for I must hold my tongue!

He can do nothing. He must lock in his heart, not any suspicion of his uncle that moves obscurely there, but that horror and loathing; and if his heart ever found relief, it was when those feelings, mingled with the love that never died out in him, poured themselves forth in a flood as he stood in his mother's chamber beside his father's marriage-bed.

If we still wonder, and ask why the effect of this shock should be so tremendous, let us observe that *now* the conditions have arisen under which Hamlet's highest endowments, his moral sensibility and his genius, become his enemies. A nature morally blunter would have felt even so dreadful a revelation less keenly. A slower and more limited and positive mind might not have extended so widely through its world the disgust and disbelief that have entered it. But Hamlet has the imagination which, for evil as well as good, feels and sees all things in one. Thought is the element of his life, and his thought is infected. He cannot prevent himself from probing and lacerating the wound in his soul. One idea, full of peril, holds him fast, and he cries out in agony at it, but is impotent to free himself ('Must I remember?' 'Let me not think on't'). And when, with the fading of his passion, the vividness of this idea abates, it does so only to leave behind a boundless weariness and a sick longing for death.

And this is the time which his fate chooses. In this hour of uttermost weakness, this sinking of his whole being towards annihilation, there comes on him, bursting the bounds of the natural world with a shock of astonishment and terror, the revelation of his mother's adultery and his father's murder, and, with this, the demand on him, in the name of everything dearest and most sacred, to arise and act. And for a moment, though his brain reels and totters, his soul leaps up in passion to answer this demand. But it comes too late. It does not strike home the last rivet in the melancholy which holds him bound.

> *The time is out of joint! O cursed spite*
> *That ever I was born to set it right,—*

so he mutters within an hour of the moment when he vowed to give his life to the duty of revenge; and the rest of the story exhibits his vain efforts to fulfil this duty, his unconscious self-excuses and unavailing self-reproaches, and the tragic results of his delay.

'Melancholy,' I said, not dejection, nor yet insanity. That Hamlet was not far from insanity is very probable. His adoption of the pretence of madness may well have been due in part to fear of the reality; to an instinct of self-preservation, a forefeeling that the pretence would enable him to give some utterance to the load that pressed on his heart and brain, and a fear that he would be unable altogether to repress such utterance. And if the pathologist calls his state melancholia, and even proceeds to determine its species, I see nothing to object to in that; I am grateful to him for emphasising the fact that Hamlet's melancholy was no mere common depression of spirits; and I have no doubt that many readers of the play would understand it better if they read an account of melancholia in a work on mental diseases. If we like to use the word 'disease' loosely, Hamlet's condition may truly be called disease. No exertion of will could have dispelled it. Even if he had been able at once to do the bidding of the Ghost he would doubtless have still remained for some time under the cloud. It would be absurdly unjust to call *Hamlet* a study of melancholy, but it contains such a study.

But this melancholy is something very different from insanity, in anything like the usual meaning of that word. No doubt it might develop into insanity. The longing for death might become an irresistible impulse to self-destruction; the disorder of feeling and will might extend to sense and intellect; delusions might arise; and the man might become, as we say, incapable and irresponsible. But Hamlet's melancholy is some way from this condition. It is a totally different thing from the madness which he feigns; and he never, when alone or in company with Horatio alone, exhibits the signs of that madness. Nor is the dramatic use of this melancholy, again, open to the objections which would justly be made to the portrayal of an insanity which brought the hero to a tragic end. The man who suffers as Hamlet suffers—and thousands go about their business suffering thus in greater or less degree—is considered irresponsible neither by other people nor by himself: he is only too keenly conscious of his responsibility. He is therefore, so far, quite capable of being a tragic agent, which an insane person, at any rate according to Shakespeare's practice, is not. And, finally, Hamlet's state is not one which a healthy mind is unable sufficiently to imagine. It is probably not further from average experience, nor more difficult to realise, than the great tragic passions of Othello, Antony or Macbeth.

Let me try to show now, briefly, how much this melancholy accounts for.

It accounts for the main fact, Hamlet's inaction. For the *immediate* cause of that is simply that his habitual feeling is one of disgust at life and everything in it, himself included,—a disgust which varies in intensity, rising at times into a longing for death, sinking often into weary apathy, but is never dispelled for more than brief intervals. Such a state of feeling is inevitably adverse to *any* kind of decided action; the body is inert, the mind indifferent or worse; its response is, 'it does not matter,' 'it is not worth while,' 'it is no good.' And the action required of Hamlet is very exceptional. It is violent, dangerous, difficult to accomplish perfectly, on one side repulsive to a man of honour and sensitive feeling, on another side involved in a certain mystery (here come in thus, in their subordinate place, various causes of inaction assigned by various theories). These obstacles would not suffice to prevent Hamlet from acting, if his state were normal; and against them there operate, even in his morbid state, healthy and positive feelings, love of his father, loathing of his uncle, desire of revenge, desire to do duty. But the retarding motives acquire an unnatural strength because they have an ally in something far stronger than themselves, the melancholic disgust and apathy; while the healthy motives, emerging with difficulty from the central mass of diseased feeling, rapidly sink back into it and 'lose the name of action.'

We *see* them doing so; and sometimes the process is quite simple, no analytical reflection on the deed intervening between the outburst of passion and the relapse into melancholy. But this melancholy is perfectly consistent also with that incessant dissection of the task assigned, of which the Schlegel-Coleridge theory makes so much. For those endless questions (as we may imagine them), 'Was I deceived by the Ghost? How am I to do the deed? When? Where? What will be the consequence of attempting it—success, my death, utter misunderstanding, mere mischief to the State? Can it be right to do it, or noble to kill a defenceless man? What is the good of doing it in such a world as this?'— all this, and whatever else passed in a sickening round through Hamlet's mind, was not the healthy and right deliberation of a man with such a task, but otiose thinking hardly deserving the name of thought, an unconscious weaving of pretexts for inaction, aimless tossings on a sick bed, symptoms of melancholy which only increased it by deepening self-contempt.

Again, *(a)* this state accounts for Hamlet's energy as well as for his lassitude, those quick decided actions of his being the outcome of a nature normally far from passive, now suddenly stimulated, and producing healthy impulses which work themselves out before they have time to subside. *(b)* It accounts for the evidently keen satisfaction which some of these actions give to him. He arranges the play-scene with lively interest, and exults in its success, not really because it brings him nearer to his goal, but partly because it has hurt his enemy and partly because it has demonstrated his own skill (III.ii.252–270). He looks forward almost with glee to countermining the King's designs in sending him away (III.iv.209–213), and looks back with obvious satisfaction, even with pride, to the address and vigour he displayed on the voyage (V.ii.1–55). These were not *the* action on which his morbid self-feeling had centred; he feels in them his old force, and escapes in them from his disgust. *(c)* It accounts for the pleasure with which he meets old acquaintances, like his 'school-fellows' or the actors. The former observed (and we can observe) in him a 'kind of joy' at first, though it is followed by 'much forcing of his disposition' as he attempts to keep this joy and his courtesy alive in spite of the misery which so soon returns upon him and the suspicion he is forced to feel. *(d)* It accounts no less for the painful features of his character as seen in the play, his almost savage irritability on the one hand, and on the other his self-absorption, his callousness, his insensibility to the fates of those whom he despises, and to the feelings even of those whom he loves. These are frequent symptoms of such melancholy, and *(e)* they sometimes alternate, as they do in Hamlet, with bursts of transitory, almost hysterical, and quite fruitless emotion. It is to these last (of which a part of the soliloquy, 'O what a rogue,' gives a good example) that Hamlet alludes when, to the Ghost, he speaks of himself as 'lapsed in *passion*,' and it is doubtless partly his conscious weakness in regard to them that inspires his praise of Horatio as a man who is not 'passion's slave.'

Finally, Hamlet's melancholy accounts for two things which seem to be explained by nothing else. The first of these is his apathy or 'lethargy.' We are bound to consider the evidence which the text supplies of this, though it is usual to ignore it. When Hamlet mentions, as one possible cause of his inaction, his 'thinking too precisely on the event,' he mentions another, 'bestial oblivion'; and the thing against which he inveighs in the greater part of that soliloquy (IV.iv.) is not the excess or the misuse of reason (which for him here and always is god-like), but this *bestial* oblivion or '*dullness*,' this 'letting all *sleep*,' this allowing of heaven-sent reason to 'fust unused':

> *What is a man,*
> *If his chief good and market of his time*
> *Be but to sleep and feed? a beast, no more.*

So, in the soliloquy in II.ii. he accuses himself of being 'a *dull* and muddy-mettled rascal,' who 'peaks [mopes] like John-a-dreams, unpregnant of his cause,' dully indifferent to his cause. So, when the Ghost appears to him the second time, he accuses himself of being tardy and lapsed in *time*; and the Ghost speaks of his purpose being almost *blunted*, and bids him not to *forget* (cf. 'oblivion'). And so, what is emphasized in those undramatic but significant speeches of the player-king and of Claudius [III.ii.170 ff., IV.vii.108ff.] is the mere dying away of purpose or of love. Surely what all this points to is not a condition of excessive but useless mental activity (indeed there is, in reality, curiously little about that in the text), but rather one of dull, apathetic, brooding gloom, in which Hamlet, so far from analysing his duty, is not thinking of it at all, but for the time literally *forgets* it. It seems to me we are driven to think of Hamlet *chiefly* thus during the long time which elapsed between the appearance of the Ghost and the events presented in the Second Act. The Ghost, in fact, had more reason than we suppose at first for leaving with Hamlet as his parting injunction the command, 'Remember me,' and for greeting him, on reappearing, with the command, 'Do not forget,' These little things in Shakespeare are not accidents.

The second trait which is fully explained only by Hamlet's melancholy is his own inability to understand why he delays. This emerges in a marked degree when an occasion like the player's emotion or the sight of Fortinbras's army stings Hamlet into shame at his inaction. '*Why*,' he asks himself in genuine bewilderment, 'do I linger? Can the cause be cowardice? Can it be sloth? Can it be thinking too precisely of the event? And does *that* again mean cowardice? What is it that makes me sit idle when I feel it is shameful to do so, and when I have *cause, and will, and strength, and means,* to act?' A man irresolute merely because he was considering a proposed action too minutely would not feel this bewilderment. A man might feel it whose conscience secretly condemned the act which his explicit consciousness approved; but we have seen that there is no sufficient evidence to justify us in conceiving Hamlet thus. These are the questions of a man stimulated for the moment to shake off the weight of his melancholy, and, because for the moment he is free from it, unable to understand the paralysing pressure which it exerts at other times.

I have dwelt thus at length on Hamlet's melancholy because, from the psychological point of view, it is the centre of the tragedy, and to omit it from consideration or to underrate its intensity is to make Shakespeare's story unintelligible. But the psychological point of view is not equivalent to the tragic; and, having once given its due weight to the fact of Hamlet's melancholy, we may freely admit, or rather may be anxious to insist, that this pathological condition would excite but little, if any, tragic interest if it were not the condition of a nature distinguished by that speculative genius on which the Schlegel-Coleridge type of theory lays stress. Such theories misinterpret the connection between that genius and Hamlet's failure, but still it is this connection which gives to his story its peculiar fascination and makes it appear (if the phrase may be allowed) as the symbol of a tragic mystery inherent in human nature. Wherever this mystery touches us, wherever we are forced to feel the wonder and awe of man's godlike 'apprehension' and his 'thoughts that wander through eternity,' and at the same time are forced to see him powerless in his petty sphere of action, and powerless (it would appear) from the very divinity of his thought, we remember Hamlet. And this is the reason why, in the great ideal movement which began towards the close of the eighteenth century, this tragedy acquired a position unique among Shakespeare's dramas, and shared only by Goethe's *Faust*. It was not that *Hamlet* is Shakespeare's greatest tragedy or most perfect work of art; it was that *Hamlet* most brings home to us at once the sense of the soul's infinity, and the sense of the doom which not only circumscribes that infinity but appears to be its offspring.

D. H. LAWRENCE

[An Aversion from Hamlet]†

* * *

I had always felt an aversion from Hamlet: a creeping, unclean thing he seems, on the stage, whether he is Forbes Robertson[1] or anybody else.

† From *D. H. Lawrence and Italy* by D. H. Lawrence. Copyright 1921 by Thomas Seltzer, Inc. Copyright renewed 1949 by Frieda Lawrence. Reprinted by permission of the publisher, Viking Penguin, a division of Penguin Books USA Inc.

and of Laurence Pollinger, Ltd.
1. Sir Johnston Forbes-Robertson (1853–1937), famous for his performances of Shakespearean roles on the London stage [*Editor*].

His nasty poking and sniffing at his mother, his setting traps for the King, his conceited perversion with Ophelia make him always intolerable. The character is repulsive in its conception, based on self-dislike and a spirit of disintegration.

There is, I think, this strain of cold dislike, or self-dislike, through much of the Renaissance art, and through all the later Shakespeare. In Shakespeare it is a kind of corruption in the flesh and a conscious revolt from this. A sense of corruption in the flesh makes Hamlet frenzied, for he will never admit that it is his own flesh. Leonardo da Vinci is the same, but Leonardo loves the corruption maliciously. Michael Angelo rejects any feeling of corruption, he stands by the flesh, the flesh only. It is the corresponding reaction, but in the opposite direction. * * *

Except in the 'great' speeches, * * * Hamlet suffered the extremity of physical self-loathing, loathing of his own flesh. The play is the statement of the most significant philosophic position of the Renaissance. Hamlet is far more even than Orestes, his prototype, a mental creature, anti-physical, anti-sensual. The whole drama is the tragedy of the convulsed reaction of the mind from the flesh, of the spirit from the self, the reaction from the great aristocratic to the great democratic principle.

An ordinary instinctive man, in Hamlet's position, would either have set about murdering his uncle, by reflex action, or else would have gone right away. There would have been no need for Hamlet to murder his mother. It would have been sufficient blood-vengeance if he had killed his uncle. But that is the statement according to the aristocratic principle.

Orestes was in the same position, but the same position two thousand years earlier, with two thousand years of experience wanting. So that the question was not so intricate in him as in Hamlet, he was not nearly so conscious. The whole Greek life was based on the idea of the supremacy of the self, and the self was always male. Orestes was his father's child, he would be the same whatever mother he had. The mother was but the vehicle, the soil in which the paternal seed was planted. When Clytemnestra murdered Agamemnon, it was as if a common individual murdered God, to the Greek.

But Agamemnon, King and Lord, was not infallible. He was fallible. He had sacrificed Iphigenia for the sake of glory in war, for the fulfilment of the superb idea of self, but on the other hand he had made cruel dissension for the sake of the concubines captured in war. The paternal flesh was fallible, ungodlike. It lusted after meaner pursuits than glory, war, and slaying, it was not faithful to the highest idea of the self. Orestes was driven mad by the furies of his mother, because of the justice that they represented. Nevertheless, he was in the end exculpated. The third play of the trilogy is almost foolish, with its prating gods. But it means that, according to the Greek conviction, Orestes was right and Clytemnestra entirely wrong. But for all that, the infallible King, the infallible male Self, is dead in Orestes, killed by the furies of Clytemnestra. He gains his peace of mind after the revulsion from his own physical fallibility, but he will never be an unquestioned lord, as Agamemnon was. Orestes is left at peace, neutralized. He is the beginning of non-aristocratic Christianity.

Hamlet's father, the King, is, like Agamemnon, a warrior-king. But, unlike Agamemnon, he is blameless with regard to Gertrude. Yet Gertrude, like Clytemnestra, is the potential murderer of her husband, as Lady Macbeth is murderess, as the daughters of Lear. The women murder the supreme male, the ideal Self, the King and Father.

This is the tragic position Shakespeare must dwell upon. The woman rejects, repudiates the ideal Self which the male represents to her. The supreme representative, King and Father, is murdered by the Wife and the Daughters.

What is the reason? Hamlet goes mad in a revulsion of rage and nausea. Yet the women-murderers only represent some ultimate judgment in his own soul. At the bottom of his own soul Hamlet has decided that the Self in its supremacy, Father and King, must die. It is a suicidal decision for his involuntary soul to have arrived at. Yet it is inevitable. The great religious, philosophic tide, which had been swelling all through the Middle Ages, had brought him there.

The question, to be or not to be, which Hamlet puts himself, does not mean, to live or not to live. It is not the simple human being who puts himself the question, it is the supreme I, King and Father. To be or not to be King, Father, in the Self supreme? And the decision is, not to be.

It is the inevitable philosophic conclusion of all the Renaissance. The deepest impulse in man, the religious impulse, is the desire to be immortal, or infinite, consummated. And this impulse is satisfied in fulfilment of an idea, a steady progression. In this progression man is satisfied, he seems to have reached his goal, this infinity, this immortality, this eternal being, with every step nearer which he takes.

And so, according to his idea of fulfilment, man establishes the whole order of life. If my fulfilment is the fulfilment and establishment of the unknown divine Self which I am, then I shall proceed in the realizing of the greatest idea of the self, the highest conception of the I, my order of life will be kingly, imperial, aristocratic. The body politic also will culminate in this divinity of the flesh, this body imbued with glory, invested with divine power and might, the King, the Emperor. In the body politic also I shall desire a king, an emperor, a tyrant, glorious, mighty, in whom I see myself consummated and fulfilled. This is inevitable!

But during the Middle Ages, struggling within this pagan, original transport, the transport of the Ego, was a small dissatisfaction, a small contrary desire. Amid the pomp of kings and popes was the Child Jesus and the Madonna. Jesus the King gradually dwindled down. There was Jesus the Child, helpless, at the mercy of all the world. And there was Jesus crucified.

The old transport, the old fulfilment of the Ego, the Davidian ecstasy, the assuming of all power and glory unto the self, the becoming infinite through the absorption of all into the Ego, this gradually became unsatisfactory. This was not the infinite, this was not immortality. This was eternal death, this was damnation.

The monk rose up with his opposite ecstasy, the Christian ecstasy. There was a death to die: the flesh, the self, must die, so that the spirit should rise again immortal, eternal, infinite. I am dead unto myself, but I live in the Infinite. The finite Me is no more, only the Infinite, the Eternal, is.

At the Renaissance this great half-truth overcame the other great half-truth. The Christian Infinite, reached by a process of abnegation, a process of being absorbed, dissolved, diffused into the great Not-Self, supplanted the old pagan Infinite, wherein the self like a root threw out branches and radicles which embraced the whole universe, became the Whole.

There is only one Infinite, the world now cried, there is the great Christian Infinite of renunciation and consummation in the not-self. The other, that old pride, is damnation. The sin of sins is Pride; it is the way to total damnation. Whereas the pagans based their life on pride.

And according to this new Infinite, reached through renunciation and dissolving into the Others, the Neighbour, man must build up his actual form of life. With Savonarola and Martin Luther the living Church actually transformed itself, for the Roman Church was still pagan. Henry VIII. simply said, 'There is no Church, there is only the State.' But with Shakespeare the transformation had reached the State also. The King, the Father, the representative of the Consummate Self, the maximum of all life, the symbol of the consummate being, the becoming Supreme, Godlike, Infinite, he must perish and pass away. This Infinite was not infinite, this consummation was not consummate, all this was fallible, false. It was rotten, corrupt. It must go. But Shakespeare was also the thing itself. Hence his horror, his frenzy, his self-loathing.

The King, the Emperor is killed in the soul of man, the old order of life is over, the old tree is dead at the root. So said Shakespeare. It was finally enacted in Cromwell. Charles I. took up the old position of kingship by divine right. Like Hamlet's father, he was blameless otherwise. But as representative of the old form of life, which mankind now hated with frenzy, he must be cut down, removed. It was a symbolic act.

The world, our world of Europe, had now really turned, swung round to a new goal, a new idea, the Infinite reached through the omission of Self. God is all that which is Not-Me. I am consummate when my Self, the resistant solid, is reduced and diffused into all that which is Not-Me:

my neighbour, my enemy, the great Otherness. Then I am perfect.

And from this belief the world began gradually to form a new State, a new body politic, in which the Self should be removed. There should be no king, no lords, no aristocrats. The world continued in its religious belief, beyond the French Revolution, beyond the great movement of Shelley and Godwin. There should be no Self. That which was supreme was that which was Not-Me, the other. The governing factor in the State was the idea of the good of others; that is, the Common Good. And the *vital* governing idea in the State has been this idea since Cromwell.

Before Cromwell the idea was 'For the King,' because every man saw himself consummated in the King. After Cromwell the idea was 'For the good of my neighbour,' or 'For the good of the people,' or 'For the good of the whole.' This has been our ruling idea, by which we have more or less lived.

Now this has failed. Now we say that the Christian Infinite is not infinite. We are tempted, like Nietzsche, to return back to the old pagan Infinite, to say that is supreme. Or we are inclined, like the English and the Pragmatist, to say, 'There is no Infinite, there is no Absolute. The only Absolute is expediency, the only reality is sensation and momentariness.' But we may say this, even act on it, *à la Sanine*. But we never believe it.

What is really Absolute is the mystic Reason which connects both Infinites, the Holy Ghost that relates both natures of God. If we now wish to make a living State, we must build it up to the idea of the Holy Spirit, the supreme Relationship. We must say, the pagan Infinite is infinite, the Christian Infinite is infinite: these are our two Consummations; in both of these we are consummated. But that which relates them alone is absolute.

This Absolute of the Holy Ghost we may call Truth or Justice or Right. These are partial names, indefinite and unsatisfactory unless there be kept the knowledge of the two Infinites, pagan and Christian, which they go between. When both are there, they are like a superb bridge, on which one can stand and know the whole world, my world, the two halves of the universe.

* * *

To be or not to be was the question for Hamlet to settle. It is no longer our question, at least, not in the same sense. When it is a question of death, the fashionable young suicide declares that his self-destruction is the final proof of his own incontrovertible being. And as for not-being in our public life, we have achieved it as much as ever we want to, as much as is necessary. Whilst in private life there is a swing back to paltry selfishness as a creed. And in the war there is the position of neutralization and nothingness. It is a question of knowing how *to be*, and how *not to be*, for we must fulfil both.

*   *   *

For the soliloquies of Hamlet are as deep as the soul of man can go, in one direction, and as sincere as the Holy Spirit itself in their essence. But thank heaven, the bog into which Hamlet struggled is almost surpassed.

*   *   *

T. S. ELIOT

Hamlet and His Problems†

Few critics have ever admitted that *Hamlet* the play is the primary problem, and Hamlet the character only secondary. And Hamlet the character has had an especial temptation for that most dangerous type of critic: the critic with a mind which is naturally of the creative order, but which through some weakness in creative power exercises itself in criticism instead. These minds often find in Hamlet a vicarious existence for their own artistic realization. Such a mind had Goethe, who made of Hamlet a Werther; and such had Coleridge, who made of Hamlet a Coleridge; and probably neither of these men in writing about Hamlet remembered that his first business was to study a work of art. The kind of criticism that Goethe and Coleridge produced, in writing of Hamlet, is the most misleading kind possible. For they both possessed unquestionable critical insight, and both make their critical aberrations the more plausible by the substitution—of their own Hamlet for Shakespeare's—which their creative gift effects. We should be thankful that Walter Pater did not fix his attention on this play.

Two writers of our time, Mr. J. M. Robertson and Professor Stoll of the University of Minnesota, have issued small books which can be praised for moving in the other direction. Mr. Stoll performs a service in recalling to our attention the labours of the critics of the seventeenth and eighteenth centuries,[1] observing that they knew less about psychology than more recent Hamlet critics, but they were nearer in spirit to Shakespeare's art; and as they insisted on the importance of the effect of the whole rather than on the importance of the leading character, they were nearer, in their old-fashioned way, to the secret of dramatic art in general.

---

† "Hamlet and His Problems" from *Selected Essays*, New Edition by T. S. Eliot, copyright 1950 by Harcourt Brace Jovanovich, Inc. and renewed 1978 by Esme Valerie Eliot, reprinted by permission of Harcourt Brace Jovanovich and Faber and Faber, Ltd.
1. I have never, by the way, seen a cogent refutation of Thomas Rymer's objections to *Othello*.

Qua work of art, the work of art cannot be interpreted; there is nothing to interpret; we can only criticise it according to standards, in comparison to other works of art; and for "interpretation" the chief task is the presentation of relevant historical facts which the reader is not assumed to know. Mr. Robertson points out, very pertinently, how critics have failed in their "interpretation" of *Hamlet* by ignoring what ought to be very obvious: that *Hamlet* is a stratification, that it represents the efforts of a series of men, each making what he could out of the work of his predecessors. The *Hamlet* of Shakespeare will appear to us very differently if, instead of treating the whole action of the play as due to Shakespeare's design, we perceive his *Hamlet* to be superposed upon much cruder material which persists even in the final form.

We know that there was an older play by Thomas Kyd, that extraordinary dramatic (if not poetic) genius who was in all probability the author of two plays so dissimilar as *The Spanish Tragedy* and *Arden of Feversham*; and what this play was like we can guess from three clues: from *The Spanish Tragedy* itself, from the tale of Belleforest upon which Kyd's *Hamlet* must have been based, and from a version acted in Germany in Shakespeare's lifetime which bears strong evidence of having been adapted from the earlier, not from the later, play. From these three sources it is clear that in the earlier play the motive was a revenge-motive simply; that the action or delay is caused, as in *The Spanish Tragedy*, solely by the difficulty of assassinating a monarch surrounded by guards; and that the "madness" of Hamlet was feigned in order to escape suspicion, and successfully. In the final play of Shakespeare, on the other hand, there is a motive which is more important than that of revenge, and which explicitly "blunts" the latter; the delay in revenge is unexplained on grounds of necessity or expediency; and the effect of the "madness" is not to lull but to arouse the king's suspicion. The alteration is not complete enough, however, to be convincing. Furthermore, there are verbal parallels so close to *The Spanish Tragedy* as to leave no doubt that in places Shakespeare was merely *revising* the text of Kyd. And finally there are unexplained scenes—the Polonius-Laertes and the Polonius-Reynaldo scenes—for which there is little excuse; these scenes are not in the verse style of Kyd, and not beyond doubt in the style of Shakespeare. These Mr. Robertson believes to be scenes in the original play of Kyd reworked by a third hand, perhaps Chapman, before Shakespeare touched the play. And he concludes, with very strong show of reason, that the original play of Kyd was, like certain other revenge plays, in two parts of five acts each. The upshot of Mr. Robertson's examination is, we believe, irrefragable: that Shakespeare's *Hamlet*, so far as it is Shakespeare's, is a play dealing with the effect of a mother's guilt upon her son, and that Shakespeare was unable to impose this motive successfully upon the "intractable" material of the old play.

Of the intractability there can be no doubt. So far from being Shakespeare's masterpiece, the play is most certainly an artistic failure. In several ways the play is puzzling, and disquieting as is none of the others. Of all the plays it is the longest and is possibly the one on which Shakespeare spent most pains; and yet he has left in it superfluous and inconsistent scenes which even hasty revision should have noticed. The versification is variable. Lines like

> Look, the morn, in russet mantle clad,
> Walks o'er the dew of yon high eastern hill,

are of the Shakespeare of *Romeo and Juliet*. The lines in Act V, sc. ii,

> Sir, in my heart there was a kind of fighting
> That would not let me sleep . . .
> Up from my cabin,
> My sea-gown scarf'd about me, in the dark
> Grop'd I to find out them: had my desire;
> Finger'd their packet;

are of his quite mature. Both workmanship and thought are in an unstable position. We are surely justified in attributing the play, with that other profoundly interesting play of "intractable" material and astonishing versification, *Measure for Measure*, to a period of crisis, after which follow the tragic successes which culminate in *Coriolanus*. *Coriolanus* may be not as "interesting" as *Hamlet*, but it is, with *Antony and Cleopatra*, Shakespeare's most assured artistic success. And probably more people have thought *Hamlet* a work of art because they found it interesting, than have found it interesting because it is a work of art. It is the "Mona Lisa" of literature.

The grounds of *Hamlet's* failure are not immediately obvious. Mr. Robertson is undoubtedly correct in concluding that the essential emotion of the play is the feeling of a son towards a guilty mother:

> [Hamlet's] tone is that of one who has suffered tortures on the score of his mother's degradation. . . . The guilt of a mother is an almost intolerable motive for drama, but it had to be maintained and emphasized to supply a psychological solution, or rather a hint of one.

This, however, is by no means the whole story. It is not merely the "guilt of a mother" that cannot be handled as Shakespeare handled the suspicion of Othello, the infatuation of Antony, or the pride of Coriolanus. The subject might conceivably have expanded into a tragedy like these, intelligible, self-complete, in the sunlight. *Hamlet*, like the sonnets, is full of some stuff that the writer could not drag to light, contemplate, or manipulate into art. And when we search for this feeling, we find it, as in the sonnets, very difficult to localize. You cannot point to it in the speeches; indeed, if you examine the two famous soliloquies you see the versification of Shakespeare, but a content which might be claimed by another, perhaps by the author of *The Revenge of Bussy d'Ambois*, Act V, sc. i. We find Shakespeare's *Hamlet* not in the action, not in any quotations that we might select, so much as in an unmistakable tone which is unmistakably not in the earlier play.

The only way of expressing emotion in the form of art is by finding an "objective correlative"; in other words, a set of objects, a situation, a chain of events which shall be the formula of that *particular* emotion; such that when the external facts, which must terminate in sensory experience, are given, the emotion is immediately evoked. If you examine any of Shakespeare's more successful tragedies, you will find this exact equivalence; you will find that the state of mind of Lady Macbeth walking in her sleep has been communicated to you by a skilful accumulation of imagined sensory impressions; the words of Macbeth on hearing of his wife's death strike us as if, given the sequence of events, these words were automatically released by the last event in the series. The artistic "inevitability" lies in this complete adequacy of the external to the emotion; and this is precisely what is deficient in *Hamlet*. Hamlet (the man) is dominated by an emotion which is inexpressible, because it is in *excess* of the facts as they appear. And the supposed identity of Hamlet with his author is genuine to this point: that Hamlet's bafflement at the absence of objective equivalent to his feelings is a prolongation of the bafflement of his creator in the face of his artistic problem. Hamlet is up against the difficulty that his disgust is occasioned by his mother, but that his mother is not an adequate equivalent for it; his disgust envelops and exceeds her. It is thus a feeling which he cannot understand; he cannot objectify it, and it therefore remains to poison life and obstruct action. None of the possible actions can satisfy it; and nothing that Shakespeare can do with the plot can express Hamlet for him. And it must be noticed that the very nature of the *données* of the problem precludes objective equivalence. To have heightened the criminality of Gertrude would have been to provide the formula for a totally different emotion in Hamlet; it is just *because* her character is so negative and insignificant that she arouses in Hamlet the feeling which she is incapable of representing.

The "madness" of Hamlet lay to Shakespeare's hand; in the earlier play a simple ruse, and to the end, we may presume, understood as a ruse by the audience. For Shakespeare it is less than madness and more than feigned. The levity of Hamlet, his repetition of phrase, his puns, are not part of a deliberate plan of dissimulation, but a form of emotional relief. In the character Hamlet it is the buffoonery of an emotion which can find no outlet in action; in the dramatist it is the buffoonery of an emotion which he cannot express in art. The intense feeling, ecstatic or terrible, without an object or exceeding its object, is something which every person of sensibility has known; it is doubtless a subject of study for pathologists. It often occurs in adolescence: the ordinary person puts these feelings to sleep, or trims down his feelings to fit the business world; the artist keeps them alive by his ability to intensify the world to his emotions. The Hamlet of Laforgue is an adolescent; the Hamlet of Shakespeare is not, he has not that explanation and excuse. We must simply admit that here Shakespeare tackled a problem which proved too much for him. Why he attempted it at all is an insoluble puzzle; under compulsion of what experience he attempted to express the inexpressibly horrible, we cannot ever know. We need a great many facts in his biography; and we should like to know whether, and when, and after or at the same time as what personal experience, he read Montaigne, II. xii. *Apologie de Raimond Sebond*. We should have, finally, to know something which is by hypothesis unknowable, for we assume it to be an experience which, in the manner indicated, exceeded the facts. We should have to understand things which Shakespeare did not understand himself.

✲   ✲   ✲

G. WILSON KNIGHT

The Embassy of Death: An Essay on *Hamlet*†

✲   ✲   ✲

It is usual in Shakespeare's plays for the main theme to be reflected in subsidiary incidents, persons, and detailed suggestion throughout. Now the theme of *Hamlet* is death. Life that is bound for the disintegration of the grave, love that does not survive the loved one's life—both, in their insistence on death as the primary fact of nature, are branded on the mind of Hamlet, burned into it, searing it with agony. The bereavement of Hamlet and his consequent mental agony bordering on madness is mirrored in the bereavement of Ophelia and her madness. The death of the Queen's love is reflected in the swift passing of the love of the Player-Queen, in the 'Murder of Gonzago.' Death is over the whole play. Polonius and Ophelia die during the action, and Ophelia is buried before our eyes. Hamlet arranges the deaths of Rosencrantz and Guildenstern. The plot is set in motion by the murder of Hamlet's father, and the play opens with the apparition of the Ghost:

> What may this mean,
> That thou, dead corse, again in complete steel

† From *The Wheel of Fire*, by G. Wilson Knight (London: Methuen & Co., Ltd., 1930), Copyright © 1930 by Methuen & Co., Ltd. Reprinted by permission. Page numbers given in parentheses refer to this Norton Critical Edition of *Hamlet*.

Revisit'st thus the glimpses of the moon,
Making night hideous; and we fools of nature
So horridly to shake our dispositions
With thoughts beyond the reaches of our souls? (19)

Those first scenes strike the note of the play—death. We hear of terrors beyond the grave, from the Ghost (21) and from the meditations of Hamlet (45). We hear of horrors in the grave from Hamlet whose mind is obsessed with hideous thoughts of the body's decay. Hamlet's dialogue with the King about the dead Polonius (68–69) is painful; and the graveyard meditations, though often beautiful, are remorselessly realistic. Hamlet holds Yorick's skull:

> *Hamlet.* . . . . Now, get you to my lady's chamber and tell her, let her paint an inch thick, to this favour she must come; make her laugh at that. Prithee, Horatio, tell me one thing.
> *Horatio.* What's that, my lord?
> *Hamlet.* Dost thou think Alexander looked o' this fashion i' the earth?
> *Horatio.* E'en so.
> *Hamlet.* And smelt so? pah!   (88)

The general thought of death, intimately related to the predominating human theme, the pain in Hamlet's mind, is thus suffused through the whole play. And yet the play, as a whole, scarcely gives us that sense of blackness and the abysms of spiritual evil which we find in *Macbeth*; nor is there the universal gloom of *King Lear*. This is due partly to the difference in the technique of *Hamlet* from that of *Macbeth* or *King Lear*. Macbeth, the protagonist and heroic victim of evil, rises gigantic from the murk of an evil universe; Lear, the king of suffering, towers over a universe that itself toils in pain. Thus in *Macbeth* and *King Lear* the predominating imaginative atmospheres are used not to contrast with the mental universe of the hero, but to aid and support it, as it were, with similarity, to render realistic the extravagant and daring effects of volcanic passion to which the poet allows his protagonist to give voice. We are forced by the attendant personification, the verbal colour, the symbolism and events of the play as a whole, to feel the hero's suffering, to see with his eyes. But in *Hamlet* this is not so. We need not see through Hamlet's eyes. Though the idea of death is recurrent through the play, it is not implanted in the minds of other persons as is the consciousness of evil throughout *Macbeth* and the consciousness of suffering throughout *King Lear*. Except for the original murder of Hamlet's father, the *Hamlet* universe is one of healthy and robust life, good-nature, humour, romantic strength, and welfare: against this background is the figure of Hamlet pale with the consciousness of death. He is the ambassador of death walking amid life. The effect is at first primarily one of separation. But it is to be noted that the consciousness of death, and consequent bitterness, cruelty, and inaction, in Hamlet not only grows in his own mind disintegrating it as we watch, but also spreads its effects outward among the other persons like a blighting disease, and, as the play progresses, by its very passivity and negation of purpose, insidiously undermines the health of the state, and adds victim to victim until at the end the stage is filled with corpses. It is, as it were, a nihilistic birth in the consciousness of Hamlet that spreads its deadly venom around. That Hamlet is originally blameless, that the King is originally guilty, may well be granted. But, if we refuse to be diverted from a clear vision by questions of praise and blame, responsibility and causality, and watch only the actions and reactions of the persons as they appear, we shall observe a striking reversal of the usual commentary.

If we are to attain a true interpretation of Shakespeare we must work from a centre of consciousness near that of the creative instinct of the poet. We must think less in terms of causality and more in terms of imaginative impact. Now Claudius is not drawn as wholly evil—far from it. We see the government of Denmark working smoothly. Claudius shows every sign of being an excellent diplomatist and king. He is troubled by young Fortinbras, and dispatches ambassadors to the sick King of Norway demanding that he suppress the raids of his nephew. His speech to the ambassadors bears the stamp of clear and exact thought and an efficient and confident control of affairs:

> . . . and we here dispatch
> You, good Cornelius, and you, Voltimand,
> For bearers of this greeting to old Norway;
> Giving to you no further personal power
> To business with the king, more than the scope
> Of these delated articles allow.
> Farewell, and let your haste commend your duty. (8–9)

The ambassadors soon return successful. Claudius listens to their reply, receives the King of Norway's letter, and hears that young Fortinbras desires a free pass through Denmark to lead his soldiers against the Poles. Claudius answers:

> It likes us well;
> And at our more consider'd time we'll read,
> Answer, and think upon this business.
> Meantime we thank you for your well-took labour:
> Go to your rest; at night we'll feast together:
> Most welcome home! (31)

Tact has found an easy settlement where arms and opposition might have wasted the strength of Denmark. Notice his reservation of detailed attention when once he knows the main issues are clear; the courteous

yet dignified attitude to his subordinates and the true leader's consideration for their comfort; and the invitation to the feast. The impression
given by these speeches is one of quick efficiency—the efficiency of the
man who can dispose of business without unnecessary circumstance,
and so leaves himself time for enjoying the good things of life: a man
kindly, confident, and fond of pleasure.

Throughout the first half of the play Claudius is the typical kindly
uncle, besides being a good king. His advice to Hamlet about his exaggerated mourning for his father's death is admirable common sense:

> Fie! 'Tis a fault to Heaven,
> A fault against the dead, a fault to nature,
> To reason most absurd; whose common theme
> Is death of fathers, and who still hath cried,
> From the first corse, till he that died to-day,
> 'This must be so.'   (10)

It is the advice of worldly common sense opposed to the extreme misery
of a sensitive nature paralysed by the facts of death and unfaithfulness.
This contrast points the relative significance of the King and his court to
Hamlet. They are of the world—with their crimes, their follies, their
shallownesses, their pomp and glitter; they are of humanity, with all its
failings, it is true, but yet of humanity. They assert the importance of
human life, they believe in it, in themselves. Whereas Hamlet is inhuman, since he has seen through the tinsel of life and love, he believes
in nothing, not even himself, except the memory of a ghost, and his
blackrobed presence is a reminder to everyone of the fact of death. There
is no question but that Hamlet is right. The King's smiles hide murder,
his mother's love for her new consort is unfaithfulness to Hamlet's father,
Ophelia has deserted Hamlet at the hour of his need. Hamlet's philosophy may be inevitable, blameless, and irrefutable. But it is the negation
of life. It is death. Hence Hamlet is a continual fear to Claudius, a
reminder of his crime. It is a mistake to consider Claudius as a hardened
criminal. When Polonius remarks on the hypocrisy of mankind, he
murmurs to himself:

> O, 'tis too true!
> How smart a lash that speech doth give my conscience!
> The harlot's cheek, beautied with plastering art,
> Is not more ugly to the thing that helps it
> Than is my deed to my most painted word:
> O heavy burthen!   (45)

Again, Hamlet's play wrenches his soul with remorse—primarily not
fear of Hamlet, as one might expect, but a genuine remorse—and gives
us that most beautiful prayer of a stricken soul beginning, 'Oh, my offence
is rank, it smells to Heaven' (58–59):

> . . . What if this cursed hand
> Were thicker than itself with brother's blood,
> Is there not rain enough in the sweet heavens
> To wash it white as snow? Whereto serves mercy
> But to confront the visage of offence?

He fears that his prayer is worthless. He is still trammelled by the enjoy-
ment of the fruits of his crime. 'My fault is past,' he cries. But what does
that avail, since he has his crown and his queen still, the prizes of murder? His dilemma is profound and raises the problem I am pointing in
this essay. Claudius, as he appears in the play, is not a criminal. He is—
strange as it may seem—a good and gentle king, enmeshed by the chain
of causality linking him with his crime. And this chain he might, perhaps, have broken except for Hamlet, and all would have been well.
But, granted the presence of Hamlet—which Claudius at first genuinely
desired, persuading him not to return to Wittenberg as he wished—and
granted the fact of his original crime which cannot now be altered,
Claudius can hardly be blamed for his later actions. They are forced on
him. As King, he cold scarcely be expected to do otherwise. Hamlet is
a danger to the state, even apart from his knowledge of Claudius' guilt.
He is an inhuman—or superhuman—presence, whose consciousness—
somewhat like Dostoievsky's Stavrogin—is centred on death. Like Stavrogin, he is feared by those around him. They are always trying in vain
to find out what is wrong with him. They cannot understand him. He
is a creature of another world. As King of Denmark he would have been
a thousand times more dangerous than Claudius. The end of Claudius'
prayer is pathetic:

> What then? What rests?
> Try what repentance can: what can it not?
> Yet what can it when one can not repent?
> O wretched state! O bosom black as death!
> O limed soul, that, struggling to be free,
> Art more engaged! Help, angels! make assay!
> Bow stubborn knees; and, heart with strings of steel,
> Be soft as sinews of the new-born babe!
> All may be well.   (59)

Set against this lovely prayer—the fine flower of a human soul in
anguish—is the entrance of Hamlet, the late joy of torturing the King's
conscience still written on his face, his eye a-glitter with the intoxication
of conquest, vengeance in his mind; his purpose altered only by the
devilish hope of finding a more damning moment in which to slaughter
the King, next hastening to his mother to wring her soul too. Which
then, at this moment in the play, is nearer the Kingdom of Heaven?
Whose words would be more acceptable of Jesus' God? Which is the
embodiment of spiritual good, which of evil? The question of the rela-

tive morality of Hamlet and Claudius reflects the ultimate problem of
this play.

✻　✻　✻

I have concentrated on Claudius' virtues. They are manifest. So are
his faults—his original crime, his skill in the less admirable kind of policy, treachery, and intrigue. But I would point clearly that, in the movement of the play, his faults are forced on him, and he is distinguished
by creative and wise action, a sense of purpose, benevolence, a faith in
himself and those around him, by love of his Queen:

> . . . and for myself—
> My virtue or my plague, be it either which—
> She's so conjunctive to my life and soul,
> That as the star moves not but in his sphere,
> I could not but by her.   (79)

In short he is very human. Now these are the very qualities Hamlet
lacks. Hamlet is inhuman. He has seen through humanity. And this
inhuman cynicism, however justifiable in this case on the plane of causality and individual responsibility, is a deadly and venomous thing.
Instinctively the creatures of the earth, Laertes, Polonius, Ophelia,
Rosencrantz and Guildenstern, league themselves with Claudius: they
are of his kind. They sever themselves from Hamlet. Laertes sternly
warns Ophelia against her intimacy with Hamlet, so does Polonius. They
are, in fact, all leagued against him, they are puzzled by him or fear
him: he has no friend except Horatio, and Horatio, after the Ghost scenes,
becomes a queer shadowy character who rarely gets beyond 'E'en so, my
lord', 'My lord——', and such-like phrases. The other persons are firmly
drawn, in the round, creatures of flesh and blood. But Hamlet is not of
flesh and blood, he is a spirit of penetrating intellect and cynicism and
misery, without faith in himself or anyone else, murdering his love of
Ophelia, on the brink of insanity, taking delight in cruelty, torturing
Claudius, wringing his mother's heart, a poison in the midst of the healthy
bustle of the court. He is a superman among men. And he is a superman
because he has walked and held converse with death, and his consciousness works in terms of death and the negation of cynicism. He has seen
the truth, not alone of Denmark, but of humanity, of the universe: and
the truth is evil. Thus Hamlet is an element of evil in the state of Denmark. The poison of his mental existence spreads outwards among things
of flesh and blood, like acid eating into metal. They are helpless before
his very inactivity and fall one after the other, like victims of an infec-
tious disease. They are strong with the strength of health—but the demon
of Hamlet's mind is a stronger thing than they. Futilely they try to get
him out of their country; anything to get rid of him, he is not safe. But
he goes with a cynical smile, and is no sooner gone than he is back again

in their midst, meditating in graveyards, at home with death. Not till it
has slain all, is the demon that grips Hamlet satisfied. And last it slays
Hamlet himself:

> The spirit that I have seen
>   May be the Devil . . .   (43)

It was.

It was the devil of the knowledge of death, which possesses Hamlet
and drives him from misery and pain to increasing bitterness, cynicism,
murder, and madness. He has indeed bought converse with his father's
spirit at the price of enduring and spreading Hell on earth. But however
much we may sympathize with Ophelia, with Polonius, Rosencrantz,
Guildenstern, the Queen, and Claudius, there is one reservation to be
made. It is Hamlet who is right. What he says and thinks of them is
true, and there is no fault in his logic. His own mother is indeed faith-
less, and the prettiness of Ophelia does in truth enclose a spirit as fragile
and untrustworthy as her earthly beauty; Polonius is 'a foolish prating
knave'; Rosencrantz and Guildenstern are time-servers and flatterers;
Claudius, whose benevolence hides the guilt of murder, is, by virtue of
that fact, 'a damned smiling villain'. In the same way the demon of
cynicism which is in the mind of the poet and expresses itself in the
figures of this play, has always this characteristic: it is right. One cannot
argue with the cynic. It is unwise to offer him battle. For in the warfare
of logic it will be found that he has all the guns.

*   *   *

Thus Hamlet spends a great part of his time watching, analysing, and
probing others. He unhesitatingly lances each in turn in his weakest
spot. He is usually quite merciless. But all he actually accomplishes is
to torment them all, terrorize them. They are dreadfully afraid of him.
Hamlet is so powerful. He is, as it were, the channel of a mysterious
force, a force which derives largely from his having seen through them
all. In contact with him they know their own faults: neither they nor we
should know them otherwise. He exposes faults everywhere. But he is
not tragic in the usual Shakespearian sense; there is no surge and swell
of passion pressing onward through the play to leave us, as in *King Lear*,
with the mightly crash and backwash of a tragic peace. There is not this
direct rhythm in Hamlet—there is no straight course. Instead of being
dynamic, the force of Hamlet is, paradoxically, static. Its poison is the
poison of negation, nothingness, threatening a world of positive assertion. But even this element is not the whole of Hamlet. He can speak
lovingly to his mother at one moment, and the next, in an excess of
revulsion, torment her with a withering and brutal sarcasm. One moment
he can cry:

> I loved Ophelia: forty thousand brothers
> Could not, with all their quantity of love,
> Make up my sum.   (90)

Shortly after he scorns himself for this outbreak. His mind reflects swift changes. He may for a moment or two see with the eyes of humour, gentleness, love—then suddenly the whole universe is blackened, goes out, leaves utter vacancy. This is, indeed, the secret of the play's fascination and its lack of unified and concise poetic statement. Hamlet is a dualized personality, wavering, oscillating between grace and the hell of cynicism. The plot reflects this see-saw motion; it lacks direction, pivoting on Hamlet's incertitude, and analysis holds the fascination of giddiness. Nor can Hamlet feel anything passionately for long, since passion implies purpose, and he has no one purpose for any length of time. One element in Hamlet, and that a very important one, is the negation of any passion whatsoever. His disease—or vision—is primarily one of negation, of death. Hamlet is a living death in the midst of life; that is why the play sounds the note of death so strong and sombre at the start. The Ghost was conceived throughout as a portent not kind but sinister. That sepulchral cataclysm at the beginning is the key to the whole play. *Hamlet* begins with an explosion in the first act; the rest of the play is the reverberation thereof. From the first act onwards Hamlet is, as it were, blackened, scorched by that shattering revelation. The usual process is reversed and the climax is at the start. Hamlet, already in despair, converses early with death. * * * Finally 'this fell sergeant, death' (99) arrests him too. This is his mysterious strength, ghost-begotten, before which the rest succumb. That is why this play is so rich in death—why its meaning is analysed by Hamlet in soliloquy, why Hamlet is so fascinated by the skulls the Grave-digger unearths; why so many 'casual slaughters' and 'deaths put on by cunning and forced cause' (101) disrupt the action, till we are propelled to the last holocaust of mortality and Fortinbras' comment:

> This quarry cries on havoc. O proud death,
> What feast is toward in thine eternal cell,
> That thou so many princes at a shot
> So bloodily hast struck?   (100)

The Ghost may or may not have been a 'goblin damned'; it certainly was no 'spirit of health' (19). The play ends with a dead march. The action grows out of eternity, closes in it. The ominous discharge of ordnance thus reverberates three times: once, before Hamlet sees the Ghost, and twice in Act v. The eternity of death falls as an abyss at either end, and Hamlet crosses the stage of life aureoled in its ghostly luminance.

HARLEY GRANVILLE-BARKER

The Five Acts of the Editors †

The long-accepted division of the play into five acts is not, of course, authentic. Here, as with other plays, the editors of the Folio were bent upon giving their author this classic dignity; and it may be, besides, that by 1623 theatrical practice had itself imposed this division upon such of his plays as were still being acted. In the private theaters it had commonly been the custom to divide plays into acts and to provide music for intervals. The practice of the public theaters is a matter of dispute. If they did observe act divisions—four of them—they are hardly likely to have done so more than formally unless or until they also had some entertaining means of filling the gaps.[1] It is possible that their practice changed, and this during Shakespeare's own lifetime. He certainly did not (except for one instance) think out his plays in five-act form; whatever the exigencies of its performance are to be, the play itself is an indivisible whole. It was the telling of a story; its shape would be dictated by the nature of the story and the need to make this dramatically effective. And that meant, among other things, that if there were to be breaks in its progress, one generally did better to minimize than to accentuate them; for the attention of an audience, once captured, must be held.

In the dividing-up of *Hamlet* the Folio editors for some reason get no further than *Actus Secundus*;[2] and not till the "Players' Quarto" of 1676, do we find an end made of their Act II, and a III, IV and V. That almost certainly represents the theatrical practice of the Restoration; but quite possibly it has an earlier origin in the performance of the play in private theaters about the date of the printing of the Folio. Rowe (who, for text, picks and chooses between Q2 and F1) adopts it, and later editors follow him.[3]

But, whatever its origin, it illustrates no consistent dramatic purpose on Shakespeare's part. It cannot but to some extent thwart his technique; and at one point—in the contriving of the end of a third act and a

†From *Preface to Hamlet*, by Harley Granville-Barker (New York: Hill & Wang, 1957), pp. 34–40. Copyright © 1957 by Hill & Wang. Reprinted by permission.

1. Or unless the strain upon the audience became too great. That might entail a definite pause or so for recovery; but hardly four pauses. The Elizabethans, moreover, could apparently support sieges from which their modern descendants shrink. Their sermons ran notably to length. While the plays could be acted through in two hours or a little longer, there would be no physical need for a pause.

2. To be quite accurate, they mark it *Scaena Secunda* and stop there. But scene-division is another matter. This is implicit in the text; for it depends, customarily, upon the incidence of a cleared stage.

3. It more certainly represents Restoration theatrical practice that this Quarto (of Davenant's editing, presumably) marks passages "to be omitted in representation," which are not included in the Folio's abbreviation of Q2. It will still be a homage to classical tradition; but there is no doubt, I think, that, whatever had been done earlier, the Restoration theater did observe the five-act division, either by formal or appreciable pauses in the performance.

beginning for a fourth—the offense is patent and the cobbling of the clumsiest.[4]

A unit of dramatic action for a first act—if there had to be one—was not hard to find; for the story, as Shakespeare tells it, carries us at a sustained stretch and upon a plainly indicated time-scheme to the Ghost's revelation and Hamlet's heartsick acceptance of his task. So definite an "act" is this, on both counts, that an editor is tempted to set down as definitely at the end of it: *Some weeks pass.* Now Shakespeare certainly suggests in the next scene that time has been passing; a remark of Ophelia's several scenes later makes it, in fact, a calculable two months. But, to realize this, we should need, as the line is spoken, to connect it mentally with another line spoken by Hamlet almost as long before, and do a small sum in subtraction—which we certainly shall not do at that moment. No such exact impression, therefore, is meant to be made on us.

The divider ends his second act upon Hamlet's resolution to put Claudius to the test of the play. This is an important milestone in the story; the scene is sure to gain applause; and in the following scene, if we are listening carefully, we shall gather that between the two a night has passed. So here, for the act-divider, are excuses enough for a few minutes' halt. Hamlet will have wrought us to share in his excitement; we shall relieve our feelings by applauding; we shall be given time to adjust our recollection of what has passed and prepare for what is promised. It may well be that Shakespeare's own actors found they had to give their audience an occasional rest from the strain of attention to such a play as *Hamlet*; it would be a greater mental-plus-emotional strain than any earlier play had exacted. It may even be that, Shakespeare consenting, they picked on this juncture as the likeliest for the purpose hereabouts; he might even pick on it himself. Nevertheless, since he did not so plan the play, the halt and the pause betray his stagecraft. He is not apt to check the impulse of his action at an emotional crisis which only anticipates a sharper crisis still, but rather to find means to relax the tension, yet without so loosening it as to lose hold on his audience. And his dramatic intention here is plain. It is to carry us straight from the deadly intent of Hamlet's

> The play's the thing
> Wherein I'll catch the conscience of the King.

to the sight of the puzzled King and Queen questioning the still equally puzzled Rosencrantz and Guildenstern, but learning with relief—that the harmless pastime of a play is in hand!

4. Dr. Johnson comments severely on it, and other editors may note its ineptitude. But Dowden (for instance) only says in the introduction to the *Hamlet* volume of the Arden Shakespeare that "the received division between III. and IV. is unfortunate," taking for granted, apparently, that for some sort of five-act form Shakespeare himself was responsible. And while he records the pertinent variants in his *apparatus criticus*, he leaves them without comment. Of so little importance did this aspect of Shakespeare's stagecraft seem even to him.

> it doth much content me
> To hear him so inclin'd.
> Good gentlemen, give him a further edge,
> And drive his purpose on to these delights.

says the unsuspecting Claudius. With the loss of the quick sequence of the scenes, the irony of this will be largely lost.

Further, not five minutes should elapse (there are fifty-five lines to speak) between that passionate soliloquy with its ringing and resolute end (the sound of it will be still in our ears) and the pessimisim of

> To be or not to be . . .

This is one of a series of such contrasts, a capital feature in the presenting of the character. Here, too, the full effect will be lost if the continuity of the action is broken.

As to the passing of a night between the scenes; at a guess, Shakespeare did not think about the matter at all till he came to write the sentence in the second scene indicating that a night has passed. (Nor, even so, is this a certain sign that it has; the performance may have been impatiently hurried forward.) It was natural in the earlier scene for Hamlet to set the play for "tomorrow night," since he had to write the "speech of some dozen or sixteen lines" to be inserted in it. But after the passionate

> O, what a rogue and peasant slave am I! . . .

what concerns Shakespeare is to see that the unavoidable anticlimax is at least given some antidote. Rosencrantz's reply to the Queen, that

> certain players
> . . . have already order
> *This night* to play before him.

provides this. It restimulates our interest. The exciting event we are expecting is already nearer. That is the dramatic worth of the statement; the chronology is incidental to it.

For a halt and a pause at the end of what is known as the closet-scene there can, as we said, be no excuse whatever. By a very usual turn of Elizabethan technique one scene simply evolves into another when the characters pass from the inner stage (the closet) to the outer (some antechamber or lobby).[5] And a change in the Folio—made by whatever hand—does but better Shakespeare's main intention, which plainly is to carry forward the action here with as little slackening as possible. It is

---

5. "Hamlet in madness hath Polonius slain,/And from his mother's closet hath he dragged him . . ."—the King tells Rosencrantz and Guildenstern; *i.e.*, from some place other than this in which he now stands speaking. The Elizabethan imagination will have responded the more readily to this changing of place by passing from inner stage to outer since it answered to the disposition of the Elizabethan house, in which one passed, as a rule, directly from room to room, not by a corridor. ° ° °

the King who is driving it ahead; for his purpose is to rid himself of his enemy without delay. And the pulse of the play has never been more feverish, nor Hamlet more beside himself; and he knows he "must to England." If somehow or other hereabouts this now lengthy third act must be brought to an end, the act-divider has but to let pass another hundred and fifty-lines. Hamlet by then will be gone, and Claudius gain a breathing-space, and we can be allowed one too.

To complete the customary tale one has now only to find an end for the fourth and as likely a beginning for a fifth act. Our act-divider could hardly have done much better than he does. We hear of Ophelia's death; there is finality in that. The ensnaring of Hamlet has been prepared against his promised return, so that the pause intervening will be an expectant one. And—since the last act is to begin with the Gravediggers—it will give the stage carpenters a good chance to open the grave-trap and make all ready. But, once again, Shakespeare's intentions (though here they may not be grossly thwarted) are falsified. The suspense between the news of Hamlet's return (brought first to Horatio, then to the King) and his actual appearance is fully provided for by the scenes which intervene. And a break in the action here can only weaken the effect of the apposition of the tragic fantasy of Ophelia's madness, the warped cunning of the King's plotting with Laertes, the lyric beauty of the tale of the girl's death on the one hand, and on the other the wholesome prose humor of the Clowns. Hamlet, when he arrives, is, by that colloquy in the graveyard, to point this contrast for us. The simple and the clever, the innocent and the guilty alike all come to the grave—to the plain prose of the grave. But how much more effective the pointing will be if we have also let Shakespeare realize the contrast for us, as he has planned to!

For our own convenience we may make pauses in the performance of the plays. Shakespeare himself had doubtless sometimes to show his audiences that consideration. If he did not at first, the growing length of his maturer work will surely have compelled him to. It would be both a sturdy and a spellbound crowd, indeed, that could—literally, as to about half of them—stand up to an uninterrupted performance of *Hamlet, King Lear* or *Antony and Cleopatra*. But he never ceased to conceive a play as a single organic whole, nor its action as a continuous progress— which a never-halted performance of the shorter *Comedy of Errors, Love's Labour's Lost* or *The Merchant of Venice* could quite well show it to be.[6]

6. I believe this to be essentially true, but subject—as with so much else to be said about his work—to qualification and exception. Among the earlier plays, the exceptional length of *Richard III* is puzzling; among the later, one seems to detect a positive effort to keep *Measure for Measure* and *Othello* within bounds. *Henry V* is definitely divided into acts. *Romeo and Juliet* shows some rudiments of a division by choruses. A *Winter's Tale* is dra-

matically divided into two parts. It may be hazarded, perhaps, that Shakespeare was indifferent to external form, though as willing to experiment in it—as he was to take a popular subject for the making of a play, or to pay a passing compliment to Elizabeth or James. But he did most eagerly experiment in the expression of the dramatic *ideas* which possessed him.

Another point. In estimating the acting-time of

And to learn how to minimize our dramatic loss, if we must interrupt a performance here and there, the Procrustean editors should first be forgotten; then the play's natural structure will appear, and divisions can at least be made to conform, as far as possible, to that.[7]

C. S. LEWIS

Hamlet: The Prince or the Poem? [†]

* * * The Hamlet formula, so to speak, is not 'a man who has to avenge his father' but 'a man who has been given a task by a ghost.' Everything else about him is less important than that. If the play did not begin with the cold and darkness and sickening suspense of the ghost scenes it would be a radically different play. If, on the other hand, only the first act had survived, we should have a very tolerable notion of the play's peculiar quality. * * *

This ghost is different from any other ghost in Elizabethan drama—for, to tell the truth, the Elizabethans in general do their ghosts very vilely. It is permanently ambiguous. Indeed the very word 'ghost,' by putting it into the same class with the 'ghosts' of Kyd and Chapman, nay by classifying it at all, puts us on the wrong track. It is 'this thing,' 'this dreaded sight,' an 'illusion,' a 'spirit of health or goblin dam'd,' liable at any moment to assume 'some other horrible form' which reason could not survive the vision of. Critics have disputed whether Hamlet is sincere when he doubts whether the apparition is his father's ghost or not. I take him to be perfectly sincere. He believes while the thing is present: he doubts when it is away. Doubt, uncertainty, bewilderment to almost

---

a play one must always consider the nature of the subject and the method of the writing; mere line measurement can be deceptive. A *Comedy of Errors* and *Love's Labour's Lost* will move far more swiftly than *As You Like It* or *Twelfth Night*. *Hamlet* moves at very varying speeds; averaged out, the pace both of *Measure for Measure* and *Coriolanus* will probably be slower. It is likely, again, that any play would then have been acted at a quicker pace than it commonly is today. The verse, and even the prose, would be spoken quicker; first, because the art of speaking was the actor's primary achievement; secondly, because in that age of little reading and much public discourse audiences would be better listeners too.

Yet another. The quickest shifting of the simplest scenes will add, say, half an hour to a quite straightforward "platform" performance of *Antony and Cleopatra*.

7. It is hard to wipe the five-act division clean from one's consciousness. Most modern editions insist

on retaining it, with a bare reference, if that, to its unauthenticity. Dover Wilson, in the new Cambridge Shakespeare, relegates it to the margin. That is a gain; and it is no doubt hard to go further, since some system of reference from text to notes and from one edition to another is needed, and this is on all counts the most convenient. The thing is to remember, when one is considering the play aesthetically, that these acts—and sometimes the scenes—have no true existence. The student must constantly have this in mind, or he will find himself still thinking of the play in acts and scenes—and thinking wrong. And it is for this reason that I have—with some difficulty for myself; I hope less for my readers—avoided all reference to acts and numbered scenes in this Preface.

† From *They Asked for a Paper* by C. S. Lewis, copyright © C. S. Lewis, 1962. Reprinted by permission of Curtis Brown Ltd., London.

any degree, is what the ghost creates not only in Hamlet's mind but in the minds of the other characters. Shakespeare does not take the concept of 'ghost' for granted, as other dramatists had done. In his play the appearance of the spectre means a breaking down of the walls of the world and the germination of thoughts that cannot really be thought: chaos is come again.

* * * I have started with the ghost because the ghost appears at the beginning of the play not only to give Hamlet necessary information but also, and even more, to strike the note. From the platform we pass to the court scene and so to Hamlet's first long speech. There are ten lines of it before we reach what is necessary to the plot: lines about the melting of flesh into a dew and the divine prohibition of self-slaughter. We have a second ghost scene after which the play itself, rather than the hero, goes mad for some minutes. We have a second soliloquy on the theme 'to die . . . to sleep'; and a third on 'the witching time of night, when churchyards yawn.' We have the King's effort to pray and Hamlet's comment on it. We have the ghost's third appearance. Ophelia goes mad and is drowned. Then comes the comic relief, surely the strangest comic relief ever written—comic relief beside an open grave, with a further discussion of suicide, a detailed inquiry into the rate of decomposition, a few clutches of skulls, and then 'Alas, poor Yorick!' On top of this, the hideous fighting in the grave; and then, soon, the catastrophe.

* * * The subject of *Hamlet* is death. I do not mean by this that most of the characters die, nor even that life and death are the stakes they play for; that is true of all tragedies. I do not mean that we rise from the reading of the play with the feeling that we have been in cold, empty places, places 'outside,' *nocte tacentia late*, though that is true. * * *

The sense in which death is the subject of *Hamlet* will become apparent if we compare it with other plays. Macbeth has commerce with Hell, but at the very outset of his career dismisses all thought of the life to come. For Brutus and Othello, suicide in the high tragic manner is escape and climax. For Lear death is deliverance. For Romeo and Antony, poignant loss. For all these, as for their author while he writes and the audience while they watch, death is the end: it is almost the frame of the picture. They think of dying: no one thinks, in these plays, of *being dead*. In *Hamlet* we are kept thinking about it all the time, whether in terms of the soul's destiny or of the body's. Purgatory, Hell, Heaven, the wounded name, the rights—or wrongs—of Ophelia's burial, and the staying-power of a tanner's corpse: and beyond this, beyond all Christian and all Pagan maps of the hereafter, comes a curious groping and tapping of thoughts, about 'what dreams may come.' It is this that gives to the whole play its quality of darkness and of misgiving. Of course there is much else in the play: but nearly always, the same groping. The characters are all watching one another, forming theories about one another, listening, contriving, full of anxiety. The world of *Hamlet* is a world where one has lost one's way. The Prince also has no doubt lost his, and we can tell the precise moment at which he finds it again. 'Not a whit. We defy augury. There's a special providence in the fall of a sparrow. If it be now, 'tis not to come: if it be not to come, it will be now: if it be not now, yet it will come: the readiness is all: since no man has aught of what he leaves, what is't to leave betimes?'[1]

If I wanted to make one more addition to the gallery of Hamlet's portraits I should trace his hesitation to the fear of death; not to a physical fear of dying, but a fear of being dead. And I think I should get on quite comfortably. Any serious attention to the state of being dead, unless it is limited by some definite religious or anti-religious doctrine, must, I suppose, paralyse the will by introducing infinite uncertainties and rendering all motives inadequate. Being dead is the unknown x in our sum. Unless you ignore it or else give it a value, you can get no answer. But this is not what I am going to do. Shakespeare has not left in the text clear lines of causation which would enable us to connect Hamlet's hesitations with this source. I do not believe he has given us data for any portrait of the kind critics have tried to draw. * * *

For what, after all, is happening to us when we read any of Hamlet's great speeches? We see visions of flesh dissolving into a dew, of the world like an unweeded garden. We think of memory reeling in its 'distracted globe.' We watch him scampering hither and thither like a maniac to avoid the voices wherewith he is haunted. Someone says 'Walk out of the air,' and we hear the words 'Into my grave' spontaneously respond to it. We think of being bounded in a nut-shell and king of infinite space: but for bad dreams. There's the trouble, for 'I am most dreadfully attended.' We see the picture of a dull and muddy-mettled rascal, a John-a-dreams, somehow unable to move while ultimate dishonour is done him. We listen to his fear lest the whole thing may be an illusion due to melancholy. We get the sense of sweet relief at the words 'shuffled off this mortal coil' but mixed with the bottomless doubt about what may follow then. We think of bones and skulls, of women breeding sinners, and of how some, to whom all this experience is a sealed book, can yet dare death and danger 'for an egg-shell.' But do we really enjoy these things, do we go back to them, because they show us Hamlet's character? Are they, from *that* point of view, so very interesting? Does the mere fact that a young man, literally haunted, dispossessed, and lacking friends, should feel thus, tell us anything remarkable? Let me put my question in another way. If instead of the speeches he actually utters about the firmament and man in his scene with Rosencrantz and Guildenstern Hamlet had merely said, 'I don't seem to enjoy things the way I used to,' and talked in that fashion throughout, should we find

---

1. I think the last clause is best explained by the assumption that Shakespeare had come across Seneca's *Nihil perdis ex tuo tempore, nam quod relinquis alienum est* (Epist. lxix).

him interesting? I think the answer is 'Not very.' It may be replied that if he talked commonplace prose he would reveal his character less vividly. I am not so sure. He would certainly have revealed *something* less vividly; but would that something be himself? It seems to me that 'this majestical roof' and 'What a piece of work is a man' give me primarily an impression not of the sort of person he must be to lose the estimation of things but of the things themselves and their great value; and that I should be able to discern, though with very faint interest, the same condition of loss in a personage who was quite unable so to put before me what he was losing. And I do not think it true to reply that he would be a different character if he spoke less poetically. This point is often misunderstood. We sometimes speak as if the characters in whose mouths Shakespeare puts great poetry were poets: in the sense that Shakespeare was depicting men of poetical genius. But surely this is like thinking that Wagner's Wotan is the dramatic portrait of a baritone? In opera song is the medium by which the representation is made and not part of the thing represented. The actors sing; the dramatic personages are feigned to be speaking. The only character who sings dramatically in *Figaro* is Cherubino. Similarly in poetical drama poetry is the medium, not part of the delineated characters. While the actors speak poetry written for them by the poet, the dramatic personages are supposed to be merely talking. If ever there is occasion to *represent* poetry (as in the play scene from *Hamlet*), it is put into a different metre and strongly stylized so as to prevent confusion.

I trust that my conception is now becoming clear. I believe that we read Hamlet's speeches with interest chiefly because they describe so well a certain spiritual region through which most of us have passed and anyone in his circumstances might be expected to pass, rather than because of our concern to understand how and why this particular man entered it. I foresee an objection on the ground that I am thus really admitting his 'character' in the only sense that matters and that all characters whatever could be equally well talked away by the method I have adopted. But I do really find a distinction. When I read about Mrs. Proudie I am not in the least interested in seeing the world from her point of view, for her point of view is not interesting; what does interest me is precisely the sort of person she was. In *Middlemarch* no reader wants to see Casaubon through Dorothea's eyes; the pathos, the comedy, the value of the whole thing is to understand Dorothea and see how such an illusion was inevitable for her. In Shakespeare himself I find Beatrice to be a character who could not be thus dissolved. We are interested not in some vision seen through her eyes, but precisely in the wonder of her being the girl she is. A comparison of the sayings we remember from her part with those we remember from Hamlet's brings out the contrast. On the one hand, 'I wonder that you will still be talking, Signior Benedick,' 'There was a star danced and under that I was born,' 'Kill Claudio'; on the other, 'The undiscovered country from whose bourne no traveller returns,' 'Use every man after his desert, and who should 'scape whippings?', 'The rest is silence.' Particularly noticeable is the passage where Hamlet professes to be describing his own character. 'I am myself indifferent honest: but yet I could accuse me of such things that it were better my mother had not borne me. I am very proud, revengeful, ambitious.' It is, of course, possible to devise some theory which explains these self-accusations in terms of character. But long before we have done so the real significance of the lines has taken possession of our imagination for ever. 'Such fellows as I' does not mean 'such fellows as Goethe's Hamlet, or Coleridge's Hamlet, or any Hamlet': it means *men*—creatures shapen in sin and conceived in iniquity—and the vast, empty vision of them 'crawling between earth and heaven' is what really counts and really carries the burden of the play.

* * *

ERNEST JONES

Tragedy and the Mind of the Infant †

* * *

As a child Hamlet had experienced the warmest affection for his mother, and this, as is always so, had contained elements of a disguised erotic quality, still more so in infancy. The presence of two traits in the Queen's character accord with this assumption, namely her markedly sensual nature and her passionate fondness for her son. The former is indicated in too many places in the play to need specific reference, and is generally recognized. The latter is also manifest: Claudius says, for instance (79), "The Queen his mother lives almost by his looks". Nevertheless Hamlet appears to have with more or less success weaned himself from her and to have fallen in love with Ophelia. The precise nature of his original feeling for Ophelia is a little obscure. We may assume that at least in part it was composed of a normal love for a prospective bride, though the extravagance of the language used (the passionate need for absolute certainty, etc.) suggests a somewhat morbid frame of mind. There are indications that even here the influence of the old attraction for the mother is still exerting itself. Although some writers, following Goethe, see in Ophelia many traits of resemblance to the Queen, perhaps just as

† Reprinted from *Hamlet and Oedipus* by Ernest Jones, by permission of W. W. Norton & Company, Inc. and Merwyn Jones. Copyright 1949 by Ernest Jones. Copyright renewed 1982 by Merwyn Jones. Page numbers given in parentheses refer to the text of this Norton Critical Edition of *Hamlet*.

striking are the traits contrasting with those of the Queen. Whatever truths there may be in the many German conceptions of Ophelia as a sensual wanton * * * still the very fact that it needed what Goethe happily called the "innocence of insanity" to reveal the presence of any such libidinous thoughts demonstrates in itself the modesty and chasteness of her habitual demeanour. Her naïve piety, her obedient resignation, and her unreflecting simplicity sharply contrast with the Queen's character, and seem to indicate that Hamlet by a characteristic reaction towards the opposite extreme had unknowingly been impelled to choose a woman who should least remind him of his mother. A case might even be made out for the view that part of his courtship originated not so much in direct attraction for Ophelia as in an unconscious desire to play her off against his mother, just as a disappointed and piqued lover so often has resort to the arms of a more willing rival. It would not be easy otherwise to understand the readiness with which he later throws himself into this part. When, for instance, in the play scene he replies to his mother's request to sit by her with the words "No, good mother, here's metal more attractive" and proceeds to lie at Ophelia's feet, we seem to have a direct indication of his attitude; and his coarse familiarity and bandying of ambiguous jests with the woman he has recently so ruthlessly jilted are hardly intelligible unless we bear in mind that they were carried out under the heedful gaze of the Queen. It is as if his unconscious were trying to convey to her the following thought: "You give yourself to other men whom you prefer to me. Let me assure you that I can dispense with your favours and even prefer those of a woman whom I no longer love." His extraordinary outburst of bawdiness on this occasion, so unexpected in a man of obviously fine feeling, points unequivocally to the sexual nature of the underlying turmoil.

Now comes the father's death and the mother's second marriage. The association of the idea of sexuality with his mother, buried since infancy, can no longer be concealed from his consciousness. As Bradley well says: "Her son was forced to see in her action not only an astounding shallowness of feeling, but an eruption of coarse sensuality, 'rank and gross,' speeding post-haste to its horrible delight". Feelings which once, in the infancy of long ago, were pleasurable desires can now, because of his repressions, only fill him with repulsion. The long "repressed" desire to take his father's place in his mother's affection is stimulated to unconscious activity by the sight of someone usurping this place exactly as he himself had once longed to do. More, this someone was a member of the same family, so that the actual usurpation further resembled the imaginary one in being incestuous. Without his being in the least aware of it these ancient desires are ringing in his mind, are once more struggling to find conscious expression, and need such an expenditure of energy again to "repress" them that he is reduced to the deplorable mental state he himself so vividly depicts.

There follows the Ghost's announcement that the father's death was a willed one, was due to murder. Hamlet, having at the moment his mind filled with natural indignation at the news, answers normally enough with the cry (21):

> Haste me to know't, that I with wings as swift
> As meditation or the thoughts of love,
> May sweep to my revenge.

The momentous words follow revealing who was the guilty person, namely a relative who had committed the deed at the bidding of lust.[1] Hamlet's second guilty wish had thus also been realized by his uncle, namely to procure the fulfilment of the first—the possession of the mother—by a personal deed, in fact by murder of the father. The two recent events, the father's death and the mother's second marriage, seemed to the world to have no inner causal relation to each other, but they represented ideas which in Hamlet's unconscious fantasy had always been closely associated. These ideas now in a moment forced their way to conscious recognition in spite of all "repressing forces", and found immediate expression in his almost reflex cry: "O my prophetic soul! My uncle?" The frightful truth his unconscious had already intuitively divined, his consciousness had now to assimilate as best it could. For the rest of the interview Hamlet is stunned by the effect of the internal conflict thus re-awakened, which from now on never ceases, and into the essential nature of which he never penetrates.

One of the first manifestations of the awakening of the old conflict in Hamlet's mind is his reaction against Ophelia. This is doubly conditioned by the two opposing attitudes in his own mind. In the first place, there is a complex reaction in regard to his mother. As was explained above, the being forced to connect the thought of his mother with sensuality leads to an intense sexual revulsion, one that is only temporarily broken down by the coarse outburst discussed above. Combined with this is a fierce jealousy, unconscious because of its forbidden origin, at the sight of her giving herself to another man, a man whom he had no reason whatever either to love or to respect. Consciously this is allowed to express itself, for instance after the prayer scene, only in the form of extreme resentment and bitter reproaches against her. His resentment against women is still further inflamed by the hypocritical prudishness with which Ophelia follows her father and brother in seeing evil in his natural affection, an attitude which poisons his love in exactly the same way that the love of his childhood, like that of all children, must have been poisoned. He can forgive a woman neither her rejection of his sexual advances nor, still less, her alliance with another man. Most

---

1. It is not maintained that this was by any means Claudius' whole motive, but it was evidently a powerful one and the one that most impressed Hamlet.

intolerable of all to him, as Bradley well remarks, is the sight of sensuality in a quarter from which he had trained himself ever since infancy rigorously to exclude it. The total reaction culminates in the bitter misogyny of his outburst against Ophelia, who is devastated at having to bear a reaction so wholly out of proportion to her own offence and has no idea that in reviling her Hamlet is really expressing his bitter resentment against his mother.[2] "I have heard of your paintings too, well enough; God has given you one face, and you make yourselves another; you jig, you amble, and you lisp, and nickname God's creatures, and make your wantonness your ignorance. Go to, I'll no more on't; it hath made me mad" (47). On only one occasion does he for a moment escape from the sordid implication with which his love has been impregnated and achieve a healthier attitude towards Ophelia, namely at the open grave when in remorse he breaks out at Laertes for presuming to pretend that his feeling for her could ever equal that of her lover. Even here, however, as Dover Wilson has suggested, the remorse behind his exaggerated behaviour springs not so much from grief at Ophelia's death as from his distress at his bad conscience that had killed his love—he acts the lover he fain would have been.

Hamlet's attitude towards Ophelia is still more complex. Dover Wilson has adduced good evidence for thinking that Hamlet is supposed to have overheard the intrigue in which Polonius "looses" his daughter to test her erstwhile lover, a suggestion which had previously been made by Quincy Adams. This is probably an echo of the old (Saxo) saga in which the girl is employed by the king to test his capacity for sexual love and so decide whether he is an imbecile or a cunning enemy. It certainly helps to explain the violence with which he attacks her feminine charms and treats her worse than a paid prostitute. He feels she is sent to lure him on and then, like his mother, to betray him at the behest of another man. The words "Get thee to a nunnery"[3] thus have a more sinister connotation, for in Elizabethan, and indeed in later, times this was also a term for a brothel; the name "Covent Garden" will elucidate the point to any student of the history of London.

The underlying theme relates ultimately to the splitting of the mother image which the infantile unconscious effects into two opposite pictures: one of a virginal Madonna, an inaccessible saint towards whom all sensual approaches are unthinkable, and the other of a sensual creature accessible to everyone. Indications of this dichotomy between love and

---

2. His similar tone and advice to the two women show plainly how closely they are identified in his mind. Cp. "Get thee to a nunnery: why wouldst thou be a breeder of sinners?" (46–47) with "Refrain to-night; And that shall lend a kind of easiness To the next abstinence" (65).

The identification is further demonstrated in the course of the play by Hamlet's killing the men who stand between him and these women (Claudius and Polonius).

3. This exhortation (with its usual connotation of chastity) may be equated with the one addressed later to his mother, "Go not to my uncle's bed", indicating Hamlet's identification of the two women in his feelings.

lust (Titian's Sacred and Profane Love) are to be found later in most men's sexual experiences. When sexual repression is highly pronounced, as with Hamlet, then both types of women are felt to be hostile: the pure one out of resentment at her repulses, the sensual one out of the temptation she offers to plunge into guiltiness. Misogyny, as in the play, is the inevitable result.

The intensity of Hamlet's repulsion against woman in general, and Ophelia in particular, is a measure of the powerful "repression" to which his sexual feelings are being subjected. The outlet for those feelings in the direction of his mother has always been firmly dammed, and now that the narrower channel in Ophelia's direction has also been closed the increase in the original direction consequent on the awakening of early memories tasks all his energy to maintain the "repression". His pent-up feelings find a partial vent in other directions. The petulant irascibility and explosive outbursts called forth by his vexation at the hands of Guildenstern and Rosencrantz, and especially of Polonius, are evidently to be interpreted in this way, as also is in part the burning nature of his reproaches to his mother. Indeed, towards the end of his interview with his mother the thought of her misconduct expresses itself in that almost physical disgust which is so characteristic a manifestation of intensely "repressed" sexual feeling.

> Let the bloat king tempt you again to bed,
> Pinch wanton on your cheek, call you his mouse,
> And let him for a pair of reechy kisses,
> Or paddling in your neck with his damn'd fingers,
> Make you to ravel all this matter out   (65)

Hamlet's attitude towards Polonius is highly instructive. Here the absence of family tie and of other similar influences enables him to indulge to a relatively unrestrained extent his hostility towards what he regards as a prating and sententious dotard.[4] The analogy he effects between Polonius and Jephthah is in this connection especially pointed. It is here that we see his fundamental attitude towards moralizing elders who use their power to thwart the happiness of the young, and not in the over-drawn and melodramatic portrait in which he delineates his father: "A combination and a form indeed, where every god did seem to set his seal to give the world assurance of a man".

It will be seen from the foregoing that Hamlet's attitude towards his uncle-father is far more complex than is generally supposed. He of course detests him, but it is the jealous detestation of one evil-doer towards his successful fellow. Much as he hates him, he can never denounce him

4. It is noteworthy how many producers and actors seem to accept Hamlet's distorted estimate of Polonius, his garrulity being presumably an excuse for overlooking the shrewdness and soundness of his worldly wisdom. After all, his diagnosis of Hamlet's madness as being due to unrequited love for Ophelia was not so far from the mark, and he certainly recognized that his distressful condition was of sexual origin.

with the ardent indignation that boils straight from his blood when he reproaches his mother, for the more vigorously he denounces his uncle the more powerfully does he stimulate to activity his own unconscious and "repressed" complexes. He is therefore in a dilemma between on the one hand allowing his natural detestation of his uncle to have free play, a consummation which would stir still further his own horrible wishes, and on the other hand ignoring the imperative call for the vengeance that his obvious duty demands. His own "evil" prevents him from completely denouncing his uncle's, and in continuing to "repress" the former he must strive to ignore, to condone, and if possible even to forget the latter; *his moral fate is bound up with his uncle's for good or ill.* In reality his uncle incorporates the deepest and most buried part of his own personality, so that he cannot kill him without also killing himself. This solution, one closely akin to what Freud has shown to be the motive of suicide in melancholia, is actually the one that Hamlet finally adopts. The course of alternate action and inaction that he embarks on, and the provocations he gives to his suspicious uncle, can lead to no other end than to his own ruin and, incidentally, to that of his uncle. Only when he has made the final sacrifice and brought himself to the door of death is he free to fulfil his duty, to avenge his father, and to slay his other self—his uncle.

There are two moments in the play when he is nearest to murder, and it is noteworthy that in both the impulse has been dissociated from the unbearable idea of incest. The second is of course when he actually kills the King, when the Queen is already dead and lost to him for ever, so that his conscience is free of an ulterior motive for the murder. The first is more interesting. It is clear that Hamlet is a creature of highly charged imagination; Vischer, for instance, quite rightly termed him a "Phantasiemensch". As is known, the danger then is that phantasy may on occasion replace reality. Now Otto Rank, who uses the same term, has plausibly suggested that the emotionally charged play scene, where a nephew kills his uncle(!), and when there is no talk of adultery or incest, is in Hamlet's imagination an equivalent for fulfilling his task.[5] It is easier to kill the King when there is no ulterior motive behind it, no talk of mother or incest. When the play is over he is carried away in exultation as if he had really killed the King himself, whereas all he has actually done is to warn him and so impel him to sign a death warrant. That his pretext for arranging the play—to satisfy himself about Claudius' guilt and the Ghost's honesty—is specious is plain from the fact that *before* it he had been convinced of both and was reproaching him-

---

5. There is a delicate point here which may appeal only to psychoanalysts. It is known that the occurrence of a dream within a dream (when one dreams that one is dreaming) is always found when analysed to refer to a theme which the person wishes were "only a dream", i.e. not true. I would suggest that a similar meaning attaches to a "play within a play", as in "Hamlet". So Hamlet (as nephew) can kill the King in his imagination since it is "only a play" or "only in play".

self for his neglect. When he then comes on the King praying, and so to speak finds him surprisingly still alive, he realizes that his task is still in front of him, but can only say "Now *might* I do it" (not "will"). He then expresses openly the unconscious thoughts of his infancy—the wish to kill the man who is lying with his mother ("in th' incestuous pleasure of his bed")—but he knows only too well that his own guilty motive for doing so would always prevent him. So there is no way out of the dilemma, and he blunders on to destruction.

The call of duty to kill his stepfather cannot be obeyed because it links itself with the unconscious call of his nature to kill his mother's husband, whether this is the first or the second; the absolute "repression" of the former impulse involves the inner prohibition of the latter also. It is no chance that Hamlet says of himself that he is prompted to his revenge "by heaven and hell".

In this discussion of the motives that move or restrain Hamlet we have purposely depreciated the subsidiary ones—such as his exclusion from the throne where Claudius has blocked the normal solution of the Oedipus complex (to succeed the father in due course)—which also play a part, so as to bring out in greater relief the deeper and effective ones that are of preponderating importance. These, as we have seen, spring from sources of which he is quite unaware, and we might summarize the internal conflict of which he is the victim as consisting in a struggle of the "repressed" mental processes to become conscious. The call of duty, which automatically arouses to activity these unconscious processes, conflicts with the necessity of "repressing" them still more strongly; for the more urgent is the need for external action the greater is the effort demanded of the "repressing" forces. It is his moral duty, to which his father exhorts him, to put an end to the incestuous activities of his mother (by killing Claudius), but his unconscious does not want to put an end to them (he being identified with Claudius in the situation), and so he cannot. His lashings of self-reproach and remorse are ultimately because of this very failure, i.e. the refusal of his guilty wishes to undo the sin. By refusing to abandon his own incestuous wishes he perpetuates the sin and so must endure the stings of torturing conscience. And yet killing his mother's husband would be equivalent to committing the original sin himself, which would if anything be even more guilty. So of the two impossible alternatives he adopts the passive solution of letting the incest continue vicariously, but at the same time provoking destruction at the King's hand. Was ever a tragic figure so torn and tortured!

Action is paralysed at its very inception, and there is thus produced the picture of apparently causeless inhibition which is so inexplicable both to Hamlet and to readers of the play. This paralysis arises, however, not from physical or moral cowardice, but from that intellectual cowardice, that reluctance to dare the exploration of his inmost soul, which

Hamlet shares with the rest of the human race. "Thus conscience does make cowards of us all."

HARRY LEVIN

An Explication of the Player's Speech †

I

The text before us (II.ii.413–479) is a purple passage, not because it has been admired, but because it stands out from the rest of the play. On the whole it has aroused, in Shakespearean commentators, less admiration than curiosity and less curiosity than bewilderment. Some of them, like Polonius, have been quite frankly bored with it; many of them, unlike Hamlet himself, have considered it highly bombastic. Those who discern the hand of another playwright, whenever Shakespeare's writing presents a problem, have fathered it upon Marlowe, Chapman, Kyd, and even unlikelier authors. Others, hesitating to assume that Shakespeare would cite a fellow playwright at such length, have interpreted the speech as parody or satire—although who is being parodied, or what is being satirized, or how or why, is again a matter of diverging opinion. Still others have explained the incongruity, between these high-pitched lines and the ordinary dialogue, by assuming that Shakespeare had taken occasion to foist upon his patient audience a fragment of his earlier journeywork. * * * More rigorous scholarship tends to support the integrity of Shakespeare's text, just as more perceptive criticism emphasizes the consciousness of his artistry. Appealing to the authority of Sir Edmund Chambers, as well as to the insight of A. C. Bradley, we can proceed from the assumption that the passage at hand is both authentic and advised. But is it well advised? is it really significant? and what, if so, does it signify?

We can scarcely become aware of its significance without some preliminary awareness of its context: not only the intrinsic place that it occupies within the dramatic economy of *Hamlet*, but the stream of extrinsic associations that it carries along with it into the drama. The player who, at Hamlet's request, gives us this demonstration of his professional skill, this 'taste' of his 'quality,' is cast in a functional role; for in the next act he and his fellows are destined to perform the play that will 'catch the conscience of the King.' Meanwhile Shakespeare, who

† From *The Question of Hamlet*, by Harry Levin (New York: Oxford UP, 1959) 141–62. Copyright © 1959 by Oxford University Press, Inc. Reprinted by permission. Page and line numbers given in parentheses for *Hamlet* are to this Norton Critical Edition.

seldom misses an opportunity to talk about his craft, indulges in two of his fullest discussions on the theater. These are often regarded as digressions, and one of them is usually cut on the stage. * * * But Goethe, who took a producer's point of view, saw how that 'passionate speech' served a psychological purpose by planting the suggestion in Hamlet's mind that leads to his experiment upon Claudius. And the late Harley Granville-Barker, perhaps the most pragmatic of all Shakespeareans, observed that the name of Hecuba was not only a necessary link between the First Player's scene and Hamlet's ensuing soliloquy, but also an implicit commentary on the Queen. To underline that observation: if the Player is nothing to Hecuba, or she to him, it follows *a fortiori* that Hamlet should feel and show a much deeper grief, and that Gertrude has failed abysmally to live up to the standard of royal motherhood.

* * * By requesting the account of 'Priam's slaughter' as it was told in 'Aeneas' tale to Dido,' Hamlet refers us to what might be called the official version: the retrospective story that Vergil tells in the second book of his *Aeneid* (506–58). * * * Further and closer scrutiny of Shakespeare's treatment reveals that—although he elaborated a few small Vergilian details, such as the useless sword *('inutile ferrum')*—he is actually less indebted to Vergil than to his favorite among the Latin poets, Ovid.
* * *

In shifting his attention from Priam to Hecuba, and his source from Vergil to Ovid, Shakespeare turns from the sphere of the epic to the lyric, and from events to emotions. It is Ovid, too, who inspires his final appeal to the gods themselves: '. . . *illius fortuna deos quoque moveret omnes.*' But the lyrical note can prevail no more than the epical, since Shakespeare's form is basically tragic. * * * The tone of [the Player's] speech is that of the *nuntius*, the Senecan messenger who enters to make a morbidly protracted recital of bad news from offstage—or, for that matter, the Sergeant in *Macbeth* (I.ii.8–42), whose sanguinary report makes the merciless Macdonwald a blood brother to the rugged Pyrrhus. Among the disheveled heroines of Seneca's tragedies, Hecuba looms particularly large as the archetype of maternal woe and queenly suffering. How she was metamorphosed into a dog, after the destruction of Troy, is recollected when, in Seneca's *Agamemnon*, she 'barketh as a bedlam bitch about her strangled chylde.' * * *

Since the Elizabethans conceived of tragedy as a spectacular descent from the heights to the depths, they could conceive of no more tragic worthies than the King and Queen of Troy. Hence the object-lesson of the first English tragedy, *Gorboduc*, is driven home by identifying the heroine with 'Hecuba, the wofullest wretch / That euer lyued to make a myrrour of.' And in the most popular of all Elizabethan plays, *The Spanish Tragedy*, the hero, instructing a painter to 'shew a passion,' volunteers to pose for his portrait 'like old *Priam of Troy*, crying: "the house is a fire . . ." ' But tragedy was more than a sad story of the death of kings and the weeping of tristful queens; it chronicled the fall of dynasties, the destruction of cities, the decline of civilizations. * * *

The matter of Troy—which Caxton had popularized, which English ballads celebrated, which poets and artists could draw upon as freely as the matter of England itself—served Shakespeare most effectively by helping to frame his characters and outline his situations. It figured upon a tapestry, as it were, backing the literal episodes of English history with a deeper dimension. The conflict between the houses of York and Lancaster was inevitably viewed in the light of the struggle between the Greeks and the Trojans. The father who accidentally slays his son in 3 *Henry VI* (II.v.120), like Northumberland when he learns of Hotspur's death in 2 *Henry IV* (I.i.70–74), is bound to see himself in Priam's role. Similarly, the Roman mother in *Coriolanus* (I.iii.43–6) and the cursing wife in *Cymbeline* (IV.ii.311–12) associate their grief with Hecuba's. It is not surprising, then, that the impassioned father wants to be painted as Priam in *The Spanish Tragedy*, or that the outraged wife in *The Rape of Lucrece* seeks consolation in a painting of the siege of Troy, more especially in its depiction of Hecuba (1450–51):

> In her the painter had anatomiz'd
> Time's ruin, beauty's wrack, and grim care's reign . . .

When Lucrece surveys the picture, discovering in it a precedent for her sorrows, its dumbness stimulates her to become vocal and its flatness puts her feelings into iconographic relief (1492): 'Here feelingly she weeps Troy's painted woes.' In similar fashion, all occasions inform against Hamlet, who rediscovers his own plight in the verbal painting, the theatrical mirror of the Player's speech. The narrator, pious Aeneas, recalls him to his filial duty. The King, his father, like Priam, has been slaughtered. The Queen his mother, ironically unlike Hecuba, refuses to play the part of the mourning wife. As for the interloping newcomer—whether you call him Pyrrhus, Neoptolemus, or Fortinbras—he too is prompted by the unquiet ghost of his father, Achilles. His destiny, too, is to bring down the revenge of a dead hero upon the unheroic heads of the living.

II

But these apparitions hover in the background until the words are pronounced that summon them. * * * The cruelty of Pyrrhus is symbolized by his heraldic trappings. Knightly prowess ordinarily finds its outward symbol in armorial panoply, which is frequently contrasted with the reality of blood, sweat, and tears—notably in the characterization of Hotspur. Here, where that situation is reversed, bloodshed is treated as if it were decoration. The sable arms of Pyrrhus resemble his funereal purpose, and also the night—which is not a generic night, but the particular, portentous, claustral night that he and his companions have just

spent in the wooden horse. The repeated adjective 'black' (1. 414, 416)
is an elementary manifestation of evil, like the 'Thoughts black' of the
poisoner in the play-within-the-play; yet it hints at that 'power of blackness' which Melville discerned more fully in Shakespeare's works than
anywhere else. But the scene does not appear in its true color until its
dark surfaces are 'o'ersized' (423), covered with sizing, dripping with
redness. Red, unrelieved by quartering, is 'total gules' in the unfeeling
jargon of heraldry, which Shakespeare deliberately invokes to describe
the clotted gore of others shed by Pyrrhus—of parents and children whose
family relationships are feelingly specified by way of contrast (419), a
contrast which ultimately juxtaposes esthetic and ethical values. He is
tricked out, dressed up in the unnatural colors of Marlowe's Tambur-
laine—in black and red and in a carbuncular brightness which flickers
against the darkness, as opposed to the hues of nature, the blues and
browns and greens that Shakespeare has more constantly in mind. Thence
the metaphor shifts from light to heat, from visual to tactile images, and
to a zeugma which holds in suspension both physical fire and psychological wrath (422). * * *

At this point, the appropriate point where Pyrrhus encounters Priam,
the Player takes up the story and—in a manner of speaking—the mono-
logue becomes a dialogue. It should not be forgotten that 'anon' (429) is
one of those adverbs whose force has been weakened by time: in this
case it means 'very soon' rather than 'later on.' It reinforces the series of
'nows,' which in their turn reinforce the employment of the present
tense, and convey the impression of breathless immediacy: we might
almost be listening to the play-by-play account of a sporting event. The
ineffectuality of the old grandsire's antique sword (430), whose fall pre-
figures his (435), is motivated by the spirit of general mutiny. The angry
swing of his assailant—which, though it goes wild, deprives the father
of his remaining strength, unnerves him—rends the air with ten ono-
matopoetic monosyllables: "But with the whiff and wind of his fell
sword . . .' (434). * * * And though the poet hesitates to indulge in a
pathetic fallacy, to attribute sensation or sensibility to the city itself, he
interprets the crash of its topless towers as a comment on the downfall
of its king. Troy, however, has its momentary and metaphorical revenge
upon Pyrrhus when the noise, by capturing his ear, arrests his motion.
At that fatal moment everything stops; the narrative is transposed to the
past tense; and the interjection 'lo!' (438) points a moral and pictorial
contrast between the bloody tyrant and his 'milky' victim (439). * * *

It is only during this uncharacteristic standstill that Pyrrhus, the
unthinking avenger, shows any likeness to his polar opposite, Hamlet.
Standing there for the nonce in a cataleptic state of neutrality, as if he
had no control over mind or body, equally detached from his intention
and his object, he 'did nothing'—and the pause is rounded out by an
unfilled line (443). Then as he swings into action by way of an epic

simile, sight is commingled with sound—or rather, with the absence of sound, since we are asked to visualize a silence (445). And as our gaze is deflected from the clouds to the earth, a second simile takes its departure from the first, and perceives an omen of death in the silent atmosphere (447). Anon—that is, suddenly—like the awaited thunderclap, vengeance is resumed; the retarded decline of the sword (453), with its Homeric reverberation (450), now parallels the dying fall of Priam and of his sword. The word 'fall,' coming twice in pairs, accentuates the rhythm and underlines the theme. The classical allusion, a preliminary glimpse of 'Vulcan's stithy,' though somewhat archaically expressed, would be commonplace if it were not for the violence of Shakespeare's application. He uses a favorite stylistic device of his predecessors, the University Wits, who seldom made a comparison without making it invidious: their characters are more beautiful than Venus, as powerful as Jove, no weaker than Hercules. After all, there could be no more remorseless task than to beat out indestructible armor for the god of war. To display as little or less remorse, while striking down a disarmed graybeard, was to be as devoid of sympathy—as ready to inflict suffering and unready to feel it—as any human being could expressibly be.

* * * Leaving the senseless Priam to the insensate Pyrrhus, after another hiatus of half a line (453), the speech addresses violent objurgations to the bitch-goddess Fortune, about whom Hamlet has lately cracked ribald jokes with Rosencrantz and Guildenstern; whose buffets and rewards he prizes Horatio for suffering with equanimity; against whom he will, in the most famous of all soliloquies, be tempted to take arms. An appeal is addressed to the gods, who are envisaged as meeting in epic conclave, to destroy the source of her capricious authority. It is urged that her proverbial wheel, whose revolution determines the ups and downs of individual lives, be itself dismantled; and that its components suffer the destiny to which they have so often carried mortals—to fall, as the angels did in the world's original tragedy, from paradise to hell. To catch the gathering momentum of that descent, Shakespeare again resorts to words of one syllable (not excepting 'heav'n'), and relies—as he does throughout—upon assonances and alliterations (457, 458): 'And bowl the round nave down the hill of heaven/As far as to the fiends.' The same image, that of 'a massy wheel,' disintegrating as it rolls down hill, is later likened by Rosencrantz to 'the cesse of majesty,' the death of the king involving 'the lives of many' attached to its spokes:

> . . . when it falls,
> Each small annexment, petty consequence,
> Attends the boist'rous ruin.

The fact that the twenty-three foregoing lines (435–458) are frequently omitted from acting versions, notably from the First Quarto, supports the view that they constitute a rhapsodic excursion from the narrative.

Shakespeare cleverly obviated boredom on the part of his audience by allowing Polonius to complain and Hamlet to gibe at him. By laughing with Hamlet at Polonius, whose own tediousness is the butt of so many gibes, the audience is pledged to renew its attention. Hamlet, of course, has personal motives for echoing the Player's mention of Hecuba. Thereupon Polonius, who fancies himself as a critic, and who has said of Hamlet's letter to Ophelia that ' "beautified" is a vile phrase,' seeks to propitiate Hamlet by voicing judicious approval of a peculiarly inept expression: ' "Mobled queen" is good.' Has impressionistic criticism ever said more?

The barefoot queen remains mobled, or muffled, for better or for worse, in spite of editors who prefer 'mob-led' or 'ennobled.' Her special poignance depends upon her abdication of queenly dignity, upon the antitheses between 'diadem' (468) and 'clout' (467) and between 'robe' (468) and 'blanket' (470). * * * The concept of royalty has been debased: 'Hyperion to a satyr,' goddess to fishwife. The sword, on its fourth and last appearance, is not unlike a kitchen-knife; while the final outburst of Hecuba is like Homer's portrayal of Helen, in one respect if in no other, since it registers its emotional impact on the spectators. Fortune, it would appear, is still so securely entrenched that the impulse to denounce her is a poisonous subversion of things as they are (472). To appeal once more to the gods is to admit—more skeptically than Ovid—that they may exhibit an Olympian disregard for the whole situation: such is the question that Shakespeare explored in *King Lear*, and which such modern writers as Thomas Hardy have reconsidered. Yet if heaven takes any interest whatsoever in man's affairs, it might be expected to respond to so harassed an incarnation of feminine frailty, and its presumptive response inspires a last downward sweep of sinking metaphor. Its tears, burning like the lurid eyes of Pyrrhus, turning into milk like the revered hair of Priam, and associated by that maternal essence with Hecuba's 'o'er-teemed loins' (469), might produce a downpour more blinding than her 'bison rheum' (467) and thereby extinguish the holocaust of Troy. What commenced in firelight concludes in rainfall. Recoiling before this bathetic *Götterdämmerung*, Dryden remarks: 'Such a sight were indeed enough to have rais'd passion in the Gods, but to excuse the effects of it [the poet] tells you perhaps they did not see it.'

III

To break off the speech is to awaken Hamlet from what he calls 'a dream of passion'—a glaring nightmare of smoke and screams and ruins—to the light of day. But somber northern daylight renews 'the motive and the cue for passion' in his own life, and the Trojan retrospect becomes a Danish omen, joining the echoes of Caesar's assassination and other portents of Hamlet's tragedy. None of the others, however, could have seemed as epoch-making or epoch-shattering as the evocation of Priam, no less a byword for catastrophe to the Elizabethans than the name of Hiroshima seems to us. 'O what a fall was there, my countrymen.' The catastrophic mood that overtook sensitive Englishmen during the latter years of Elizabeth's reign, particularly after the downfall of Essex, had set the key for the play. From the long-echoing lament of Hecuba, as enunciated by Ovid, Shakespeare had learned the rhetorical lesson of copiousness. It is also probable that his books of rhetoric had taught him an old argument of Quintilian's: that the orator who pens his own speeches would move his hearers more profoundly than the mere elocutionist who recites what someone else has felt and thought and written. At all events, the surface of the drama is undisturbed by the Player's elocution. Again he is merely a player; Polonius is quite unaffected; and Hamlet completes his arrangements for the morrow's performance of the play that will affect Claudius as—it soon appears—this foretaste has affected him. Hitherto constrained from weeping or speaking his mind, he now reveals that the player has wept and spoken for him. The deeply reveal-ing soliloquy that completes the Second Act and sets the scene for the Third, 'O what a rogue and peasant slave am I,' pulls aside the curtain of heavily figured declamation that has just been spread before us for that very purpose.

   To be more precise, the soliloquy is the mirror-opposite of the speech. Both passages are very nearly of the same length, and seem to be subdi-vided into three movements which run somewhat parallel. But where the speech proceeds from the slayer to the slain, and from the royal victim to the queenly mourner, the soliloquy moves from that suggestive figure to another king and finally toward another villain. And where the speech leads from action to passion, the soliloquy reverses this direction. Where the Player's diction is heavily external, underlining the funda-mental discrepancy between words and deeds, Hamlet's words are by convention his thoughts, directing inward their jabs of self-accusation. Midway, where the Player curses Fortune as a strumpet, Hamlet falls 'a-cursing like a very drab.' Well may he hesitate, 'like a neutral to his will and matter,' at the very point where even the rugged Pyrrhus paused and did nothing. Though we need not go so far as Racine, who refined that model of bloody retribution into the gallant lover of Andromaque ('vio-lent mais sincère'), we may cite the precedent as a justification—if fur-ther justification still be needed—for Hamlet's often criticized delay. While he must hold his tongue, so long as he 'cannot speak' his genuine sentiments, the Player is vocal on his behalf. Since he is all too literally 'the observed of all observers,' he must enact a comedy and so must they: the courtly comedy of fashionable observance. He offers Rosencrantz and Guildenstern the same treatment that he accords the Players, to whom he also must 'show fairly outwards.' Polonius, who has acted in his youth, ends—all too ironically—as Hamlet's 'audience.' And while the courtiers watch Hamlet, he watches Claudius, the most subtle impersonator of them all, who conceals his villainy behind a smile and only reveals it while watching a dramatic performance.

Afterwards, when Hamlet confronts his mother with her 'act,' he undertakes to show her 'a glass / Where you may see the inmost part of you.' The Elizabethan conception of art as the glass of nature was ethical rather than realistic; for it assumed that, by contemplating situations which reflected their own, men and women could mend their ways and act with greater resolution thereafter. To the observer who is painfully learning the distinction between *seems* and *is*, the hideous pangs of the Trojan Queen are the mirrored distortions of Gertrude's regal insincerities. The 'damn'd defeat' of Priam, reminding Hamlet of his father, prompts him to denounce his hitherto passive role, to soliloquize on the Player's example, and finally to evolve his plan of action. Thus his soliloquy departs from, and returns to, the theatrical sphere. 'The play's the thing'—the play-within-the-play, where the Player's 'passionate speech' will be crowned by the Play Queen's 'passionate action,' and the crime will be metaphorically ('tropically') reenacted, beginning and ending with Hamlet's echoed quotations from two notorious tragedies of revenge. Meanwhile the situation at hand is transcended by the searching question in Hamlet's mind—a question which ponders not only the technique of acting, but the actual nature of the esthetic process. * * * What is the relationship of the player to the play, of the dancer to the dance, of the work of art to its interpretation, or of the interpreter to the audience? How, Shakespeare asks himself in effect, can emotion be communicated by my dramaturgy?

Observe—and here I beg leave to reduce our text for the moment to a paradigm (see Figure 1, page 216)—that he does not present Hecuba's emotions directly. Her passion, unlike Thisbe's, is neither presented nor described. Instead he describes her appearance and appeals to the spectator: 'Who, O who,' he opines—or even more lugubriously, as the Quartos would have it, 'Who, ah woe!'—whoever viewed that spectacle would repudiate destiny itself. Thence the poet appeals the case to a higher court:

> But if the gods themselves did *see* her, then,
> When she [Hecuba] *saw* Pyrrhus make malicious sport,
> In mincing with his sword her husband's [Priam's] limbs—

even they (the GODS) might feel an emotional response, though such a prospect is conditionally stated. Let us meet the condition by recognizing their existence on a highly figurative plane, and by characterizing their attitude as *compassion*: a sympathetic participation in the feelings of Hecuba. * * * HECUBA is likewise an onlooker, tense though the bond of sympathy must be that unites her to the agonies of Priam; it is he who feels, who suffers physically when Pyrrhus acts. PYRRHUS is

your man of *action*, in the most epical and extroverted signification of
the term: the key to this passage is the emphasis that Shakespeare places
upon his insensibility. Furthermore, no effort is made to present the
sufferings of PRIAM: his falling city sympathizes with him, his animistic
sword rebels against him, but he himself remains inanimate. Tradition
depicts him slain upon the altar of Apollo, and—although Shakespeare
makes no point of this circumstance—it sheds the light of religious ritual
upon his sacrifice, and helps to explain why so many generations could
identify it with their experience. In terms of sheer brutality, or ritualistic
fulfilment, the murder might be regarded as a *passion*, and differentiated
by an exclamation-point from the question-mark that might appropriately designate the psychological *passion* of Hecuba. But even the
burden of her grief, as we have noticed, is relayed to higher authorities:
if the gods exist and look down, perhaps their compassionate overview
will gather up the vicarious passions of the dead Priam, the unfeeling
Pyrrhus, and the muffled queen. And we are left confronting a dizzying
hierarchy of externalized emotion, which continues to refer our query
upwards until it is out of sight.

Let us therefore look in the other direction, downwards—from the
eyes of the gods, past Hecuba and the murderer and the murdered, to
the voice of the narrator. When all is said and done, we must not forget
that it is AENEAS who speaks: a surviving eye-witness who relives the
tale as he tells it to Dido. Since she is not represented, its impact on her
goes unregistered. But since the epic has been adapted to the drama,
narration has become *action* in quotation-marks, simulated actuality;
while Aeneas is enacted by the PLAYER. Shakespeare exploits the
ambiguity of the verb 'to act,' which alternates between 'doing' and
'seeming,' between the brutal deeds of Pyrrhus and the verbal hypocri-
sies that Hamlet dwells on: 'For they are actions that a man might
play . . .' By means of his acting, the Player simulates *passion*, again in
quotation-marks; he functions as a surrogate for the various mythical
figures whose respective sorrows he personifies, and bridges the gap
between their world and Hamlet's. * * *

Since the theater perforce exaggerates, amplifying its pathos and styl-
izing its diction, it takes a specially marked degree of amplification and
stylization to dramatize the theatrical, as Schlegel realized. Conversely,
when matters pertaining to the stage are exhibited upon the stage, to
acknowledge their artificiality is to enhance the realism of everything
else within view. The contrasting textures of the Player's fustian and
Hamlet's lines, like the structural contrast between the prevailing blank
verse and the rhyming couplets of the play-within-the-play, bring out
the realities of the situation by exposing its theatricalities. By exaggeration of drama, by 'smelling a little too strongly of the buskin' in Dryden's
phrase, Shakespeare achieves his imitation of life. Yet the play itself—
not 'The Murder of Gonzago' but *The Tragedy of Hamlet, Prince of*

Denmark—is 'a fiction,' an illusion which we accept on poetic faith. Hamlet's passion is sincere and sentient as compared to the Player's, which—though externalized and factitious—has aroused Hamlet from passivity to action. And of course he is not, in the very last analysis, 'passion's slave'; he is, he becomes, an agent of revenge; he suits 'the word to the action.' Nor is he a recorder to be played upon, though he succeeds in playing upon Claudius. The implied comparison with Aeneas would be completed by Dido's counterpart in the neglected person of Ophelia, but dalliance in either case is resolutely cut off. When Hamlet hits upon his ingenious plot, it projects him in two directions at once: back to the plane of intradramatic theatricals, and forward to the plane of his audience. A spectator of the players, he has his own spectators, who turn out to be ourselves, to whom he is actually an ACTOR. Here we stand in relation to him—that is, to his interpreter, be he Garrick or Gielgud—where he stands in relation to the Player. The original emotion, having been handed down from one level to another of metaphor and myth and impersonation and projection, reaches the basic level of *interpretation*, whence the expression can make its impression upon our minds. There the reality lodges, in the *reaction* of the AUDIENCE: the empathy that links our outlook with a chain of being which sooner or later extends all the way from the actors to the gods.

*   *   *

GODS	*compassion*
↑	
HECUBA	*passion?*
↑	
PYRRHUS	*action*
↑	
PRIAM	*passion!*
↑	
AENEAS	*narration*
↓	
PLAYER	*"action"*
↓	
HAMLET	*"passion"*
↓	
ACTOR	*interpretation*
↓	
AUDIENCE	*reaction*

FIGURE 1

PETER J. SENG

[Dramatic Function of the Songs in *Hamlet*]†

I

How should I your true love know
   From another one?
By his cockle hat and staff,
   And his sandal shoon.

(72)

He is dead and gone, lady,
   He is dead and gone;
At his head a grass-green turf,
   At his heels a stone.

(72–73)

White his shroud as the mountain snow

(73)

Larded all with sweet flowers;
   Which bewept to the grave [Q2: "ground"] did not go
With true-love showers. (73)

* * * The surface irony detected by most of the commentators—that the ballad relates to the death of Polonius—is not wrong; it simply does not go far enough. The song does, after all, tell of a loved one who has unexpectedly died and who has been buried without loving rites. . . . [But] the next level of interpretation ought to relate Ophelia's song more closely to its context. Ophelia's appearance on her entrance confirms what the audience has already heard about her, that she is mentally deranged. . . . Her first question is, "Where is the beauteous Majesty of Denmark?" We can echo with Granville-Barker, "Aye, indeed, where is she?" Certainly not in the wretched and haggard Queen confronting the mad girl. In timid words that betray her apprehension Gertrude responds, "How now, Ophelia?" Her nondescript question receives its only answer in [ll. 1-2 of] the song. It is easy to imagine the Queen's guilty start, her sudden dread of what the crazed girl may say. We sense it in her appalled question: "Alas, sweet lady, what imports this song?" . . . [It] clearly imports, among other things, that Gertrude once had a true-love whom she failed to distinguish from "another one." . . . [But]

† †Reprinted by permission of the publishers from *The Vocal Songs in the Plays of Shakespeare: A Critical History* by Peter J. Seng, Cambridge, Mass.: Harvard University Press. Copyright © 1967 by the President and Fellows of Harvard College. Songs are quoted from the text of this Norton Critical Edition. Bracketed words and phrases in the quoted passages that follow are found in the original. Page numbers given in parentheses refer to the text of this Norton Critical Edition of *Hamlet*.

"He is dead and gone, lady." "Nay, but Ophelia—" the Queen inter-
rupts, only to be told . . . that the true-love was one "Which bewept to
the grave did not go With true-love showers." That obviously interpolated negative chides Gertrude for her inadequate mourning for King
Hamlet, and perhaps for worse offences as well. * * *

                          *   *   *

Coleridge alone, among commentators on this song, seems to have
divined the memories that may underlie it in Ophelia's deranged mind.
In his lectures on Shakespeare he called attention to the conjunction in
her songs of

> two thoughts that had never subsisted in disjunction, the love for
> Hamlet and her filial love, and the guileless floating on the surface
> of her pure imagination of the cautions so lately expressed and the
> fears not too delicately avowed by her father and brother concern-
> ing the danger to which her honor lay exposed.[1]

The last the audience has seen of Ophelia before she enters deranged,
singing and playing on a lute, is the time when she sat beside Hamlet, a
naive auditor of the play-within-the-play. Prior to this occasion she has
known herself to be in love with Hamlet and has thought that Hamlet
loved her. Laertes' cautions on the perils of such a relationship she had
accepted with charming good humor, her father's strictures with loving
and dutiful obedience. She must have known as well as either of them
that Lord Hamlet was a prince out of her star, yet she was willing to bide
her time patiently, waiting his formal proposals. She had good reason to
expect them. The remarks made by Gertrude at her funeral,

> I hop'd thou shouldst have been my Hamlet's wife;
> I thought thy bride-bed to have deck'd, sweet maid,
> And not have strew'd thy grave   (89),

cannot have been unique on this occasion. And long before her death
Polonius himself admitted that his own earlier judgement of Hamlet's
"tenders of affection" might have been in error.

But the events which have transpired between the time of her appearance at the court play and her entrance "with her haire downe singing"
have undone her world. Her father has been killed—by her mad lover
as she believes—and hastily interred. Her brother is abroad at school in
a foreign land. Hamlet has been hustled out of Denmark and been put
aboard ship for England. The distraught girl could hardly turn to King
Claudius, and the "beauteous Majesty of Denmark," Gertrude, has
apparently been avoiding her. For Ophelia, as for Hamlet, Denmark
has become a prison, and she is all alone at Elsinore. It is the realization

---

1. For the quotation from Coleridge, see above, p. 162 [Editor].

of this fact, coming on top of all the earlier horrors, that destroys her sanity.

In the light of such a background the "true-love" of the ballad is now seen to be Hamlet. He has gone across the seas on a mysterious voyage whose import is unknown to her. Yet the song that she sings fancifully explains to her the mystery of his disappearance, illuminates in her deranged mind the few paltry facts she possesses. Hamlet has left Elsinore to make a pilgrimage to Walsingham—he has reason enough to do penance—and he can be recognized on the road by the habiliments of the pilgrim. To her, so much, at least, must seem plausible. But the old song has its own inexorable logic, and the romantic fiction of its tragic story becomes the only reality Ophelia knows: "He is dead and gone, Lady." For an audience viewing this scene, irony is added to the pathos. The nightmare delusion which assails the poor girl's mind is, in fact, the very reality which Claudius had intended.

Ophelia's song begins with an imaginary wayfarer's echo of her simple query about her missing lover; it ends with the equally simple statement about his burial in a foreign land. Hamlet has been laid to earth by strangers, and without the tribute of Ophelia's true-love tears. Such a burial is a foreshadowing of her own barren rites a few scenes later in the unconsecrated plot of Elsinore churchyard.

II

To-morrow is Saint Valentine's day,
    All in the morning betime,
And I a maid at your window,
    To be your Valentine.
Then up he rose, and donn'd his clo'es,
    And dupped the chamber-door,
Let in the maid, that out a maid
    Never departed more.
                (73)

By Gis and by Saint Charity,
    Alack, and fie for shame!
Young men will do't, if they come to't;
    By Cock, they are to blame.
Quoth she 'Before you tumbled me,
    You promised me to wed'.

He answers:

'So would I 'a done, by yonder sun,
    An thou hadst not come to my bed'.
                (73)

Ophelia may have learned her song from a "free-spoken" nurse-maid—or from almost anyone else in that free-spoken age; but the critics who are so concerned to salvage her innocence tend frequently to forget that it was not Hamlet alone who sullied it. Ophelia's father and brother have had their share in the spoliation of her mind's purity and her child-like trust. The cynicism of Laertes' remark (15),

> For Hamlet, and the trifling of his favour,
> Hold it a fashion, and a toy in blood;
> A violet in the youth of primy nature,
> Forward, not permanent—sweet, not lasting;
> The perfume and the suppliance of a minute;
> No more,

must have come as a shock to her gentle nature which believed men were what they seemed to be. Nor is Laertes content with a mere generalized admonition in his efforts to school her in lack of trust. He goes on to express in the plainest terms his suspicions about Hamlet's intentions, suspicions which, as far as Ophelia is concerned, nothing in Hamlet's conduct to her thus far would ever have occasioned (15):

> Then weigh what loss your honour may sustain
> If with too credent ear you list his songs,
> Or lose your heart, or your chaste treasure open
> To his unmast'red importunity.

Her brother's little lecture Ophelia charmingly turns aside, but he has sown doubts in her mind which Polonius' cruder tactics and language exploit to the full. The very abruptness and impatience with which her father catechizes her is an accusation of guilt where no guilt has been (17):

> I must tell you
> You do not understand yourself so clearly
> As it behooves my daughter and your honour.
> What is between you? Give me up the truth.

Between Hamlet and Ophelia have been only "tenders of his affection," as she submissively responds. But her words only warm her father to the subject at hand (17):

> Affection? Pooh! You speak like a green girl,
> Unsifted in such perilous circumstance.
> Do you believe his tenders, as you call them?

His remarks bear the same implications as his son's: no one is to be trusted or taken at face value. Ophelia's confused reply, "I do not know, my lord, what I should think," is clear evidence that the habit of mistrust, so ingrained in her father and brother, is something new to her. For, indeed, she had believed Hamlet; and, as it turns out, though tragically and too late, her trust was not misplaced. Yet father and son are concerned to throw a lurid light across the relationship. Polonius' bitter joke, "Tender yourself more dearly, Or . . . you'll tender me a fool" (*i.e.*, "Behave yourself more carefully or you will (1) make a fool of me (2) bring a bastard grandchild to me") is not lost on Ophelia. Its slander on her honor and on her love for Hamlet stirs her to rebellious protest: "My lord, he hath importun'd me with love In honourable fashion." Polonius, however, is not one to brook rebellion in a green slip of a girl. "Ay, fashion you may call it. Go to, go to!" Ophelia makes one further effort to keep her vision of the world undefiled. She cannot believe that she could have been so mistaken in Hamlet, nor Hamlet so base in his protestations of love. Her appeal is to religion, for Hamlet "hath given countenance to his speech, my lord, With almost all the holy vows of heaven." But Polonius is not to be shaken from his own unlovely view of man and the world. Those "holy vows of heaven" are mere "springes to catch woodcocks." Years of politicking at court have taught him better than to believe in men's words, no matter how buttressed with religious oaths, and he rides roughshod over her trustful nature. He orders her to "be scanter" henceforth of her maiden presence, to set her entreatments at a higher rate than "a command to parley"; as for those "holy vows" (18),

> they are brokers,
> Not of that dye which their investments show,
> But mere implorators of unholy suits,
> Breathing like sanctified and pious bawds,
> The better to beguile.

The very diction in which he couches his warning is a slander.

It may be argued that Laertes and Polonius are merely exercising the prudent judgement of men of the world, men who know something of Renaissance courts and courtiers; and only the briefest acquaintance with the social history of Elizabeth I's court suggests that even in that stronghold of Diana a father would need be wary about his daughter. Yet those critics who would urge that Polonius is merely prudent here will be hard put to defend him a few scenes later when he tells Claudius that he will "loose" his daughter to Hamlet for purposes of entrapment; and how is Polonius to be defended at all for the role of *agent provocateur* that he suggests Reynaldo take with Laertes' friends about the son's sexual morals?

The fact of the case seems to be that Polonius is only too willing to sacrifice morals to political expediency; and it is his spying, sneaking, and eavesdropping that finally brings about his own death. The interview with Ophelia may have begun as a rash and frightened father's attempt to warn his daughter about the ways of the world, but it ends as a groundless slander. Even during the interview there is no question in an audience's mind that the relations between Hamlet and Ophelia have been other than honest. Any niggling doubts about the matter are surely resolved by Gertrude's remark at Ophelia's grave, "I hop'd thou shouldst have been my Hamlet's wife," and Hamlet's equally open declaration (90),

> I lov'd Ophelia. Forty thousand brothers
> Could not (with all their quantity of love)
> Make up my sum.

This is not the language of trifling, beguilement, or seduction.

The relative importance of these successive interviews of Ophelia to the rest of the play can be gauged by the fact that Shakespeare gives almost the entire scene (I.iii) to them. The distorted vision of the world that Polonius and Laertes impress on Ophelia in this episode is clearly the beginning of her tragedy. That vision is reinforced by Hamlet's later "brutal" treatment of her, but his actions are motivated by the sense that she has already betrayed him. Thus the heroine of the song is far from being the Ophelia that Hamlet knew; rather she is the Ophelia that Polonius and Laertes, without real cause, had feared their daughter and sister might become.

III

> They bore him barefac'd on the bier;
> Hey non nonny, nonny, hey nonny;
> And in his grave rain'd many a tear—
> (76)

> For bonny sweet Robin is all my joy.
> (77)

> And will 'a not come again?
> And will 'a not come again?
>   No, no, he is dead,
>   Go to they death-bed,
> He never will come again.

> His beard was as white as snow,
> All flaxen was his poll;
>   He is gone, he is gone,
>   And we cast away moan;
> God-a-mercy on his soul!
> (77)

*   *   *

* * * Between . . . two funeral dirges Ophelia once more alludes in song to the circumstances of her relationship with Hamlet. For her brother, who was not present to hear her Valentine's song, she now has another, very similar in its implications. . . . Much of the relevance that this little fragment may have had for Shakespeare's audience is lost on us, since the ballad from which the line comes has apparently not survived. Yet . . . a great deal may be inferred. It is very likely that the source of Ophelia's lyric was a Robin Hood ballad. By Shakespeare's time these stories had already long undergone epic degeneration, and the name Maid Marian had become a by-word for promiscuity. Hence if Ophelia in this song is picturing herself as Marian to Hamlet's Robin Hood, she is merely envisioning once again the nightmare world of her Valentine's song.

All three of these songs can be seen to be intimately related to the tragic fortunes of the family of Polonius. Two are dirges for the dead father, while the ballad-fragment reminds the audience of the love between Ophelia and Hamlet, and of Polonius' and Laertes' fears and warnings concerning that love. Rash and distraught, Laertes wholly fails to comprehend his own measure of responsibility for the events that have befallen. Yet a close examination of this episode seems to show that Shakespeare has taken pains to make the irony clear.

Laertes storms onto the stage midway in IV.v. filled only with thoughts of avenging his father's death. As yet he knows nothing of his sister's madness. Claudius promises the angry youth the revenge he seeks, and at the same time absolves himself from any guilt or complicity in Polonius' death. It is at this point that Ophelia enters. Stunned with horror, Laertes looks at the crazed girl. Almost as if anticipating her language of flowers a few moments later he cries out, "O rose of May," and then,

> is't possible a young maid's wits
> Should be as mortal as an old man's life? (76)

Immediately after her first dirge he reverts—now with renewed purpose—to thoughts of revenge:

> Hadst thou thy wits, and didst persuade revenge,
> It could not move thus.

Ophelia's only reply to her brother is to assign him a part—the refrain—in a ballad she will sing of a "false steward that stole his master's daughter." Her words mean nothing to Laertes; he fails to recall that it was just such false lovers that he had once warned her against. He is heedless of every thought except revenge: "This nothing's more than matter," he says, meaning that the nonsense she speaks, a symptom of her madness, is more than a material cause to prompt his vengeance. There is appalling irony in Ophelia's next words:

> There's rosemary, that's for remembrance. Pray
> you, love, remember. And there is pansies,
> that's for thoughts. (76)

But this, too, falls on a wooden understanding.

Some months earlier Laertes had told Ophelia to regard Hamlet's attentions as

> a fashion, and a toy in blood;
> A violet in the youth of primy nature. (15)

Now she pays him back in verbal kind:

> I would give you some violets, but they
> wither'd all when my father died. (77)

And then, finally, as if in summary of all the earlier hints and allusions, the wild and incredible song: "For bonny sweet Robin is all my joy." That she should sing such a song in the midst of her imaginative funeral rites for her father, and in the actual presence of her brother, is Shakespeare's final bitter irony. She "speaks things in doubt, That carry but half sense," says an anonymous "Gentleman" at the beginning of IV.v. Ophelia's "half sense," however, carries just about as much poignancy as an audience can bear.

IV

> In youth, when I did love, did love,
>   Methought it was very sweet,
> To contract-O-the time for-a-my behove,
>   O, methought there-a-was nothing-a-meet.
>   (85)

> But age, with his stealing steps,
>   Hath clawed me in his clutch,
> And hath shipped me intil the land,
>   As if I had never been such.
>   (85)

> A pick-axe and a spade, a spade,
>   For and a shrouding sheet:
> O, a pit of clay for to be made
>   For such a guest is meet.
>   (86)

The gravedigger's song is a garbled and fragmentary version of a poem by Thomas Lord Vaux titled, "The aged louer renounceth loue." It was first printed in Richard Tottel's *Songs and Sonettes*, 1557 * * *, but also

exists in a number of early manuscript copies. * * * The text which
follows is from [Hyder E.] Rollins' edition of Tottel [Cambridge, Mass.
1928–29, I, 165 ff.].

The aged louer renounceth loue.

I Lothe that I did loue,
    In youth that I thought swete:
As time requires for my behoue
Me thinkes they are not mete,

    My lustes they do me leaue,   5
My fansies all be fledde:
And tract of time begins to weaue,
Gray heares vpon my hedde.

    For age with stelyng steppes,
Hath clawed me with his cowche: 10
And lusty life away she leapes,
As there had bene none such.

    My muse dothe not delight
Me as she did before:
My hand and pen are not in plight,   15
As they haue bene of yore.

    For reason me denies,
This youthly idle rime:
And day by day to me she cryes,
Leaue of these toyes in time.   20

    The wrincles in my brow,
The furrowes in my face:
Say limpyng age will hedge him now,
Where youth must geue him place.

    The harbinger of death,   25
To me I see him ride:
The cough, the colde, the gaspyng breath,
Dothe bid me to prouide.

    A pikaxe and a spade,
And eke a shrowdyng shete,   30
A house of claye for to be made,
For such a gest most mete.

Me thinkes I heare the clarke,
That knols the careful knell:
And bids me leaue my wofull warke,   35
Er nature me compell.

My kepers knit the knot,
That youth did laugh to scorne:
Of me that clene shalbe forgot,
As I had not ben borne.   40

Thus must I youth geue vp,
Whose badge I long did weare:
To them I yelde the wanton cup
That better may it beare.

Loe here the bared scull,   45
By whose balde signe I know:
That stoupyng age away shall pull,
Which youthfull yeres did sowe.

For beauty with her bande
These croked cares hath wrought: 50
And shipped me into the lande,
From whence I first was brought.

And ye that bide behinde,
Haue ye none other trust:
As ye of claye were cast by kinde,   55
So shall ye waste to dust.

It is either a failing memory or an ill acquaintance with the original song—perhaps a little of both—which accounts for the gravedigger's mangling of his text. From the very outset he confuses the metrical pattern (in the original it is 3-3-4-3, a perfectly respectable meter), and attempts to impose on it instead a common ballad meter (4-3-4-3) that may have been more familiar to him. Once off stride, he never recaptures the original with any accuracy; when he cannot remember what follows the lines or stanzas he sings, he fills in with fragments from other parts of the song.

He begins his song by borrowing "In youth" from the second line of his source, but bridges the gap which that borrowing leaves by repeating the "Me thinkes" of Vaux's fourth line as the "Me thought" of his own second and fourth lines. He then drops a whole stanza of the original, only to resume with the first two lines of the third quatrain in the original, and quotes with fair accuracy until he arrives at "cowche," itself a misprint in Tottel's 1557 *Songs and Sonettes* (all the manuscripts and later editions give the correct reading, "crutch"), when he makes a not so crude emendation of his own, "clutch." For the seventh line of his song he goes to the fifty-first line of his source, leaving the first rhyme blind, but returns to the proper stanza to complete his second quatrain with the correct rhyme, even if he does garble the last line. He next omits four stanzas in the original to hit on a fifth that is appropriate to his activities. This stanza he again throws into ballad meter by repeating the final foot of the first line. In the second line he anticipates the last one by beginning with "for," but corrects himself, and in the third he substitutes the simpler and more direct "pit" for the metaphor "house."

The incongruity of the song with the task which prompts it—a grave being dug for Ophelia—is a reflection of the disordered moral universe of the whole play. The lives of all the characters seem to have been infected by Claudius' original crime. First to fall victim to the general moral sickness are those very institutions which were intended in their origins to confer dignity on important human occasions. King Hamlet himself has had no decent period of mourning, since

> The funeral bak'd meats
> Did coldly furnish forth the marriage tables

for the hasty wedding of Claudius and Gertrude. The courtship of Hamlet and Ophelia is next blasted. Polonius dies without dignity behind an arras, and with even less dignity is hastily interred in his grave. The drowned Ophelia receives but "maimed rites," and these only a few minutes after the gravedigger has been callously singing, and Hamlet bitterly jesting, over her grave.

The song and its setting—the grisly quibbles and speculations by the two clowns and by Hamlet and Horatio about death—dominate the scene. Three fourths of V.i. is given over to evoking the "metaphysical shudder." The song tells of love and death, youth and old age, and so echoes those earlier songs of Ophelia. The scene has its antecedents in the medieval Dance of Death, but also sounds the great seventeenth-century diapason that is heard in Donne's sermons and meditations, Browne's *Urn-Burial*, and in the sweeping peroration that closes Ralegh's fragmentary *History of the World*.

REBECCA WEST

The Nature of Will†

Yet Hamlet recognizes the value of tradition. That is made clear by the courage he shows in choosing to meet the ghost and in casting off the

---

† From *The Court and the Castle* (New Haven: Yale UP, 1958) 17–32. Copyright © 1958 by Yale University Press. Reprinted by permission of Yale University Press. Page numbers given in parentheses refer to the text of this Norton Critical Edition of *Hamlet*.

hands of his companions when it bids him follow it and they seek to
hold him back. But he feels no real reverence for tradition. That is a
very strange scene, when he swears his companions to secrecy on his
sword, and the ghost raps upward on the earth they stand on, and Hamlet says, "You hear this fellow in the cellarage" (25). The root of this
disrespect becomes explicable when we inquire into Hamlet's attitude to
humanity. For tradition is the distillation of human experience, and it
must be condemned if humanity is condemned; and Hamlet was disgusted by his own kind.

There are other crimes afoot in Elsinore, in the world, as well as
murder. The ghost wishes Hamlet to avenge his murder and also to put
an end to the unholy offense of the marriage between his widow and his
murderer. But when Hamlet talks of these matters with his mother he
loses all interest in that part of the command which relates to his father's
murder, and in the course of over eighty lines addressed to her he devotes
only three to a perfunctory mention of the fact that her present husband
murdered her previous husband, and when she shows that she did not
know that any such crime had been committed he does not take the
opportunity of enlightening her. He simply tells her that she is behaving
reprehensibly in living with her present husband, not because he had
murdered her dead husband and his own brother, but because he was
not so good looking as her dead husband. It is not surprising, though it
is always comic, that the ghost should then reappear in order to ask
Hamlet to stick to the point. "Do not forget: this visitation Is but to whet
thy almost blunted purpose" (63). But a revelation is made in the course
of the scene. The Queen admits the charge of sensuality (62–63):

> Oh, Hamlet, speak no more,
> Thou turn'st mine eyes into my very soul,
> And there I see such black and grained spots
> As will not leave their tinct.

Claudius is guilty, the Queen is guilty, and so as this scene makes quite
plain, is Hamlet. All that he says is smeared with a slime which is the
mark of sexual corruption. His curious emphasis on the physical difference between the dead King and the living Claudius hints at a homosexual element in his nature, but that is irrelevant. Hamlet could be neither
a heterosexual nor a homosexual lover. Such an egotist would be restricted
to lust, for he could not afford the outgoings of love.

This has been indicated earlier in the play by his scenes with Ophelia.
There is no more bizarre aspect of the misreading of Hamlet's character
than the assumption that his relations with Ophelia were innocent and
that Ophelia was a correct and timid virgin of exquisite sensibilities.
Probably the conception would not have lasted so long in England had
it not been for the popularity of the pre-Raphaelite picture by Sir John
Millais which represents her as she floated down the glassy stream, the

weeping brook; for his model was his friend Rossetti's bride, the correct, timid, sensitive, virginal, and tubercular Miss Siddal, and she was, poor thing, especially wan during the painting of the picture, for she was immersed in a tin bath full of water kept warm by a lamp placed underneath, like an old-fashioned hot-water dish. We have certainly put Ophelia into the wrong category and into the wrong century. She was not a chaste young woman. That is shown by her tolerance of Hamlet's obscene conversations, which cannot be explained as consistent with the custom of the time. If that were the reason for it, all the men and women in Shakespeare's plays, Romeo and Juliet, Beatrice and Benedict, Miranda and Ferdinand, Antony and Cleopatra, would have talked obscenely together, which is not the case. "The marriage of true minds" would hardly, even in the most candid age, have expressed itself by this ugly chatter, which Wilson Knight has so justly described as governed by "infra-sexual neurosis." The truth is that Ophelia was a disreputable young woman: not scandalously so, but still disreputable. She was foredoomed to it by her father, whom it is a mistake to regard as a simple platitudinarian. Shakespeare, like all major writers, was never afraid of a good platitude, and he would certainly never have given time to deriding a character because his only attribute was a habit of stating the obvious. Polonius is interesting because he was a cunning old intriguer who, like an iceburg, only showed one-eighth of himself above the surface. The innocuous sort of worldly wisdom that rolled off his tongue in butter balls was a very small part of what he knew. It has been insufficiently noted that Shakespeare would never have held up the action in order that Polonius should give his son advice as to how to conduct himself abroad, unless the scene helped him to develop his theme. But "This above all—to thine own self be true; And it must follow, as the night the day, Thou canst not then be false to any man" (16), has considerable contrapuntal value when it is spoken by an old gentleman who is presently going to instruct a servant to spy on his son, and to profess great anxiety about his daughter's morals, when plainly he needed to send her away into the country if he really wanted her to retain any.

There is no mistaking the disingenuousness of his dealings with his daughter. When Ophelia comes to him with her tale of how Hamlet had come to her as she was sewing in her chamber, "with his doublet all unbraced," and had looked madly on her, Polonius eagerly interprets this as "the very ecstasy of love," and asks her "What, have you given him any hard words of late?" Ophelia answers (28):

> No, my good Lord; but as you did command
> I did repel his letters, and denied
> His access to me.

At that Polonius purrs in satisfaction (28–29):

That hath made him mad.
I am sorry that with better heed and judgment
I had not quoted him: I fear'd he did but trifle,
And meant to wrack thee; but beshrew my jealousy!
It seems it is as proper to our age
To cast beyond ourselves in our opinions
As it is common for the younger sort
To lack discretion. Come, go we to the king.
This must be known; which, being kept close, might move
More grief to hide than hate to utter love.
Come.

This is the Court Circular version of Pandarus. The girl is not to be kept out of harm's way. She is a card that can be played to take several sorts of tricks. She might be Hamlet's mistress; but she might be more honored for resistance. And if Hamlet was himself an enemy of the King, and an entanglement with him had ceased to be a means of winning favor, then she can give a spy's report on him to Claudius. Surely Ophelia is one of the few authentic portraits of that army of not virgin martyrs, the poor little girls who were sacrificed to family ambition in the days when a court was a cat's cradle of conspiracies. Man's persuasion that his honor depends on the chastity of his women folk has always been liable to waste away and perish within sight of a throne. Particularly where monarchy had grown from a yeasty mass of feudalism, few families found themselves able to resist the temptation to hawk any young beauty in their brood, if it seemed likely that she might catch the eye of the king or any man close to the king. Unfortunately the king's true favorite was usually not a woman but an ideology. If royal approval was withdrawn from the religious or political faith held by the family which had hawked the girl, she was as apt to suffer fatality as any of her kinsmen. The axe has never known chivalry. Shakespeare, writing this play only three reigns from Henry the Eighth, had heard of such outrages on half-grown girls from the lips of those who had seen the final bloodletting. He wrote elsewhere of Anne Boleyn; and he must have heard much of the worse case, which did not excite so much compassion because the edge of the tragedy had been taken off by repetition, the case of Katherine Howard. She, who had been beheaded half a century before, was one of the Catholic Howards, a poor relative of the Duke of Norfolk, and had grown up in the attics and passages and antichambers of a disordered country seat, where maturing beauty brought her several lovers, one of whom she loved. But she did not marry him, because she was presently procured for the King, whom she pleased so well that he made her Queen. Pleasure, however, was not the most important issue involved. The marriage was a token of Henry's temporary softening toward Rome. But he hardened his heart again and turned again toward the innovators of Protestantism, and so the Howards fell out of favor, and Katherine's head was cut off when she was twenty years old.

Shakespeare had pondered on such massacres of the innocent, and he had thought it one of the worse offenses of the court (and he hated courts) that by the time the innocents were massacred, they were no longer innocent. The scene between Anne Boleyn and the bawdy old lady in the part-Shakespearean *Henry the Eighth* has an obvious pathos, because he knows and we know that the girl is doomed to die by the headsman's axe. But it is even more pathetic that she is deprived not only of her life, but of a noble death; for however bravely she bore herself when she laid her head on the block, she had nevertheless found her way there by a greedy intrigue which sought to snatch profit from the fall of an authentic queen. Like Anne Boleyn, Ophelia has lost her integrity. She fiddles with the truth when she speaks of Hamlet to her father, and she fiddles with the truth when she talks to Hamlet as her father and Claudius eavesdrop; and she contemplates without surprise or distaste Hamlet's obscenity, the scab on his spiritual sore.

Surely the picture of Ophelia shows that Shakespeare, who wrote more often of cruelty than any other great writer, was not a cruel man, and was great in pity, that rare emotion. He shows the poor little creature, whom the court had robbed of her honesty, receiving no compensation for the loss, but being driven to madness and done to death. For the myth which has been built round Hamlet is never more perverse than when it pretends that Ophelia went mad for love and killed herself. No line in the play suggests that she felt either passion or affection for Hamlet. She never mentions him in the mad scene, and Horatio says of her, "She speaks much of her father." Indeed she was in a situation which requires no sexual gloss. Her father had been murdered by a member of the royal house, and she found herself without protection, since her brother Laertes was in France, in the midst of a crisis such as might well send her out of her wits with fear. For the Danes hostile to the royal house made of her wrong a new pretext for their hostility, and the royal house, noting this, turned against her, helpless though she was. Claudius speaks of a general resentment (74):

> . . . The people muddied,
> Thick and unwholesome in their thoughts and whispers,
> For good Polonius' death; and we have done but greenly
> In hugger-mugger to inter him . . .

When Ophelia wanders to the Castle and asks that the Queen should receive her, she is refused. The Queen says, "I will not speak with her." But Horatio tells her she is not wise (72):

> She speaks much of her father; says she hears
> There's tricks i' th' world; and hems, and beats her heart;

Spurns enviously at straws; speaks things in doubt,
That carry but half sense; her speech is nothing.
Yet the unshaped use of it doth move
The hearers to collection; they aim at it,
And botch the words up fit to their own thoughts;
Which, as her winks and nods and gestures yield them,
Indeed would make one think there might be thought,
Though nothing sure, yet much unhappily.
'Twere good she were spoken with; for she may strew
Dangerous conjectures in ill-breeding minds.

Courts thus threatened had their own ways of dealing with the threats, as all courtiers knew; and Shakespeare must have heard of women thus dealt with who had been frightened into madness. Lady Rochford, who had helped Katherine Howard to meet her cousin Culpepper after her marriage, was raving mad when she went to her execution.

But neither from fear nor from love did Ophelia kill herself. She did not kill herself at all. The Queen describes her drowning as an accident. "An envious sliver broke," she says, and there is no indication that she was lying. Many things are packed into the passage which begins "There is a willow grows aslant a brook," but insincerity is not among them. These lines achieve a double dramatic value not often exploited in the theater. They are beautiful and expressive verse: their sound suggests heaviness submerging lightness, the soaked clothes dragging down the fragile body they encase, the inanimate flesh grown leaden round the spirit. But the lines are also in character. The Queen is one of the most poorly endowed human beings which Shakespeare ever drew. Very often he created fools, but there is a richness in their folly, whereas Gertrude is simply a stately defective. The whole play depends on her not noticing, and not understanding; and in this passage there are samples of her stupidity. The botanical digression about the long purples is ill-timed, and the epithet "mermaid-like" is not applicable to someone saved from drowning by an amplitude of skirts or to the skirts themselves. But the fusion of perception and obtuseness in these lines, and the contrast between their distinction and the empty rotundity of all the Queen's other speeches, convince us that just once this dull woman was so moved that her tongue became alive. It is not credible that at that moment she would have taken thought to deceive Laertes about the object of her emotion; nor indeed does Shakespeare suggest that she practiced any such deception.

For that Ophelia drowned herself is stated definitely only by two people: the clowns in the graveyard, typical examples of the idiot groundlings gorged on false rumor who appear so often in Shakespeare's plays. Whether we like it or not, we must admit that there is very little in the works of Shakespeare which could be used as propaganda for adult suffrage. For the rest, the priest declares that "her death was doubtful" (89), and that the doubt was enough to make it necessary that she should be buried with "maimed rites" (89). But surely we are not intended to believe him, for he is drawn as a bigot, who finds it possible to answer her brother coldly when he asks, "What ceremony else?" (89), and it is to be presumed that such lack of charity would invent a doubt. Shakespeare will not allow anyone in the graveyard scene, even to the priest, to be without sin. Each of them has helped to dig the girl's grave. Hamlet was the most guilty, for he had been her spurious lover and a tyrant prince, giving her no protection as a mistress or as one of his people; but it was the whole court that had destroyed her. She was a victim of society, which abandons principle for statecraft, for politics, for intrigue, because of its too urgent sense that it must survive at all costs, and in its panic loses cognizance of all the essentials by which it lives. Even her brother Laertes was not fully aware of his sister's tragedy, for he was tainted with the vice which Shakespeare feared most as a distraction: he was subject to lust.

This is indicated clearly enough in the early scene when Laertes warns Ophelia against the nature of Hamlet's courtships and she mocks him (16):

> But, good my brother,
> Do not as some ungracious pastors do,
> Show me the steep and thorny way to heaven,
> Whilst like a puft and reckless libertine,
> Himself the primrose path of dalliance treads,
> And recks not his own rede.

To this Laertes replies:

> Oh, fear me not.
> I stay too long. But here my father comes.

If Ophelia offers a *tu quoque* defense which we do not usually offer unless we are guilty, Laertes does not trouble to put up a defense at all. These two are no better than they should be; and Polonius, when he instructs his servant Reynaldo to spy on his son in Paris, speaks of drabbing and visiting "a house of sale, Videlicet, a brothel" (27), as if these were fairly certain to be among his son's activities. When Laertes leaps into his sister's grave, he cries (89–90):

> Now pile your dust upon the quick and the dead
> Till of this flat a mountain you have made
> To' o'ertop old Pelion or the skyish head
> Of blue Olympus.

For Shakespeare there was a connection between this outburst and the primrose path, the drabs, and the house of sale, Videlicet, a brothel. In his analysis of love that is not love, the hundred and twenty-ninth sonnet, he uses the word "extreme."

> The expense of spirit in a waste of shame
> Is lust in action; and till action, lust
> Is perjured, murd'rous, bloody, full of blame,
> Savage, extreme, rude, cruel, not to trust.

Laertes' expressions of grief are extreme. His mind rushes away from the dead girl on too long a journey, all the way to blue Olympus, and forgets its true grief in the excitement of travel. The essence of Ophelia has again been ignored, and the waste of a human being not appropriately resented.

It is Shakespeare's contention that the whole of the court is corrupt: society is corrupt. There is a flaw running horizontally through humanity wherever it is gathered together in space. It would seem natural therefore that Hamlet should obey the ghost and punish Claudius, who controls the court, who is an emblem of society. But the flaw runs vertically also; it runs through time, into the past. For Hamlet's father, the ghost, is in purgatory, doing penance for his sins, which were of the same gross kind as those he desires his son to punish. Shakespeare tells us this, stating the fact, and again using bombast to suggest immoderation (21):

> I am thy father's spirit,
> Doom'd for a certain term to walk the night,
> And for the day confined to fast in fires,
> Till the foul crimes done in my days of nature
> Are burnt and purged away. But that I am forbid
> To tell the secrets of my prison-house,
> I could a tale unfold, whose lightest word
> Would harrow up thy soul; freeze thy young blood;
> Make thy two eyes, like stars, start from their spheres,
> Thy knotted and combined locks to part,
> And each particular hair to stand an end,
> Like quills upon the fretful porpentine.

The ghost was indeed a sinner; the voice of tradition speaks from a tainted source. The evil in the world is not the product of the specially corrupt present generation, it has its roots in the generations that went before and also were corrupt; it has its roots in the race. There is no use pretending that we can frustrate our sinful dispositions by calling on tradition, because that also is the work of sinful man. This is the situation of our kind as it is shown to us in *Hamlet*, which is as pessimistic as any great work of literature ever written. The theme of the play could never appear to any reader who kept his eye on the text as the irresolution of Hamlet, his lack of the nerve which forms a hero (as Goethe put it), his failure to achieve a virtue which would consist simply of capacity for action. For what excites Shakespeare in this play is the impossibility of conceiving an action which could justly be termed virtuous, in view of the bias of original sin.

What does Shakespeare see written on the other side of the ledger? Nothing but beauty. This is the play which more than any of the others reminds us of the extraordinary advantages which he enjoyed. For it was his luck to see the human race at one of the moments, in one of the places, when it blossomed into a state of exceptional glory; and he moved among men and women who were beautiful, intelligent, learned, and fearless beyond the habit of our kind, and whose way of life, with its palaces and its pageants, was a proper setting for the jewels that they were. Here we ourselves enjoy an extraordinary advantage. Literature cannot always do its business of rendering an account of life. An age of genius not of the literary sort must go inadequately described unless there should happen to exist at the same time a literary genius of the same degree, who works in circumstances enabling him to accumulate the necessary information about his non-literary contemporaries. It happened that the Renaissance man was observed by Shakespeare. "What a piece of work is man! How noble in reason! How infinite in faculty! In form and moving how express and admirable! In action how like an angel! in apprehension how like a god! The beauty of the world! The paragon of animals!" (36). Here is a coincidence. Shakespeare was himself "the paragon of animals," therefore he could describe to us the man who was "the beauty of the world." He could write this description and make the whole character of Hamlet as shown from scene to scene bear out what he said about man.

All through the play Hamlet speaks with a quick, springing harmony recognizable as the voice of physical and mental splendor; his mind travels like lightning yet strikes below the surface, and is impulsive not in surrender to folly but in search of wisdom. How superior, to use Turgenev's words, he is in mind and temperament, how daring, how proud. In fact, Shakespeare has given us a picture of the Renaissance man, without the lacunae noticeable in the other attempts to portray him made by the Elizabethan and Jacobean dramatists, notably Ford and Webster. They tried to depict the new man created by the new wealth of Europe, the new community and continuity of culture, the new opening of windows on far parts of the globe and on the minutiae of matter. But they fall into the trap of showing the Renaissance man at his experiments without explaining why he felt free to experiment, without bringing forward the good reasons he had for thinking that he might tamper with the existing moral world. Even Marlowe took the Faust legend for his great work, and accounted for his Renaissance man by devil-dealing; but Shakespeare in Hamlet makes the Renaissance man his own Mephistopheles, and depicts a being so gifted that he needs no supernatural being to raise him above the common lot. But Shakespeare, the supreme artist observing this supreme man, immediately adds, "And yet to me what is the quintessence of dust?" And his genius has been asking that question throughout the play. Scene after scene has demonstrated the paragon of animals to be an animal, the world to be so diseased that even its beauty is infected. This speech of homage to man is indeed an example of teasing ambiguity; it can be read without irony or with irony; each reading is equally faithful to the text.

Shakespeare hopes for little from the dust. It is quite certain that he wished to present Hamlet as a bad man, because he twice makes him rejoice at the thought of murdering men who had not made their peace with God. He might have killed Claudius when he came on him at prayer. But he decided this might mean that Claudius would go straight to heaven (60):

> Up, sword; and know thou a more horrid hent;
> When he is drunk, asleep, or in his rage;
> Or in th'incestuous pleasure of his bed;
> At gaming, swearing or about some act
> That has no relish of salvation in't;
> Then trip him, that his heels may kick at heaven;
> And that his soul may be as damn'd and black
> As hell, whereto it goes.

Later on, when he tells Horatio of his peculiarly cold-blooded murder of Rosenkrantz and Guildenstern, his description of the letter he forged to the King of England shows traces of a like perverse determination to kill the soul as well as the body (92):

> An earnest conjuration from the king,—
> As England was his faithful tributary;
> As love between them like the palm might flourish;
> As peace should still her wheaten garland wear,
> And stand a comma 'tween their amities;
> And many such-like As-es of great charge,—
> That, on the view and knowing of these contents,
> Without debatement further, more or less,
> He should the bearers put to sudden death,
> Not shriving-time allow'd.

There would be no question at all in the minds of an Elizabethan audience that a murderer who could cheat his victims of their chance of salvation was a very bad man indeed; and indeed most of us would think with repulsion of such an action, if, through the hazards of war or dictatorship, it came within our experience.

But to this bad man Shakespeare ascribes one virtuous action; and the nature of that action is determined by his most lasting preoccupation. It is a political action. Hamlet gives his dying breath to thought for the future of his people; his last words choose a ruler for them (100):

O, I die, Horatio;
The potent poison quite o'ercrows my spirit;
I cannot live to hear the news from England;
But I do prophesy th' election lights
On Fortinbras: he has my dying voice.
So tell him, with the occurents, more and less,
Which have solicited—the rest is silenced.

Hamlet was never more the Renaissance man—who was a statesman, a true Macchiavellian, a prince careful for the safety of his subjects. Even if one be disillusioned with the race, and suspect paragons and the beauty of the world, this is still admirable. These fragile creatures, so little changed from dust that they constantly revert to it, show bravery in their intention that their species shall survive as if it were marble. Yet, all the same, how horrid is the sphere in which they show their excellence. The court was saved by its political conscience; yet it was damned by it too.

ARNOLD KETTLE

[Hamlet in a Changing World]†

*   *   *

I will first put, as a hypothesis, a description of *Hamlet* which, though obviously oversimplified, I think gets somewhere near the heart of the play, what it is about.

Hamlet is a sixteenth-century prince who, because of certain extremely disturbing personal experiences, the death of his father and his mother's marriage to his uncle, comes to see his world in a different way. This new vision affects everything: his attitude to his friends and family, his feelings about sex, his view of the court and its politics, his image of himself. The experience is so all-embracing and so shattering that he is not at first sure that his new vision can be true or, if it is, whether he can endure it. But as the situation clarifies he becomes convinced of its validity and comes to understand its implications better. In this he is helped by two things: his education, which has predisposed him towards a humane and rational approach to life, and his friendship with Horatio, another young man who, though much less brilliant than Hamlet, is also a humanist scholar and who stands firm in loyalty and affection when the rest of the world treats him as a pitiable or dangerous neurotic.

† From "From *Hamlet* to *Lear*," by Arnold Kettle in *Shakespeare in a Changing World*, (London, 1964) 146–157. Reprinted by permission of the publisher, Lawrence and Wishart. Page numbers given in parentheses refer to the text of this Norton Critical Edition of *Hamlet*.

At first Hamlet, though of an active disposition, is almost over-whelmed by the difficulty of solving his problems—especially with regard to his uncle—in terms of his new way of looking at things. He more or less deliberately prolongs the business of testing-out his well-founded suspicions and allows his uncle to get back the initiative and ship him out of the country. At this point, however, he comes to the conclusion that he cannot avoid acting, even if the actions he takes cannot satisfac-torily meet all the problems he has unearthed. He acts very decisively therefore on the voyage to England, returns to Denmark and, moved beyond measure by the suicide of Ophelia and the reactions of her stupid but not ineffectual brother, puts on once more the bearing and respon-sibilities of a prince and solves the situation in action in the only way he can, by killing the king, leaving Prince Fortinbras to reign in his place, and begging Horatio to live on to tell the tale.

The degree to which Hamlet, in the last act, capitulates to the values he has previously rejected—the extent to which he gives up the battle to act as a man rather than as a prince—corresponds, I suggest, to the actual possibilities in the year 1600 of putting into practice the ideas of the new humanism or, perhaps more accurately, holds the mirror up to nature in the sense that certain limitations in sixteenth-century human-ism and discrepancies between humanist theory and practice are revealed.

Hamlet's new view of the world he lives in is, essentially, the view of the world of the most advanced humanists of his time. It rejects as intol-erable the ways of behaviour which formed the accepted standards of the contemporary ruling class. The basic view of man of the feudal ruling class had been, in theory, a metaphysical one which saw man as a fallen creature seeking to win redemption through submission to and service of God, in practice a highly conservative one which saw each man as having a specific, appointed place within existing society, and wisdom as acceptance of this fact. Within this view abuses of responsibility—tyranny, cruelty, murder—were theoretically condemned but in practice sanctioned by political custom. There was no lack of all three in Eliza-bethan England. The revolutionary nature of Hamlet's view of the world is that he sees tyranny and murder and inhumanity not as unfortunate abuses but as the norm and essence of the court of Denmark, not as blots on a society he can accept but as integral parts of a way of life he now finds intolerable.

In other words, Hamlet can no longer base his values and actions on the accepted assumptions of the conventional sixteenth-century prince. He ceases to behave as a prince ought to behave and begins behaving as a man, a sixteenth-century man, imbued with the values and caught up in the developing and exciting potentialities of the new humanism. The words which Hamlet comes back to in his deepest moments of need and trouble are the words man and friend.

> He was a man, take him for all in all   (12)

is the best he can say of the best of men, his father. And when, dying, he stretches out his hand to Horatio it is with the words 'As thou art a man, Give me the cup'. He scarcely speaks, even in the two great solil- oquies most relevant to his public position and behaviour ('O, what a rogue and peasant slave am I!' and 'How all occasions do inform against me') of his duties and obligations as a prince, except in so far as he happens to be the son of a murdered father who was also a king; always the question is, what should a *man* do? He scarcely refers to what, in any of the Histories, would have been uppermost in the thoughts of a prince whose father has been murdered: his own claims to the throne.

Throughout the play he is obsessed by the contradiction between his own desperate unease and his vital sense of the potentialities of man, so noble in reason, infinite in faculty, 'the beauty of the world, the paragon of animals'. (36). It is this contradiction that provides the underlying dramatic and verbal tensions of the soliloquies and makes them so much more than exercises in melancholic introspection. It is Hamlet's opti- mism and vitality that give his pessimism and misery their unique power to move us. He is so unbearably horrified by a man like Claudius because he has recognized the possibility of being a different kind of man. What most disgusts him about Rosencrantz and Guildenstern is their betrayal of friendship, but when Horatio uses the conventional 'your poor servant ever' he at once replies

> Sir, my good friend. I'll change that name with you.
> (12)

When Polonius is asked to see the players well bestowed, he says, think- ing to please the Prince who has been expatiating on their virtues,

> My lord, I will use them according to their desert

and Hamlet cuts back with

> God's bodykins, man, much better. Use every man after
> his desert, and who shall scape whipping?
> (41)

Obviously Hamlet is not a twentieth-century democrat; his thinking remains deeply sixteenth-century in its flavour. But within the context in which he is operating his humanism has very definite democratic implications—as any able actor doing the part before a modern audience quickly discovers—especially when it is contrasted with the social and political attitudes of Claudius, Laertes, Polonius and Fortinbras.

At the centre of any discussion of *Hamlet* must always be what he himself calls his 'mystery'. I think it is important to recognize that this mystery, though it includes a psychological 'state', cannot be adequately described in purely psychological terms. It involves not only Hamlet but the world he lives in. If his view of that world had no real basis, if it were at bottom a delusion, then one would be justified in seeing Hamlet, as his interpreters on the stage often seem to see him, as a 'case', a neurotic. But Shakespeare is at pains to show that Hamlet's view of his world in the opening scenes of the play is not a delusion. It is the worldly-wise of the play, in particular the Queen and Polonius, who are time and time again shown to be deluded. In his very first speech, after his three sardonic puns, Hamlet states the problem. The King and Queen are trying to persuade him to be sensible about his father's death. Everyone dies. To die is common.

> If it be,
> Why seems it so particular with thee?

asks his mother, immediately treating Hamlet as the queer one. But he, whose experience has made him aware of the double edges of words as well as deeds, immediately seizes on her least-considered assumption and throws it back:

> Seems, Madam! Nay, it is; I know not seems.

It is not his superficial behaviour, the forms, moods and shows of grief, that can denote him truly.

> These, indeed, seem;
> For they are actions that a man might play;
> But I have that within which passes show—
> These but the trappings and the suits of woe.
> (10)

The contrast between 'seems' and 'is' is a key question in the play. And it is not treated metaphysically. The contrast between appearance and reality which Hamlet at once emphasizes is not at all an abstract philosophical problem: it is a problem of behaviour and human values. When he cries out agonizingly

> That one may smile, and smile, and be a villain;

he adds at once

> At least I am sure it may be so in Denmark.
> (23)

The phrase 'I have that within that passes show' means not only 'I cannot express what I feel' but 'What I have experienced makes further pretence at conformity impossible'. Hamlet is putting the issue quite bluntly: which way of feeling and behaving corresponds most fully to the situation? The Queen's and the court's, or his? Who is putting on a show? Is it the conventional, 'normal' behaviour of the court that 'is', so that he 'seems' the odd man out, or is it *their* behaviour that involves dissimulation and self-deception, the rejection of reality?

Hamlet, at the beginning of the play, is on the verge of suicide, seeing life as entirely weary, stale, flat and unprofitable. The delineation of this state of mind is so convincing and indeed so clinically precise that it immediately entitles Shakespeare to an honoured place in the history of psychology. But the limitation of Freudian interpretations of the play[1] is that, though they can throw light on the nature of Hamlet's experience and reactions—the effects on him of his father's murder (which he already half-suspects) and his mother's marriage—they tend to draw attention away from the real dramatic significance of that experience, that it makes him see the world differently in ways which have little to do with the experience itself. The personal crisis Hamlet has been through is the *occasion* of his new vision but does not explain it or help us to judge its ultimate validity. We are so used to separating 'personal' from 'public' issues in our thinking that it is not easy for us to recognize that Hamlet's discontent is not merely private: on the contrary, it is deepened and validated by his perception that the values and attitudes which corrupt personal relationships are essentially the same values and attitudes which reside at the corrupt core of the public world.

Shakespeare goes out of his way to emphasize that what Hamlet is up against is not a problem of personal relationships simply but a whole society. 'Something is rotten in the state of Denmark'. The rottenness is not psychological (though it has its psychological manifestations all right) but social. This is stressed right through the play. The King and the state are reflections of one another.[2] It is the *time* that is out of joint, not Hamlet. The difficulty of his dilemma is that he sees all too clearly for his comfort that it is only by setting the time right that he can set himself right. This and not some metaphysical mole is the 'cursed spite' behind his mystery.

That is why it is unforgiveable to act Hamlet as though he were a neurotic instead of a hero and why one must reject as hopelessly on the wrong track any interpretations of the play which offer us a 'negative' Hamlet skulking in the wings of a sanity represented by the Court of Denmark.

What Hamlet has come to see, as a result of the goings-on in his family, is, I would suggest, nothing less than what, from the point of view of an advanced sixteenth-century humanist, the Renaissance court of Denmark is actually like. The King, whom a generous-minded modern critic like Professor Wilson Knight can describe as 'a good and gentle king'[3] he sees as a drunken, lecherous murderer. The Queen is 'stew'd

1. As, for instance, Ernest Jones, *Hamlet and Oedipus* (1949) [see pp. 200–207, above—*Editor*].
2. This is brought out particularly in Act I. Sc. 4.
3. *The Wheel of Fire* (1930). Professor Knight rec-

ognizes, of course, that this is only one side of Claudius; but he argues that Claudius is presented as being 'human', Hamlet 'inhuman'. Hamlet is no doubt in the right but his philosophy is the

in corruption'. The politicians are time-servers and machiavels, without a decent principle between them, to whom the lives of the common people mean nothing except as a factor in personal struggles for power. The women are mere pawns in the intrigues of the court, generally willing pawns reducing themselves to the status of whores. Friends cannot be trusted. The values of love are those of the stud or the stock-market.

And all this does not 'seem' but 'is'. Shakespeare makes sure that we are in a position to check up on Hamlet's judgments, to see whether he is deluded or not. It is not only the authenticity of the Ghost and the conscience of the King that are tested out in the play scene but also the moral values of the Danish court. Shakespeare leaves much to the imagination but nothing to chance, permitting no escape into metaphysical generalities about 'the human condition'. We are spared no detail of Polonius's attitude to his son's taste of *la dolce vita* in Paris or of Claudius's complex political manoeuvres at home and abroad. The predatory Norwegian army crosses Denmark on its way to Poland before our eyes and we are left to choose between two comments, the cynical acceptance of the Norwegian captain who sees this as the way of the world (Claudius has already expressed his attitude succinctly with 'It likes us well') and Hamlet's immediate linking of the project with the rottenness in the state of Denmark:

> This is th' imposthume[4] of much wealth and peace,
> That inward breaks, and shows no cause without
> Why the man dies.   (71)

The pitiless humiliation of Ophelia is revealed in pitiful detail. In one of the most painful scenes in all literature the words of human dignity and rationality enter like daggers into the ears of the wretched Queen and cleave in twain her corrupt but human heart.

The state of Denmark that unfolds before our eyes is presented with extraordinary realism and at the same time against an almost continuous undercurrent of thoroughgoing criticism. The criticism comes, of course, largely from Hamlet himself, especially in the soliloquies and the graveyard scene, but in some form or other it impregnates every scene in which he appears. It is this deep, insistent strain of irreverent, daring and radical criticism that represents the essential change wrought by Shakespeare upon his sources—the Danish chronicle from which, via an earlier 'revenge' play, he took his plot.[5] In the earlier play Hamlet's

---

negation of life. I think Professor Knight grants Claudius far too much and underemphasizes Hamlet's realism.

4. imposthume = boil or ulcer

5. The chronicle was the *Historica Danica* of Saxo Grammaticus, a 12th-century Dane whose work was translated in the sixteenth century into French, German and possibly English. The old *Hamlet* revenge-play, which may have been by Kyd, has never come to light but we know it to have existed from contemporary references and a German play *Der Bestrafte Brudermord* based on it. Some critics, like J. M. Robertson, have tried to explain the difficulties of Shakespeare's *Hamlet* primarily in

problems had been purely physical—how, when and where to get a revenge, the implications of which were never questioned. Shakespeare's rejection of the old feudal concepts of revenge (based on the feudal lord's refusal to accept any justice other than his own) first in *Romeo and Juliet* and then in *Hamlet* shows how far he had come from the more primitive morality which Kyd, only a few years earlier, had accepted as the moral and dramatic driving-force of his plays.[6]

Not that there is anything abstract or schematic about the insistent note of social criticism that gives *Hamlet* its particular flavour. On the contrary, the solid and detailed realism of the presentation of the Danish court is such that it is not surprising that readers and audiences who take the ways and values of class-divided society for granted should have tended to take Claudius's Denmark at its face value as the human norm.[7] Yet if one examines, say, Polonius's speech of advice to the departing Laertes—a speech which generations of schoolboys have had to get by heart as one of the ultimates in human wisdom—it turns out to be (quite appropriately in the context) a compound of stuffy platitudes and unconscious ironies culminating in the words (which I remember a worthy uncle inscribing in my autograph book as a child)

> This above all—to thine own self be true,
> And it must follow, as the night the day,
> Thou canst not then be false to any man.
> (16–17)

The glib simile should be warning enough. If it followed as inevitably as that there would be no problem, and it is not the only time in the play that Polonius uses this particular image to reinforce his quarter-truths.[8] The 'moral' of his speech simply enshrines the cheerful self-deception of the individualist who cannot face the fact that his individualism brings him to an insoluble impasse.

Hamlet has seen through Polonius. His contempt for him is so complete that he cannot even spare him a moment's pity when he has run his sword through him by accident.[9] For Hamlet, who knows that a tear is an intellectual thing, has come to see the horror, in terms of human misery and betrayal, of what Polonius stands for. That is why it is wrong

---

terms of the unsuitable plot Shakespeare was saddled with. There is, of course, something in this, but it does not touch the principal point—why Shakespeare made the changes he did in his original source material.

6. While there is still no central national state strong enough to enforce its law and order, revenge is the individual's only means of getting justice. The decline of the 'revenge-tragedy' and changes in the feudal concept of 'honour' run parallel to the strengthening of a centralized state apparatus in the later years of Elizabeth's reign.

7. Alternatively, like Laurence Olivier in the film,

they abstract the significance of the play by offering an Elsinore in the clouds, a *Hamlet* with plenty of Prince but no Denmark.

8. See Polonius's sycophantic speech in Act II. Sc. 2. after the exit of the Ambassadors from Norway.

9. He does say, a little later, "For this same lord I do repent", but adds immediately "but heaven hath pleased it so" (III. 4.). For the death of Rosencrantz and Guildenstern he feels even less remorse:

> Why, man, they did make love to this employment;
> They are not near my conscience; . . . (92)

for an actor to play the Lord Chamberlain simply as a clown: he is a responsible figure who, in the context within which he works, knows perfectly well what he is doing and boasts of how skilfully he can 'By indirections find directions out'.[1] Politically he is a machiavel: morally, as Hamlet tells him to his face, a fishmonger. Before he has 'loosed' his daughter to Hamlet (a good stock-breeder's term) he has expatiated at length to her on her value on the marriage-market, fearing she has taken Hamlet's 'tenders for true pay Which are not sterling' and describing his vows as 'brokers, Not of that dye which their investments show.'

It is not, of course, only Polonius that Hamlet has seen through but the morality of a whole society which sees nothing wrong with Polonius except his garrulousness. Hamlet has loved Ophelia, but now, in the light of his new vision of the Danish world, he sees her as, though personally innocent, a pawn in the corrupt intrigues of the court. This is what lies behind his contradictory and paradoxical shifts in his scene with her (III. 1.). 'I did love you once' and then, immediately, 'I loved you not'. He loved her, but now he sees her—and women in general—differently, and what he sees he cannot love. She were better in a nunnery. That is before he realizes that Ophelia has been 'loosed' to him. After that he is pitiless and in the play scene treats her with the utmost brutality as a prostitute, humiliating both himself and her.

Hamlet's problem is the appallingly difficult one of finding actions commensurate with his new vision of what 'is', what the world he lives in is actually like. He is not afraid of action as such. He has been, we are told more than once, a capable and popular prince. All through the play he acts boldly and decisively whenever he needs to—in following the ghost, in organizing the play, in facing his mother with the brutal facts, in killing the old man behind the arras, in coping effectively with the situation on the ship bound for England: and about none of these actions does his conscience bother him particularly, though his enigmatic display immediately after the death of Polonius shows his awareness of the moral complexities of that act. But it is really only over the killing of the King that he hesitates and that is certainly not because he dare not do it or looks on the killing as in some absolute way 'wrong'. The 'Now might I do it pat' speech (59) expresses as clearly as any of his utterances his sense of the inadequacy of *merely* killing the King, of achieving nothing but the minimal formalities of revenge.

It is not good enough to describe Hamlet as a man who cannot make up his mind. More adequately one might say that he is faced with a situation which it is almost impossible for him to resolve satisfactorily in action. For, to put it crudely, what adequate actions could a young man take who, in the year 1600, could no longer look at society from the

1. Act II. Sc. 1. Professor Harry Levin in his *The Question of Hamlet* (1959) is good on Polonius and the court's political morality.

point of view of the ruling class? He might kill the king (as was, within fifty years, to happen in Britain) recognizing him as the source not only of his personal ills but of the corrupt state, the prison that is Denmark. But what then? Especially if young Fortinbras, just back from a successful mopping-up operation in Poland, is to reign in his stead.

It seems to me essential to see Hamlet's problem historically. To do so helps resolve one of the issues that has always worried actors who tackle the part: how can Hamlet be at the same time—what almost everyone feels instinctively he must be—a hero, yet also ineffective? It is this problem that has led to the tendency to sympathize with Hamlet *because* he is ineffective. I think this tendency, though wrong, is a tribute to the significance of the situation Shakespeare has put his finger on, a situation of great general interest in the modern world and the one which makes everyone recognize the typicality as well as the uniqueness of Hamlet. Hamlet is not merely a Renaissance prince. Along with Marlowe's Faustus he is the first modern intellectual in our literature and he is, of course, far more modern as well as much more intelligent than Faustus. And his dilemma is essentially the dilemma of the modern European intellectual: his ideas and values are in a deep way at odds with his actions. Thinking and doing have got separated, basically because power is in the hands of a class whose values humane people feel they must repudiate. Power and effectiveness tend therefore to be suspected by the intelligentsia who retreat physically into a world removed from vital power-decisions and mentally into a realm of ideas and art which they value above the world of action and try to defend from the corrupting inroads of cynical expediency.

In Hamlet all these tendencies and temptations are to be found, though, being a sixteenth-century prince, the practical possibilities of an escape from the world of action are not, for him, very great. But the lost young man of the opening acts, acutely conscious of 'not belonging', contemptuous, sardonic, even a bit exhibitionist, talking a language different from those around him,[2] speaks directly to the experience of the modern intellectual who proceeds to idealize this unhappy young man into the supreme expression of the eternal human condition epitomized in being an intellectual.

Shakespeare does not permit this idealization. Hamlet, having stood on the brink of despair, comes back to the court of Denmark, refusing to continue to contemplate the possibility of a separation of thought from action. From the moment at which, recalled to actuality in the graveyard by the death of Ophelia, he leaps into the grave with a cry 'This is I, Hamlet the Dane!', he puts behind him the most desperate of his haunting doubts.[3] The atmosphere of the fifth act, with its tense,

2. Literally as well as metaphorically, as his baiting of Osric (v. 2.) shows.
3. It is worth noticing that Shakespeare delays

Hamlet's description of his adventures on the voyage to England (V. 2.) until *after* this moment, though the events occurred before and could quite

controlled, unemphatic prose statements, is one of sad, almost (but not quite) passive acceptance of the need to act.

The readiness is all. Hamlet is not taken in, nor has he become cynical: in his heart there remains a kind of fighting that will not let him sleep. Although all's ill about his heart he will meet the challenges that come bravely, without cynicism and without humbug.

The fifth act does not involve, it seems to me, a dramatic resolution of Hamlet's dilemmas in any full sense of the word, but rather some kind of salvaging of human decency and a rejection of philosophic idealism. Hamlet, the prince who has tried to become a man, becomes a prince again and does what a sixteenth-century prince ought to do— killing the murderer of his father, forgiving the stupid, clean-limbed Laertes, expressing (for the first time) direct concern about his own claims to the throne but giving his dying voice to young Fortinbras, the kind of delicate and tender prince that Hamlet himself could never again have been. Horatio, it is true, lives on, pledged to tell the truth and bearing the aspirations of the humanist cause; but Horatio without Hamlet will not be, we feel, a decisive force. The end then, is, in one sense, almost total defeat for everything Hamlet has stood for. But it is an acceptance of the need to act in the real world, and that is a great human triumph.

*   *   *

MARGARET W. FERGUSON

Hamlet: Letters and Spirits†

"The letter killeth," said Saint Paul (2 Cor. 3:6). His words can serve as an epigraph—or epitaph—to my essay, which approaches some broad questions about the genre of Shakespearean tragedy by exploring the connections between certain techniques of wordplay in *Hamlet* and a process of dramatic literalization that is associated, in this play, with the impulse to kill. In the early part of the play, Hamlet frequently uses language to effect a divorce between words and their conventional meanings. His rhetorical tactics, which include punning and deliberately undoing the rhetorical figures of other speakers, expose the arbitrariness, as well as the fragility, of the bonds that tie words to agreed-upon significations. His language in dialogues with others, though not in his soliloquies, produces a curious effect of *materializing* the word,

plausibly have been related to Horatio in the graveyard (V.1.) This is surely because Shakespeare wants Hamlet to emerge as a man of action only after the funeral of Ophelia, thus linking the two.

†From *Shakespeare and the Question of Theory*, ed. Patricia Parker and Geoffrey Hartman (New York and London, 1985) 292–309. Reprinted by permission of the publisher, Routledge, Chapman & Hall. Page numbers given in parentheses refer to the text of this Norton Critical Edition of *Hamlet*.

materializing it in a way that forces us to question the distinction between literal and figurative meanings, and that also leads us to look in new ways at the word as a spoken or written phenomenon. Hamlet's verbal tactics in the early part of the play—roughly through the closet scene in Act III—constitute a rehearsal for a more disturbing kind of materializing that occurs, with increasing frequency, in the later part of the drama. This second kind of materializing pertains to the realm of deeds as well as to that of words; in fact it highlights the thin but significant line that separates those realms, while at the same time it reminds us that all acts performed in a theater share with words the problematic status of representation. This second type of materializing might be called *performative*,[1] and since in *Hamlet*, in contrast to the comedies, it almost always results in a literal death, it might also be described as a process of "incorpsing"—to borrow a term that is used once in *Hamlet* and nowhere else in Shakespeare's corpus.

Hamlet begins his verbal activity of materializing words with the first line he speaks: "A little more than kin, and less than kind" (9).[2] With this riddling sentence, spoken aside to the audience, Hamlet rejects the social and linguistic bond that Claudius asserted when he addressed Hamlet in terms of their kinship: "But now, my cousin Hamlet, and my son" (9). Hamlet not only refuses to be defined or possessed by Claudius's epithets, the second of which confuses the legal relation of stepson with the "natural" one of son; he also refuses to accept the principle of similarity that governs Claudius's syntax, which here, as elsewhere, employs the rhetorical figure of *isocolon:* balanced clauses joined by "and."[3] Claudius's isocolonic style is also characteristically oxymoronic: opposites are smoothly joined by syntax and sound, as for instance in these lines from his opening speech:

> Therefore our sometime sister, now our queen,
> Th'imperial jointress to this warlike state,
> Have we, as 'twere with a defeated joy,
> With an auspicious and a dropping eye,
> With mirth in funeral and with dirge in marriage,
> In equal scale weighing delight and dole,
> Taken to wife.
>
> (8)

1. I borrow the term "performative" from J. L. Austin, *How To Do Things With Words* (1962), 2nd edn (Cambridge, Mass., 1975), 5 and *passim*. Austin, however, notoriously seeks to exclude from his discussion the type of performative utterance that interests me here, namely that which occurs on a stage or in a literary text. Such performatives, he writes, "will be *in a peculiar way* hollow or void" (22, Austin's italics).

2. All quotations from *Hamlet* and other Shakespeare plays are from the New Arden editions,

general editors Harold F. Brooks, Harold Jenkins and Brian Morris (London and New York). The Arden *Hamlet*, ed. Harold Jenkins, was published in 1982.

3. See Stephen Booth's excellent discussion of the syntactic and rhetorical devices Claudius uses to achieve "equation by balance"; "On the value of *Hamlet*," in *Reinterpretations of Elizabethan Drama*, ed. Norman Rabkin (New York, 1969), esp. 148–9.

Hamlet's remark "A little more than kin, and less than kind" unbalances the scale Claudius has created through his rhetoric—a scale in which opposites like "delight" and "dole" are blandly equated. Hamlet's sentence disjoins what Claudius has linked; it does so through its comparative "more" and "less," and also through the play on "kin" and "kind" which points, by the difference of a single letter, to a radical difference between what Claudius seems or claims to be, and what he is. The pun on the word "kind" itself, moreover, works, as Hamlet's puns so often do, to disrupt the smooth surface of another person's discourse. Hamlet's pun, suggesting that Claudius is neither natural nor kindly, is like a pebble thrown into the oily pool of the king's rhetoric. As Lawrence Danson observes in *Tragic Alphabet*, Hamlet's puns challenge Claudius's "wordy attempts at compromise" by demanding "that words receive their full freight of meaning."[4] If the puns work to increase semantic richness, however—the Elizabethan rhetorician George Puttenham characterized the pun or *syllepsis* as "the figure of double supply"[5]— they do so by driving a wedge between words and their ordinary meanings. The pun, Sigurd Burckhardt argues, characteristically performs "an act of verbal violence. . . . It asserts that mere phonetic—i.e., material, corporeal—likeness establishes likeness of meaning. The pun gives the word as entity primacy over the word as sign."[6]

If Hamlet's punning wit makes an oblique attack on Claudius's rhetorical penchant for "yoking heterogeneous ideas by violence together"— to borrow the phrase Dr Johnson used in a similar attack on what he felt to be indecorous conceits—Hamlet is, of course, attacking much more than Claudius's rhetorical style. For Claudius has yoked not only words but bodies together, and it therefore seems likely that Hamlet's style reflects his (at this point) obscure and certainly overdetermined desire to separate his uncle from his mother. His dialogue with Polonius in II.ii offers further support for my hypothesis that Hamlet's disjunctive verbal techniques constitute not only a defense against being entrapped by others' tropes but also an aggressive, albeit displaced, attack on the marriage union of Gertrude and Claudius. By the time Hamlet speaks with Polonius, of course, he has not only had his worst suspicions about the king confirmed by the Ghost, but has also met with a rebuff from Ophelia, a

4. Lawrence Danson, *Tragic Alphabet: Shakespeare's Drama of Language* (New Haven and London, 1974), 27.

5. See George Puttenham's *The Arte of English Poesie*, ed. Gladys Willcock and Alice Walker (Cambridge, 1936), 136. "Syllepsis" is the classical trope that corresponds most closely to the modern notion of the pun—a term that did not appear in English until the eighteenth century, according to the OED. Oswald Ducrot and Tzvetan Todorov define syllepsis as "the use of a single word that has more than one meaning and participates in more than one syntactic construction"; they cite as

an example Falstaff's remark, from *The Merry Wives of Windsor*, "At a word, hang no more about me; I am no gibbet for you" (*Encyclopedic Dictionary of the Sciences of Language*, tr. Catherine Porter (Baltimore, 1979), 278). I am indebted for this citation and for my general understanding of punning tropes to Jane Hedley's unpublished essay on "Syllepsis and the problem of the Shakespeare sonnet order."

6. Sigurd Burckhardt, *Shakespearean Meanings* (Princeton, 1968), 24–5. Burckhardt's comment is cited in part by Danson, op. cit., 27, n. 2.

rebuff dictated by Polonius's and Laertes' suspicions. It is no wonder, then, that his rhetoric is now directly deployed against the very idea of fleshly union. "Have you a daughter?" he asks Polonius (34), and goes on to draw Ophelia into his morbid train of thought, which has been about the sun's power to breed maggots in the dead flesh of a dog. "Let her not walk i'th' sun," he says, echoing his earlier statement, in the opening scene with Claudius, "I am too much in the sun" (9). The echo hints that Ophelia is already in some sense Hamlet's double here: both are endangered by the sun which is an emblem of kingly power, and both are also endangered—though in significantly different ways— by Hamlet's terrible burden of being a biological son to a dead king and a legal son to Claudius. As if dimly aware that his own way of thinking about Ophelia is tainting her with maggoty conceptions about sonship, Hamlet says to her father, "Conception is a blessing, but as your daughter may conceive—friend, look to't" (34). It is at this point that Hamlet strikes yet another rhetorical blow against union in the realm of discourse: "What do you read, my lord?" asks Polonius. "Words, words, words," Hamlet replies. "What is the matter, my lord?" Polonius persists. "Between who?" is the perverse, ungrammatical, and fascinating reply, not an answer but, characteristically, another question. In this peculiar dialogue Hamlet disjoins words from their conventional meanings both rhetorically and thematically; in so doing, he breaks the social contract necessary to ordinary human discourse, the contract which mandates that there be, in Roman Jakobson's words, "a certain equivalence between the symbols used by the addressor and those known and interpreted by the addressee."[7]

In his first answer, "Words, words, words," Hamlet deliberately interprets Polonius's question literally; in his second reply, however, he does something more complicated than substituting a literal sense for a figurative one: he points, rather, to the problem that has always plagued classical theories of metaphor, which is that a word or phrase may not *have* a single, "literal" sense.[8] And it seems strangely appropriate that Hamlet should expose the problem of distinguishing between multiple—and perhaps equally figurative—meanings through the example of the word *matter*—a word that appears 26 times in the play, more than in any other by Shakespeare, in locutions ranging from Gertrude's acerbic remark to Polonius, "More matter with less art" (31), to Hamlet's poignant comment to Horatio in the last act: "Thou wouldst not think

7. Roman Jakobson and Morris Halle, *Fundamentals of Language* (The Hague, 1956), 62; cited by Danson, op. cit., 27, n. 3.
8. See, e.g., Paul de Man's discussion of Locke's condemnation of *catachresis*, the trope that most notoriously dramatizes the difficulty of grounding a theory of figurative language in a concept of referential correspondence between words and "reality"; "The epistemology of metaphor," in *On*

Metaphor, ed. Sheldon Sacks (Chicago and London, 1979), 11–28. Locke's condemnation of catachresis, in *The Essay Concerning Human Understanding*, eventually "takes all language for its target," de Man argues, "for at no point in the course of the demonstration can the empirical entity be sheltered from tropological deformation" (19–20).

how ill all's here about my heart; but it is no matter" (96).

As is apparent from even a cursory examination of the play's manifold uses of this word, the relation between matter and spirit, matter and art, matter and anything that is "no matter," is altogether questionable for Hamlet; he is therefore quite accurate in presenting matter as an obstacle to unity of opinion: "Between who?" suggests only that any definition of matter will be a matter for dispute. Hamlet has indeed effectively disjoined this word from any single conventional meaning we or Polonius might want to give it; and it is no accident, I think, that Hamlet's rapier attack on the word "matter" foreshadows the closet scene in which he both *speaks* daggers to his mother and literally stabs Polonius, mistaking him, as he says to the corpse, "for thy better." In this scene, the concept of matter is linked to that of the mother by a pun that marries Shakespeare's mother tongue to the language known, in the Renaissance, as the *sermo patrius*: the language of the Church fathers and also of the ancient Romans.[9] "Now, mother, what's the matter?" asks Hamlet at the very outset of the closet scene (60), and this query makes explicit an association of ideas already implied by a remark Hamlet made to Rosencrantz: "Therefore no more, but to the matter. My mother, you say—" (56).

As we hear or see in the word "matter" the Latin term for mother, we may surmise that the common Renaissance association between female nature in general and the "lower" realm of matter is here being deployed in the service of Hamlet's complex oedipal struggle.[1] The mother is the matter that comes between the father and the son—and it is no accident that in this closet scene Hamlet's sexual hysteria rises to its highest pitch. Dwelling with obsessive, disgusted fascination on his mother's unseemly passion for her second husband, Hamlet appears to be struggling with his own feelings about her body even as he argues for his dead father's continuing rights to her bed. Hamlet's act of stabbing Polonius through the curtain, which occurs almost casually in the middle of the tirade against Gertrude's lust, seems only to increase his passionate desire to make her *see* her error in preferring Claudius to her first husband. For Hamlet, however, the problem of seeing a genuine *difference* between his original father and the man Gertrude has called his father assumes

9. On Latin as a *sermo patrius*, see my *Trials of Desire: Renaissance Defenses of Poetry* (New Haven and London, 1983), 24, and Leo Spitzer, "Muttersprache und Muttererziehung," in *Essays in Historical Semantics* (New York, 1948), 15–65.

1. See Ian Maclean, *The Renaissance Notion of Woman* (Cambridge, 1980), for a survey of Renaissance authors who adopted the Aristotelian scheme of dualities "in which one element is superior and the other inferior. The male principle in nature is associated with active, formative, and perfected characteristics, while the female is passive, material, and deprived" (8). See also Linda Woodbridge, *Woman and the English Renaissance: Literature and the Nature of Womankind, 1540–1620* (Urbana and Chicago, 1984), esp. ch. 3. It seems likely that an association between baseness, "matter," and his mother is at work even earlier in the play, when Hamlet vows that the Ghost's "commandment all alone shall live / Within the book and volume of my brain, / Unmix'd with baser matter. Yes, by heaven! / O most pernicious woman!" (23). Cf. Avi Erlich's comments about this passage in *Hamlet's Absent Father* (Princeton, 1977), 218.

enormous significance at precisely this juncture in the drama; immediately before Hamlet refers to Claudius as a "king of shreds and patches,"
the Ghost appears, or rather reappears, with a dramatic entrance that
allows the phrase "king of shreds and patches" to refer to the Ghost as
well as to Claudius. As if to underscore the fact that Hamlet's dilemma
here is a hermeneutic as well as an ethical one, Shakespeare has him
address the Ghost with the pregnant question, "What would your gracious figure?" (63). If Claudius is a figure of the father, so is the Ghost;
according to what standard of truth, then, is Hamlet to distinguish between
them?

Shakespeare gives this problem a further turn of the screw, as it were,
by making the Ghost invisible and inaudible to Gertrude. Like the gov-
erness in Henry James's tale, who sees the ghostly figure of Miss Jessell
when the "gross" housekeeper does not, Hamlet is forced to confront
and deny the possibility that the Ghost may be a figment of his own
imagination. He, and the audience, must at least fleetingly experience
a conflict between the evidence provided by their eyes and ears and
Gertrude's statement that she perceives "nothing." And even if this scene's
stage directions confirm the Ghost's existence and support Hamlet's
argument that what he has seen is not, as Gertrude insists, a "bodiless
creation" of "ecstasy," we may well not feel entirely easy about giving
credence to Hamlet here; after the Ghost exits, Hamlet declares to Gertrude that his "pulse" keeps time just as "temperately" as hers does (64).
Then, having claimed to be no less (but also no more) sane than is the
woman whose perceptions we have just been forced to discount, Hamlet
proceeds to promise that "I the matter will re-word, which madness /
Would gambol from." The relation between the "matter" of the Ghost
and the matter Hamlet will "re-word" in the ensuing passionate dialogue
with Gertrude remains deeply mysterious.

By stressing the epistemologically doubtful status of the Ghost, we can
usefully supplement the classic psychoanalytic explanation for why Hamlet
defers performing the deed of revenge. That explanation, outlined by
Freud in a famous footnote to the *Interpretation of Dreams* and elaborated by Ernest Jones, suggests that Hamlet obscurely knows that in killing Claudius he would be satisfying his repressed oedipal desire to be
like Claudius, who has become a king and husband by killing the elder
Hamlet.[2] Jacques Lacan, in his brilliant, albeit elliptical, essay on "Desire
and the interpretation of desire in *Hamlet*," speculates that Hamlet's

2. Freud's famous discussion of Hamlet as a "hysteric" whose guilt about his own repressed oedipal
wishes prevents him from taking vengeance "on
the man who did away with his father and took
that father's place with his mother" was originally
published as a footnote to ch. 5 of *The Interpretation of Dreams* (1900); from 1914 onward the passage was included in the text. See *The Standard
Edition of the Complete Psychological Works of*
Sigmund Freud, ed. James Strachey *et al.*, 4 (London, 1953), 264–6. See also Ernest Jones, *Hamlet
and Oedipus* (Garden City, 1949) [pp. 200–207,
this edition—*Editor*]. But see also, for a critique
of the "Freud–Jones" interpretation and a discussion of other psychoanalytic readings of *Hamlet*,
Theodore Lidz, *Hamlet's Enemy: Madness and
Myth in "Hamlet"* (New York, 1975), esp. 9–13,
184–6.

invectives against Claudius in the closet scene are an example of *déné-gation*, that is, the words of dispraise and contempt are indications of repressed admiration.[3] Building on both Freud and Lacan, we might read Hamlet's frantic efforts to draw a clear epistemological distinction between his father and Claudius as a defense against his perception of an excessive degree of *likeness* between himself and Claudius, or, more precisely, between his desires and Claudius's. In fact, the distinctions Hamlet draws between Claudius and Old Hamlet seem no less question-able, in their hyperbole, than the distinction he draws between himself and his mother when, alluding to the simple moral system of medieval religious drama, he calls her a vice and himself a virtue. A parallel dualistic oversimplification informs his sermon-like speech on the pic-tures of the two kings, "The counterfeit presentment of two brothers," as he calls them:

> See what a grace was seated on this brow,
> Hyperion's curls, the front of Jove himself,
> An eye like Mars to threaten and command,
> A station like the herald Mercury
> New-lighted on a heaven-kissing hill
>
> (62)

He doth protest too much, methinks, in this plethora of similitudes designed, as he says, to make his mother relinquish that passion which is blind to difference. Hamlet's own passion, we might say, is making him blind to similarity. His description of his father's incomparable vir-tue hardly accords with what the Ghost himself said to his son when he lamented having been "Cut off even in the blossoms of my sin" and "sent to my account / With all my imperfections on my head" (22–23). Nor does it accord with what Hamlet himself said in III.iii, where he described his father dying with "all his crimes broad blown, as flush as May" (59).

Hamlet's doubts about his father's character, about the Ghost's status as a figure, and about his own relation to both his father and Claudius, constitute one reason why he cannot resolve the matter of his mother or his revenge. Another and related reason is that he is too filled with dis-gust at female flesh to follow the path Freud describes for those who

---

3. Jacques Lacan, "Desire and the interpretation of desire in *Hamlet*," tr. James Hulbert, French text ed. Jacques-Alain Miller from transcripts of Lacan's seminar, in *Literature and Psychoanaly-sis, The Question of Reading: Otherwise*, ed. Sho-shana Felman (*Yale French Studies*, 55–6 (1977), 11–52). The mention of *dénégation* occurs on p. 50; my explanation of the term draws on the trans-lator's note 6. I should observe, however, that Lacan's analysis departs from Freud's, or rather claims to "shed light on what Freud [had to] . . . leave out" (48), by interpreting the play with reference to the Lacanian theory of the "phal-lus." The fundamental reason why Hamlet cannot raise his arm against Claudius, Lacan argues, is that "he knows that he must strike something other than what's there" (51). That "something other" is the phallus, the symbolic object which, for Lacan, signifies "the law of the father," and which cannot be mastered by the individual subject because it is an *effect* of repression and of one's insertion into a cultural system of meaning. "[O]ne cannot strike the phallus," Lacan asserts, "because the phallus, even the real phallus, is a *ghost*" (50).

eventually emerge, however scarred, from the oedipal complex. That path leads to marriage with a woman who is not the mother. In Hamlet's case, the obvious candidate is Ophelia, whom Hamlet actually seems to prefer to his mother in the play within the play scene. "Come hither, my dear Hamlet, sit by me," says Gertrude, and Hamlet replies, "No, good mother, here's metal more attractive" (50–51). The metaphor is misogynistically reductive—and ominously allied to Hamlet's pervasive concern with debased currency; nonetheless, for a moment it seems that he may find in Ophelia a matter to replace his mother. "Lady, shall I lie in your lap?" he asks, and when she says no, taking him literally, he specifies his meaning, offering to lay in her lap only that part of him which houses the higher faculties: "I mean, my head upon your lap?" "Ay, my lord," she answers; but he twists her affirmation by indicating that his head is filled with thoughts of her—and his—lower parts: "Do you think I meant country matters?" he asks, punning on the slang term for the female genitals. "I think nothing, my lord," Ophelia replies; and Hamlet once again bawdily literalizes her words: "That's a fair thought to lie between maids' legs" (51). While his speeches in this dialogue seem like an invitation to sexual union (in one sense he is enticing her to realize that the matter between *his* legs is not nothing but something), the final effect of this exchange, as of all the encounters between Ophelia and Hamlet we see in this play, is to separate her from him, to push her naive love away and reduce her to incomprehension of what he later calls his "mystery." Hamlet's relation to Ophelia seems aptly epitomized a little later in this scene, when he leaves off interpreting the tropical ambiguities of the *Mousetrap* play being presented before them to say to her, "I could interpret between you and your love if I could see the puppets dallying" (54). The role of the interpreter who stands *between* others and their loves is the role he has at once had thrust upon him by fate and which he chooses to continue to play. It is dangerous to suggest that he had any alternative, for the play notoriously foils critics who think themselves ethically or intellectually superior to this tragic hero.[4] Nonetheless, I would like to argue that the play does provide a critical perspective on Hamlet, a perspective that implies a questioning of the genre of tragedy itself more than a moral critique of the hero as an individual subject.

The critical perspective I hope to trace does not result in our feeling that Hamlet *should* have done something else at any point in the play; rather, it heightens our awareness that the drama itself is the product of

4. Many critics have succumbed to the temptation to reproach Hamlet for incompetence (Bradley) or for possessing "a moral sensibility inferior to our own," as Helen Gardner characterizes T. S. Eliot's rebuke to Hamlet for "dying fairly well pleased with himself" despite the fact that he has made "a pretty considerable mess of things" ("The stoicism of Shakespeare and Seneca," cited in Gardner's useful survey of the problems critics have encountered in trying to find ethical or logical "consistency" in the drama; see her chapter on "The historical approach: Hamlet," in *The Business of Criticism* (Oxford, 1959), 35–51).

certain choices which *might have been different*. Like many students of
Shakespeare, I have often felt that certain of his plays strongly invite the
audience to imagine how the play would go if it were written according
to a different set of generic rules. Certain turns of plot are made to seem
somehow *arbitrary*, and the effect of such moments is to shift our attention from the story-line to the invisible hand manipulating it; we are
reminded that the dramatist's decisions about his material are *not* wholly
preordained. A strange sense of potentiality arises at such moments; we
enter a metadramatic realm where movements of plot and characterization no longer seem simply given or "necessary." The death of Mercutio
in *Romeo and Juliet* is an example of the kind of moment I have in
mind; it seems so accidental, so unmotivated, that we may well wonder
how the play would have turned out had he been allowed to live. The
play *could* have been a comedy—as Shakespeare later explicitly indicated by including a parody of it in Act V of *A Midsummer Night's
Dream*. Shakespeare's tendency to blur generic boundaries throughout
his career has often been remarked; but critics have not, to my knowledge, related this phenomenon to the peculiar way in which Shakespearean tragedy, in contrast to Greek or classical French examples of the
genre, seems so often to imply a questioning of the necessity of casting
a given story *as* tragedy.

The critical perspective on Hamlet—or on *Hamlet* as a "piece of
work"—begins to emerge, I think, with the first death in the play, the
stabbing of Polonius in the pivotal closet scene of III.iv. Here we see a
darker, literalized version of Hamlet's verbal technique of separating others'
words from their conventional meanings. That technique was dissocia-
tive but also semantically fecund; now, however, a spirit is definitively
separated from its body, which becomes mere matter. "It was a brute
part of him to kill so capital a calf," Hamlet had punningly remarked
apropos of Polonius's fate when he played Julius Caesar in a university
theatrical (50); now, by killing Polonius, Hamlet makes the earlier insult
seem prophetic; he "realizes" it, transforming the old man into a sacri-
ficial calf on another stage. This performative mode of materializing a
figure, with its grim effects of tragic irony, is what I want to call "incorpsing."

Although the play raises all sorts of questions about the boundary
between speaking and doing, in the closet scene there is no doubt that
Hamlet passes from speaking daggers to using them. But he has stabbed
Polonius only through a curtain—yet another figure for that position of
"in betweenness" Hamlet himself is structurally bound to occupy. That
curtain may also be seen, I think, as a material emblem not only for
Hamlet's ignorance of Polonius's identity, but also for his inability to
pursue a certain ethical line of interpreting the meaning of his deed.
Hamlet does not inquire very deeply either here or later, when he kills
Rosencrantz and Guildenstern, into the meaning of his action. This

seems odd, since he has shown himself so remarkably capable of inter-
rogating the meaning of his *inaction*. There is a thinness, even an
uncharacteristic patness, to his response to his killing of Polonius: "For
this same lord / I do repent," he says, adding, "but heaven hath pleas'd
it so, / To punish me with this and this with me, / That I must be their
scourge and minister" (65). It seems to me that the play questions this
kind of self-justification, supplementing if not altogether invalidating
Hamlet's view of himself as a divinely appointed "scourge." The questioning occurs most generally through the play's scrutiny of kingship;
kings, like divinely appointed "scourges," may easily abuse their power
by seeing themselves as heavenly instruments, beyond the authority of
human laws. Shakespeare, I would argue, invites us to see that one
meaning of Hamlet's "incorpsing" activity is that through it he becomes
more and more like a king—or, perhaps, like a playwright. Indeed, with
the killing of Polonius—the "rat" Hamlet mistakenly takes for the king
he had already symbolically caught in the *Mousetrap* play—Hamlet takes
a crucial step towards occupying the place of the king as the play defines
it: not in terms of an individual, but in terms of a *role* associated both
with the power to kill and with the tendency to justify killing with lines
of argument unavailable to lesser men. Horatio darkly suggests this in
V.ii. Hamlet has just described how he disposed of Rosencrantz and
Guildenstern. "They are not near my conscience," he says:

> 'Tis dangerous when the baser nature comes
> Between the pass and fell incensed points
> Of mighty opposites.
>
> (93)

"Why, what a king is this!" Horatio ambiguously exclaims or queries.
Does he refer to Hamlet or to Claudius? It doesn't much matter, Shakespeare seems to say: a king is one who thinks himself capable of literally
disposing of whatever comes between him and his desires.

It is no accident that Hamlet kills Rosencrantz and Guildenstern by
means of a forged letter. For Claudius's letter ordering the king of England to kill Hamlet, Hamlet substitutes a letter ordering the king to kill
Rosencrantz and Guildenstern. He seals that letter with his father's ring,
the signet or sign of royal power; Claudius of course possesses a copy of
this ring, and it is worth noting that there is no difference between the
effect of Claudius's copy and that of the original seal. Both have the
power to order instant death. Communication among kings in this play
would, indeed, appear to be a grim illustration of Saint Paul's dictum
that the letter killeth. The play suggests, however, that it is not only the
letter, but the desire to *interpret* literally, to find one single sense, that
leads to murder. The Ghost that appeared "In the same figure like the
King that's dead" commands Hamlet to take action by means of several
equivocal and mutually contradictory phrases, including "bear it not,"

"Taint not thy mind," and "Remember me" (23); even when he reappears to whet Hamlet's almost blunted purpose, all the Ghost commands is "Do not forget" (63). So long as Hamlet remains perplexed by the multiple potential meanings of these commands, he remains in a realm where destruction of meanings goes hand in hand with the creation of new ones: the verbal and hermeneutic realm of his puns. Unyoking words from their conventional meanings is not the same thing as unyoking bodies from spirits. In coming to resemble Claudius, Hamlet is driven to forget this distinction, and Shakespeare, I think, asks us to see the cost of this forgetting. He does so by giving the audience a letter (of sorts) that invites a radically different interpretation from those which Claudius and Hamlet take from the messages they receive from mysterious places.

Shakespeare's "letter to the audience," as I want to characterize it, appears in a passage immediately following Claudius's receipt of Hamlet's letter announcing his return—naked and alone—to the shores of Denmark (80): let me try to show why the juxtaposition of passages is significant. Claudius says that he cannot understand Hamlet's letter ("What should this mean?" he asks Laertes (80)); but he recognizes Hamlet's "character" in the handwriting and proceeds quickly enough to give it a kingly interpretation. For he immediately tells Laertes of his "device" to work Hamlet's death in a way that will appear an accident. His response to the letter—which comes, after all, from someone he believed he had sent to the country from which no traveler returns—is eerily similar to Hamlet's response to the Ghost's message from the land of the dead. Like Hamlet, Claudius wonders about the ambiguity of the message: "is [the letter] some abuse?" he asks Laertes (80), echoing Hamlet's earlier question to himself about whether "The spirit that I have seen" is or is not a devil that "perhaps . . . / Abuses me to damn me" (43). Also like Hamlet, although much more quickly, Claudius chooses a single interpretation of the message, finding in it an incentive to kill. It hardly seems to matter whether the message comes from a spirit or a letter: the interpreter's *decision* about its meaning creates the deadliness. But in the passage that follows, Shakespeare offers an oblique criticism of the kind of interpretive decision that the kings or would-be kings make in this play. He does so by using Claudius as the unwitting spokesman for a greater king, the one who will really win the duel in the final scene. This is the king whom Richard II describes in Act III of his play:

> within the hollow crown
> That rounds the mortal temples of a king,
> Keeps Death his court, and there the antic sits
> Scoffing his state and grinning at his pomp,
> Allowing him a breath, a little scene,
> To monarchize, be fear'd, and kill with looks;
> Infusing him with self and vain conceit,

> As if this flesh which walls about our life
> Were brass impregnable.
>
> (*Richard II*, III.ii.160–8)

With wonderful irony, Shakespeare has Claudius metaphorically describe this king of kings while *thinking* he is pursuing his own aims—devising his own plot—by manipulating Laertes' competitive spirit to transform his rage against Claudius for Polonius's death into anger against Hamlet. "Two months since," Claudius says,

> Here was a gentleman of Normandy—
> I have seen myself, and serv'd against, the French,
> And they can well on horseback, but this gallant
> Had witchcraft in't. He grew unto his seat,
> And to such wondrous doing brought his horse
> As had he been incorps'd and demi-natur'd
> With the brave beast. So far he topp'd my thought
> That I in forgery of shapes and tricks
> Come short of what he did.
>
> (81)

"A Norman was't?" Laertes asks, and then, in one of the subtlest non-recognition scenes in all of Shakespeare, Laertes tells us the Norman's name: "Upon my life, Lamord" (81).[5] The spirit behind these letters from the text of the Second Quarto is invisible to Laertes and Claudius; it was also invisible to the compilers of the First Folio, who spelled the Frenchman's name "Lamound," and to eighteenth-century editors like Pope and Malone; the former gave the name as "Lamond," the latter, citing the phrase which describes the character as "the brooch and gem of all the nation," suggested "Lamode," fashion.[6] But I contend that Shakespeare meant us to hear or see the word "death" in and through the letters of this name; "Upon my life, Death," is the translation we are invited to make[7]—and for those who are uncertain of their French but willing to suspect that puns which depend on mere changes of letters have metaphorical significance, Shakespeare provides an English pun in the word "Norman," which is all too close for comfort to the phrase used by the gravedigger in the next scene: "What man dost thou dig it for?" Hamlet asks. "For no man, sir," is the equivocal reply (87).

---

5. The Norman's name is spelled "Lamord" in the Second Quarto and in many modern editions of the play, e.g., the Arden, the Signet, the Riverside; the entire passage is absent from the First ("Bad") Quarto.

6. See the variants and notes for IV.vii.93 in the New Variorum *Hamlet*, ed. H. H. Furness, 5th edn (Philadelphia, 1877), 1, 363. The Variorum itself prints the name as "Lamond."

7. Although most modern editors who use the Second Quarto's spelling of the name do so without explaining their choice, Harold Jenkins in the New Arden edition does comment on his decision, suggesting that "the name of the 'wondrous' messenger (91) is a presage of fatality" and is most plausibly interpreted as a play on "La Mort" (see his note to IV.vii.91, p. 369, and his longer note about the passage on 543–4). To the best of my knowledge, Harry Levin is the only other modern commentator who has devoted much attention to the passage; in *The Question of Hamlet* (New York, 1959), Levin discusses the "easily possible slip of typography or pronunciation" that would make "La Mort" into the Second Quarto's "Lamord" (95).

The play offers other intratextual clues to the identity of "Lamord." Laertes' phrase "Upon my life, Lamord," echoes a phrase Horatio used in his discussion of the Ghost in I.i:

> Let us impart what we have seen tonight
> Unto young Hamlet; for *upon my life*
> *This spirit*, dumb to us, will speak to him.
>   (7; my italics)

Horatio here unwittingly exposes the same eerie truth that Laertes does in Act IV: the "spirit" of Death, whether in the figure of the Ghost or in the figure of Lamord, sits upon the lives of all the characters in the play. And the scene which introduces Lamord seems deliberately designed not only to make Death's past and future presence manifest, but to link it, ominously and obscurely, to the playwright's own activities of "forging shapes," of persuading, and of creating elegiac song: immediately after Claudius successfully persuades Laertes to envenom his sword so that if he "galls" Hamlet in the duel "It may be death" (82), the queen enters with news of Ophelia's fate of being pulled, by her garments, from her "melodious lay / To muddy death" (83).

In the description of the mysterious Norman, Shakespeare paradoxically insists on the presence of Death by animating the dead metaphor in the common phrase "upon my life"; he also creates a new adjective, "incorpsed," which editors (and the *OED*, citing this line as the first use of the term) gloss as "made into one body," but which may also evoke the image of a dead body if we hear the Norman's name as "Death." The lines make us "see" Death, as it were, in a strangely materialized and emblematic figure: that of the rider sitting on—and controlling— the horse that traditionally represents human passion and ambition: "A horse, a horse, my kingdom for a horse," Richard III famously cries, when he is about to lose the powerful vitality that animal symbolizes.[8] The figure of Lamord sitting on his horse as if he were "incorps'd and demi-natur'd / With the brave beast" is richly evocative, reminding us, as Harry Levin suggests, both of the apocalyptic image of Death as a rider on a "pale horse" (Revelation 6:8), and of Hamlet's broodings on the inherently double or centaur-like nature of man, the angel and beast, the "beauty of the world" and the "quintessence of dust" combined into one "piece of work" (36).[9]

The description of Lamord, which I would like to see as Shakespeare's figurative letter to the reader, is somber and mysterious, a *memento mori*

---

8. The common Renaissance allegorization of the horse as a symbol for those passions which need to be controlled by reason (figured in the rider or driver) frequently harks back to Plato's image of the soul as a charioteer with two winged horses (*Phaedrus*, 246–8). Shakespeare uses the horse as a figure for uncontrolled anger in 2 *Henry IV*, I.i.9–11, and again in *Henry VIII*, I.i.133.

9. See Levin, op. cit., 95; see also Harold Jenkins's editorial comment (op. cit., 544) that the description of Lamord recalls the image of Claudius as a satyr (11) and "kindred animal images, even while the horseman, in contrast with the satyr, is invested with a splendour of which no touch is ever given to Claudius."

admonition. But it contrasts in a curious way with the other messages
and admonitions in this play; for there is all the difference in the world
between a message that asks us, with the paradoxical temporality of literature and dream, to *remember* our own future death, and messages
that ambiguously incite characters to kill and thereby to forget, as it
were, the potential future of another. It seems to me significant, therefore, that Shakespeare uses the trope of personification—the animation
of inanimate things—to describe Lamord. A premonitory and admoni-
tory figure he certainly is—but how interestingly different from the literalized *memento mori* that appears in the next scene, in Yorick's skull.
I do not think Hamlet grasps the meaning of Yorick's skull very completely because he so quickly forgets its implications for the fate of kings.
Although seeing the skull leads him to brood on the idea that great men
such as Alexander and Caesar finally become, like commoners, no more
than dust to stop a bunghole, in the very next scene (93) we find Hamlet
still thinking of *himself* as a "mighty opposite" in a kingly war that makes
humble men like Rosencrantz and Guildenstern irrelevant to conscience. Paradoxically, the death drive in Hamlet seems too strong to
allow him to understand either a graphic *memento mori* such as Yorick's
skull or the more unusual, figurative one offered to the audience (but
not to Hamlet) in the Lamord passage. For truly to understand a *memento
mori*, one must have at least some love of life—on earth or beyond. And
Hamlet lacks this love; he was speaking truly when he told Polonius that
there was nothing he would prefer to lose more than Polonius's company
"except my life, except my life, except my life" (34).[1] It is therefore
appropriate that, in the description of Lamord that Hamlet can neither
read nor hear, Shakespeare asks us to remember not only death, but also
love and life—particularly the life of Hamlet as Ophelia remembers it
from a time before the play began. Lamord, Laertes admiringly says, is
"the brooch indeed / And gem of all the nation" (81); the phrasing and
rhythm recall Ophelia's description of Hamlet as "Th'expectancy and
rose of the fair state, / The glass of fashion and the mould of form" (47).

The implied parallel between Lamord and Hamlet—not the gloomy
and disheveled prince we see throughout most of the play, a man obsessed
with a sense of sexual impotence, but rather a prince made present to us
only through the mediation of Ophelia's memorializing description—
this parallel suggests that there is yet another way of interpreting Lamord's
name and symbolic significance. If one listens closely to his name, one
may hear in it a pun not only on Death but also on Love—there is, after
all, only the slightest difference in pronunciation between the French
"la mort" and "l'amour"; and the Latin *amor* is contained within the

<hr />

1. Cf. Lacan's remarks on Hamlet's rejection of
Ophelia once she becomes, in his eyes, "the child-
bearer to every sin"; she is then "the phallus, exte-
riorized and rejected by the subject as a symbol
signifying life" (Lacan, op. cit., 23).

Norman's name. French Renaissance poets often punned on "l'amour" and "la mort" in ways that suggest the two forces are no less "demi-natured" than Lamord and his horse.[2]

In a play as concerned as this one is with problems of translation, it seems quite plausible that Shakespeare would pun bilingually here no less richly than he does in the bawdy "French lesson" scene of *Henry V.* It also seems plausible that he would be particularly interested in puns that strike the reader's eye even more than the listener's ear; *Hamlet* is after all a play that broods on the relation between elite and "general" audiences, and also on the relation between written texts and dramatic performances of them.[3] The play on Lamord's name suggested by the Second Quarto in any case invites those of us who read *Hamlet* now, knowing all the problems presented by the existence of its different textual versions, to imagine the playwright asking of himself a question similar to the one Horatio voices in Act V, apropos of Osric's inability to understand Hamlet's parody of the inflated courtly style Osric himself uses: "Is't not possible to understand in another tongue?" (94). Horatio's question, like so many questions in this play, is left unanswered. But even if most of Shakespeare's later readers and editors have *not* understood the other tongue, or tongues, spoken by the text in the Lamord passage, that passage is nonetheless significant as a kind of window that allows us briefly to look out from the dark and claustrophobic world of *Hamlet* to another verbal universe, one whose metaphysical economy is less depressed than the one we see in *Hamlet.* The description of Lamord, often cut in production and apparently so irrelevant to the play's plot that it is sometimes described as a "personal allusion" on Shakespeare's part,[4] seems to me a significant digression from the world of tragedy

2. My favorite example, for which I am indebted to Joseph Shork, of the University of Massachusetts at Boston, is the following:

Amour en latin faict amor;
Or donc provient d'amour la mort,
Et par avant, soulcy qui mord,
Deuils, plours, pieges, forfaitz, remords.

Stendhal uses this *blason* as an epigraph to chapter 15 of *Le Rouge et le Noir.* I have been unable to locate a Renaissance source for this epigraph and it may of course have been composed by Stendhal himself; nonetheless, "se non è vero, è ben trovato." Its play on "mordre" as "to bite" makes it a particularly apt gloss on the Lamord passage, since one editor of *Hamlet,* Edward Dowden, connects the Second Quarto's Lamord with the French *mords,* a horse's bit. For simpler examples of wordplay on love and death in sixteenth-century French poetry, see *Poètes du XVIe siècle,* ed. Albert-Marie Schmidt (Paris, 1953), 725 (Jodelle's *Les Amours,* Sonnet 35), and 827, 823, 820 (poems from Philippe Desportes's *Les Amours d'Hippolyte*).

3. For whatever reasons—one possibly having to do with the complex publication and production history of *Hamlet* in Shakespeare's own lifetime— the play emphasizes the difference between written scripts and actors' versions of them in a way unique in Shakespeare's canon; see, e.g., Hamlet's remark to the Player in (39) apropos the speech that "was never acted" ("'twas caviare to the general") and his later directive, again addressed to the Player, that "your clowns speak no more than is set down for them" (49). The play is also unusually full of references to books, tablets, letters, and forgeries of written texts; some critics have suspected that Hamlet's letter to Ophelia (32) is a forgery by Polonius. For a discussion of the theme of writing in the play, see Daniel Sibony, "*Hamlet:* a writing effect" (*Yale French Studies,* 55–6 (1977), 53–93). On other passages in the text that contain bi- and trilingual puns, see Lidz, op. cit., 23–5.

4. As Harold Jenkins notes (Arden *Hamlet,* 369), a number of editors have suggested a "personal allusion" in the passage to the cavalier in Castiglione's *The Courtier* named Pietro Monte (ren-

itself. The language of this passage is strangely foreign to *Hamlet* because here letter and spirit are joined in a message that insists on the union of life and death but does not present that union as a horror. For Hamlet, questioner of tropes and incorpser of bodies, all unions are tainted with poison, like the literal "union" (the pearl) in the cup Claudius prepares for Hamlet in the final scene. After Gertrude has mistakenly drunk from that cup and Claudius has been wounded with the envenomed sword, Hamlet ironically offers the poisoned vessel to Claudius, asking bitterly, "Is thy union here? / Follow my mother" (99).

There is a different perspective on unions in the personification of Lamord. Shakespeare explores that perspective more fully in some of his later plays, notably the romances; one might indeed see the passage on Lamord as a kind of prophecy of Shakespeare's later career, when he experimented with a genre characterized by "wondrous" escapes from potentially tragic plots. In the romances, and in a play like *Antony and Cleopatra* which blurs the boundary between tragedy and romance, we find a vision of the relation between death and life that sharply contrasts with the tragic vision represented in *Hamlet*. Characters like Antony, Florizel *(The Winter's Tale)* and Ferdinand *(The Tempest)* inhabit verbal universes in which the verb "to die" often has a double meaning; and the playwright himself exploits the theatrical analogue to this pun by reminding us, as he does conspicuously in *Antony*, that actors, like lovers, may die many times and come again to life.[5] Antony's marvelous dialogue with Eros envisions death as a dissolving of boundaries that is more erotic than terrible, and that may well be compared to the image of Lamord "incorps'd and demi-natur'd" with his horse. "Thou hast seen these signs, / They are black vesper's pageants," Antony tells Eros after describing to him the various forms clouds take; he goes on to conjure an image that anticipates Prospero's famous "cloud-capp'd towers" speech in *The Tempest* (IV.i.148ff.). Antony says:

> That which is now a horse, even with a thought
> The rack dislimns, and makes it indistinct
> As water is in water.
>
> (IV.xiv.9–11)

Such a way of conceiving death allows for the possibility of new shapes rising from the dissolution of old ones; death is acknowledged but also, one might say, embraced, in a romance vision similar to the one incarnated in a dialogue in Act IV of *The Winter's Tale*. Speaking of the spring flowers she lacks (for the pastoral world of Shakespearean romance

---

dered by Hoby in his Tudor translation as Peter Mount; cf. the Folio's "Lamound"). I do not dispute the idea of an esoteric allusion; I am simply arguing what can never be definitively proved, that

an allusion to Death is more plausible.
5. See, for examples of erotic puns on "die," *Antony and Cleopatra*, I.ii.138–42 and IV.xv.38–9; *The Tempest*, III.i.79–84.

is never an Eden of timeless spring), Perdita says that if she had such
flowers she would use them on her lover, "To strew him o'er and o'er."
"What, like a corpse?" he asks, and she replies:

> No, like a bank, for love to lie and play on:
> Not like a corpse; or if—not to be buried,
> But quick, and in mine arms.
>   (IV.iv.130–2)

Here again is language like that in the Lamord passage, which speaks of
something "incorps'd" and lively at once, the quick and the dead "demi-
natur'd." In such visions there is a kind of sublime punning, an equivocation that holds life and death in solution or delicate balance. "We
must speak by the card or equivocation will undo us," Hamlet says in
the graveyard scene (87). Shakespeare, I think, infuses this statement
with an irony Hamlet cannot see; for Hamlet is undone, and undoes
others, not because he equivocates, but because he inhabits a world
where equivocation tends, as if by a fatal entropy, to become "absolute
for death." The play, however, renders its own generic drive toward
death just equivocal enough to make us question the rules of tragedy.

JACQUELINE ROSE

Sexuality in the Reading of Shakespeare: *Hamlet* and *Measure for Measure* †

I

What fantasy of the woman has figured in readings—psychoanalytic and
other—of *Hamlet* and *Measure for Measure*, plays which have repeatedly been defined as a 'problem', as requiring an interpretation which
goes beyond their explicit, or manifest, content? How far has the woman
been at the centre, not only of the internal drama, but also of the critical
drama—the controversy about meaning and language—which each of
these plays has provoked? In this essay, rather than apply psychoanalysis
to literature, as if psychoanalysis were a method to be mapped onto the
literary text, I will try to show how psychoanalytic and literary criticism
share with the literature they address a terrain of language, fantasy and
sexuality—a terrain in which the woman occupies a crucial, but difficult, place. In both of these plays, the central woman character finds

† From *Alternative Shakespeares*, ed. John Dra-
kakis (London and New York, 1985) 95–118, 229–
31. Reprinted by permission of the publisher,
Methuen & Company, Inc. Page numbers to
Hamlet given in parentheses refer to the text of this
Norton Critical Edition of *Hamlet*.

herself accused—Gertrude in *Hamlet* of too much sexuality, Isabella in *Measure for Measure* of not enough. In both cases, the same notion of excess or deficiency has appeared in the critical commentaries on the plays. *Hamlet* and *Measure for Measure* have each been described as aesthetic failures which ask too much of—or offer too little to—the act of interpretation itself. By focusing on the overlap of these two accusations, of the woman and of the play, we might be able to see how the question of aesthetic form and the question of sexuality are implicated in each other.

T. S. Eliot linked the two plays when he described their material as 'intractable', resistant to interpretation and infringing the proper boundaries of dramatic form. In his famous essay (1919) on *Hamlet* (Eliot 1975), which was later picked up by Ernest Jones in his psychoanalytic reading of the play (Jones 1949), Eliot first put forward his central concept of the 'objective correlative' in the form of a critique: of *Hamlet* for its aesthetic failure and of Gertrude for being its cause. For Eliot, the aesthetic matching of emotion to object, which is the pre-condition of proper aesthetic form, fails in *Hamlet* because Gertrude is not sufficient as a character to carry the weight of the affect which she generates in the chief character of the play. Without this correlation, emotion in literature, or drama, becomes too insistent. Unless it can be seen as the inevitable response to the character presented on stage, it draws attention to itself, uneasily suggestive of something in the artist which he has failed to get under control. The deficiency of the character is therefore not only the cause, but also the result of an emotional excess. In *Hamlet*, the failing is Gertrude's, who thus deprives not only her son, but also the play, of the proper emotional support.

In his essay, Eliot lays down the terms for a way of assessing literature and its values whose influence has by no means been restricted to Shakespeare, but it is important that he first does so with reference to Shakespeare, and that the formulation centres so crucially on a woman. The importance of the woman in Eliot's theory appears as more than arbitrary when we notice that he uses another image of a woman to embody what he sees as the consequent failure of the play. *Hamlet*, Eliot writes, is 'the *Mona Lisa* of literature' (Eliot 1975, p. 47), offering up in its enigmatic and undecipherable nature something of that maimed or imperfect quality of appeal which characterizes Leonardo's famous painting. Like the *Mona Lisa*, *Hamlet* is a flawed masterpiece whose very failing acts as a pull on spectator and critic alike. Its very imperfection brings with it the power to seduce. Thus the idea of emotional excess shifts across the different levels of analysis—from drama to author to spectator. The appearance of the *Mona Lisa* in Eliot's essay suggests that the problem with *Hamlet* is that the 'inexpressibly horrible' content which he identifies beneath the surface of the text fascinates as much as it repels. The danger which *Hamlet* poses to Eliot's definition of proper aesthetic form resides—as much as in the play's origins—in its effect. [1]

To this extent, Eliot's analysis—like other readings which will take their authority from his conception of literature—repeats the drama which is acted out inside the plays he describes. In both *Hamlet* and *Measure for Measure*, sexuality entails danger and violates propriety, or form. Gertrude's impropriety (her 'o'erhasty' marriage) and Isabella's excessive propriety (her refusal to comply with Angelo's sexual demand) produce an image of sexuality as something unmanageable which cannot be held in its place. In both plays, it is the woman who provokes a crisis which overturns the sexual identity of the central male character of the drama. Hamlet, in response to his mother's 'flagrancy', projects that same flagrancy onto the image of the innocent Ophelia whom he then spurns along with life itself. Angelo places sexual licence under penalty of death and then, provoked into desire by the total virtue of Isabella, he shifts from his role of legislator into that of 'vice'. In both plays, sexuality appears as infringement, and in each case it is the woman who is the cause. For Hamlet, Gertrude's blatant sexuality makes her less than human, less even than a beast lacking 'discourse of reason' (11) (Isabella also hurls the epithet 'beast' at her brother Claudio when he asks her to submit to Angelo's sexual demand [III.i.135]). But it is Angelo who states most clearly the *more* and *less* that the woman becomes when she fails to contain for the man the sexuality which she provokes:

> Be that you are,
> That is, a woman; if you be more, you're none.
> (II.iv.133–4)

In relation to *Hamlet*, the charge of failure, as well as the horror, can be lifted straight out of the play: Hamlet and his dead father united in their reproach of Gertrude for her sexual failing ('O Hamlet what a falling off was there' [22]), and horror as the old Hamlet's exact response to the crime which precedes the play and precipitates its drama ('O horrible! O horrible! most horrible!' [23]).

Eliot's essay suggests that the question of the woman and the question of meaning go together. The problem with *Hamlet* is not just that the emotion it triggers is unmanageable and cannot be contained by the woman who is its cause, but that this excess of affect produces a problem of interpretation: how to read, or control by reading, a play whose inscrutability (like that of the *Mona Lisa*) has baffled—and seduced—so many critics. Eliot's criticism is normative in two senses which he himself makes explicit. It demands a particular aesthetic of formal constraint (this demand is part of his critique of Romanticism) and it entails pref-

---

1. See also on this image of the text as seducer and threat, Shoshana Felman's important psychoanalytic reading of responses to, and movement of, Henry James's *The Turn of the Screw* (Felman 1977).

erences—a particular selection of texts as the model of what literature should be (Eliot later had to qualify his essay on *Hamlet* by stating that his critique did not detract from the value and unity of Shakespeare's work as a whole [Eliot 1933, p. 44]). The objective of Eliot's critical writing is therefore to validate literature at the same time as holding it to account. The task of the writer, and the critic, is ethical. Emotion must be controlled by meaning, and an always potentially chaotic and fragmentary reality must be ordered by art. In Eliot's writing, the objective correlative carries the burden of social order itself. Gertrude's weakness as a character provokes a crisis in which the chaos latent in social cohesion refuses to submit itself to form.

Paradoxically, the importance of psychoanalysis for a questioning of this critical tradition lies not in its distance from it, but in the proximity of its terms, in the striking similarities and echoes which connect the psychoanalytic account of subjectivity to the drama of representation and its dangers which Eliot so graphically describes. That there is risk in the human utterance, and uncertainty behind its apparent security of form, could be seen as the most fundamental discovery of Freud. For psychoanalysis, speech is always a drama which contains something in excess. It always bears the traces of a conflict of positions and identities which can only ever momentarily be arrested or resolved. The unconscious upsets the proper order of representation most clearly in dreams, in slips of the tongue and in jokes, but it can also threaten the most normal or seemingly ordered protocols of representation and speech. Eliot identifies in *Hamlet* something 'excessive', 'inexpressibly horrible' and 'unknowable' which, because it cannot be managed, brings 'buffoonery' in its train. But by linking his demand for artistic coherence so closely to a recognition of its demise, Eliot suggests in this essay on Shakespeare not an incompatibility, but a relation, between these two extremes. The supremacy of the artist (the most supreme *of* artists) and the ideal conception of form come together at the precise point of their collapse. Instead of looking down on chaos from the heights of artistic mastery and control, Shakespeare in *Hamlet* slips off the edge of representation itself.

Order for psychoanalysis is also sexual order: the division of human subjects into male and female and the directing of desire onto its appropriate objects, but again this is effected only partially and at a cost. This process is also described by psychoanalysis as a drama—the Oedipal drama which allocates subjects to their sexual place while also showing that the norm can be violated by the one who most firmly believes that he is submitting to its law. As with language, so with sexuality, an insistence on order always speaks the other and more troubled scenario which it is designed to exclude. Again the link can be made with Eliot. In 'Tradition and the individual talent', published in the same year (1919) as the *Hamlet* essay (Eliot 1975), Eliot provides the complement to his concept

of aesthetic form in what can fairly be described as an 'Oedipal' reading
of literary tradition itself. In order to control his disordered subjectivity
and transmute it into form, the artist must give himself up to something
outside himself and surrender to the tradition which precedes and sur-
rounds him. Only by capitulating to his literary ancestors can the artist
escape his oppressive individuality and enter into historical time: 'Set
[the artist] for contrast and comparison among the dead' for 'the most
individual parts of his work may be those in which the dead poets, his
ancestors, assert their immortality most vigorously' (p. 38). Thus, just as
in the psychoanalytic account the son pays his debt to the dead father,
symbol of the law, in order fully to assume his own history, so for Eliot,
the artist pays his debt to the dead poets and can only become a poet by
that fact.

Eliot's conception of literary tradition could therefore be described as
a plea for appropriate mourning and for the respecting of literary rites.
Once again the echo of *Hamlet* is striking. But, as has been pointed out
by Jacques Lacan (Lacan 1959), it is the shameful *inadequacy* of mourning which is the trigger and then the constant refrain of the play: the old
Hamlet cut off in the 'blossom' of his sin, Polonius interred 'hugger
mugger', Ophelia buried—wrongly because of her suicide—in sacred
ground.

In this context, where order is constantly both asserted and fails, the
fact that it is a woman who is seen as the cause of the excess and deficiency in the play, and again, a woman who symbolizes its aesthetic
failure, takes on a further resonance, seeming to echo another fundamental drama of psychic experience as described by Freud. This is the
drama of sexual difference where the woman appears as the cause of just
such a failure in representation, as something deficient, lacking or
threatening to the systems and identities which are the precondition not
only of integrated artistic form but also of so-called normal adult psychic
and sexual life. Located by Freud at the point where the woman is first
seen to be different (Freud 1924, 1925), this moment can then have its
effects in that familiar mystification (or fetishization) of the woman which
makes of her something both perfect and dangerous or obscene (obscene
if not perfect). And perhaps no image has embodied this process more
clearly than that of the *Mona Lisa* itself, which at exactly this historical
moment (the time of Eliot and Freud alike) started to be taken as the
emblem of an inscrutable femininity, cause and destination of the whole
of human mystery and its desires:

> The lady smiled in regal calm: her instincts of conquest, of ferocity,
> all the heredity of the species, the will to seduce and to ensnare,
> the charm of deceit, the kindness that conceals a cruel purpose,—
> all this appeared and disappeared by turns behind the laughing veil

and buried itself in the poem of her smile. Good and wicked, cruel
and compassionate, graceful and feline, she laughed.

(Angelo Conti, *cit.* Freud 1910, p. 109)[2]

The enigma of the woman and the enigma, or undecipherability, of
the image are inseparable: 'No one has solved the riddle of her smile,
no one has read the meaning of her thoughts' (Muther, *cit.* Freud 1910,
p. 108). It is their combination which produces the excess: 'a presence . . . expressive of what in the ways of a thousand years men had
come to desire' (Walter Pater, *cit.* Freud 1910, p. 110), as well as the
danger: 'the kindness that conceals a cruel purpose' (p. 109). Freud also
picks up the tone, in one of his most problematic observations on femininity, when he allows that writers have recognized in this painting:

> the most perfect representation of the contrasts which dominate the
> erotic life of women; the contrast between reserve and seduction,
> and between the most devoted tenderness and a sensuality that is
> ruthlessly demanding—consuming men as if they were alien beings.
>
> (Freud 1910, p. 108)

What other representation, one might ask, has more clearly produced a
set of emotions without 'objective correlative', that is, in excess of the
facts as they appear? The place of the *Mona Lisa* in Eliot's reading of
Hamlet suggests that what is felt as inscrutable, unmanageable or even
horrible for an aesthetic theory which will only allow into its definition
what can be controlled or managed by art, is nothing other than femininity itself.

What requires explanation, therefore, is not that Gertrude is an inadequate object for the emotions generated in the play, but the fact that
she is expected to support them. Hamlet's horror at Gertrude (like the
horror Eliot sees behind the play) makes her a focus for a set of ills which
the drama shows as exceeding the woman *at the same time* as it makes
of her their cause. It has often been pointed out that Hamlet's despon-
dency seems to centre more on his mother's remarriage than it does on
his father's death even after the revelation of his uncle's crime. Eliot
does suggest that it is in the nature of the sentiments dealt with in *Hamlet*—a son's feelings towards a guilty mother—that they are unmanageable by art. But he does not ask why it is, in the play as in his own
commentary, that the woman bears the chief burden of the guilt.

At the end of Eliot's essay, he refers to Montaigne's 'An Apologie of
Raymond Sebond' as a possible source for the malaise of Shakespeare's
play (its discourse on the ephemeral, contradictory and unstable nature

2. All page references to Freud are to *The Standard Edition of the Complete Psychological Works
of Sigmund Freud*, edited by James Strachey, with
references to *The Pelican Freud*, where available,
in italics.

of man has often been taken as the origin of Hamlet's suicide soliloquy)
(Florio 1885, pp. 219–310). In relation to the woman, however, another
smaller essay by Montaigne—'Of three good women'—is equally striking, not necessarily as a source, but for the exact reversal which it represents *vis-à-vis* Gertrude herself, each of these women choosing self-
imposed death at the point where her husband is to die (pp. 378–82).
The image is close to the protestations of the Player Queen in the
Mousetrap scene of *Hamlet* who vows her undying love to her husband,
whereupon Gertrude, recognizing perhaps in the Player Queen's claims
a rebuke or foil to her own sexual laxness, comments 'The Lady doth
protest too much' (54) (a familiar cliché now for the sexual 'inconstancy'
of females). So what happens indeed to the sexuality of the woman
when the husband dies, who is there to hold its potentially dangerous
excess within the bounds of a fully social constraint? This could be seen
as one of the questions asked by *Hamlet* the play, and generative of its
terrible effect. Behind Eliot's reading we uncover a whole history of the
fantasies that the woman embodies and the order that she is required to
uphold.

The presence of sexuality to this concept of aesthetic form has important implications for recent literary debate whose terms echo, from the
opposite side, those of Eliot's critique. Taking their cue from psychoanalysis, writers like Roland Barthes (1970 and 1971) and Julia Kristeva
(1974 and 1980) have seen the very stability of the sign as index and
precondition for that myth of linguistic cohesion and sexual identity
which we must live by, but under whose regimen we suffer, with literature as one of the chief arenas in which that struggle is played out.
Writing which proclaims its integrity, and literary theory which demands
such integrity (objectivity/correlation) of writing, merely repeat that
moment of repression when language and sexuality were first ordered
into place, putting down the unconscious processes which threaten the
resolution of the Oedipal drama and of narrative form alike. In this
contrast, Eliot's critical writing with its stress on the ethical task of writer
and critic becomes nothing less than the most accomplished (and influ-
ential) case for the interdependency and centrality of language and sexuality to the proper ordering of literary form. Much recent literary theory
can be seen as an attempt to undo the ferocious effects of this particularly
harsh type of literary super-ego—one whose political repressiveness in
the case of Eliot became more and more explicit in his later allegiance
to Empire, Church and State.

Hamlet fails, therefore, at the two precise points where Eliot calls
literature to account—the coherence of the aesthetic object and the proper
ordering of historical time. What in his terms is the play's failure could
be taken now as the sign of the oppressiveness—for criticism and for
literature—of these very demands, of their aesthetic and moral constraint. It is as if the woman becomes both scapegoat and cause of the

dearth or breakdown of (Oedipal) resolution which the play enacts, not only at the level of its theme, but also in the disjunctions and difficulties of its aesthetic form. Much has been made of the aesthetic problem of *Hamlet* by critics other than Eliot, who have pondered on its lack of integration or single-purposiveness, its apparent inability to resolve itself or come to term (it is the longest of Shakespeare's plays), just as they have pondered on all these factors in the character of Hamlet himself.

Hamlet therefore poses a problem for Eliot at the level of both matter and form. Femininity is the image of that problem; it seems in fact to be the only image through which the problem can be conceptualized or thought. Femininity thus becomes the focus for a partly theorized recognition of the psychic and literary disintegration which can erupt at any moment into literary form.

II

The overlap of aesthetic and sexual failing appears again in commentaries on *Measure for Measure* in which Isabella has become the focus of a generally acknowledged sense of deficiency in the play's dramatic form. F. R. Leavis saw the play as one of the most 'consummate and convincing of Shakespeare's achievements' (Leavis 1942, p. 234), but in doing so, he set himself explicitly against a list of critics which include 'Hazlitt, Coleridge, Swinburne, the Arden editor, Sir Edmund Chambers, Mr Desmond McCarthy, the editors of the New Cambridge Shakespeare and innumerable others' (p. 234). Isabella is not the only 'problem' in this play (the term 'problem' was introduced at the turn of the century by analogy with the naturalist dramas of Ibsen and Shaw); but criticism has alternatively revered and accused her in such a way that her sexual identity has become the site on which dissatisfaction with the play, and disagreement about the play, have turned. No character in the play has produced a 'wider divergence of opinion' (R. M. Smith 1950, p. 212), opinions which, despite the differences between them, once again have in common their *excess*. Isabella has been the object of 'excessive admiration' and 'excessive repugnance' (Smith, p. 212) uniting in her person those extremes of attraction and recoil which were latent in T. S. Eliot's comparison of the *Mona Lisa* with *Hamlet*.

Strangely, the accusations against Isabella have, if anything, been stronger than those against Gertrude, suggesting that it is the desire provoked by the woman which is above all the offence, and that the woman who refuses to meet that desire is as unsettling as the one who does so with excessive haste. Isabella has been described as a 'hussy' (Charlton, *cit.* R. M. Smith 1950, p. 213), 'hysterical' (Lever, Introduction to Arden edition, Shakespeare 1965, p. lxxx), as suffering 'inhibition' (Knight 1930, p. 102) or 'obsession' (Jardine 1983, p. 192) about sex. She has also been revered as divine. The two positions are, however, related and the second can easily tip over into the first. Angelo himself makes the link:

> Shall we desire to raze the sanctuary
> And pitch our evils there?
>
> What is't I dream on?
> O cunning enemy, that, to catch a saint,
> With saints dost bait thy hook!
> (II.ii.171–2, 180–1)

Wilson Knight's essay on *Measure for Measure*, which Leavis refers to as the only adequate account which he knows of the play (Knight 1930), gives the strongest illustration of the proximity between Isabella's evil and her sainthood. 'More saintly than Angelo' with a 'saintliness that goes deeper, is more potent than his', Isabella gradually turns in the course of the analysis into a 'fiend'. Her rejection of Angelo's sexual demand and her refusal to sacrifice herself for the life of her brother makes that same sanctity 'self-centred', 'ice-cold', lacking 'humanity', 'feeling' or 'warmth'. In the face of this refusal criticism blows hot and cold, becoming in itself a participation in the act. Isabella's 'sex inhibitions' show her 'horribly as they are, naked'. Shakespeare 'strikes mercilessly against her once and deep' and she is 'stung', 'lanced on a sore spot of her soul'. Her final intercession for Angelo's life shows the response beneath the denial: 'his strong passions have moved her . . . thawed her ice-cold pride' (Knight 1930, pp. 100–3).

In the case of Isabella, it is lack of sexuality which is the failing, but as with Gertrude it is the woman who bears the burden of the reproach. The basic accusation, which is shared by Lever in the Arden edition of the play, does not greatly differ from the more measured interpretations of Isabella's slow growth into humanity which have been offered against it (Traversi, *cit.* Maxwell 1947; R. M. Smith 1950; French 1982).

The critical premises on which this interpretation rests are, however, as important as its content, and these can be related back to Eliot. One implication of the objective correlative is that drama relies on the credibility of the character to give coherence to its form. If the character fails, then meaning cannot be pinned down or drawn into its proper bounds. It starts to circulate and goes out of control. For Eliot, such lack of control is ultimately that of the author himself who, like the character on stage, has failed to hold together. The aesthetic consistency of the character and the psychological cohesion of the author are interdependent. If meaning is not properly ordered through the dramatic personae, it is therefore the very limits of human subjectivity which are put at risk.

The critical investment in Isabella, of which Wilson Knight's essay is only one of the most extreme instances, can be seen as deriving from this way of conceptualizing literature, which is of course not restricted

to Eliot alone. Eliot's assessment of Gertrude was predominantly an aesthetic one (he distanced himself from criticism of Hamlet as a character
by insisting that the problem was the play), but it does contain within it
the idea of a norm. To judge Isabella—whether positively or nega-
tively—is already to pre-judge the issue of meaning and subjectivity by
transposing it into moral terms. If the problem is *how* a character behaves,
then the limits of characterization are not called into question. Given
that *Measure for Measure* is one of Shakespeare's plays where it is generally recognized that his method of characterization cannot fully be
grasped psychologically (the weakness of Claudio as a character, the alle-
gorical role of the Duke), then the extent to which Isabella has been
discussed in terms of consistency, credibility and ethics is striking. In the
critical debates about Isabella, it is as if we can see anxiety about aesthetic or representational cohesion turning into a sexual reproach.[3]

The fact that there is a question of language and meaning at stake in
relation to *Measure for Measure* is made explicit by Leavis himself whose
article 'The greatness of *Measure for Measure*' was written as a reply to
an article by L. C. Knights called 'The ambiguity of *Measure for Measure*', both of which were published in *Scrutiny* in 1942.[4] For Leavis,
the charge of ambiguity must be answered if Shakespeare is not to be
seen as the 'victim of unresolved contradiction, of mental conflict or
uncertainty' (Leavis 1942, p. 240). His critical task is therefore to establish the integrity of the text, which entails aesthetic and moral certainty,
that is, the power to identify and judge. The easiest identification is with
Angelo ('it is surely easier for us to put ourselves in Angelo's place and
imagine ourselves exposed to his temptations', p. 247), while the supreme
judgement falls on Isabella herself ('a supreme test on Isabella' at the end
of the play). Lack of ambiguity therefore involves unequivocal sexual
identity and a corresponding (and uneven) distribution of moral roles.[5]

If we overturn this certainty—as L. C. Knights does in his article—
we can therefore expect to find an ambiguity or dislocation at the heart
of sexuality itself—one which upsets the very form of judgement which
this type of character-based analysis enshrines. What is sexuality in *Measure for Measure?* Who bears the responsibility for the problem posed to
ethics by desire? What is it that criticism is forced to leave aside when it

---

3. See also G. K. Hunter's introduction to the
Arden edition of *All's Well That Ends Well*
(Shakespeare 1967) which again traces the problem of interpretation to the woman: 'To fit Helena
into the play or adapt the play to Helena is obviously
the central problem of interpretation in *All's Well*
(p. xlviii), and makes explicit reference to Eliot's
aesthetic concept: 'Her role is a complex one, but
there is an absence of adequate external correla-
tives to justify this complexity' (p. xlix).

4. See Mulhern 1979 for a full discussion of the
socio-political context of *Scrutiny* from 1932 to 1953
and its significance for British literary culture.

5. See also Harold Brooks's judgement on Titania
in the introduction to the Arden edition of *A Midsummer Night's Dream* (Shakespeare 1979): 'it is
of course she who is principally at fault' (p. cvi),
'her obstinacy has to be overcome' (p. cviii), a
judgement which gives moral legitimation to, and
even cancels out, the sinister and disturbing aspects
of fairyland and of Oberon's actions: 'his ill-feeling
does not grate so much as it would without this
context. As a rule, the context is a complete control when anything sinister is introduced' (p. cviii)
(as if control could not be sinister . . .).

asks the woman to transform sexuality from outrage into something moral and human and safe? It would seem to be the excess of sexuality itself, an excess which disrupts linguistic, fully as much as ethical, form. Apologetically—given his own commitment to the idea of Shakespeare's mastery—L. C. Knights identifies such a dislocation in these lines:

> Our natures do pursue,
> Like rats that ravin down their proper bane,
> A thirsty evil; and when we drink, we die.
>   (I.ii.120–2)

The problem with these lines (like those of Sonnet 129 to which Knights also refers) is that sexuality is given as an evil which belongs to the act, to the desire, to the object and to nature itself, but it can be limited to none of them. Instead Shakespeare's language shifts awkwardly across them all:

> The illustrative comparison has, we notice, three stages: (i) rats 'ravin down' poison, (ii) which makes them thirsty, (iii) so they drink and—the poison taking effect—die. But the human parallel has, it seems, only two stages: prompted by desire, men quench their 'thirsty evil' in the sexual act and—by the terms of the new proclamation—pay the penalty of death. The act of ravening down the bane or poison is thus left on our hands, and the only way we can dispose of it is by assuming that 'our natures' have no need to 'pursue' their 'thirsty evils' for it is implanted in them by the mere fact of being human. This is of course pedantry and—you may say—irrelevant pedantry, for Shakespeare's similes do not usually demand a detailed, point by point, examination, and the confusion between desire (thirst) and that from which desire springs does not lessen the general effect. The fact remains, however, that there is some slight dislocation or confusion of feeling, comparable, it seems to me, to the wider confusion of Sonnet 129, 'An expense of spirit in a waste of shame . . .' (for not even the excellent analysis by Robert Graves and Laura Riding in their *Survey of Modernist Poetry*, pp. 63–81, can make me feel that the sonnet forms a coherent whole). And even if you accept the simile as completely satisfactory, nothing can prevent 'our natures' from receiving some share of the animus conveyed by 'ravin', a word in any case more appropriate to lust than to love.
>   (Knights 1942, pp. 226–7)[6]

L. C. Knights' analysis of these lines moves as far from Leavis's (and Eliot's) conception of artistic cohesion as the more recent analyses of

---

6. Lever in the Arden edition (Shakespeare 1965) annotates the line and L. C. Knights's commentary by stating that there is no confusion since the 'thirsty evil' refers, not to lechery, but to the 'liberty' of the preceding lines (I.ii.118–20), although he does acknowledge the sexual connotation of ratsbane (p. 15n.); for Lever's relegation, or diminishing, of the sexual, see also the note on the meaning of 'torches' (I.i.32, pp. 5–6 n.).

Shakespeare's *Sonnets* and of the language of the first scene of *Hamlet* given by Stephen Booth (Booth 1977 and 1969b), where what is always at stake is the insecurity of meaning which Shakespeare imposes on the reader of the *Sonnets* and on the spectator of his play (*Hamlet* as 'the tragedy of an audience which cannot make up its mind', Booth 1969b, p. 152). The two critical positions—the one which would contain and the one which would explode the text—confront each other around *Hamlet* in that it is precisely the first twenty-two lines of the play that Eliot describes as masterly for being *transparent* to the dramatic meaning of the play (Eliot 1951, p. 135). Language as something transparent or as something which calls attention to itself has been another issue of recent critical debate. What is interesting in relation to *Hamlet* and *Measure for Measure* is that the concentration on the woman seems to siphon off or distract attention from the difficulty of language itself. Slippage of meaning and sexuality as excess seem therefore to be the subtext of the critical focus on Isabella and Gertrude. If they fail as characters and/or as women, then what is required of criticism, and of dramatic form, is their moral aesthetic *completion*.

III

One remark of Isabella has been especially condemned. When Claudio asks her to submit to Angelo in order to save his life, she reacts:

> Is't not a kind of incest, to take life
> From thine own sister's shame? What should I think?
> Heaven shield my mother play'd my father fair:
> For such a warped slip of wilderness
> Ne'er issued from his blood.
>
> (III.i.138–42)

Lever calls this a 'hysterical conceit . . . in keeping with the speech as a whole' (Shakespeare, 1965, p. 75 n.); Charlotte Lennox in 1753 criticized it for 'its coarse and unwomanly reflections on the virtue of her mother' (Lennox, *cit*. R. M. Smith 1950, p. 213). In relation to these lines, Isabella is 'hysterical' and 'unwomanly', not through lack of humanity (her refusal to relent), but because of the aspersion which she casts on the proper sexual ordering of humanity itself. Accusing her brother of incest (if he takes his life from her sexual act), she then immediately releases him from the charge by claiming that he cannot—because of this very demand—be her legitimate brother. The sexual scandal shifts generations and becomes a mother's sexual crime (like Gertrude's). This way of thinking makes Isabella 'hysterical' and 'unwomanly' because it overturns the most fundamental of sexual laws.

The charge of neurosis is brought to bear, therefore, on behaviour and language which is an affront to—or does not make—sense. Leavis ended his article on *Measure for Measure* by objecting to a recent Cambridge production which had presented Angelo as a 'twitching study in neurosis'. If the meaning of the play is coherent and unambiguous there must be *no* neurosis, just as the charge of neurosis (or hysteria) is brought to classify and organize meaning which goes out of control. Refusal of difficulty and diagnosis of disorder become complementary ways of managing the literary text, each one subjecting the text to the control of an ego which denies, or surveys at a distance, any trouble of meaning which it might present.

Ernest Jones's famous psychoanalytic reading of *Hamlet* (Jones 1949) seems to put interpretation firmly on this path of diagnosis, which then works in the service of critical and artistic control. Jones makes it explicit that his intention is also to establish the integrity of the literary text, that is to uncover factors, hidden motives and desires, which will give back to rationality what would otherwise pass the limits of literary understanding and appreciation itself: 'The perfect work of art is one where the traits and reactions of a character prove to be harmonious, consistent and intelligible when examined in the different layers of the mind' (p. 49). Jones's reading therefore belongs with that psychoanalytic project which restores to rationality or brings to *light*, placing what was formerly unconscious or unmanageable under the ego's mastery and control. It is a project which has been read directly out of Freud's much contested statement '*Wo es war, soll Ich werden*', translated by Strachey 'Where id was, there ego shall be' (Freud 1933 (1932), p. 80; 2, *p. 112*). Lacan, for whom the notion of such conscious mastery is only ever a fantasy (the fantasy of the ego itself) retranslates or reverses the statement 'There where it was, so I must come to be' (Lacan 1957, p. 524; my translation).

For Jones, as for Eliot therefore, there must be no aesthetic excess, nothing which goes beyond the reaches of what can ultimately be deciphered and known. In this context, psychoanalysis acts as a key which can solve the enigma of the text. The chapter of Jones's book which gives the Oedipal reading of the text, the one which tends to be included in the anthologies (for example, Lerner 1963), is accordingly entitled 'The psychoanalytic solution'. Taking his reference from Freud's comments in *The Interpretation of Dreams* (Freud 1900, pp. 264–6; *4, pp.* 366–8), Jones sees Hamlet as a little Oedipus who cannot bring himself to kill Claudius because he stands in the place of his own desire, having murdered Hamlet's father and married his mother. The difference between Oedipus and Hamlet is that Oedipus unknowingly acts out this fantasy, whereas for Hamlet it is repressed into the unconscious, revealing itself in the form of that inhibition or inability to act which has baffled so many critics of the play. It is this repression of the Oedipal drama beneath the surface of the text which leads Freud to say of *Hamlet*, comparing it with Sophocles' drama, that it demonstrates 'the secular advance of repression in the emotional life of mankind' (Freud 1900, p. 264; 4, *p.* 366).

If Hamlet cannot act, therefore, it is because he is locked into an unconscious drama which has not been elucidated, or resolved. The psychoanalytic solution therefore answers not only Hamlet's but also the critic's dilemma. The diagnosis of the character's *disorder* produces for the reader the *order*, or intelligibility, of the text.

Jones's reading involves a psychological interpretation of character, but it cannot, by its own definition, stop there. If Hamlet's dilemma is to be understood in terms of a failing, then that failing must have a cause. Jones's interpretation has often been discredited for its psychological speculations about Hamlet's early childhood as well as for its conjectures about Shakespeare's personal life, both of which lead him necessarily off the edge of the text. But these are in a sense only the logical consequence of a critical method which takes the reality or consistency of the character as its norm. Just as Eliot read into *Hamlet* a momentary loss by Shakespeare of the self-possession which is the precondition of art, so Jones reads Shakespeare's private psychic drama out of that of the character on the stage (Jones 1949, pp. 115 ff.). (Psycho-) analysis of the author is latent to the concept of the aesthetic inadequacy or breakdown of the text. Inside the play, Eliot located this inadequacy in Gertrude. Jones sees this same failing as psychological—Gertrude's too great possessiveness and her too little constraint produce those overwhelming feelings in Hamlet which then threaten to engulf the character and the play. In Jones's reading, Hamlet also bears the guilt of his own desire (the mind of the infant is, Jones writes in a less known chapter, 'tragic' under the weight of this desire—chapter IV, pp. 81–103), but Gertrude none the less becomes the vanishing point of the problem represented in the play.

Yet the drift of this analysis also starts to give an opposite impression, which is that responsibility for the psychological drama cannot in fact be pinned down. At the very moment when psychoanalysis produces its Oedipal reading, with the implied account of what could—or should— have been the successful resolution or norm, then, as was the case with Eliot, the origin or source of the failure starts to move across the different levels of text. From Hamlet to Shakespeare and back to Gertrude, the question arises as to what would be needed, precisely, to get matters straight? Or is it that what is felt as the *deviation* of *Hamlet* exposes the futility of asking this question at all? Another look at the psychoanalytic engagement with *Hamlet* suggests that the second of these questions might be closer to the point.

The relationship of psychoanalysis to *Hamlet* has in fact always been a strange and repetitive one, in which Hamlet the character is constantly given the status of a truth. When Hamlet is described as Oedipus, psychoanalysis has been brought in to solve a problem of reading or aesthetic form. But when he is described as melancholic or hysteric, the relationship works in reverse. Then literature becomes the place where psychoanalysis can seek illustration for those aspects of subjectivity which bring us up against the limits of interpretation and sexual identity alike. The interpretative distinction between rationality and excess, between normality and abnormality, starts to crumble for instance when the melancholic is defined as a madman who also speaks the truth. Freud uses *Hamlet* with this meaning in 'Mourning and melancholia' written in 1915:

> We can only wonder why a man has to be ill before he can be accessible to a truth of this kind. For there can be no doubt that if anyone holds an opinion of himself such as this (an opinion which Hamlet holds of himself and everyone else) he is ill, whether he is being more or less unfair to himself.
>
> (Freud 1917, pp. 246–7; 2, p. 255)

Taken in this direction, *Hamlet* illustrates not so much a failure of identity as the precarious distinction on which this notion of identity rests. In 'Psychopathic characters on the stage' (Freud 1942 [1905 or 1906]), Freud includes *Hamlet* in that group of plays which rely for their effect on the neurotic in the spectator, inducing in her or him the neurosis watched on the stage, crossing over the boundaries between onstage and offstage, and breaking down the habitual barriers of the mind.[7] A particular *type* of drama, this form is none the less effective only through its capacity to implicate us *all*: 'A person who does not lose his reason under certain conditions can have no reason to lose' (Lessing, *cit.* Freud 1942 (1905 or 1906), p. 30 n.). Jones makes a similar point, and underscores its fullest social import, when he attributes the power of *Hamlet* to the very edge of sanity on which it moves, and the way that it confuses the division which 'until our generation (and even now in the juristic sphere) separated the sane and responsible from the irresponsible insane' (Jones 1949, p. 76). T. S. Eliot also gave his version of this, but from the other side, when he described poetry in 'Tradition and the individual talent' as an escape from emotion and personality, and then added 'but, of course, only those who have personality and emotion can know what it means to want to escape from these things' (Eliot 1975, p. 43). So instead of safely diagnosing Hamlet—his Oedipal drama, his disturbance—and subjecting them to its mastery and control, the psychoanalytic interpretation turns back onto the spectator and critic, and implicates the observer in those forms of irrationality or excess which Jones and Eliot, in their different ways, seem to be ordering into place.

Calling Hamlet a hysteric, which both Freud and Jones also do (Freud

---

7. André Green gives an important discussion in psychoanalytic terms of the division of stage space (1969, pp. 11–29). See also note 9 below.

1887–1902, p. 224; Jones 1949, p. 59), has the same effect in relation to the question of sexual difference, since it immediately raises the issue of femininity and upsets the too tidy Oedipal reading of the play. Freud had originally seen the boy's Oedipal drama as a straightforward desire for the mother and rivalry with the father, just as he had first considered the little girl's Oedipal trajectory to be its simple reverse. The discovery of the girl's pre-Oedipal attachment to the mother led him to modify this too easy picture in which unconscious sexual desires in infancy are simply the precursors in miniature of the boy's and the girl's later fitting sexual and social place (Freud 1924, 1925, 1931). This upset of the original schema led Freud to re-think the whole issue of feminine sexuality, but it also has crucial effects on how we consider the psychic life of the boy. In a section called 'Matricide' (Jones 1949, chapter V, pp. 105–14), which tends to be omitted from the anthologies, Jones talks of Hamlet's desire to kill not the father, but the mother. He takes this from Hamlet's soliloquy before he goes to his mother's bedchamber in Act III, scene ii of the play:

> Let not ever
> The soul of Nero enter this firm bosom;
> Let me be cruel, not unnatural.
> I will speak daggers to her, but use none.
>
> (57)

and also from Gertrude's own lines: 'What wilt thou do? Thou wilt not murder me. Help, Ho!' (61) (the murder of Polonius is the immediate consequence of this). Thus desire tips over into its opposite and the woman becomes guilty for the affect which she provokes.

This is still an Oedipal reading of the play, since the violence towards the mother is the effect of the desire for her. But desire then starts to trouble the norms of identification, involving Jones in a discussion of the femininity in man (not just desire *for* the woman but identification *with* her), a femininity which has been recognized in Hamlet by more than one commentator on the play (Jones 1949, pp. 88, 106).[8] Thus Hamlet, 'as patient as the female dove' (91), becomes Renaissance man only to the extent that he reveals a femininity which undermines that fiction (the image of the female dove was objected to by Knight in 1841 as a typographical error (Shakespeare 1877, I, p. 410 n.)). Femininity turns out to be lying behind the Oedipal drama, indicating its impasse or impossibility of resolution, even though Freud did talk of its 'dissolution', as if it suddenly went out of existence altogether. But this observation contradicts the basic analytic premiss of the persistence of unconscious desire.

Thus on either side of the psychoanalytic solution we find something

8. The concept of femininity in relation to Hamlet's character appears again in French 1982, p. 149, and in Leverenz 1980.

which makes of it no 'solution' at all. The ascription of melancholia and
hysteria to Hamlet appear at first as traditional diagnoses of the character
and the text. In fact they entail a different interpretative scenario altogether, one which exposes not the failure of the play, but of the fantasy
which lies behind the aesthetic critique—that there could be a straightforward resolution to the drama of our own psychic and sexual life. For
Jones, as for Eliot, this problem of *Hamlet*, the challenge which it poses
to interpretation, is then best embodied by femininity itself: 'The central
mystery [of *Hamlet*] has well been called the Sphinx of modern literature' (Jones 1949, pp. 25–26). What seems most important is not, therefore, whether Hamlet suffers from an excess of femininity (what form of
diagnosis would that be?), but the way that femininity itself functions *as*
excess, the excess of this particular interpretative schema (hence presumably its omission from the extracts and summaries of Jones), and the very
image once again for the troubled and troubling aesthetic boundaries of
the play.

IV

It should therefore come as no surprise that the opposite of this disturbance—an achieved aesthetic or even creativity itself—then finds its most
appropriate image again in femininity, but this time the reverse: the
good enough mother herself. As if completing the circuit, André Green
turns to D. W. Winnicott's concept of the maternal function as the basis
for his recent book on *Hamlet* (Green 1982).[9] In this psychoanalytic
reading, femininity appears as the very principle of the aesthetic process.
Shakespeare's Hamlet forecloses the femininity in himself, but by pro-
jecting onto the stage the degraded and violent image of a femininity
repudiated by his character, Shakespeare manages to preserve in himself
that other femininity which is the source of his creative art:

> Writing *Hamlet* had been an act of exorcism which enabled its
> author to give his hero's femininity—cause of his anxieties, self-
> reproaches and accusations—an acceptable form through the pro-
> cess of aesthetic creation. . . . By creating *Hamlet*, by giving it
> representation, Shakespeare, unlike his hero, managed to lift the
> dissociation between his masculine and feminine elements and to
> reconcile himself with the femininity in himself.
>
> (Green 1982, p. 256)

9. In *Hamlet et HAMLET* (1982), André Green continues the work he began in *Un Oeil en trop (The Tragic Effect)* (1969) on the psychoanalytic concept of representation in relation to dramatic form, and argues that, while the explicit themes of *Hamlet* (incest, parricide, madness) have the clearest links with the concerns of psychoanalysis, the play's central preoccupation with theatrical space and performance also fall within the psychoanalytic domain through the concept of psychic represen-tation and fantasy. Green examines the way that theatricality, or show, and femininity, are con-stantly assimilated throughout the play (pp. 9–10, 43, 45); in the remarks which follow I concentrate on the concept of femininity which he sets against this negative assimilation in his final section on Shakespeare's creative art (pp. 255–62).

The reading comes from Winnicott's paper 'Creativity and its origins' (Winnicott 1971, pp. 65–85) which ends with a discussion of Shakespeare's play. It is a fully psychological reading of the author, but its interest, once again, lies in the way that femininity appears as the enigma and source of the analysis, as of the play. More clearly and explicitly for Winnicott than for the other writers discussed here, aesthetic space itself is now conceptualized in terms of sexual difference and the place of femininity within it. Creativity *per se* (the creativity in all of us, so this is not just the creativity of the artist) arises out of a femininity which is that primordial space of being which is created by the mother alone. It is a state of being which is not yet a relationship to the object because there is as yet no self, and it is, as Green defines it, '*au delà de la représentation*', that is, the other side of representation, before the coming of the sign (this comes very close to French feminists such as Luce Irigaray on femininity and language).[1] But it is worth noting how the woman finds herself thus situated either at the point where language and aesthetic form start to crumble or else where they have not yet come to be.

'Masculinity does, femininity is'[2]—Winnicott's definition, like Green's, and that of Eliot before them, starts once again to look like a repetition, which reproduces the fundamental drama of *Hamlet*, cleaving the image of femininity in two, splitting it between a degradation and an idealization which, far from keeping each other under control (as Green suggests), set each other off, being the reverse sides of one and the same mystification. And like Eliot, Green also gets caught in the other face of the idealization, the inevitable accusation of Gertrude: 'Is the marriage of Gertrude consequence or cause of the murder of Hamlet's father? I incline towards the cause'. ('*Je pencherai pour la cause*', Green 1982, p. 61); and at the end of the book, he takes off on a truly wild speculation which makes Gertrude the stake in the battle between the old Fortinbras and the old Hamlet before the start of the play.

But the fact that *Hamlet* constantly unleashes an anxiety which returns to the question of femininity tells us above all something about the relationship of aesthetic form and sexual difference, about the fantasies they share—fantasies of coherence and identity in which the woman appears repeatedly as both wager and threat.

1. See especially Irigaray 1974 and 1977; Montrelay 1970.
2. Winnicott first presented this paper to the British Psycho-Analytic Society in 1966 under the title 'Split-off male and female elements found clinically in men and women: Theoretical inferences' (Winnicott, 1972). In the discussion which followed, which was not reprinted in the final publication, one objection raised to the definition 'Masculinity does, femininity is' pointed to its literary affinity, if not source, by referring to Winnicott's recent interest in Robert Graves's writings on Greek mythology and, specifically, the poem 'Woman Is, Man Does'. Winnicott's discussion of sexual difference in this paper is, however, far more complex and interesting than this final descent (ascent) into mythology, although it is this concept of femininity, with its associated emphasis on mothering, which has recently been imported directly into psychoanalytic readings of Shakespeare (see especially Leverenz 1980 and the whole anthology in which the article appears, Schwarz and Kahn 1980).

Lacan, in his essay on *Hamlet* (1959) (see p. 266 above), puts himself resolutely on the side of the symbolic—reading the play in terms of its dearth of proper mourning, and the impossibility for Hamlet of responding to the too literal summons of the dead father, who would otherwise represent for the hero the point of entry into his appropriate symbolic place (the proximity between this article and Eliot's 'Tradition and the individual talent' is truly striking). Lacan therefore places the problem of the play in the symbolic, on the side of the father; Green in the 'before' of representation where the mother simply *is*. The difference between them is another repetition, for it is the difference between the law of the father and the body of the mother, between symbol and affect (one of Green's best-known books in France was an exposition of the concept of 'affect' in Freud and a critique of Lacan's central premiss that psychic life is regulated by the exigencies of the linguistic sign (Green 1973)). But it is a difference with more far reaching implications, which link back to the question—of the fantasy of the woman and her guilt—with which this investigation started. For the concentration on the mother—on her adequacies and inadequacies—was the development in psychoanalytic theory itself which Lacan wanted to redress, precisely because, like *Hamlet*, it makes the mother cause of all good and evil, and her failings responsible for a malaise in all human subjects, that is, in men and in women, which stems from their position in the symbolic order of culture itself (Lacan 1957–8 and 1958). The problem of the regulation of subjectivity, of the Oedipal drama and the ordering of language and literary form—the necessity of that regulation and its constant difficulty or failing—is not, to put it at its most simple, the woman's fault.

Finally the reference to the *Mona Lisa* and to the Sphinx have another relevance to psychoanalysis, one which refers to the act of interpretation itself. The Sphinx presents meaning as a riddle, the *Mona Lisa* seems to hold a meaning which it refuses to divulge. The psychoanalytic concept of resistance also assumes that meaning is never simply present to the subject, but is something which disguises itself, is overwhelming or escapes. Freud came to recognize that its very intractability was not a simple fault to be corrected or a history to be filled. It did not conceal a simple truth which psychoanalysis should aim to restore. Instead this deviation or vicissitude of meaning was the 'truth' of a subject caught in the division between conscious and unconscious which will always function at one level as a split. Paradoxically, interpretation can only advance when resistance is seen not as obstacle but as process. This simultaneously deprives interpretation of its own control and mastery over its object since, as an act of language, it will necessarily be implicated in the same dynamic.

In both *Hamlet* and *Measure for Measure*, the play itself presents this deviant and overpowering quality of meaning which appears in turn as something which escapes or overwhelms the spectator. In Act III of *Hamlet* the two effects are staged, the one fast upon the other, in the Mousetrap scene: the Dumbshow discloses its meaning only partially or postpones its effects, while the spoken and too explicit words of the play which follows send their chief spectator into crisis. The Dumbshow gives the shadow of a meaning, the play speaks its meaning too loud. Together they divide the play in two, forcing us to ask for whom is meaning intended and does it always unfailingly reach its goal (does the King see the Dumbshow or is it intended for the audience and not for his eyes?). The disparity between these two moments also reflects the Renaissance division between nonrepresentational and illusionistic stage space (Weimann 1978), but the problem of interpretation they have provoked (Jenkins, in Shakespeare 1982a, pp. 501–5) equally points to repetition, discontinuity and excess, all of which run right through the fabric of the play. In *Hamlet*, the murder of the old King is represented three times over—in the Ghost's speech, in the Dumbshow and in the play, although the chief horror is directed at the sexual act (the one act that cannot be staged). Hamlet himself hovers between the word and a deed whose sole meaning, when it comes, is to bring death. The dilemma of Hamlet (character and play) could also be seen in terms of an analytic scenario in which focus brought to bear on the problem and difficulty of meaning leaves the relationship between word and action held in unbearable suspense.

In *Measure for Measure*, speech is also offered as a drama which can be too present—in this case the drama of a woman who dares to speak and show her face. When Isabella is called upon to plead for her brother, she is poised on the edge of a vow which will forbid her to speak with her face uncovered to a man (I.iv.10–13). The play therefore opens with a sexual danger which it places within the utterance itself. This danger— to which Angelo's desire comes as the immediate and anticipated response—resides in something given as the too physical voice of the woman, the overwhelming presence of her speech.

In *Measure for Measure*, sex unlegitimated by marriage is therefore forbidden, but speech itself in relation to the woman is placed under the weight of a law. The penalty which falls on the too blatant sexuality of Juliet and Claudio is matched by this injunction against the act of expression which can also be felt as too glaring or exposed. As if, by analogy, the sexuality of the utterance will by definition be overpowering unless it disguises itself or is covered from view.

In *Hamlet* and *Measure for Measure* words either fail to complete themselves in action or else they reach their destination too fast. This may be at least part of the discomfort which is aroused for interpretation by these plays. More than the theme of an illicit or adulterate sexuality, this tension may be what is felt as intractable to a form of analysis which wants meaning to be balanced or to be held in its proper bounds. The same tension could perhaps explain why Gertrude and Isabella have, in their different ways, served so much as the critical focus of these plays. Failing in a woman, whether aesthetic or moral, is always easier to point to than a failure of integration within language and subjectivity itself. If we try to read Shakespeare in terms of the second, however, it might be possible to lift the onus off the woman, who has for so long now been expected to take the responsibility, and to bear the excessive weight.

Works Cited

Barthes, Roland (1970) S/Z. Paris: Seuil. In English: S/Z, trans. Richard Miller. New York: Hill & Wang, 1974.
——— (1971) 'La mythologie aujourd'hui', Esprit. April. In English: 'Change the object itself', in Image-Music-Text, trans. Stephen Heath. London: Fontana, 1977, 165–9.
Booth, Stephen (1969) 'On the value of Hamlet', in Rabkin, Norman (ed.) Reinterpretation of Elizabethan Drama. New York and London: Columbia University Press, 137–76.
——— (ed). (1977) Shakespeare's Sonnets, edited with an analytic commentary. New Haven and London: Yale University Press.
Charlton, H. B. (1938) Shakespearian Comedy. London: Methuen.
Eliot, T. S. (1933) The Use of Poetry and the Use of Criticism. London: Faber & Faber.
——— (1951) Selected Essays. London: Faber & Faber.
——— (1975) Selected Prose of T. S. Eliot, ed. Frank Kermode. London: Faber & Faber.
Felman, Shoshana (1977) 'Turning the screw of interpretation', in Felman, S. (ed.) Literature and Psychoanalysis. The Question of Reading: Otherwise. Yale French Studies 55/56. New Haven: Yale University, 94–207.
Florio, John (trans.) (1885) The Essays of Michael, Lord of Montaigne [1603]. London: Routledge & Sons.
French, Marilyn (1982) Shakespeare's Division of Experience. London: Jonathan Cape.
Freud, Sigmund (1887–1902) The Origins of Psychoanalysis, letters to Wilhelm Fliess, Drafts and Notes, ed. by Marie Bonaparte, Anna Freud and Ernst Kris. Reprinted 1954, London: Imago.
——— (1900) The Interpretation of Dreams, in Strachey, James (ed.) The Standard Edition of the Complete Psychological Works of Sigmund Freud. Reprinted 1955–74, London: Hogarth, vols IV–V. Reprinted 1976, in The Pelican Freud, vol. 4. Harmondsworth: Pelican.
——— (1910) 'Leonardo da Vinci and a memory of his childhood', Standard Edition, vol. XI, 57–137.
——— (1917) [1915] 'Mourning and melancholia', Standard Edition, vol. XIV, 237–58. Reprinted in The Pelican Freud, vol. 2, 245–68.
——— (1924) 'The Dissolution of the Oedipus Complex', Standard Edition, vol. XIX, 173–9. Reprinted in The Pelican Freud, vol. 7, 313–22.
——— (1925) 'Some psychical consequences of the anatomical distinction between the sexes', Standard Edition, vol. XIX, 243–58. Reprinted in The Pelican Freud, vol. 7, 323–43.
——— (1931) 'Female sexuality', Standard Edition, vol. XXI, 223–43. Reprinted in The Pelican Freud, vol. 7, 367–92.
——— (1933) [1932] 'The dissection of the psychical personality', New Introductory Lectures, Standard Edition, vol. XXII, 57–80. Reprinted in The Pelican Freud, vol. 2, 88–122.
——— (1942) [1905 or 1906] 'Psychopathic characters on the stage', Standard Edition, vol. VII, 303–10.
Green, André (1969) Un Oeil en trop. Paris: Minuit. In English: The Tragic Effect: Oedipus Complex and Tragedy, trans. Alan Sheridan. Cambridge: Cambridge University Press, 1979.
——— (1973) Le discours vivant, le concept psychanalytique de l'affect. Paris: Presses Universitaries de France.
——— (1982) Hamlet et HAMLET, une interprétation psychanalytique de la réprésentation. Paris: Ballard.
Irigaray, Luce (1974) Speculum de l'autre femme. Paris: Minuit. In English: Speculum of the Other Woman, trans. Gillian C. Gill. Ithaca, NY: Cornell University Press, 1985.
——— (1977) 'Women's exile: an interview with Luce Irigaray', Ideology and Consciousness, 1, 24–39.
Jardine, Lisa (1983) Still Harping on Daughters: Women and Drama in the Age of Shakespeare. Brighton: Harvester Press.
Jones, Ernst (1949) Hamlet and Oedipus. New York: Norton. Anchor edition, 1954.
Knight, G. Wilson (1930) The Wheel of Fire. Reprinted London: Methuen, 1964.

Knights, L. C. (1942) 'The ambiguity of *Measure for Measure*', *Scrutiny*, X, 3, 222–33.

Kristeva, Julia (1974) *La Révolution du langage poetique*. Paris: Seuil.

—— (1980) *Desire in Language. A Semiotic Approach to Literature and Art*, ed. Leon S. Roudiez, trans. Thomas Gora, Alice Jardine and Leon Roudiez. Oxford: Blackwell.

Lacan, Jacques (1957) 'L'instance de la lettre dans l'inconscient ou la raison depuis Freud', in *Ecrits*. Paris. Seuil, 1966, 725–36. In English: 'The agency of the letter in the unconscious', trans. Alan Sheridan, in *Ecrits, a Selection*. London: Tavistock Publications, 1977, 146–78.

—— (1957–8) 'Les formations de l'inconscient', *Bulletin de Psychologie*, II, 1–15.

—— (1958) "Propos directifs pour un Congrès sur la sexualité feminine', in *Ecrits*. Paris: Seuil, 1966, 725–36. In English: Guiding remarks for a congress on feminine sexuality', trans. Jacqueline Rose, in Mitchell, J. and Rose, J. (eds) *Feminine Sexuality, Jacques Lacan and the Ecole Freudienne*. London: Macmillan, 1982, 86–98.

—— (1959) 'Desire and the interpretation of desire in *Hamlet*', in Felman, Shoshana (ed.) *Literature and Psychoanalysis, the Question of Reading: Otherwise*. Yale French Studies 55/56. New Haven: Yale University Press, 11–52.

Leavis, F. R. (1942) 'The greatness of *Measure for Measure*', *Scrutiny*, X, 3, 234–47.

Leverenz, David (1980) 'The woman in Hamlet: An interpersonal view', in Schwarz, Murray M. and Kahn, Coppélia (eds) *Representing Shakespeare, New Psychoanalytic Essays*. Baltimore, Md. and London: Johns Hopkins University Press.

Maxwell, J. C. (1947) '*Measure for Measure*: A footnote to recent criticism', *Downside Review*, 65, 45–59.

Montrelay, Michèle (1970) 'Recherches sur la féminité', *Critique*, 26, 654–74; revised 'Inquiry into femininity', trans. and intro. by Parveen Adams, *m/f*, 65–101.

Mulhern, Francis (1979) *The Moment of 'Scrutiny'*. London: New Left Books. Reprinted Verso, 1981.

Schwarz, Murray M. and Kahn, Coppélia (1980) *Representing Shakespeare, New Psychoanalytic Essays*. Baltimore, Md. and London: Johns Hopkins University Press.

Shakespeare, William (1877) *Hamlet*. Variorum Edition, ed. H. H. Furness, 15th edn. Philadelphia: Lippincott.

—— (1965) *Measure for Measure*, ed. J. W. Lever. London: Methuen.

—— (1967) *All's Well That Ends Well*, ed. G. K. Hunter. London: Methuen.

—— (1979) *A Midsummer Night's Dream*, ed. Harold F. Brooks. London: Methuen.

—— (1982) *Hamlet*. ed. H. Jenkins. London: Methuen.

Smith, Robert M. (1950) 'Interpretations of *Measure for Measure*', *Shakespeare Quarterly*, I, 208–18.

Weimann, R. (1978) *Shakespeare and the Popular Tradition in the Theater*, ed. R. Schwartz. Baltimore, Md. and London: Johns Hopkins University Press.

Winnicott, D. W. (1971) *Playing and Reality*. London: Tavistock Publications.

—— (1972) [1966] 'Split-off male and female elements found clinically in men and women: theoretical inferences'. *Psychoanalytic Forum*, 4, (ed.) J. Linden. New York: International Universities Press.

WILLIAM EMPSON

[Up-dating Revenge Tragedy]†

One feels that the mysteries of Hamlet are likely to be more or less exhausted, and I have no great novelty to offer here, but it has struck me, in the course of trying to present him in lectures, that the enormous panorama of theory and explanation falls into a reasonable proportion if viewed, so to speak, from Pisgah, from the moment of discovery by Shakespeare. To do that should also have a relation with the impressions of a fresh mind, meeting the basic legend of the play at any date. I was

† From *Essays on Shakespeare*, by William Empson, ed. David B. Pirie (Cambridge, 1986), pp. 79–92. Reprinted with the permission of Cambridge University Press.

led to it from trying to answer some remarks of Hugh Kingsmill, in *The Return of William Shakespeare*, who said that Hamlet is a ridiculously theatrical and therefore unreal figure, almost solely concerned with scoring off other people, which the dialogue lets him do much too easily, and attractive to actors only because "they have more humiliations than other men to avenge". A number of critics seem to have felt like this, though few have said it so plainly; the feeling tends to make one indifferent to the play, and over-rides any "solution of its problems", but when followed up it leads to more interesting country. I think it allows of a reconsideration of the origins, along which one might even take fresh troops into the jungle warfare over the text.

The experts mostly agree that Kyd wrote a play on Hamlet about 1587, very like his surviving *Spanish Tragedy* except that it was about a son avenging a father instead of a father avenging a son. In any case there was some early play on Hamlet. The only record of a performance of it is in 1594, under conditions which make it likely to have become the property of Shakespeare's Company; jokes about it survive from 1589, 1596, and 1601, the later two regarding it as a standard out-of-date object. A keen sense of changing fashion has to be envisaged; when Shakespeare's Company were seduced into performing *Richard II* for the Essex rebels they said they would have to be paid because it was too old to draw an audience, and it wasn't half as old as *Hamlet*. A gradual evolution of *Hamlet*, which some critics have imagined, isn't likely under these conditions. We have to consider why Shakespeare rewrote a much-laughed-at old play, and was thus led on into his great Tragic Period, and the obvious answer is that he was told to; somebody in the Company thumbed over the texts in the ice-box and said "This used to be a tremendous draw, and it's coming round again; look at Marston. All you have to do is just go over the words so that it's *life-like* and they can't laugh at it." Kyd had a powerful but narrow, one might say miserly, theatrical talent, likely to repeat a success, so his *Hamlet* probably had a Play-within-the-Play like *The Spanish Tragedy*; we know from a joke it had a Ghost; and he would have almost all the rest of the story as we know it from the sources. For all we know, when Shakespeare created a new epoch and opened a new territory to the human mind, he did nothing but alter the dialogue for this structure, not even adding a scene. The trouble with this kind of critical approach, as the experienced reader will already be feeling with irritation, is that it can be used to say "That is why the play is so muddled and bad." On the contrary, I think, if taken firmly enough it shows how, at the time, such a wonderful thing as Shakespeare's *Hamlet* could be conceived and accepted.

The real "Hamlet problem", it seems clear, is a problem about his first audiences. This is not to deny (as E. E. Stoll has sometimes done) that Hamlet himself is a problem; he must be one, because he says he is; and he is a magnificent one, which has been exhaustively examined in the last 150 years. What is peculiar is that he does not seem to have become one until the end of the eighteenth century; even Dr Johnson, who had a strong grasp of natural human difficulties, writes about Hamlet as if there was no problem at all. We are to think, apparently, that Shakespeare wrote a play which was extremely successful at the time (none more so, to judge by the references), and continued to hold the stage, and yet that nearly two hundred years had to go by before anyone had even a glimmering of what it was about. This is a good story, but surely it is rather too magical. Indeed, as the Hamlet Problem has developed, yielding increasingly subtle and profound reasons for his delay, there has naturally developed in its wake a considerable backwash from critics who say "But how can such a drama as you describe conceivably have been written by an Elizabethan, for an Elizabethan audience?" Some kind of mediating process is required here; one needs to explain how the first audiences could take a more interesting view than Dr Johnson's, without taking an improbably profound one.

The political atmosphere may be dealt with first. Stoll has successfully argued that even the theme of delay need not be grasped by an audience, except as a convention; however, Dover Wilson has pointed out that the first audiences had a striking example before them in Essex, who was, or had just been, refusing to make up his mind in a public and alarming manner; his attempt at revolt might have caused civil war. One need not limit it to Essex; the Queen herself had long used vacillation as a major instrument of policy, but the habit was becoming unnerving because though presumably dying she still refused to name a successor, which in itself might cause civil war. Her various foreign wars were also dragging on indecisively. A play about a prince who brought disaster by failing to make up his mind was bound to ring straight on the nerves of the audience when Shakespeare rewrote *Hamlet*; it is not a question of intellectual subtlety but of what they were being forced to think about already. It seems to me that there are relics of this situation in the text, which critics have not considered in the light of their natural acting power. The audience is already in the grip of a convention by which Hamlet can chat directly to them about the current War of the Theatres in London, and then the King advances straight down the apron-stage and urges the audience to kill Hamlet:

> *Do it*, England,
> For like the hectic in my blood he rages,
> And *thou* must cure me.

None of them could hear that without feeling it was current politics, however obscure; and the idea is picked up again, for what seems nowadays only an opportunist joke, when the Gravedigger says that Hamlet's madness won't matter in England, where all the men are as mad as he. Once the idea has been planted so firmly, even the idea that England is paying Danegeld may take on some mysterious weight. Caroline Spurgeon and G. Wilson Knight have maintained that the reiterated images of disease somehow imply that Hamlet himself is a disease, and this gives a basis for it. Yet the audience might also reflect that the character does what the author is doing—altering an old play to fit an immediate political purpose. This had to be left obscure, but we can reasonably presume an idea that the faults of Hamlet (which are somehow part of his great virtues) are not only specific but topical—"so far from being an absurd old play, it is just what you want, if you can see what is at the bottom of it". The insistence on the dangers of civil war, on the mob that Laertes does raise, and that Hamlet could raise but won't, and that Fortinbras at the end takes immediate steps to quiet, is rather heavy in the full text though nowadays often cut. Shakespeare could at least feel, when the old laughingstock was dragged out and given to him as a new responsibility, that delay when properly treated need not be dull; considered politically, the urgent thing might be not to let it get too exciting.

Such may have been his first encouraging reflection, but the political angle was not the first problem of the assignment, the thing he had to solve before he could face an audience; it was more like an extra gift which the correct solution tosses into his hand. The current objection to the old play *Hamlet*, which must have seemed very hard to surmount, can be glimpsed in the surviving references to it. It was thought absurdly theatrical. Even in 1589 the phrase "whole Hamlets, I should say handfuls, of tragical speeches" treats Hamlet as incessantly wordy, and the phrase of 1596, "as pale as the vizard of the ghost which cried so miserably at the Theatre, like an oyster wife, Hamlet Revenge", gets its joke from the idea that her dismal bawling may start again at any moment, however sick of her you are (presumably she is crying her wares up and down the street). The objection is not against melodrama, which they liked well enough, but against delay. You had a hero howling out "Revenge" all through the play, and everybody knew the revenge wouldn't come till the end. This structure is at the mercy of anybody in the audience who cares to shout "Hurry Up", because then the others feel they must laugh, however sympathetic they are; or rather, they felt that by the time Shakespeare rewrote *Hamlet*, whereas ten years earlier they would only have wanted to say "Shush". This fact about the audience, I submit, is the basic fact about the rewriting of *Hamlet*.

The difficulty was particularly sharp for Shakespeare's Company, which set out to be less ham than its rivals, and the Globe Theatre itself, only just built, asked for something impressively new. And yet there was a revival of the taste for Revenge Plays in spite of a half-resentful feeling that they had become absurd. No doubt, the old ones had gone on to being occasionally revived; though Henslow records a performance of *The Spanish Tragedy* in 1597 as "new", with no record of previous performance since 1592; but also new ones were now being written with a rather different tone. Clifford Leech (*Shakespeare's Tragedies*, p. 51) has pointed out that the "induction" was revived in four plays around the turn of the century, and argues that it marks a new kind of self-consciousness about the situation of being in a theatre; one which led to greater realism but rather began by excusing the absence of it (*Antonio and Mellida, The Malcontent, Every Man Out of his Humour* and *Cynthia's Revels*). Indeed, J. M. Nosworthy has suggested, Hamlet's scenes with the Players are rather like an Induction put in the middle. Now, Kyd had been writing before the destruction of the Spanish Armada, therefore while facing a more immediate probability of conquest with rack and fire; the position had remained dangerous, but 1588 had made the Elizabethans feel sure that God was on their side. I think the wheel seemed to be coming round again, chiefly because of the succession problem (there was a considerable scare in 1599 that the Queen was dead and the Spaniards had landed), so that we ought not to regard this vague desire to recover the mood of ten years earlier as merely stupid. Perhaps the fashion for child actors, the main complaint of the Players in *Hamlet*, came back at this moment because children could use the old convention with an effect of charm, making it less absurd because more distanced. E. K. Chambers quotes a complaint by Jonson, when the Children of the Queen's Chapel started acting in 1600, that "the umbrae of ghosts of some three or four plays, departed a dozen years since, have been seen wailing on your stage here".

Shakespeare himself had hardly written a tragedy before. To have written or had a hand in *Titus Andronicus*, ten years before, only brings him closer to his current audience; his own earlier tastes, as well as theirs, were to be re-examined. Romeo does not suggest an Aristotelian "tragic flaw"; the source poem by Brooke blames the lovers for haste and greed, but Shakespeare though increasing their haste has a short prologue putting the blame on their families; the moral is against feuds. As a writer of comedies, his main improvement in technique had been to reduce the need for a villain so that the effect was wholly un-tragic, and meanwhile the series of History Plays had been on the practical or hopeful theme "How to Avoid Civil War"; even so he had manoeuvred himself into ending with the cheerful middle of the series, having written its gloomy end at the start when the public was grim and anxious. What Shakespeare was famous for, just before writing *Hamlet*, was Falstaff and patriotic stuff about Henry V. *Julius Caesar*, the play immediately previous to *Hamlet*, is the most plausible candidate for a previous tragedy or indeed Revenge Play, not surprisingly, but the style is dry and the interest mainly in the politics of the thing. One can easily imagine that the external cause, the question of what the audience would like, was prominent when the theme was chosen. If Essex came into the background of the next assignment, Shakespeare's undoubted patron Southampton was also involved. I am not trying to make him subservient to

his public, only sensitive to changes of taste in which he had an important part; nor would I forget that the misfortunes of genius often have a
wild luck in their timing. But he must have seemed an unlikely person
just then to start on a great Tragic Period, and he never wrote a Revenge
Play afterwards; we can reasonably suppose that he first thought of *Hamlet* as a pretty specialised assignment, a matter, indeed, of trying to satisfy
audiences who demanded a Revenge Play and then laughed when it was
provided. I think he did not see how to solve this problem at the committee meeting, when the agile Bard was voted to carry the weight, but
already did see how when walking home. It was a bold decision, and
probably decided his subsequent career, but it was a purely technical
one. He thought: "The only way to shut this hole is to make it big. I
shall make Hamlet walk up to the audience and tell them, again and
again, 'I don't know why I'm delaying any more than you do; the moti-
vation of this play is just as blank to me as it is to you; but I can't help
it.' What is more, I shall make it impossible for them to blame him.
And *then* they daren't laugh." It turned out, of course, that this method,
instead of reducing the old play to farce, made it thrillingly life-like and
profound. A great deal more was required; one had to get a character
who could do it convincingly, and bring in large enough issues for the
puzzle not to appear gratuitous. I do not want to commit the Fallacy of
Reduction, only to remove the suspicion that the first audiences could
not tell what was going on.

Looked at in this way, the plot at once gave questions of very wide
interest, especially to actors and the regular patrons of a repertory company; the character says: "Why do you assume I am theatrical? I particularly hate such behaviour. I cannot help my situation. What do you
mean by theatrical?" Whole areas of the old play suddenly became so
significant that one could wonder whether Kyd had meant that or not;
whether Hamlet really wants to kill Claudius, whether he was ever really
in love with Ophelia, whether he can continue to grasp his own motives
while "acting a part" before the Court, whether he is not really more of
an actor than the Players, whether he is not (properly speaking) the only
sincere person in view. In spite of its great variety of incident, the play
sticks very closely to discussing theatricality. Surely that is what critics
have long found so interesting about *Hamlet*, while an occasional voice
like Kingsmill's says it is nasty, or Stoll tries to save the Master by arguing
it was not intended or visible at the time. But, so far from being innocent
here, what the first audiences came to see was whether the Globe could
revamp the old favourite without being absurd. To be sure, we cannot
suppose them really very "sophisticated", considering the plays by other
authors they admired; to make *The Spanish Tragedy* up-to-date enough
for the Admiral's Company (which was paid for in September 1601, and
June 1602, in attempts to catch up with Shakespeare's *Hamlet* presumably—indeed I think with two successive *Hamlets*) only required some

interesting "life-like" mad speeches. But that they *imagined* they were too sophisticated for the old *Hamlet* does seem to emerge from the surviving jokes about it, and that is all that was required. We need not suppose, therefore, that they missed the purpose of the changes; "he is cunning past man's thought" they are more likely to have muttered into their beards, as they abandoned the intention to jeer.

As was necessary for this purpose, the play uses the device of throwing away dramatic illusion much more boldly than Shakespeare does anywhere else. (S. L. Bethell, in *Shakespeare and the Popular Dramatic Tradition,* has written what I take to be the classical discussion of this technique.) A particularly startling case is planted early in the play, when the Ghost pursues Hamlet and his fellows underground and says "Swear" (to be secret) wherever they go, and Hamlet says

> Come on, you hear this fellow in the cellarage,
> Consent to swear.

It seems that the area under the stage was *technically* called the cellarage, but the point is clear enough without this extra sharpening; it is a recklessly comic throw-away of an illusion, especially for a repertory audience, who know who is crawling about among the trestles at this point (Shakespeare himself, we are told), and have their own views on his style of acting. But the effect is still meant to be frightening; it is like Zoo in *Back to Methuselah,* who says "This kind of thing is got up to impress you, not to impress me"; and it is very outfacing for persons in the audience who come expecting to make that kind of joke themselves.

Following this plan, there are of course satirical misquotations of the Revenge classics, as in "Pox! leave thy damnable faces and begin. Come— 'the croaking raven doth bellow for revenge' " (probably more of them than we realise, because we miss the contrast with the old *Hamlet*); but there also has to be a positive dramatisation of the idea, which is given in *Hamlet's* scenes with the Players. Critics have wondered how it could be endurable for Shakespeare to make the actor of Hamlet upbraid for their cravings for theatricality not merely his fellow actors but part of his audience (the term "groundlings" must have appeared an insult and comes nowhere else); but surely this carries on the central joke, and wouldn't make the author prominent. I agree that the Player's speech and so forth was a parody of the ranting style of the Admiral's Company (and when Hamlet praised it his actor had to slip in and out of real life, without turning the joke too much against the Prince); but even so the situation is that the Chamberlain's Company are shown discussing how to put on a modern-style Revenge Play, which the audience knows to be a problem for them. The "mirror" was being held close to the face. As to the talk about the War of the Theatres, people were curious to know what the Globe would say, and heard its leading actor speak for the Company; they were violently prevented from keeping their minds on "buried Denmark". What is technically so clever is to turn this calculated collapse of dramatic illusion into an illustration of the central theme. The first problem was how to get the audience to attend to the story again, solved completely by "O what a rogue" and so on, which moves from the shame of theatrical behaviour and the paradoxes of sincerity (Hamlet first blames himself for not feeling as much as the actors do and then for over-acting about it, feeling too much) into an immediate scheme to expose the king. Yet even here one might feel, as Dover Wilson said (with his odd power of making a deep remark without seeing its implications), that "the two speeches are for all the world like a theme given out by the First Violin and then repeated by the Soloist"—Hamlet has only proved he is a better actor, and indeed "rogue" might make him say this, by recalling that actors were legally rogues and vagabonds. We next see Hamlet in the 'To be or not to be" soliloquy, and he has completely forgotten his passionate and apparently decisive self-criticism—but this time the collapse of interest in the story comes from the Prince, not merely from the audience; then when Ophelia enters he swings away from being completely disinterested into being more disgracefully the-atrical than anywhere else (enjoying working up a fuss about a very excessive suspicion, and thus betraying himself to listeners he knows are present); next he lectures the Players with grotesque hauteur about the art of acting, saying that they must always keep cool (this is where the word "groundlings" comes); then, quite unexpectedly, he fawns upon Horatio as a man who is not "passion's slave", unlike himself, and we advance upon the Play-within-the-Play. The metaphor of the pipe which Fortune can blow upon as she pleases, which he used to Horatio, is made a symbol by bringing a recorder into bodily prominence during his moment of triumph after the Play scene, and he now boasts to the courtiers that he is a mystery, therefore they cannot play on him—we are meant to feel that there are real merits in the condition, but he has already told us he despises himself for it. Incidentally he has just told Horatio that he deserves a fellowship in a "cry" of players (another searching joke phrase not used elsewhere) but Horatio only thinks "half of one". The recovery from the point where the story seemed most com-pletely thrown away has been turned into an exposition of the character of the hero and the central dramatic theme. No doubt this has been fully recognized, but I do not think it has been viewed as a frank treat-ment of the central task, that of making the old play seem real by making the hero life-like.

Dover Wilson rightly points out the obsessive excitability of Hamlet, as when in each of the scenes scolding one of the ladies he comes back twice onto the stage, each time more unreasonable, as if he can't make himself stop. "But it is no mere theatrical trick or device", he goes on, "it is meant to be part of the nature of the man"; and meanwhile psy-chologists have elaborated the view that he is a standard "manic-depressive" type, in whom long periods of sullen gloom, often with actual forgetfulness, are followed by short periods of exhausting excitement, usually with violence of language. By all means, but the nature of the man grows out of the original *donnée*; his nature had (first of all) to be such that it would make the old story "life-like". And the effect in the theatre, surely, is at least prior to any belief about his nature, though it may lead you on to one; what you start from is the *astonishment* of Hamlet's incessant changes of mood, which also let the one actor combine in himself elements which the Elizabethan theatre usually separates (e.g. simply tragedy and comedy). Every one of the soliloquies, it has been pointed out, contains a shock for the audience, apart from what it says, in what it doesn't say: the first in having no reference to usurpation; the second ("rogue and slave") no reference to Ophelia, though his feelings about her have been made a prominent question; the third ("To be or not to be") no reference to his plot or his self-criticism or even his own walk of life—he is considering entirely in general whether life is worth living, and it is startling for him to say no traveller returns from death, however complete the "explanation" that he is assuming the Ghost was a devil; the fourth ("Now might I do it pat") no reference to his obviously great personal danger now that the King knows the secret; the fifth ("How all occasions do inform") no reference to the fact that he can't kill the King now, or rather a baffling assumption that he still can; and one might add his complete forgetting of his previous self-criticisms when he comes to his last words. It is this power to astonish, I think, which keeps one in doubt whether he is particularly theatrical or particularly "life-like"; a basic part of the effect, which would be clear to the first audiences.

However, the theme of a major play by Shakespeare is usually repeated by several characters in different forms, and Hamlet is not the only theatrical one here. Everybody is "acting a part" except Horatio, as far as that goes; and Laertes is very theatrical, as Hamlet rightly insists over the body of Ophelia ("I'll rant as well as thou"). One might reflect that both of them trample on her, both literally and figuratively, just because of their common trait. And yet Laertes is presented as opposite to Hamlet in not being subject to delay about avenging his father or to scruples about his methods; the tragic flaw in Hamlet must be something deeper or more specific. We need therefore to consider what his "theatricality" may be, and indeed the reader may feel I am making too much play with a term that Elizabethans did not use; but I think it makes us start in the right place. The Elizabethans, though both more formal and more boisterous than most people nowadays, were well able to see the need for sincerity; and it is agreed that Shakespeare had been reading Montaigne about how quickly one's moods can change, so that to appear consistent requires "acting", a line of thought which is still current. But to understand how it was applied here one needs to keep one's mind on the immediate situation in the theatre. The *plot* of a Revenge Play seemed theatrical because it kept the audience waiting without obvious reason in the characters; then a theatrical *character* (in such a play) appears as one who gets undeserved effects, "cheap" because not justified by the plot as a whole. However, "theatrical behaviour" is never only "mean" in the sense of losing the ultimate aim for a petty advantage, because it must also "give itself away"—the idea "greedy to impress an audience" is required. Now the basic legend about Hamlet was that he did exactly this and yet was somehow right for it; he successfully kept a secret by displaying he had got one. The idea is already prominent in Saxo Grammaticus, where it is presented as wholly successful (the eventual bad end of Hamlet had a different cause). Many scholars recently have argued that Shakespeare looked up his sources more than we have supposed, and I imagine the text of Saxo could be borrowed for him when he was given the assignment, if he wanted a rapid check on the French version; "the Saxon who could write Latin" in 1200 would be an evidently impressive source of primitive legend. The differences from the French are not important, but if Shakespeare did look up Saxo he would get an even firmer reassurance that his natural bent was the right one; the brief pungent Latin sentences about Hamlet are almost a definition of Shakespeare's clown, and Dover Wilson is right in saying that Shakespeare presented Hamlet as a kind of generalisation of that idea ("they fool me to the top of my bent" he remarks with appalling truth). Here we reach the bedrock of Hamlet, unchanged by the local dramas of reinterpretation; even Dr Johnson remarks that his assumed madness, though entertaining, does not seem to help his plot.

Kyd would probably give him powerful single-line jokes when answering other characters; the extreme and sordid pretence of madness implied by Saxo would not be used. I think that Shakespeare's opening words for Hamlet, "A little more than kin and less than kind", are simply repeated from Kyd; a dramatic moment for the first-night audience, because they wanted to know whether the new Hamlet would be different. His next words are a passionate assertion that he is *not* the theatrical Hamlet—"I know not seems." Now this technique from Kyd, though trivial beside the final Hamlet, would present the inherent paradox of the legend very firmly: why are these jokes supposed to give a kind of magical success to a character who had obviously better keep his mouth shut? All Elizabethans, including Elizabeth, had met the need to keep one's mouth shut at times; the paradox might well seem sharper to them than it does to us. Shakespeare took care to laugh at this as early as possible in his version of the play. The idea that it is silly to drop hints as Hamlet does is expressed by Hamlet himself, not only with force but with winning intimacy, when he tells the other observers of the Ghost that they must keep silence completely, and not say "We could an if we would. There be an if they might" and so on, which is precisely what he does himself for the rest of the play. No doubt he needs a monopoly of this technique. But the first effect in the theatre was another case of "closing the hole by making it big"; if you can make the audience laugh *with* Hamlet about his method early, they aren't going to laugh *at* him for it afterwards. Instead they can wonder why he is or pretends to be mad, just as the other characters wonder; and wonder why he delays, just as he himself wonders. No other device could raise so sharply the question of "what *is* theatrical behaviour?" because here we cannot even be sure what Hamlet is aiming at. We can never decide flatly that his method is wrong, because the more it appears unwise the more it appears courageous; and at any rate we know that he sees all round it. There seem to be two main assumptions, that he is trying to frighten his enemies into exposing themselves, and that he is not so frightened himself as to hide his emotions though he hides their cause. I fancy Shakespeare could rely on some of his audience to add the apparently modern theory that the relief of self-expression saved Hamlet from going finally mad, because it fits well enough onto their beliefs about the disease "melancholy". But in any case the basic legend is a dream glorification of both having your cake and eating it, keeping your secret for years, till you kill, and yet perpetually enjoying boasts about it. Here we are among the roots of the race of man; rather a smelly bit perhaps, but a bit that appeals at once to any child. It would be absurd to *blame* Shakespeare for accentuating this traditional theme till it became enormous.

The view that Hamlet "is Shakespeare", or at least more like him than his other characters, I hope falls into shape now. It has a basic truth, because he was drawing on his experience as actor and playwright; these professions often do puzzle their practitioners about what is theatrical and what is not, as their friends and audiences can easily recognise; but he was only using what the theme required. To have to give posterity, let alone the immediate audiences, a picture of himself would have struck him as laying a farcical extra burden on an already difficult assignment. I think he did feel he was giving a good hand to actors in general, though with decent obscurity, when he worked up so much praise for Hamlet at the end, but you are meant to be dragged round to this final admiration for Hamlet, not to feel it all through. To suppose he "is Shakespeare" has excited in some critics a reasonable distaste for both parties, because a man who models himself on Hamlet in common life (as has been done) tends to appear a mean-minded neurotic; whereas if you take the *plot* seriously Hamlet is at least assumed to have special reasons for his behaviour.

We should now be able to reconsider the view which Stoll has done real service by following up: Hamlet's reasons are so good that he not only never delays at all but was never supposed to; the self-accusations of the revenger are always prominent in Revenge Plays, even classical Greek ones, being merely a necessary part of the machine—to make the audience continue waiting with attention. Any problem we may invent about Shakespeare's Hamlet, on this view, we could also have invented about Kyd's, but it wouldn't have occurred to us to want to. In making the old play "life-like" Shakespeare merely altered the style, not the story; except that it was probably he who (by way of adding "body") gave Hamlet very much better reasons for delay than any previous revenger, so that it is peculiarly absurd of us to pick him out and puzzle over his delay. I do not at all want to weaken this line of argument; I think Shakespeare did, intentionally, pile up all the excuses for delay he could imagine, while at the same time making Hamlet bewail and denounce his delay far more strongly than ever revenger had done before. It is the force and intimacy of the self-reproaches of Hamlet, of course, which ordinary opinion has rightly given first place; that is why these legal arguments that he didn't delay appear farcical. But the two lines of argument are only two halves of the same thing. Those members of the audience who simply wanted to see a Revenge Play again, without any hooting at it from smarter persons, deserved to be satisfied; and anyhow, for all parties, the suspicion that Hamlet was a coward or merely fatuous had to be avoided. The ambiguity was an essential part of the intention, because the more you tried to translate the balance of impulses in the old drama into a realistic story (especially if you make Hamlet older which you want to if he is to understand what he is doing) the more peculiar this story had to be made. The old structure was still kept firm, but its foundations had to be strengthened to carry so much extra weight. At the same time, a simpler view could be taken; whatever the stage characters may say, the real situation in the theatre is still that the audience knows the revenge won't come till the end. Their own foreknowledge is what they had laughed at, rather than any lack of motive in the puppets, and however much the motives of the Revenger for delay were increased he could still very properly blame himself for keeping the audience waiting. One could therefore sit through the new *Hamlet* (as for that matter the eighteenth century did) without feeling too startled by his self-reproaches. But of course the idea that "bringing the style up to date" did not involve any change of content seems to me absurd, whether held by Shakespeare's committee or by Stoll; for one thing, it made the old theatrical convention appear bafflingly indistinguishable from a current political danger. The whole story was brought into a new air, so that one felt there was much more "in it".

※　※　※

Selected Bibliography

The volume of Shakespearean scholarship and criticism is enormous. Each of the plays now has attached to it its own private mountain of critical and scholarly opinion and conjecture, amid which the bibliography of works dealing with *Hamlet* towers like a very Everest. The present list can do little more than suggest the range of studies that the play has occasioned and direct the reader to some of the more significant sources of information concerning *Hamlet*, Shakespeare, and the background of the Elizabethan period. That the list should not seem even more arbitrary than it inevitably must, it is limited to works published during the past seventy years. For the earlier criticism of the play, the student is referred to the Variorum edition of *Hamlet*, edited by H. H. Furness (Philadelphia, 1877), which provides a generous selection of commentary on the play through the third quarter of the nineteenth century. For the years between the Variorum and the mid-1930s, a full account of publications dealing with the play is given in A. A. Raven's A *Hamlet Bibliography and Reference Guide*, 1877–1935 (Chicago, 1935). Useful accounts of later criticism of the play are given by Clifford Leech, "Studies in *Hamlet*," (*Shakespeare Survey*, 1956), and G. K. Hunter, "*Hamlet* Criticism," (*Critical Quarterly*, 1959). For studies of *Hamlet* published since 1960, the annual bibliography of the *Shakespeare Quarterly* should be consulted.

Abbreviations

SS	Shakespeare Survey
PMLA	Publications of the Modern Language Association
SQ	Shakespeare Quarterly
ELH	Journal of English Literary History
JHI	Journal of the History of Ideas
RES	Review of English Studies
SP	Studies in Philology
SB	Studies in Bibliography

I. ELIZABETHAN BACKGROUND.

Shakespeare's England (Oxford, 1916) is a vast store of information concerning the life of the times: social customs, pastimes, trades and professions, education, and the like. A more recent collection of similar materials is *William Shakespeare: His World, His Work, and His Influence*, edited by John F. Andrews, 3 vols. (New York, 1985). J. Dover Wilson's *Life in Shakespeare's England* (Cambridge, 1911) is a useful guide, as is A *Companion to Shakespeare Studies*, edited by Harley Granville-Barker and G. B. Harrison (Cambridge, 1934). This has been revised as A *New Companion to Shakespeare Studies*, edited by Kenneth Muir and S. Schoenbaum (Cambridge, 1971).

II. THE ELIZABETHAN THEATER.

All studies of this begin with the four volumes of E. K. Chambers's *The Elizabethan Stage* (Oxford, 1923). T. W. Baldwin, *The Organization and Personnel of the Shakespearean Company* (Princeton, 1926) is another pioneer study of lasting importance. More recent investigations include C. Walter Hodges, *The Globe Restored: A Study of the Elizabethan Theatre* (London, 1953); A. M. Nagler, *Shakespeare's Stage* (New Haven, 1958); Richard Hosley, "The Discovery-Space in Shakespeare's Globe" (*SS*, 1959), and "Was there a Music Room in Shakespeare's Globe?" (*SS*, 1960). The results of recent research into the Globe Theater (its site, its dimensions and design, its audiences) are reported by Andrew Gurr in *The Shakespearean Stage, 1574–1642* (Cambridge, 1980, 2nd ed.), in *Rebuilding Shakespeare's Globe* (New York, 1989, with John Orrell), and in Gurr's *Playgoing in Shakespeare's London* (Cambridge, 1987), where the conclusions reached by Ann Jennalie Cook in her *The Privileged Playgoers of Shakespeare's London, 1576–1642* (Princeton, 1981) are challenged.

III. SHAKESPEAREAN BIOGRAPHY.

The essential documents were first set forth in the two volumes of E. K. Chambers's *William Shakespeare: A Study of Facts and Problems* (Oxford, 1930) but the definitive works are now S. Schoenbaum's *Shakespeare's Lives* (Oxford, 1970), and his *William Shakespeare: A Documentary Life* (Oxford, 1975). E. A. J. Honigmann's *Shakespeare: The 'Lost' Years* (Manchester, 1985) is a conjectural account of the dramatist's early, pre-London career.

IV. SHAKESPEAREAN TRAGEDY.

Hamlet of course looms large in all accounts of the tragedies. The play receives extended treatment in each of the following: Lily B. Campbell, *Shakespeare's Tragic Heroes: Slaves of Passion* (Cambridge, 1930); H. B. Charlton, *Shakespearean Tragedy* (Cambridge, 1948); G. Wilson Knight, *The Wheel of Fire* (London, 1948, rev. ed.), and *The Imperial Theme* (London, 1931); Theodore Spencer, *Shakespeare and the Nature of Man* (New York, 1942); E. E. Stoll, *Art and Artifice in Shakespeare: A Study in Dramatic Contrast and Illusion* (Cambridge, 1933); G. B. Harrison, *Shakespeare's Tragedies* (London, 1951); Harold S. Wilson, *On the Design of Shakespearean Tragedy* (Toronto, 1957); Brents Stirling, *Unity in Shakespearean Tragedy: The Interplay of Theme and Character* (New York, 1957); Paul N. Siegel, *Shakespearean Tragedy and the Elizabethan Compromise* (New York, 1957); John Vyvyan, *The Shakespearean Ethic* (London, 1959); John Lawlor, *The Tragic Sense in Shakespeare* (London, 1960); John Holloway, *The Story of the Night: Studies in Shakespeare's Major Tragedies* (London, 1961); Irving Ribner, *Patterns in Shakespearean Tragedy* (London, 1960); A. P. Rossiter, *Angel With Horns* (London, 1961); Robert Speaight, *Nature in Shakespearean Tragedy* (London, 1955); H. M. V. Matthews, *Character and Symbol in Shakespeare's Plays* (Cambridge, 1962). E. M. W. Tillyard treats *Hamlet* in *Shakespeare's Problem Plays* (London, 1950) as do D. A. Traversi in *An Approach to Shakespeare* (London, 1957, rev. ed.) and Terence Hawkes, *Shakespeare and the Reason: A Study of the Tragedies and the Problem Plays* (London, 1964). There are important discussions of *Hamlet* in Francis Ferguson's *The Idea of a Theater* (Princeton, 1949), H. D. F. Kitto's *Form and Meaning in Drama* (London, 1956), and Helen Gardner's *The Business of Criticism* (Oxford, 1959) and her *Religion and Literature* (Oxford, 1983). Other recent treatments include those by Bernard McElroy in *Shakespeare's Mature Tragedies* (Princeton, 1973), John Bayley in *Shakespeare and Tragedy* (London, 1981), Jonathan Dollimore in *Radical Tragedy: Religion, Ideology, and Power in the Drama of Shakespeare and His Contemporaries* (Chicago and London, 1983), Gordon Braden in *Renaissance Tragedy and the Senecan Tradition: Anger's Privilege* (New Haven and London, 1985), and Michael Goldman in *Acting and Action in Shakespearean Tragedy* (Princeton, 1985).

V. SEPARATE STUDIES OF *HAMLET*.

These include the following: J. Dover Wilson, *What Happens in Hamlet* (Cambridge, 1935); Harley Granville-Barker, *Prefaces to Shakespeare, Third Series: Hamlet* (London, 1937); E. E. Stoll, *Hamlet: An Historical and Comparative Study* (Minneapolis, 1919); J. M. Robertson, *The Problem of "Hamlet"* (London, 1919) and *"Hamlet" Once More* (London, 1923); L. L. Schücking, *The Meaning of Hamlet* (Oxford, 1937); A. J. A. Waldock, *Hamlet: A Study in Critical Method* (Cambridge, 1931); J. W. Draper, *The Hamlet of Shakespeare's Audience* (Durham, N.C., 1938); Richard Flatter, *Hamlet's Father* (London, 1949); Bertram Joseph, *Conscience and the King: A Study of Hamlet* (London, 1953); Roy Walker, *The Time is Out of Joint: A Study of*

Hamlet (London, 1948); G. R. Elliott, *Scourge and Minister: A Study of Hamlet as a Tragedy of Revengefulness and Justice* (Durham, N. C., 1951); D. J. James, *The Dream of Learning: An Essay on "The Advancement of Learning," "Hamlet," and "King Lear"* (Oxford, 1951); Maynard Mack, "The World of *Hamlet*," *Yale Review* 41 (1951–52); Peter Alexander, *Hamlet, Father and Son* (Oxford, 1955); L. C. Knights, *An Approach to Hamlet* (London, 1960); Stephen Booth, "On the Value of *Hamlet*," *Selected Papers from the English Institute: Reinterpretations of Elizabethan Drama*, ed. Norman Rabkin (New York and London, 1969); Maurice Charney, *Style in "Hamlet"* (Princeton, 1969) and *Hamlet's Fictions* (New York and London, 1988); Nigel Alexander, *Poison, Play, and Duel: A Study in "Hamlet"* (London, 1971); Eleanor Prosser, *Hamlet and Revenge* (Stanford, 1971, 2nd ed.); Mark Rose, *Shakespearean Design* (Cambridge, Mass., 1972); Jacques Lacan, "Desire and the Interpretation of Desire in *Hamlet*," *Literature and Psychoanalysis, The Question of Reading: Otherwise*, ed. Shoshana Felman, *Yale French Studies* 55–56 (1977); Arthur C. Kirsch, "Hamlet's Grief," *ELH* 48 (1981); Walter N. King, *Hamlet's Search for Meaning* (Athens, Ga., 1982); James L. Calderwood, *To Be and Not to Be: Negation and Metadrama in "Hamlet"* (New York and London, 1983); Roland Mushat Frye, *The Renaissance Hamlet: Issues and Responses in 1600* (Princeton, 1984); Martin Dodsworth, *"Hamlet" Closely Observed* (London, 1985); Elaine Showalter, "Representing Ophelia: Women, Madness, and the Responsibilities of Feminist Criticism," *Shakespeare and the Question of Theory*, ed. Patricia Parker and Geoffrey H. Hartman (New York and London, 1985); Stanley Cavell, *Disowning Knowledge in Six Plays of Shakespeare* (Cambridge and New York, 1987); Arthur McGee, *The Elizabethan "Hamlet"* (New Haven and London, 1987); Jonathan Goldberg, "Hamlet's Hand," *SQ* 39 (1988); John Hunt, "A Thing of Nothing: The Catastrophic Body in *Hamlet*," *SQ* 39 (1988).

VI. SOURCES.

These are discussed by Kemp Malone, *The Literary History of Hamlet: I. The Early Tradition* (Heidelberg, 1923); by Israel Gollancz in the introduction to his *The Sources of Hamlet* (Oxford, 1926); by Kenneth Muir, *Shakespeare's Sources* (London, 1957; rev. ed. as *The Sources of Shakespeare's Plays*, New Haven, 1978). Texts of sources and analogues for *Hamlet* are printed in *Narrative and Dramatic Sources of Shakespeare*, vol. 7, ed. Geoffrey Bullough (London and New York, 1973).

VII. TEXTUAL STUDIES.

The fullest account of Q1 is G. I. Duthie's *The 'Bad' Quarto of Hamlet* (Cambridge, 1941). J. Dover Wilson's *The Manuscript of Shakespeare's Hamlet* (Cambridge, 1934) is important for having established the authority of Q2, but details of Wilson's reconstruction of the textual problem have been much modified, and later work should be taken into account, e.g., Fredson Bowers, "The Printing of *Hamlet*, Q2" (*SB* 1955) and "The Textual Relation of Q2 to Q1 *Hamlet* (*SB* 1956); Harold Jenkins, "The Relation between the Second Quarto and the Folio Text of *Hamlet*" (*SB* 1955). All three texts and their relationship are discussed by W. W. Greg, *The Shakespeare First Folio* (Oxford, 1955), and by the editors of recent editions, e.g., Harold Jenkins in the Introduction to his Arden Shakespeare edition (London and New York, 1982), Philip Edwards in his New Cambridge Shakespeare edition (Cambridge, 1985), Stanley Wells and Gary Taylor in A *Textual Companion* to the Oxford Shakespeare (Oxford, 1987), and George Hibbard in his Oxford edition (London and New York, 1987). Paul Werstine's "The Textual Mystery of *Hamlet*," *SQ* 39 (1988) is the most closely reasoned of recent discussions of the subject.

VIII. SHAKESPEAREAN PRODUCTION AND STAGING.

Bernice W. Kliman, "Kozintsev's *Hamlet*: A Flawed Masterpiece," *Hamlet Studies* 1 (1979), and *Hamlet: Film, Television, and Audio Performance* (Rutherford, N.J., 1988); Jean E. Howard, *Shakespeare's Art of Orchestration: Stage Technique and Audience Response* (Urbana and Chicago, 1984); Ralph Berry, "Hamlet's Doubles," *SQ* 37 (1986); J. C. Bulman and H. R. Coursen, eds., *Shakespeare on Television: An Anthology of Essays and Reviews* (Hanover, N.H. and London, 1988).